THE WITCH DOCTORS

WINNER OF THE 1996 *FINANCIAL TIMES*/BOOZE • ALLEN & HAMILTON GLOBAL BUSINESS BOOK AWARD FOR THE BEST BOOK ABOUT BUSINESS STRATEGY AND LEADERSHIP.

'*The Witch Doctors* is a gem of debunking'   *The Times*

'One of the few sensible management books in print. Written in the sharp prose you would expect from two *Economist* journalists, it guides a course through the overcrowded field of management writers, gurus, consultants *et al*'   *Financial Times*

'Clear, useful, pithy and wise . . . good entertainment'
The Economist

'They have performed a great public service . . . Their book brings clarity, humour and historical perspective to a field that rewards gibberish [and] pomposity'   *Wall Street Journal*

'Clearly written, level-headed advice that hasn't been shipped from over the rainbow and is this inexpensive is hard to come by. Here's a rare case where the advice is worth a lot more than what you'll pay for it. Spend some time with this one; you'll come away richer for it'
Chief Information Officer

'John Micklethwait and Adrian Wooldridge skewer the pretensions of the modern management-consulting business. This book is brimming with ideas for the global marketplace'   *Success*

'Possibly the best-written business book of the decade. The authors' polished, concise and witty style is a pleasure to read'
Journal of Business Strategy

'A worthy contribution: it is broad in its range of information and insights'   *Harvard Business Review*

'This book is excellent and a must for those who currently run companies but also for those who would aspire to great heights'
British Journal of Administrative Management

'Read it before buying any other business book!'
Rosabeth Moss Kanter, *Harvard Business School*

John Micklethwait is the award-winning Business Editor of *The Economist*. He has previously worked for the magazine in America and Asia.

Dr Adrian Wooldridge is a former Management Editor of *The Economist*. He is now the magazine's West Coast correspondent in Los Angeles. He is a quondam Fellow of All Souls College, Oxford, and the author of *Measuring the Mind: Education and Psychology in England c. 1860–1990* (Cambridge University Press, 1994).

THE
WITCH
DOCTORS

What the management gurus
are saying, why it matters
and how to make sense of it

JOHN MICKLETHWAIT
ADRIAN WOOLDRIDGE

Mandarin

For Fevronia and Amelia

Published in the United Kingdom in 1997 by
Mandarin Paperbacks

1 3 5 7 9 10 8 6 4 2

Copyright © John Micklethwait and Adrian Wooldridge

The right of John Micklethwait and Adrian Wooldridge to be identified as the
authors of this work has been asserted by them in accordance with the Copyright,
Designs and Patents Act, 1988

First published in the United Kingdom in 1996 by William Heinemann

Mandarin Paperbacks
Random House UK Limited
20 Vauxhall Bridge Road, London SW1V 2SA

Random House Australia (Pty) Limited
20 Alfred Street, Milsons Point, Sydney, New South Wales 2061, Australia

Random House New Zealand Limited
18 Poland Road, Glenfield, Auckland 10, New Zealand

Random House South Africa (Pty) Limited
Endulini, 5A Jubilee Road, Parktown 2193, South Africa

Random House UK Limited Reg. No. 954009

A CIP catalogue record for this book is available from the British Library

Some passages of this book have appeared in different form in articles the authors
have written for *The Economist*. They are reprinted by kind permission of The
Economist Newspaper Ltd.

Papers used by Random House UK Limited are natural, recyclable products made
from wood grown in sustainable forests. The manufacturing processes conform to
the environmental regulations of the country of origin

Typeset by Deltatype Ltd, Birkenhead Merseyside
Printed and bound in the United Kingdom by
Cox & Wyman Ltd, Reading, Berkshire

ISBN 0 7493 2645 X

CONTENTS

ACKNOWLEDGEMENTS

There are two long, equally inglorious traditions in management theory. The first is for books to come complete with a list of acknowledgements long enough to make a decent chapter in any other sort of book: every person at every conference, every research student, every corporate public-relations manager has somehow delivered a valuable insight to the writer. The second tradition is to mention nobody, thereby presumably reiterating the message that the great ideas that await the reader are the author's alone. What follows is something of a compromise.

Our primary thanks go to *The Economist* for giving us the time to write *The Witch Doctors* and also for giving us permission to use articles that we have written for the newspaper. In particular, we should thank Bill Emmott, the editor of *The Economist*, and Peter David, the business affairs editor, for their tolerance and support. A small squadron of colleagues kindly agreed to read all or parts of this book, including Brian Barry, Barbara Beck, Matthew Bishop, Victor Earl, Carol Mawer and Nick Valery; Victor was particularly helpful in checking facts and Carol in reading proofs. We are also grateful to Jenny Geddes, for providing invaluable help, and to Gideon Rachman, for acting as a source of encouragement in the darkest moments.

Three non-*Economist* readers were kind enough to offer their comments when the book was in preparation: Partha Bose, Joel Kurtzman and Alan Kantrow. They all work for the same 'vested interests' which we claim in *The Witch Doctors* make management theory such an un-self-critical business. Perhaps seeking to prove us wrong, they proved to be remarkably objective critics, often urging us to be harsher.

When it came to writing the book, we were helped in the very first instance by Allegra Huston, who convinced us – perhaps wrongly – that it was not an insane project. We have been enormously lucky to have Gillon Aitken and Andrew Wylie as our agents; the book would not have been written without Gillon's help in particular. Our good fortune continued when we ended up with two excellent editors, Tom Weldon, at Heinemann, and Peter Smith, at Random House. They have not only helped us to clarify confusions and cut out nonsense, but also contrived to leave us with the impression that we had come up with the improvements in the first place.

Finally, we should thank our families – and particularly our wives, Fevronia and Amelia. Amongst the various promises extracted from them on their wedding days, there was no mention of management theory. For that hideous betrayal alone, this book is dedicated to them.

THE WITCH DOCTORS

'You can resist an invading army; you cannot resist an idea
whose time has come.'
>Victor Hugo

'The new authority will be: member led, officer driven,
customer focused; a team environment where the whole is
greater than the sum of its parts; a flat management structure
where employees and managers are fully empowered and
decisions are devolved close to the customer; a culture of
learning rather than blame; a clear sense of direction and
purpose. A firm commitment to delivering high quality public
services through a combination of direct-provision and
effective partnerships.'
>*Recruitment advertisement, Bath and North East Somerset
>District Council. Quoted in 'Birtspeak', a column in* Private
>Eye *devoted to 'management drivel in all spheres', 22
>September 1995.*

'Only the paranoid survive.'
>*Andy Grove, Chief Executive Officer, Intel.*

The average big company used twelve of the twenty-five most
common management tools in 1993; in 1994 they used
thirteen; they expect to use fourteen tools in 1995. Seventy-
two per cent of managers believe that companies who use the
right tools are more likely to succeed; 70 per cent say that the
tools promise more than they deliver.
>*A survey of 787 companies around the world by Bain &
>Company, April 1995.*

'Guru? You find a gem here or there. But most of it's fairly obvious, you know. You go to Doubleday's business section and you see all these wonderful titles and you spend $300 and then you throw them all away.'

> Rupert Murdoch, on being asked whether there was any management guru he followed or admired, March 1996.

After the Republican landslide in the 1994 elections, Newt Gingrich told his new storm-troopers to prepare for government by reading Peter Drucker. Meanwhile Bill Clinton, who had already conducted a time-and-motion study on his own personal disorganisation (resulting in a 62.5 per cent increase in the time he spent shaping domestic and economic policy), sought succour from two peak-performance gurus, Anthony Robbins and Stephen Covey. The first meeting with Robbins, a former janitor and author of *Awaken the Giant Within*, was supposed to take less than an hour; it lasted most of the day.

> Various news reports 1994–95.

'These bold new ideas vault business people *beyond* re-engineering, *beyond* total quality management, *beyond* empowerment, and even *beyond* change and toward nothing less than reinvention and revolution ... In presenting a radical new view of how businesses can work, Peters offers the following challenge: "If you're not irate in the first thirty minutes of reading, if you don't throw this book down at least once in the first hour, and if you don't reach for the Maalox by the two-hour mark, then I and this book have utterly failed you." '

> Publisher's blurb, The Tom Peters Seminar: Crazy Times Call for Crazy Organizations *(1994). For the uninitiated, this is the book with Peters wearing his boxer shorts on the cover.*

'China needs managers more than anything else.'

> *Candidate for place at China Europe International Business
> School, Shanghai. The school offers sixty-four places. It
> receives 4,000 applications.*

'Employees will have four primary reactions: denial, sadness,
anger, withdrawal. Be certain to recognise and acknowledge
the employee's feelings. However, you may need to restate
the message to ensure that the employee knows that the
decision is final and has been made at the highest level. Notify
your Human Resources Generalist if you anticipate strong
reactions. If necessary, he/she will alert Security and Medical.'

> *'Communication guidelines, manager meeting with employees
> not selected for the new organisation', Chase Manhattan
> Bank, following merger with Chemical Bank which resulted in
> 10,000 job losses. Chase's directors, none of whom lost their
> jobs, referred to the jobs eliminated as 'saves'.*

'At one point so many copies of *Discipline* were pouring into
Paragon's office that they had to be stored in a tractor trailer
the database marketing firm maintained outside its former
office on College Corner Pike . . . Paragon ultimately received
10,000 copies of the book, all paid for by CSC. Total cost to
CSC: About $200,000.'

> Business Week, *7 August 1995, which exposed the dubious
> tactics that CSC Index, a management consultancy, had used
> to propel* The Discipline of Market Leaders *up the* New
> York Times *best-seller lists. Discipline had received mixed
> reviews. The phenomenal success of another management book,*
> Reengineering the Corporation, *had helped CSC Index
> double in size.*

The management consultancy business generated $11.4 billion
worth of fees in 1994; it is on course to bring in $21 billion
in 1999. At McKinsey, the biggest strategic consultancy, each
partner accounted for $468,000 of revenues. More than half of
today's leading consulting firms did not exist five years ago.

> *The Gartner Group; Management Consultant International.*

Even in a city full of surprises and unintentional ironies, the billboard came as something of a shock. There, surrounded by the familiar yellow flags of the Hezbollah and the pock-marked machine-gunned buildings, stood a huge advertisement summoning the faithful of Beirut to a 'Total Quality Management' seminar.

Our driver saw our interest.

'Oh yes, management. The future. But only once we get rid of these Syrian pigs.'

Lebanon, January 1995.

'You know what worries me about your book about management theory: that you'll talk to all the people and read all the books; that you will detail all its incredible effects – the number of jobs lost, the billions of dollars spent and so on. And you won't say the obvious thing: that it's 99 per cent bullshit. And everybody knows that.'

Senior editor, The Economist, summer 1995.

INTRODUCTION
The World of the Witch Doctors

The unacknowledged legislators

Shelley once claimed that poets are 'the unacknowledged legislators of mankind'. Today that honour belongs to management theorists. Names such as Drucker and Peters may not have the same ring as Wordsworth or Keats; yet, wherever we look, management theorists are laying down the law, reshaping institutions, refashioning our language and, above all, reorganising people's lives. Indeed, at its most extreme fringe, where management theory merges with the self-help industry, gurus are actually ordering people's minds, teaching them how to think about everything from organising their desk to reassessing their love-life. In late 1994 the revelation that Princess Diana had sought help from Anthony Robbins, a 'business-motivation guru' who encourages his clients to 'unleash the power within' by walking on red hot coals, caused barely a flicker of surprise in Fleet Street. On the other side of the Atlantic, the simultaneous news that Newt Gingrich, the new speaker-elect of the House of Representatives, was preparing for his new job 'by reading Peter Drucker' was greeted with relief.

At the same time as the Princess and the Speaker were seeking out management theory, millions of more mundane human beings were having it done unto them. Some 43m jobs were eliminated in America in 1979–95 (though many more were created). In paternalist Germany, 'downsizing' had pushed unemployment to above four million by early 1996 – the highest since the Second World War. In Japan, the home of lifetime employment, temporary and part-time workers now account for one in four of the workforce. In Britain, figures from the

Department of Employment, leaked in December 1994, showed that 6.6m men – or 44 per cent of the male workforce – had been unemployed at some time since 1990; 3.9m women – or roughly a third of the female workforce – had suffered the same fate.[1]

Blue-collar workers everywhere are used to being laid off when times get tough. Nowadays, the victims are often managers; and a company does not have to be in dire financial trouble to start slimming or worrying about its 'core competencies'. Three-quarters of the American companies in a survey carried out in April 1995 by Watson Wyatt, a London-based consultancy, admitted to restructuring in the previous two years.

In America, things came to a head in early 1996 when AT&T, formerly cuddly old Ma Bell, announced 40,000 redundancies. Not only was the company making healthy profits but its share price soared (enriching its then boss, Bob Allen, by some $5m). People joked that the acronym of the company, which had been a passionate follower of management fads and had already laid off 70,000 people over the past decade, would one day stand for Allen & Two Temps. As various presidential candidates attacked the greed of corporate America, *Business Week*'s cover worried about 'America's Economic Anxiety'.[2] The *New York Times* ran a seven-part series on 'The Downsizing of America'.[3] 'Firing people has got to be trendy in corporate America,' moaned *Newsweek*, which ran a cover story headlined 'Corporate Killers' contrasting the rising salaries of bosses with their shortening payrolls. 'You can practically smell the fear and anger in white-collar America because nobody in CEO-land seems to care.'

From Ohio to Oslo and Osaka, many of those laid off in the first half of the 1990s, including a good portion of those at AT&T, were 're-engineered' out of their jobs. Although ugly names – 'downsizing', 'outsourcing' and so on – have always been used to disguise routine corporate bloodletting, 'business process re-engineering', to give it its full title, was actually outlined in a book, *Reengineering the Corporation* published in 1993 by two management theorists, Michael Hammer and James Champy. Since then the re-engineering creed, which involves reorganising businesses around 'processes', such as selling, rather than administrative fiefs, such as marketing departments, has spread far around the world. In Japan, Nomura's Research Institute keeps an index measuring the use of the word in news stories to chart the country's willingness to change. In Britain re-engineering theories are now being applied to the National Health Service.

So far *Reengineering the Corporation* has sold almost two million copies, and various lacklustre follow-ups, such as Champy's *Reengineering Management* and Hammer's *The Reengineering Revolution*, have reached the *New York Times* business best-seller list. The re-engineering movement has spawned specialist consultancies, endless conferences, dozens of 'do-it-yourself' videos, and countless courses at business schools. Now there are signs of a backlash – of re-engineering revisionists questioning how easy the theory is to put into practice and complaining about 'corporate anorexia'; in time, there will doubtless be re-engineering re-revisionists reaffirming the faith.

An industry is born

The re-engineering craze is merely the latest, most potent example of the bewildering power of management gurus throughout this century. Although some antiquarians argue that Niccolò Machiavelli was the first management thinker and others that that honour belongs to whichever Egyptian organised the construction of the pyramids, the first recognisable guru was Frederick Taylor, the father of stop-watch-based 'scientific management'. In the early 1900s his books sold in their millions and Taylor's consultancy fees were $35 a day – or $630 in today's money. Taylor's worker-as-machine theories always had their critics (Charlie Chaplin, for example, lampooned them memorably in *Modern Times*) but that did not stop them from being adopted by many leading American businessmen, including Henry Ford, and spread around the world. Since then, a steady procession of management thinkers have followed in Taylor's path. After the Second World War, W. Edwards Deming, who pioneered 'total quality management', was dubbed the most revered American in Japan after General Douglas MacArthur.

However, interest in management theory went into overdrive in the 1980s, as the rich world in general, and America in particular, tried to come to terms with the rise of Japan, the spread of computers, and radical changes in working patterns. For a new breed of increasingly evangelical management theorists, led by Tom Peters, the accompanying corporate self-analysis proved a bonanza. In the summer of 1982 Peters and a colleague, Robert Waterman, from a management consultancy, McKinsey, published *In Search of Excellence*, which boldly (and correctly) told American businessmen that they were in better shape than they thought. The book became a runaway success, selling more than five million copies, staying at the top of the *New York Times* bestseller list for more than two years, and turning its authors into millionaires.

Ever since *In Search of Excellence*, the guru industry has boomed. Some $750m worth of business books are currently sold in America alone every year, and the market for tapes, videos, courses and seminars is even bigger. Not only are the latest theories such as re-engineering more rapidly and zealously applied than their predecessors, but the wealth and status accruing to those who promote them have increased exponentially. Peters, now much copied by other gurus, charges $60,000 for a day-long seminar and conducts around sixty a year. His newspaper column, where he opines on subjects from personal hygiene to Zen Buddhism, is syndicated around the world. It is rare to meet a guru who has houses in only one continent.

The gurus themselves are only the most visible tip of a much larger management iceberg, which incorporates business schools, management consultancies and much of the business press. It is hard to think of any other academic discipline that has built such an industry around itself as management theory. American firms alone now spend $20 billion a year on outside advice. Guru-breeding grounds, such as McKinsey, now have offices wherever firms lose money. Around the world, executives who thought they knew it all are being encouraged to take training courses in everything from assertiveness to ethical management. Even in self-conscious, cynical Britain some forty companies now provide adventure-based management training courses where fat merchant bankers and balding bond traders swing across rivers and tell their colleagues what they really think about each other around camp fires.[4] Every year more than 75,000 students are awarded MBAs in America – fifteen times the total in 1960. And every year a quarter of a million people around the world sit the 'GMAT' entrance exam for MBA courses. Business schools are spreading throughout the newly liberated economies of Eastern Europe and Asia; they have even reached Oxford and Cambridge.

As we shall explain, management theory, more than any other branch of academia, is propelled by two primal human instincts: fear and greed. It is usually one of these two emotions that persuades a middle manager at Heathrow Airport to pick up yet another book on leadership or tempts a chief executive in Ohio to blow yet another million dollars on consultancy fees. However, it is also clear that management theory is bound up with three revolutions that directly or indirectly affect all of us: the reinvention of companies, the reinvention of careers and the reinvention of government.

Nowadays, companies everywhere are going through contortions which their predecessors could scarcely have imagined. The attrition rate of companies is spectacular – only around a third of America's 500 leading companies in 1970 still exist today. Even the best companies, terrified that they will end up in this ever more crowded corporate graveyard, are forever reorganising themselves. This not only applies to job-slashers such as AT&T but to fast-growing companies such as Electronic Data Systems (EDS), a computer-services firm that seems to be addicted to management rethinks despite the fact that it has barely put a foot wrong since Ross Perot founded it with $1,000 in 1962.

Even when such contortions are not directly inspired by management theory, they tend to drive managers back into the gurus' arms. Management theory, after all, is the study of business. It explains not just what this or that firm is doing, but what whole groups of firms are doing, and why. The old excuse that a business person knew his or her own industry and did not need to know about anybody else's no longer holds water. Industry borders are blurring everywhere: between commercial banking, investment banking and brokerages; between computer hardware and software vendors; and between publishers, broadcasters, telecommunication companies and film studios. Even the most hard-headed managers are having to get to grips with ideas like synergy and alliances – and the challenge of managing disparate, multicultural organisations. All these paths lead to management theory.

As companies change, so do careers. Jobs are being reinvented in much the same way that businesses are. Gone are the days when a man (and it usually was a man) could expect to spend his entire career working for the same company, starting as an apprentice, climbing up through the ranks, and retiring, after forty years of uninterrupted employment, to enjoy an index-linked pension, a corporate carriage-clock and a mention in the company history. As both companies and employees try to deal with this more unstable age, it is not surprising that they are drawn to books with titles like *The Age of Unreason* (by Charles Handy), *The Change Masters* (Rosabeth Moss Kanter) and *Managing in a Time of Great Change* (Peter Drucker).

What is more, the number of people who have to know something about management is growing. Of the eight million new jobs created in America in 1991–95, 60 per cent belonged to the category of 'managers and other professionals', now the largest group in the workforce. Nor is it just white-collar workers who have to know their TQM from their JIT: nowadays even the lowliest western factory worker knows that his most valuable asset is his brain rather than his hands.

Just as companies have been forced by competitors and shareholders to question how they manage themselves, so have governments, prodded by budget deficits and tax-payers. In many cases this has simply meant privatisation. In Argentina, for instance, a group of state-owned businesses that used to cost tax-payers money were sold for over $20 billion. Some governments have moved from privatisation to what might be called the next stage of public-sector management: trying to reorganise those institutions that have to remain in government hands. Britain's former Conservative government redesigned large parts of one of the country's most cherished institutions, the welfare state. It devolved power to individual schools and hospitals, gave doctors and teachers their own budgets, linked those budgets to the number of pupils taught or patients treated, and compiled and published league tables of 'productivity' (i.e. lives saved and exams passed). These reforms owed much more to management theorists such as Peter Drucker and Alain Enthoven than they did to Tory philosophers such as David Hume and Edmund Burke, which helps to explain why the Labour government has been content to leave the bulk of these charges intact.

Across the Atlantic, the Clinton White House, with its obsession with think-tanks, Renaissance weekends and the like, is even more steeped in management theory. (Indeed, Bill Clinton's interest in management goes back a long way: it was whilst attending a conference on 'total quality management' that he allegedly propositioned Paula Jones.) In early 1995 it emerged that Clinton had consulted both Princess Diana's mentor, Anthony Robbins, and Stephen Covey, another motivational expert. Hillary Clinton's incomprehensible but apparently omniscient health plan was largely written by a management fanatic, Ira Magaziner. Vice-President Al Gore spends most of his time reinventing government in line with the latest management thinking. And a belief in the power of management is one of the few ideas that crosses party lines – as the Drucker-reading Speaker Gingrich bears witness.

The age of anxiety

Wherever management theory has been invoked, fear and anxiety seem to have followed. Ask for an explanation at a shuttered factory in Bavaria or a reorganised hospital in Newcastle, and you will begin to hear a familiar anodyne language that makes laying people off sound more like a scientific decision than a human tragedy: sacked workers are 'downsized', 'separated', 'severed', 'unassigned' and 'proactively outplaced'. (In AT&T's case, it was carrying out a 'force management programme' to reduce 'an imbalance of forces or skills'.)

Despite their invariable presence at the scene of the crime, the gurus have not yet been rounded up for questioning. The list of suspects compiled by Pat Buchanan in his populist campaign for the Republican presidential nomination, for instance, included the fiendish José (the symbolic foreign worker out to steal your job) and 'Goldman and Sachs' (the symbolic Jewish investment bank); there was no Drucker or Peters. More sober commentators have tended to talk about economics.

In one way, this is right. The underlying reasons why people have lost their jobs (or feel more insecure in them) have to do with competition, technological change and government budgets. However, it is not quite enough for the management gurus to claim that they were 'only following orders', that they were the servants of macroeconomic forces beyond their control. For better or worse, management theory has played an enormous role in how those forces have affected people. American companies would still have shed jobs without re-engineering. But the discipline, alongside several other management techniques, probably increased the carnage and certainly affected the way that the cutting was done.

It cannot have been a coincidence that many of the most enthusiastic downsizers have also been the most enthusiastic consumers of management theory. AT&T, for example, has long been a playground for the gurus, forever calling in consultants or sending staff members on management courses; indeed the telephone giant is responsible for arguably the most baffling management slogan of all time – 'Putting the moose on the table' – which had something to do with flattening hierarchies and empowering workers, and was one of several (disastrous) attempts to inject modern management thinking into AT&T's NCR subsidiary.

Moreover, a good deal of 'anxiety' has nothing to do with losing your job, but with the way that the workplace is being reorganised. 'Delayering', for instance, not only affects those who are sacked. It increases pressure on shop-floor workers who now have to make more decisions for themselves. It also disrupts people's careers: with fewer rungs to climb, managers have to be content with moving sideways. Similarly, the gurus have been unabashed supporters of ways to measure individuals' contribution to a company, from performance pay to newer devices such as '360-degree evaluation' (where people evaluate each other). Once again, they tend to see these things as 'empowering'; but survey after survey suggests that most workers find them frightening. Indeed, one of the ironies of management theory is that although it was invented to make managers' jobs easier, it has often made their lives much more difficult.

The management theory paradox

Does the gurus' influence – their apparent status as the unacknowledged legislators of mankind – make sense? One obvious answer is that management theory matters because management matters. Put simply, it changes companies and the way that people work; and in a world where many companies are bigger than some countries and where most people spend more of their waking hours at work than at home, that changes lives – often dramatically. While most other academics – even scientists and economists – have to wait decades to see their work have any practical impact, the gurus' ideas are often tested immediately. There are few other academic disciplines that can claim to be so 'alive'.

Yet there is a catch. Management theory is bedevilled by a paradox: how can an academic discipline which matters so much be so unrespected? Management theory, even its foremost thinkers admit, is still far from respectable. As Peter Drucker puts it, people use the word 'guru' only because they do not want to say 'charlatan'. Another guru, Henry Mintzberg, has the motto 'the higher a monkey climbs the more you see its arse' pinned to his wall. Even in America, academics at business schools are regarded with condescension – and with suspicion. Outside America, the reaction in common rooms and Grandes Ecoles is far more vicious. Management gurus often throw out intellectual grappling hooks to older disciplines, such as economics, philosophy and history; other academics seldom return the favour.

At first sight, this looks like a cover for academic jealousy. What underfunded medieval historian, toiling away in an ancient library for an audience of hundreds and a bus conductor's salary, could fail to be annoyed by the corporate-jet-and-speaking-tour lifestyle of a 'human-resources management expert'? There is a little in this, but not enough to explain the management theory paradox. The hard fact remains that most academics are rude about management theory simply because they do not think that it is very profound. And these doubts are not confined to snooty ivory towers. Talk to virtually any publisher privately about management books and you will probably unearth the attitude: 'Isn't it incredible that this stuff sells?' (This is more than just literary prejudice against 'boring' business books: by some counts, managers fail to finish four in every five business books they buy.)[5] Nor are those who deal more directly with management theory any more flattering. Corner a consultant, charge him or her up with alcohol, and the chances are that he or she will admit the same thing as the publisher. Even ordinary business people – including those who have sacked thousands in the name of one of these theories – will blush awkwardly when asked how 'intellectual' management theory is. Sooner or later, in virtually every case, the word 'bullshit' appears.

Perhaps a better word would be an older Anglo-Saxon equivalent: management theory lacks what Yorkshire folk used to call 'bottom'. Even if it is not all 'bullshit', then enough of it is to disqualify the rest. In many cases, the blame lies with the dismal range of tub-thumping charlatans ('Transform your company in three days for $10,000') who have jumped on to the management theory bandwagon because there is no longer any room left on the bandwagons peddling advice on sex or dieting. Such people make convenient scapegoats, but (to mix metaphors with the same enthusiasm as they do) they are basically red herrings when it comes to the management theory paradox. There are plenty of appalling economics papers and unspeakable poems published every year, but the thinking world does not turn up its nose at economics or literature. The real problem is that there are grave doubts over the serious canon of management theory.

Witnesses for the prosecution

Management theory, according to the case against it, has four defects: it is constitutionally incapable of self-criticism; its terminology usually confuses rather than educates; it rarely rises above basic common sense; and it is faddish and bedevilled by contradictions that would not be allowed in more rigorous disciplines. The implication of all four charges is that management gurus are conmen, the witch doctors of our age, playing on business people's anxieties in order to sell snake oil. The gurus, many of whom have sprung suspiciously from the 'great university of life' rather than any orthodox academic discipline, exist largely because we let them get away with it. Modern management theory is no more reliable than tribal medicine. Witch doctors, after all, often got it right – by luck, by instinct or by trial and error.

The first charge against management theory – its lack of self-criticism – we happily accept. Indeed, one of the points of this book is to provide just such criticism. The second charge – that much of it is incomprehensible gobbledegook – we also happily accept. Another of the purposes of this book is to translate 'managementese' into something approaching English. There seems to be something in the water in business schools or at management conferences that destroys people's capacity to speak plainly or write clearly. Read the following paragraph, for example, written by Gary Hamel and C.K. Prahalad, two of the better gurus:

Wave participants involved their direct reports in the discovery process. Each wave appointed a few 'linking pins' responsible for interacting the wave's work with that of the other waves. Change team members acted as coaches to each wave. The output of every wave was thoroughly debated by the other waves and with the Leadership Council. Finally, an 'integration team', made up of some of the more 'convergent thinkers' across the waves, boiled the work down to its essence and produced a draft strategic architecture that again was widely debated in the company.[6]

Obfuscation and jargon is not just confined to the printed word. The idea for this book sprang out of a symposium held at a Swiss management forum, where a room full of German businessmen endeavoured heroically to understand what an American guru was on about. Every direct, practical query from the floor received an ever vaguer response from the podium. Specific questions, along the lines of 'How should we apply your ideas?' were answered by philosophical musings about what words such as 'apply' meant and an invitation to the whole room to discuss 'apply'. A few incomprehensible diagrams were produced 'just as a loose framework'. Interestingly, the German businessmen blamed themselves for not understanding.

What then of the third, more substantial charge: that, underneath this convenient cloud of obfuscation, most of what the gurus say is blindingly obvious? Too often to outside eyes, management gurus seem to be dealing in applied common sense ('the customer is king'); many of their catch phrases ('total quality management') now seem trite. They often claim to be predicting the future when all they are doing is describing the present. Just as Lenin's *Imperialism: the Highest Stage of Capitalism* predicted the outbreak of the First World War three years after it had actually happened, management gurus are forever prophesying a future that has already arrived.

There is an element of truth in this, but less than critics allege. Some of the things that strike us nowadays as blindingly obvious were anything but obvious when far-sighted management theorists began to talk about them. Peter Drucker, for example, was predicting the decline of the blue-collar worker and the rise of the 'knowledge worker' back in the 1950s. People have stopped preaching about 'total quality management' not because quality has gone out of fashion, but because everybody is striving for it. Besides, there is nothing inherently wrong with stating the obvious. One of the arguments for hiring management consultants is that they can see what is obvious to an outsider but incomprehensible to an insider.

However, the most common criticism of management theory focuses on the fourth charge: its faddishness. Management theorists have a passion for permanent revolution that would have made Trotsky or Mao Ze Dong green with envy. Theorists are forever unveiling ideas, christened with some acronym and tarted up in scientific language, which are supposed to 'guarantee competitive success'. A few months later, with the ideas tried out and 'competitive success' still as illusory as ever, the theorists unveil some new idea. The names speak for themselves: Theory Z, Management by Objectives, Brainstorming, Managerial Grid, T Groups, Intrapreneurship, Demassing, Excellence, Managing By Walking Around and so on.

The fashion in theories is mirrored by a fashion in companies. Gurus are constantly discovering companies that seem to have found the secret of competitive success. A few years later these miracle organisations are faltering, troubled or even bankrupt. In 1982 Tom Peters' *In Search of Excellence* identified forty-three excellent American companies and tried to distil the sources of their success. But fewer than five years after the book's publication two-thirds of the companies studied had ceased to be excellent. Some, such as Atari and Avon, were in serious trouble; others, like Wang and Du Pont, were no longer outstanding. IBM was well advanced in its serious decline. But, rather than taking a vow of silence, Tom Peters produced yet more books, advocating different solutions to America's problems.

These theories seem to have a large and willing (if confused) audience among managers. In 1995 a survey by Bain & Co, a consultancy, of what use managers around the world made of twenty-five leading management techniques found that the average company used 11.8 of these techniques in 1993 and 12.7 in 1994. The managers were on course to use 14.1 techniques in 1995.[7] Though Americans are usually singled out as the worst offenders, their consumption rate (12.8) was only slightly higher than France (11.4) and Japan (11.5) and behind the biggest binger, Britain (13.7).

Management fashions seem to be growing ever more fickle: the life-cycle of an idea has now shrunk from a decade to a year or less. Humble businessmen trying to keep up with the latest fashion often find that, by the time they have implemented the new craze, it looks outdated. The only people who win out of this are the theorists, who just go on getting richer and richer. Indeed it is not hard to construct an Oliver Stone movie out of the available evidence for a concerted conspiracy. Established gurus, with jet-set lifestyles to support, are always looking for ways to update their arguments; would-be gurus, be they overworked management consultants dreaming of spending some time with their families or under-employed business professors dreaming of first-class travel, are always trying to invent the revolutionary ideas that will establish their reputations; and everybody in the business is desperate to keep the wheel turning.

The contradictory corporation

All the complaints about faddism miss the point. There is nothing necessarily wrong about trying out ideas. Rather like jogging or pumping iron, a new theory forces companies to exercise their corporate muscles. (General Electric's Jack Welch even dubs one of his management systems 'Work-Out', implying that managerial change is good for corporate health.) The problem comes when these ideas contradict each other. The real problem with management theory is that it is pulling institutions and individuals in conflicting directions.

For every theory dragging companies one way there are two other theories dragging it another. One moment, the gurus are preaching total quality management – and the importance of checking quality and reducing defects; the next, they are insisting that what matters is speed (which means being a little less painstaking about checking quality). One moment, they are saying that what gives a company its edge is its corporate culture, the more distinctive the better; the next they are ordering companies to become more 'multicultural' in order to be able to hold up a mirror to the rest of society. One moment, companies are urged to agree upon and then follow a single strong 'vision'; the next they are being warned that they live in an 'age of uncertainty' where following any single vision can be suicidal. Most management theorists have not worked out whether it is important to be global or local, to be big or small, to be run in the interests of shareholders or stakeholders. Usually, they end up by telling managers to do both.

The contradictions are particularly poisonous when they involve a company's relations with its staff. One of the more fashionable words in management theory is 'trust' – it is this, we are told, that will keep 'knowledge workers' loyal and inspire them to come up with ideas. Yet all the gurus also preach the virtue of 'flexibility', which is usually shorthand for sacking people. Indeed, there is a growing contradiction between the interests of companies and those of their employees. What companies do to make themselves secure – laying off workers, putting them on short-term contracts or introducing flexible schedules – is precisely what makes those workers feel insecure. Meanwhile, the only person who could sort out these contradiction is the one who – thanks to all that delayering – has the least time to do it: the boss.

These contradictions within firms reflect a deeper intellectual confusion at the heart of management theory, which has left it not so much a coherent discipline as a battleground between two radically opposed philosophies. Management theorists usually belong to one of two rival schools, each of which is inspired by a different philosophy of human nature; and management practice has oscillated wildly between these two positions. Scientific management is based on the idea that the average worker is a lazy dolt who is redeemed only by greed. The job of the manager is to break down jobs into their component parts, so that even the dumbest can master them, and design incentive systems, so that even the laziest will exert himself. Humanistic management, on the other hand, is based on the idea that the average worker is a model human being, intelligent, creative and self-motivating. The job of the manager is to ensure that work is interesting enough to bring out the best in his employees, by dint of devolving decisions to shop-floor workers, creating self-managing teams, and encouraging workers to make suggestions about how the company might be improved. This, in essence, is the debate between 'hard' and 'soft' management.

The first theory held sway until the Second World War, in the guise of scientific management; the second gained ground in the 1950s and 1960s, under the banner of the 'human-relations movement'. In the 1980s the humanists pointed to Japan as a country that devolved power to workers and eschewed scientific management. This soft approach was increasingly overshadowed by hard realities: for all their kind words companies everywhere began to chop back staff. By the early 1990s the dominant management theory was re-engineering, which tried to adapt Taylorism to the age of the computer.

The contradictory corporation has had two alarming effects. The first has been to reinforce anxiety, from the boardroom down. American managers have an acronym which captures the effect of all the changes: BOHICA – or bend over, here it comes again. *Business Week* quoted one American manager delivering his verdict on management fashion: 'Last year it was quality circles . . . this year it will be zero inventories. The truth is, one more fad and we will all go nuts.'[8] That was in 1986, and since then the velocity of fads – and their ability to contradict one another – has increased considerably.

The second problem is to do with language – and commitment. As contradictory theories zip past them, managers have learned how to pay lip service to theories without really understanding them, let alone bothering to implement them. Many managers are rather like Soviet bureaucrats, living in a dual world – the real world and the world of officially sanctioned ideology. Thus they talk about 'empowerment' but habitually hoard power, or proclaim that they are 're-engineering' their organisations when they are really just sacking a few of the more lacklustre workers.

This doublespeak matters because management theory is the

language of the international élite. An increasing number of people who rule our companies and our countries speak in its terms. For the young and ambitious, a business-school education is looking more and more of a necessity (and a spell at a consultancy more of a probability). Eavesdrop in the business-class lounge of any airport from Shanghai to San Francisco and you will hear a familiar vernacular. In politics, the old battles between left and right no longer seem to matter. Bill Clinton and Tony Blair won office largely by adopting the right's policies on everything from welfare to job-creation. Instead the battleground has become one of managerial efficiency: who will 'manage' the economy, who will 'restructure' government, who has the necessary 'leadership skills', and so on. If this debate is carried out in terms that are contradictory or empty, then we all suffer.

With a scalpel not a hatchet

Some would argue that all these contradictions mean that management theory is itself a contradiction in terms. We would rather see it as an immature discipline, prevented from growing up partly by its enormous financial success.

Management theory, we maintain, is in roughly the same sort of state that economics was a century ago. Many of its fundamental tenets have yet to be established. The discipline still awaits its John Maynard Keynes, Friedrich Hayek or Milton Friedman. It lacks rules of debate, so that the discipline remains open to anybody with an axe to grind – much as economics was open to the likes of Karl Marx. However, just as anybody wanting to know about economics 100 years ago could draw on writers such as Alfred Marshall, Adam Smith and David Ricardo, management theory already has its founding fathers, among them Alfred Sloan and Peter Drucker. Management theory has also generated debates on such momentous subjects as globalisation, the nature of work, and the changing structure of companies. Perhaps even more importantly, the discipline has generated ideas that work. Japanese manufacturers trounced American ones in the 1980s because they embraced 'quality'.

Dig into virtually any area of management theory and you will find, eventually, a coherent position of sorts. The problem is that in order to extract that nugget you have to dig through an enormous amount of waffle. This book is an attempt to extract those nuggets.

Needless to say, it would have been much easier (and often far more pleasurable) to have trashed the industry. There is a wealth of material for anybody hoping to produce a hatchet job. We would rather see *The Witch Doctors* as a 'scalpel job', an attempt to separate the good (or, at any rate, the influential) from the bad and the irrelevant – and to look at its effect on companies and societies around the world. By definition this has been an exclusive rather than an inclusive task. If ideas or thinkers fail the test completely we have usually left them out, rather than waste ink on debunking them.

We begin by looking at the life-cycle and influence of one of the most influential fads: re-engineering (Chapter One). We then take a look at the enormous industry that produces and sells management theory (Chapter Two). Next come two chapters devoted to individual gurus: Peter Drucker (Chapter Three) is the father of modern management and a natural introduction to most of the big debates of our time. Tom Peters (Chapter Four) has been the most influential guru of the past two decades – not just because of what he has said but also because of the way in which he has said it.

'Rethinking the Company' (Chapter Five), which looks at the way that traditional corporate structures have collapsed over the past decade, introduces a series of chapters on the contortions taking place within companies: the difficulties of trying to combine knowledge, learning and innovation (Chapter Six); and the conflict between 'vision' and other forms of strategy (Chapter Seven). Chapter Eight looks at how all these ideas, many of them imposed by bosses, are actually putting increasing pressure on the boardroom, making leadership ever more difficult; it also deals with the debates about what companies are for and whether they are responsible to their shareholders alone or to a wider group of stakeholders. We close this section with a look at how all these corporate gyrations are changing the world of work, and with it the lives of ordinary people (Chapter Nine).

Our next subject is globalisation and the extent to which geography determines what companies do and how they do it (Chapter Ten). Management theory itself is now a global industry. Lean production, an idea invented in America but developed in Japan, has changed the way that factories around the world operate; now Japanese companies are struggling to learn from the West – but do they still have something to teach the rest of us (Chapter Eleven)? In Chapter Twelve we move to management's new frontier, developing Asia, where the overseas Chinese are pioneering a new sort of organisation but where there is also enormous demand for western management ideas. Will a new hybrid emerge just as it once did in Japan?

Finally we look at two areas where management theory is making fast – and often frightening – headway. The first is the public sector (Chapter Thirteen) – a place where doctors now have to decide whether treating people is within their core competencies, teachers issue mission statements and generals talk about war being 'the ultimate benchmarking exercise'. Another area is the wilder (but extremely profitable) realm of management, where the discipline mixes with self-help, futurology and downright quackery (Chapter Fourteen).

We have conducted our audit with two groups of readers in mind. The first group is the huge number of people who already buy business books, but who find them confusing and faddish – and usually never finish them. More and more people are assuming some sort of managerial responsibility; and managers are more and more frightened of losing their jobs. These people need to know about management – and not just American management. The case-studies we use stretch from Stockholm to Shanghai and Seoul. The second group are 'normal' readers who are only just becoming aware of management theory. This category should encompass virtually every intelligent reader, but it could include: a government worker in Derby who wants to know why her husband has been re-engineered out of his job at Rolls-Royce (and wonders if she will soon be re-engineered out of her job too); a sociology professor at the London School of Economics curious to inspect a wealthy neighbouring discipline; or a political activist who wants to know why the British government became obsessed by 'internal markets'.

Our aim has been to challenge the specialist readers without confusing the generalists. If any piece of jargon has somehow slipped through our net, we apologise. Time and again, confronted by a theory or a passage in a book, we have returned to three questions. Is it intelligible? Does it add more than mere common sense? And is it relevant? In short we have tried to judge the gurus on the same terms by which the foremost of them – such as Peter Drucker and Michael Porter – have themselves insisted to us that they wish to be judged – as part of a serious 'intellectual' discipline.

PART ONE

How it Works

THE FAD IN PROGRESS:
RE-ENGINEERING

There is something heartening about the sight of people practising what they preach and thriving on it: astrologers making millions on lotteries or marriage-guidance counsellors wallowing in uxoriousness. So when Fred Wiersema, a management consultant at CSC Index, an ambitious young consultancy, and Michael Treacy, an independent consultant with strong links to the same firm, published a book called *The Discipline of Market Leaders* in early 1995, it seemed entirely appropriate that, despite indifferent reviews, the book became a market leader in its own right. It stayed on the *New York Times* best-seller list for fifteen weeks, climbing as high as number five and selling 250,000 copies.

This rosy version of events lasted only until the 7 August edition of *Business Week*, which published a long article about how the two consultants, working in conjunction with CSC Index, had used tactics more commonly associated with the grubbier parts of the music industry to get their book into the charts. It has long been common for consultancies to buy large quantities of books written by their employees to distribute to their clients and prospective clients as freebies, or just to decorate the office. At around the same time Gemini Consulting was buying 5,000 copies of *Transforming the Organization*, a book written by two of its own men, Francis Gouillart and James Kelly. However, these purchases are normally done in the open, so that the *New York Times* can take account of such corporate largesse. With *The Discipline of Market Leaders*, shadowy people connected with the consultancy spent $250,000 buying some 10,000 copies of the book in small quantities at bookshops all around the country, paying special attention to those thought to be followed by the *New York Times*. The purchases were often not made in CSC Index's name or in those of the two authors; instead other employees and third parties bought the books and were then reimbursed. Another 40,000 copies that were bought by CSC Index clients were also funnelled through hundreds of small bookshops. A database marketing company called Paragon, which bought 10,000 copies of the book (for which it was fully reimbursed by CSC Index), had to store copies in a tractor trailer parked outside its office.

Treacy and Wiersema denied any wrongdoings, claiming simply that it was 'smart marketing'. Other publishers called it 'disgusting'. Although, at first sight, there is little to be gained from spending $250,000 buying your own book in the most expensive way possible, there are considerable spin-offs from getting a book into the *New York Times* best-seller lists. It increases the value of the book's overseas rights and also of the likely advances on any future books. It also makes the authors a more valuable commodity on the speaker circuit (Treacy was charging $30,000 for a talk when the scandal broke). And the aura of success itself increases sales: people who had earlier dismissed *Discipline of Market Leaders* as trite decided that there must be something in it to justify the fuss. However, the chief potential gainer had been CSC Index, which shared the copyright to the ideas behind the book with the authors, and was just beginning to introduce the theories to its customers. It stood to gain tens of millions of dollars in consulting fees.

Business Week's article had a crushing effect. The *New York Times* adjusted its best-seller list. Other newspapers and magazines picked up the story (which might have grown still bigger had Disney not decided to bid for ABC/Capital Cities on the following Monday, monopolising American business pages for most of the next week). One conference organiser who had booked the authors to speak complained about having to deal with angry telephone calls from participants. It also emerged that CSC Index had used similar tactics to buy 7,500 copies of another book published at about the same time, called *Reengineering Management*. This time the author was James Champy, one of the consultancy's founders. To complete a bad month, CSC Index also lost the second phase of a lucrative consulting project at the *New York Times*.

Reversing the industrial revolution

The scandal over *Market Leaders* is actually a chapter – some would call it an epilogue – in a much bigger story also involving CSC Index and Champy: re-engineering. (Champy left Index for Perot Systems in 1996, but was the firm's presiding genius throughout re-engineering's glory days.) Re-engineering is arguably the most ambitious management theory of our time. The movement's founders, James Champy and Michael Hammer, a mathematician turned computer scientist who now sells re-engineering full-time, insist that re-engineering is the most radical change in business thinking since the industrial revolution. Re-engineering teaches that managers need to tear up their old blueprints and start with a clean sheet of paper if they are to stand any chance of surviving. Asked what he does for a living, Hammer, who combines a mathematician's logic with a prose-lyte's enthusiasm, replies, quite simply, 'Reversing the industrial revolution.'[1]

Re-engineering has established itself as the first great management fad of the 1990s, contributing to millions of people losing their jobs and millions more working in entirely new ways. Having reorganised corporate America, the discipline's apostles are now carrying its message to the public sector, and around the world. By 1996 several surveys showed that more European firms than American ones were engaged in re-engineering. The Japanese edition of Hammer and Champy's book, *Reengineering the Corporation*, sold 250,000 copies in its first three months.

Why was re-engineering so wildly popular? To answer this question, a little scene-setting is necessary. By the mid-1990s, most managers found themselves in a quandary. They felt let down by two ideas in which they had invested near-blind devotion. The first was technology – particularly the personal computer, a machine that now sat accusingly on every manager's desk. Computers were becoming faster, cheaper and much easier to use. However, there was a hitch – officially discovered by economists, but long suspected by every corporate treasurer who could count: all this splendid new technology was not making people any more productive. Despite enormous investment in information technology throughout the 1980s, most of the available numbers showed that companies had gained very little from it.

The other treacherous friend was the fad that had preceded re-engineering: 'total quality management'. By the early 1990s, it had become an act of managerial heresy to argue against 'quality'. To simplify a little, TQM meant getting products and services right the first time, rather than waiting for them to be finished before checking them for errors. As every manager knows, it was through such devilish techniques that Japanese companies, such as Toyota, had built more reliable cars and 'stolen' the American market from Detroit. By the early 1990s western manufacturers were imitating those methods, and beginning to see improvements in customer satisfaction and employee morale.

But 'information technology' and 'quality' shared a more fundamental problem: they seemed to involve doing much the same things as before, with much the same workforce – only doing them with the help of computers and doing them more painstakingly. The machine had not been redesigned; rather, it had simply had a few new gadgets added to it. TQM was a particularly tricky business. Joseph Juran, a quality expert, estimated in 1993 that only fifty of the top 500 American companies had attained 'world class quality'. And since virtually everybody was doing it, quality had become more of a basic necessity than a competitive advantage. In such an environment, managers began to sense that continued gains in productivity, market share, and profitability were going to have to come from somewhere else. As it happened, a new management theory had begun to make the rounds of the business schools and consultancies just as this uneasy realisation announced itself in corporate boardrooms across the United States. The theory had the added virtue of combining technology and quality into one package.

Disposing of Adam Smith

'Business-process re-engineering', as the name implies, is an attempt to break an organisation down into its component parts and then put some of them back together again to create a new machine. That means asking what the machine is expected to do in the first place – in the jargon, what the 'processes' are supposed to achieve. In a typical re-engineering project ten to twenty young consultants descend on a company, draw up maps of process flows, propose ripping up old accounting procedures and suggest that people from different departments work together in one team (with a good portion of them losing their jobs). Rather than focusing on what comes out of the machine at the end, a re-engineered company's edge comes from its efficiency. Process is more important than product; indeed good products should naturally follow good processes.

This involves slaughtering a number of sacred cows. The first is Adam Smith. In *Wealth of Nations* Smith advocated a system based on employee specialisation and economies of scale. Famously, he observed that a group of pin makers who each concentrated on a particular part of the task could make more pins than a group in which each worker made the whole pin. Industrialists such as Henry Ford and Alfred Sloan perfected this system, building assembly lines and splitting workers into different departmental fiefs, such as marketing and design. Mass production always had its downside, leaving many workers bored and alienated; more recently, its whole *raison d'être* has begun to disappear, according to the re-engineers, as demand has become more uneven and machines have taken over more and more menial jobs.

One of re-engineering's discoveries is that, as a result of information technology, it is often more efficient to turn back to the system Adam Smith rejected. Why should it take six weeks to process a credit form, with each specialist filling out a single line before passing it on to a colleague, when a single clerk, armed with a computer to deal with any specialised problems, could get the job done in ninety minutes? What matters, argue the re-engineers, is the customer, and the customer could not care a fig which departmental manager is supposed to sign a form: all he or she wants is a quick answer and somebody who can be held responsible for it.[2]

Re-engineers blame a lot of corporate inertia on the great 'functional chimneys', such as marketing departments or even IT departments, which dominate most big organisations. Re-engineering consultants have repeatedly discovered that most of the time wasted on any particular process is frittered away during the transfer from one department to another. Re-engineering prefers to group people from different functions into teams dedicated to carrying out processes that span several functions. Thus people from marketing, design and research can be gathered together in a team devoted to the 'new product development process'.

Such a reorganisation also gets rid of that other pet hate-figure for re-engineers, the middle manager: if a firm uses information technology correctly, there is no need to have a connecting layer of people between the powers on high and the shop floor. Information should just zip around 'horizontally' rather than filter down 'vertically'.

Don't automate, obliterate

Put in its own strident, devastating tones, re-engineering can sound a little mad. However, it is easy to see why even perfectly sane managers have latched on to the idea. At a time when business seems to be getting more complicated and the answers more uncertain, when other gurus order you to surrender to your circumstances by learning how to live in 'an age of unreason' or to 'thrive on chaos', re-engineering offers the promise of certainty and control. Here, at last, is a clear-cut, no-nonsense guide to rebuilding your business and beating the competition. It is also engagingly modern: arguably the first management theory to use computers as a starting point, rather than just a neat addition. And it has been marketed with rare panache.

Re-engineering, like Hammer and Champy, was the product of two institutions that are just around the corner from each other in Cambridge, Massachusetts, and which feed off each other's ideas and personnel: CSC Index, the consulting arm of the giant Computer Sciences Corporation, and the Massachusetts Institute of Technology's Sloan School of Management. Both institutions were obsessed with working out what the computer revolution meant for the nature of work and the structure of organisations. The term 're-engineering' was first coined in the mid-1980s when a group of young MIT-trained consultants at the Index Group, one of CSC Index's antecedents, masterminded a major restructuring of their own 'business processes'. Thomas Gerrity, who then held jobs with both CSC Index and MIT and is now Dean of Wharton Business School, recalls dismissing the term as far too 'techie' to catch on.[3] But it turned out that 'techie' was just what American business wanted.

The first place most businessmen heard about 're-engineering' was in an article by Michael Hammer in the July/August 1990 edition of the *Harvard Business Review*, appropriately entitled 'Re-engineering Work: Don't Automate, Obliterate'. Three years later Hammer and Champy laid out the ideas more carefully in a book. *Reengineering the Corporation* sold almost two million copies in seventeen languages, making it one of the biggest-selling business books since Peters' *In Search of Excellence*. The business press latched on to the word with extraordinary enthusiasm: the number of articles using 're-engineering' in the title increased from ten in 1990 to well over 800 in 1994.[4]

Soon every consultancy worth its flipchart was marketing some form of re-engineering. Arthur D. Little, a management consultancy, called it 'high performance business'; Gemini used the word 'transformation.' And the business rolled in. A survey in 1994 by Price Waterhouse, an accountancy and consultancy firm, found that 78 per cent of Fortune 500 companies and 68 per cent of British ones were engaged in some form of re-engineering. A survey by CSC Index at the same time produced nearly identical figures, but also found that the average number of re-engineering projects for each company was 3.3 in America and 3.8 in Europe.

Re-engineering has also been spreading in two directions. The first is out of its manufacturing heartland and into service businesses, utilities and the public sector. One of the boldest apostles of the discipline in America was William Bratton, the head of New York's Police Department (see page 313–5). The other direction is geographic. In Japan, for instance, the discipline was first pioneered by the local subsidiaries of American companies, such as IBM Japan. But it spread quickly: in December 1993 a lecture session by a Japanese consultancy on 'Proposal for re-engineering – Japanese style' drew such a large crowd that the consultancy put on two more lectures. In early 1994 the *Yomiuri Shimbun*, a popular newspaper, cited 're-engineering' alongside 'China' as the two key words for that year.

Worse than the disease?

Inevitably, a discipline that made such a fuss about obliteration soon became associated with just one word: downsizing. A fairly typical survey of eighty main financial officers at big American companies in May 1995 found that the main reason for wanting to re-engineer was cost-cutting (29 per cent) followed closely by 'someone important said we should do it' (26 per cent). Only a tenth did it primarily to improve service or quality.[5]

In 1994 corporate America's profits rose 11 per cent, yet it also eliminated 516,069 jobs and announced $10 billion of restructuring charges.[6] The most dramatic slimmers included some of the biggest money-machines: Mobil, Procter & Gamble, American Home Products and Sara Lee. Edwin Artzt, P&G's chief, said that his firm was cutting 13,000 of its 106,000 workers to stay competitive – and he scolded the public for thinking that corporate restructuring was a sign of trouble: 'That is definitely not our situation.'[7] The stock market certainly no longer reached that conclusion: when Mobil announced its plan to shed a tenth of its workforce in early 1995, the oil company's shares jumped to a fifty-two-week high. The same association of restructuring with corporate virility seemed to be developing in other countries: Britain's stock market reached a new peak in September 1995, in the same week as a blitz of job-loss announcements, including the disappearance of 9,000 people at the pharmaceuticals giant, Glaxo-Wellcome.

To what extent was re-engineering responsible for this bloodletting? In many cases, the slimmers cited the discipline directly. In early 1994, for example, GTE, an American telephone company, gave details of a re-engineering programme that would cut its customer-service centres from 171 to eleven, and its revenue-collection centres from five to one. In all, 17,000 jobs would go in the next three years, and some $1.2 billion would be invested in new sorts of technology, but the potential cost savings would be around $1 billion per year.[8] What is beyond doubt is that, as the predominant management fad of the time, re-engineering set the agenda. Even those companies that were shedding weight in their own way were still thinking about rivals that were re-engineering. Like a pair of omnipresent television-aerobic instructors, Hammer and Champy did not actually need to be at a manager's shoulder to make him feel overweight.

The question of responsibility is a moot one because by late 1994 there were doubts about just how good for the patient all this slimming was proving to be. True, it had helped make America more competitive, at least for a while. America's unit-labour costs were falling whilst those of Japan and Germany had risen. Unfortunately, by 1994 there were also signs that it had gone too far, with people beginning to talk about 'the anorexic corporation'. One study by the American Management Association showed that two-thirds of firms cutting back in any given year did so again the next year; and a quarter of those surveyed had done so in three or more of the past five years. Another study by Mitchell & Co, a Massachusetts-based consultancy, found that the shares of downsizing companies outperformed the stock market for six months after a downsizing was announced. Three years later they lagged.

The first response of any re-engineer to such statistics is, of course, to claim that there is a sizeable difference between downsizing and re-engineering proper. However, the available evidence on re-engineering proper is only slightly better than that on downsizing. True, there are examples of confirmed re-engineered successes, notably Bell Atlantic, Federal Express, Ford and Hallmark Cards. There is also plenty of hype from consultants about how much their clients have increased their productivity. CSC Index claims that studies of its clients show that fundamentally changing a business process produced 'an average improvement of 48 per cent in costs, 80 per cent in time and 60 per cent in defects'. (In a typical piece of re-engineering hyperbole, the consultancy then goes on to say: 'The results are startling – but then re-engineering is defined in part by the outrageousness of its goals and the ambition of its scope.')[9]

However, as soon as surveys widen to include other people's clients such results evaporate. A survey by Arthur D. Little in the summer of 1994 found that only 16 per cent of managers were fully satisfied; and 68 per cent were encountering unexpected problems. By late 1994, even Michael Hammer and James Champy were admitting that many attempts at re-engineering were falling short of their goals.

Move over Mainwaring

So how successful is re-engineering? The answer, unsurprisingly, is that the discipline is good at some things, not so good at others. Consider a case-study of a company regarded as one of re-engineering's successes.

In September 1992 Britain's Lloyds Bank embarked on a massive re-engineering effort: by mid-1995 it had changed operations accounting for two-thirds of the costs at each of its branches and involving nearly all its 29,000 employees.[10] In many ways Lloyds was a model re-engineer (and not just because it was advised by CSC Index, then Champy's consultancy). Although cost-cutting was a motive, the clearing bank turned to re-engineering principally because of worries about the quality of its service – particularly in comparison with building societies. Another related problem was organisation – or rather the lack of it. During the 1980s countless new services had been bolted on to local branches, simply by adding more staff. 'We saw the branch system as an enormous bucket into which things could just be dropped,' Gordon Pell, the general manager of Lloyds' retail operations, recalls.

As in other industries, re-engineering proved a good way to remodel Lloyds' back office so that it made better use of technology. Under the bank's old system, staff were slotted into narrow jobs in an administrative hierarchy. Countless people and bits of paper were involved in jobs which, from the customer's point of view, were part of the same process. Under the old system of opening an account, for instance, a piece of paper could spend a month being shuffled from desk to desk as different staff ordered bank cards, checked credit details and so on. Re-engineered so that one person was responsible for a largely paperless (though absurdly named) 'quality-welcome' process, it took well under a week.

Five other processes were also broken down and reassembled in a mock 'laboratory' before being spread across the network in a series of 'waves'. In some cases the processes look a little contrived. For instance, before re-engineering, a customer moving their account to another bank simply told Lloyds where their new account was. Under the 'customer retention process' they are interviewed and sometimes persuaded to stay. This looks like no more than common-sense marketing, but Lloyds bosses insist that it was only thanks to re-engineering that they thought of it.

All the processes are monitored closely (once again, using technology). For instance, Kate Pepper, a young assistant at Lloyds' branch in London's Regent Street, used to send out forms for opening an account the day after she met a customer; by sending them out immediately, she increased the branch's computer-generated score for this process from 45 per cent to 90 per cent. The performance of people like Pepper is also now closely monitored by 'mystery shoppers' – spies sent by Lloyds to check on performance. And an increasing proportion of Pepper's salary and those of her colleagues is tied to their performance.

But did it work? The bank's most obvious gain from re-engineering has been financial. Lloyds will not give any exact details of the figures, but it claims that the project has comfortably cleared the bank's 12 per cent return on capital. Many of the changes introduced by re-engineering paid for themselves rapidly. For instance, the number of faulty cheque-book orders fell by 30 per cent – enough to pay for all the computers bought to monitor that activity.

On the other hand, for all the timely cheque books, there is much less evidence that Lloyds met its primary goal of making customers happy. Britain's high-street banks, including Lloyds, were even less loved at the beginning of 1996 than they had been at the start of the decade. One reason for this is that customers increasingly encountered grumpy staff demoralised by downsizing. All the British banks were struggling to cut costs and to automate jobs previously done by humans. The high-street banks shed some 80,000 people in 1989–95, and they were talking of laying off another 70,000.

Did re-engineering contribute to this unease? Lloyds avoided using the word re-engineering ('too many people associated it with obliteration'), opting instead for a 'service quality improvement programme' – or SQIP. Nevertheless, the pain and worry was obvious. In the Regent Street branch alone SQIP, combined with other changes, saw numbers decline from forty-two to eighteen by mid-1995. Overall the number of branches had been cut from 2,100 to 1,800. As elsewhere re-engineering was particularly tough on middle managers: forty-one out of eighty area-manager jobs went.

And when will it stop? Re-engineering helped reduce Lloyds' ratio of operating costs to revenues from 64.3 per cent in 1990 to 63.6 per cent in 1994, but many financial firms have ratios below 60 per cent. In America, banks have begun to charge people for using human tellers rather than ATMs; in Britain telephone banking companies such as First Direct are drawing people away from high-street banks that customers perceive as being no more friendly than a voice at the other end of the telephone. The staff at Lloyds plainly think that they need a breather; it is equally apparent that the next re-engineering wave will have to be more fundamental, and might even have to ask whether Lloyds needs a branch network at all.

The backlash begins

Although it is stuck in an industry that seems to need ever fewer people, Lloyds is, in re-engineering terms, a fairly bloodless case-study. In January 1994 Nynex, New York's telephone company, embarked on a $3 billion programme that got rid of 16,800 people or 22 per cent of its workforce.[11] As with Lloyds, any cost-benefit analysis would show that the exercise paid for itself several times over. However, as a cover story in *Business Week* in 1995 made clear, the changes badly damaged morale. 'The officers are in charge of their own fates,' said a Nynex worker. 'We're not involved. We're affected.' The plan's architect, Robert Thrasher – now known as 'Thrasher the slasher' – had to turn off his answering machine at home because he received so many abusive messages. At another telephone company, GTE, unions have been so enraged by cutbacks that they have run radio advertisements detailing its alleged declining service.

It was against this background that many management thinkers started damning re-engineering. Calling it 'a polite word for downsizing', Charles Handy declared that 'blowing organisations apart is not conducive to a state of commitment and euphoria . . . The trouble with re-engineering when it is done badly – which it mostly is – is that it leaves people shattered, even the people left behind.'[12] The most influential book of the mid-1990s, *Competing for the Future* by Gary Hamel and C.K. Prahalad, argues that re-engineering has 'more to do with shoring up today's businesses than creating tomorrow's industries. Any company that succeeds at restructuring and re-engineering, but fails to create the markets of the future will find itself on a treadmill, trying to keep one step ahead of the steadily declining margins and profits of yesterday's businesses.'[13]

The re-engineers have tried to fight back. One tactic is to query the statistics. It is still an article of faith for CSC Index that re-engineering itself did not lead to huge job losses. According to a CSC Index study, each re-engineering initiative resulted in only 282 jobs (or 22 per cent of the total involved in each reorganisation) disappearing. In Europe the figure was 1,001. In many cases, the jobs were shed voluntarily or the people were moved to other parts of the organisation. By the time all these moves are averaged out, CSC Index puts the figure for lay-offs at just 336 employees per firm in America and 760 in Europe.

However, the most common defence was that people just weren't doing it right. Some people were just slashing their workforces and calling it re-engineering; others were trying to go by the book but failing to read past the first few chapters. Champy claimed that only around one in ten companies undergoing re-engineering was doing the business properly. 'Much of the criticism is based on a misconception of what re-engineering really is,' Michael Hammer wrote in *The Economist* on 5 November 1994, 'and much of the rest reflects a limited assessment of its significance.'

Apologias aside, there do appear to be real problems with re-engineering. Ironically, one of the biggest is that the discipline is far too close to the type of stop-watch management that the re-engineers affected to despise. Management pioneers such as Frederick Taylor and Henry Ford were fascinated by processes; they were both also lousy practitioners of the softer, human side of management. Re-engineering – a little like Taylorism – would work well if we were all unthinking automatons, without hearts or souls. However, simply telling a marketing man that he is no longer part of the marketing department but of the 'product-development process' does not stop him thinking like a marketing man.

Re-engineering's obsession with process rather than product also looks less than convincing. Trying to shift a firm's competitive advantage from what it makes to how it makes it might be a sensible strategy in a mature, stable business – manufacturing milk cartons for instance. However, if a firm in a faster-changing industry is making the wrong product then no amount of downsizing is going to help it. IBM's mainframe division may be a case in point. One of the first victims of many re-engineering efforts is the strategy department; but without some degree of strategic thought or vision, re-engineering always risks building a superb machine whose only purpose is to churn out antiquated products.

If strategy has made something of a comeback, so too has another favourite whipping boy of re-engineering, the middle manager. Re-engineers see middle managers as barriers to horizontal organisations. Yet they can also be the source of a company's culture, and the repositories of valuable information. Computers, it emerges, are often less successful at connecting the strategists in the boardroom to operational staff in the field than managers with long experience of the organisation. In many cases, firms that have downsized and produced big cost savings in the first year have seen those savings evaporate as they have had to train people to do jobs that many middle managers knew by heart.

A study of American companies, published in late 1995 by the *California Management Review*, found that downsizing had an adverse effect on innovation.[14] That does not necessarily mean that re-engineering makes research and development departments stop producing ideas; the more likely problem is that it destroys the informal network of contacts that allow a product to gain acceptance within an organisation. In some cases where jobs have been contracted out the chief beneficiaries are those same middle managers, now hired as contract labour. Indeed, ripping out middle management has made it hard to get long-term commitment from workers: it is very difficult to devise a career structure if all the middle rungs of the ladder are missing.

Re-engineered people feel that their employers have broken the implicit moral contract between bosses and workers – we'll work as hard as we can for you just so long as you only sack us if it's absolutely necessary. Xerox saw its reputation for paternalism destroyed when it sacked about one in ten of its workers between the beginning of 1994 and the middle of 1995, a period when it was making a profit. At about the same time, one boss at AT&T, an enthusiastic re-engineer, confessed to *The Economist* that trust levels at his firm had plummeted: 'In the past we said to employees, "Do as you're told and you have a job for life." Then we betrayed them.'[15] Any warm feeling AT&T's staff felt for Ma Bell would have disappeared in January 1996 when it laid off another 40,000 people (and were hardly restored when it later reduced the lay-offs to 28,000). British Telecom cut its workforce from 232,000 in 1990 to 148,000 in 1995, with devastating effect on morale. Internal surveys in 1995 suggested that only one-fifth of employees thought that managers could be relied upon to do what they said.

Employees in companies which are undergoing re-engineering often spent more time discussing potential job losses than they do thinking about their work. In March 1995 CoreStates Financial Corporation of Philadelphia announced it would fire 890 people – 6 per cent of its staff. 'Everybody is thinking "What is my future, what am I doing here?",' one employee told the *Wall Street Journal*. 'For the last month people have been talking more than 50 per cent of the time. Its water-cooler talk all day long.'[16] At leaving parties at Westinghouse people joked that 'the winners get to leave; the losers get to stay'. A survey by the American Management Association in mid-1995 found that more than half those asked felt more overwhelmed by work than they had done in 1993, before the recovery really started. A similar poll in Britain found that 70 per cent of workers felt less secure than they had done two years before; 44 per cent felt pressure to work late and 31 per cent said people were afraid to take time off if they were sick.[17]

In other words, re-engineering is less than it was originally cracked up to be. But that does not mean that it is useless. Re-engineering tends to work particularly well in things such as logistics and order fulfilment, because it forces a company to concentrate on speed and service – the two things which most interest customers. Thus, through re-engineering, the manufacturing and distribution side of EMI Records in North America managed to increase the number of CDs being delivered on time to retailers during their peak selling period from 90 per cent to over 99 per cent (the peak selling time matters because, as with *The Discipline of Market Leaders*, many people will only buy a record or book when it is a hit). EMI also claimed that the annual cost of transporting CDs fell by 30 per cent; and labour productivity at the distribution sites increased by 70 per cent.

Occasionally, re-engineering can galvanise an entire industry. Thanks to the discipline, America's freight-carrying railway companies recast themselves as the logistical arm of their customers. Rather than just ferrying boxes from one point to another, the railroads have begun to use computers to keep their customers informed about the whereabouts of each box. They have also begun to link up with their old foes, the truckers, to provide a more seamless service. Now companies such as Chrysler hire railway companies to take their cars all the way from the factory gate to the dealer's doors.

Even when critics consider re-engineering at its most bloody, they tend to forget what the alternatives are. British Telecom, AT&T and Nynex may be bruised but they are surely in a better state than France Télécom or NTT. It was easy to chuckle at Lou Gerstner, IBM's chairman, for declaring, 'We enter 1995 with the bulk of our right sizing behind us' (which was his way of describing 1994's 35,000 redundancies at IBM); but IBM still looked in better shape than, say, France's Bull. And Big Blue also illustrates another point that critics of re-engineering may have exaggerated. The computer maker is often included alongside firms such as General Motors and Digital in lists of firms that have downsized and still not solved their problems. That is true. But the real reason why they got into trouble in the first place had nothing to do with re-engineering.

Re-engineering re-engineered

What is needed is not to abandon re-engineering completely, but to refine it. In 1996 there was talk of taking a more 'holistic' or 'organic' approach to the discipline, involving managers as well as workers. Such compromises do not come easily for such an all-encompassing discipline. However, for an example of what a 'holistic' version of re-engineering looks like consider Corning, a technology company headquartered in the eponymous small town in the foothills of the Appalachian mountains in up-state New York.[18] Corning is the quintessential paternalist company (though the term 'paternalist' is frowned on by Corningites as being too politically incorrect). The company chairman from 1983 until 1996 was James Houghton, the great-grandson of the founder; his brother, Amory, was his predecessor as chairman and now represents the area in Congress. (If you get a hair-cut on Main Street, you stare up at a poster of 'Amo's' smiling face.) Half the town's 12,000 adult inhabitants work for Corning. Whole families have worked for the company for decades, and cannot remember a time when Corning did not pay their salary cheques. Everything about Corning ('the biggest company in the smallest town in the United States,' according to James Houghton) proclaims its commitment to good corporate citizenship, from its splendid new headquarters deliberately built low so as not to overshadow the town, to the leaflets in the lavatories warning of the dangers of herpes, smoking and bulimia nervosa.

Houghton refused categorically to consider re-engineering if it meant destroying his home town. But by the end of 1993 senior managers, some of whom also sat on the boards of companies that were undergoing re-engineering, felt that Corning could not ignore the new management theory any longer. The company's share price had fallen by a quarter. The ostensible problem was Dow Corning, a stand-alone joint-venture with Dow Chemicals to produce silicone breast-implants, which was being sued by thousands of women for potential damages. But Corning's underlying problems were two-fold. Organisationally it was a mess – it had some 150 different businesses, each with its own legal status. And those businesses – fibre optics, medical services, catalytic converters and so on – were not making money.

In the past the company, which is notorious for its enthusiasm for management theories, had had surprisingly little difficulty in combining its zest for profits with its commitment to paternalism. Corning had avoided laying off local workers by transforming itself from a glassmaker (it once made the glass for Edison's electric lights) into a technology company. Recent fashions such as total quality management, high-performance workplaces and employee empowerment essentially meant being nice to workers. Re-engineering had a very different reputation. The job of Corning's management was to see if they could introduce re-engineering without destroying a small town's economy and breaking a century-long commitment to enlightened industrial relations.

By coming to the discipline fairly late, Corning had a huge amount of experience to draw on – not least the 70 per cent of re-engineering efforts that Micheal Hammer admits have failed. It thus took a different approach. One of the biggest causes of failure in other companies is lack of consistent involvement from the top; Corning, on the other hand, made sure that senior managers sponsored each group of re-engineers, and that the company's president, Roger Ackerman (who became chairman when James Houghton retired in early 1996), took personal responsibility for each programme. Re-engineering has often failed because companies are keener on slaking the stock market's thirst for quick fixes, usually by sacking workers, than on introducing structural changes. To Wall Street's chagrin, Corning refused, point blank, to announce any immediate redundancies.

Elsewhere re-engineering had been imposed by computer-wielding consultants. At Corning the consultants were told to stay in the background. Indeed, rather than imposing re-engineering on a hostile workforce, Corning got the workers to do their own re-engineering. In January 1994, it asked key employees, many of them from middle management (a group normally despised by re-engineers), to forsake their proper jobs for a few months in order to redesign their company from top to bottom. The company put a building at their disposal (known as the 'Donut-U', because it was next to a Dunkin' Donuts store), told them to turn up in casual clothes (now policy throughout the company) and divide themselves into teams to look at processes such as 'manufacturing' and 'innovation'.

Corning made sure that the re-engineers had easy access to senior management. It also put a huge amount of effort into explaining what was going on to the workforce. Roger Ackerman held regular town meetings at which he and his colleagues explained what was happening and why. (The meetings were also videotaped and distributed to those who could not attend.) The company magazine ran frequent articles on the process. Workers were encouraged to express their worries by e-mail – anonymously if they preferred – and they were offered 'stress counselling'.

The re-engineers introduced a number of changes that are almost par for the course in re-engineering, such as reorganising its tangle of businesses (they found that 95 per cent of its sales came from only half its products). Re-engineering cut the number of levels of managers between Houghton and the shop floor from seven to five, simplified decision-making and got rid of two senior vice-presidents and their staffs. Though it is always difficult to put a figure on such things, the company calculated that re-engineering could produce $50m–60m in savings in 1996–97.

But the Corning re-engineers also used their freedom to introduce two important modifications to the discipline. First, they made sure that re-engineering applied in the boardroom just as much as on the factory floor. The bulk of the cuts in manpower came from management: and one of the biggest structural changes was to the corporate headquarters, which had to hand over more power to the operating units. Second, the Corning re-engineers made sure that change was evolutionary rather than revolutionary. Far from starting with Hammer and Champy's clean sheet of paper, the Corningites tried to build on what the company was already doing right.

Nobody at Corning pretends that re-engineering has been free of friction. The word has been the subject of nervous, often angry discussions in the town's churches and bars. When one of the authors jokingly asked what would happen if he went into one of the local bars posing as a management consultant, he was flatly told not to entertain the thought. The two local newspapers have repeatedly hinted that the company has a secret plan to re-engineer the community out of existence. The local union argued that re-engineering hangs over the valley like a skull-and-crossbones. An in-house survey concluded that 33 per cent of workers were suffering from stress, and only 12 per cent of those were coping with it.

Still, by mid-1995, when we visited the company, the overall feeling was one of relief. Corningites were acutely conscious that they had introduced the most feared management technique of their time without suffering the massive lay-offs or bitter industrial disputes that often accompanied it. Yes, the company had been forced to get rid of some workers, but most of them had gone through early retirement. Profits were improving, meaning that the jobs of those who remained were much more secure. A century's worth of paternalism may have meant that Houghton and Ackerman started with a considerable advantage over other re-engineers. All the same, they did seem to have found a middle way where words such as 'obliteration' were not necessary.

Above all, they had rejected one of the fundamental parts of the re-engineering creed that had first made the discipline so appealing to other managers: the idea that it is a mechanical, scientific process. Rather than regarding it as a retooling manual on how to reorganise your company, Houghton and Ackerman had looked on it more as a form of background music: sometimes they listened to it; and sometimes they turned it off.

The desperation of fading market leaders

The reinvention of re-engineering as a discipline in places like Corning may not be enough to save re-engineering as a business. After all, it is much easier to sell a medicine with a label saying 'This will cure you, no matter what your complaint', than it is to sell one with a label saying 'This treatment may or may not succeed, depending on your circumstances. It is likely to be painful and could well have unintended side-effects.'

To make things worse, by 1995 – the year when *The Discipline of Market Leaders* appeared – re-engineering had become a commodity business. Big consultancy firms – particularly Andersen Consulting – had moved into the market. By mid-1995 CSC Index was only the fourth largest re-engineering specialist in America. It was against this background that CSC Index threw its weight behind both Champy's lacklustre follow-up, *Reengineering Management*, and the ill-fated *Discipline of Market Leaders*. But even with the help of vigorous marketing neither book filled the gap.

What is needed is a new fad, a new idea that can be branded, preached, sold and spread all around the world.

But then with the management theory industry that is always the case.

2

THE MANAGEMENT THEORY INDUSTRY

Anyone who meets the Dean of the Wharton Business School at the University of Pennsylvania expecting an unworldly academic who lives for nothing but ideas is in for a surprise. Thomas Gerrity is as smooth as they come, immaculately tailored and perfectly coiffed. He litters his conversation not with scholarly references but with business buzzwords, even referring to his university's president as 'the CEO'.

Gerrity's business patois is not just affectation. He is one of a new breed of deans: businessmen who have been roped back into academia in order to force business schools to practise what they preach. In his previous life, Gerrity was one of the founders of CSC Index, the consultancy which invented re-engineering (see previous chapter). As dean of Wharton, Gerrity has tried to put his own creed into practice, dividing both his students and his professors into specially varied teams: each student team includes at least two non-Americans; each faculty team includes professors from different academic disciplines. He has also changed the system for gaining tenure and awarding annual pay rises in order to shift the emphasis from publishing academic articles (once the only road to success) to teaching and 'leadership'.

Many of these changes cost money, but with an annual budget of $135 million, Gerrity can afford to experiment. Over at Harvard Business School, where the annual budget is $195 million, a new dean, Kim Clark, is implementing similar reforms of his own, including a plan to put 500 case-studies on-line. Ever since *Business Week* started publishing a ranking of business schools in November 1988, deans such as Gerrity and Clark have had a licence to tamper with the syllabus, reform teaching methods and recruit expensive 'star' professors. Thanks to Gerrity's reforms, Wharton, a financially-minded school where the students have been known to throw dollar bills rather than caps into the air on graduation, has powered its way to the top of these league tables.

As Gerrity's own career suggests, business schools, consultancies and the ideas they trade in are really part of the same prosperous industry. Virtually everybody involved in management theory is making money out of it in one way or another. Indeed, the 'management theory industry' seems immune to economic cycles: consultancies take on ever more staff as their clients employ ever fewer, business schools become ever more ornate and numerous as the universities around them crumble.

This success, as we shall see, is largely a reflection of the seemingly endless demand for the industry's product. Management theory has always appealed to the thousands of people who want to get ahead; now it has tapped into the market of the millions who are scared of being left behind. However, the success and scope of the industry has also had an effect on the sort of ideas produced. With such huge vested interests, self-criticism is almost unheard of. And the industry's relentless appetite for more fuel – more ideas to process, print, sell and regurgitate – has helped to make it a peculiarly faddish discipline, where ideas are grabbed at rather than matured. In other words, the industry has often driven the theory rather than the other way round.

The breadth of the industry

The management industry can be divided a little crudely into three parts. The most obvious of these is the management consulting business, which employs at least 100,000 people full-time around the world and has been growing more than twice as fast as the world economy for the past decade. In 1996, according to *Consultancy News*, an industry newsletter, it generated about $40 billion in revenues. The biggest firm, Andersen Consulting, brought in just under $3.1 billion in 1996 – not counting another $1.38 billion of consultancy fees booked by its sister accountancy firm, Arthur Andersen.[1] Four other consultancy-accountancy combines collected over $1 billion in consultancy fees: Ernst & Young, Coopers & Lybrand, KPMG Peat Marwick and Deloitte & Touche. However the most profitable (and also the second biggest with revenues of $2.6 billion) is McKinsey: its revenue per consultant was $532,000 – compared with Andersen's $71,000. The other big 'strategic' consultants – Booz Allen & Hamilton, Gemini Consulting, Mercer Management, the Boston Consulting Group, Arthur D. Little, Bain & Co – all booked over $200,000 per partner. A measure of the youthful vitality of the industry is that more than half of today's leading consulting firms did not exist five years ago.

Consultancies have replaced Oxbridge and the Ivy League as the nurseries of the powerful. Indeed students from the latter jostle to get into the former. With good reason. The list of companies headed by ex-McKinseyites stretches from America's IBM, Levi Strauss and American Express to France's Bull and Britain's Asda. Even Ben & Jerry's, that symbol of countercultural commerce, was run for a while by an ex-consultant from the firm. In Britain, the consultancy's old-boy list includes the present head of the Confederation of British Industry (and both his immediate predecessors), the chairman of the new Securities and Investments Board, the boss of London Transport and William Hague, John Major's Welsh Secretary and now the youngest leader of the Tory party for 200 years. Alumni are going out of their way to keep in contact, giving McKinsey a much broader reach than its office network, which stretches across thirty-five countries, would suggest.

The second part of the management industry is made up of business schools. There are about 700 business schools in the United States alone. All these institutions are full of academics desperate to make their name as management theorists: the 1996 meeting of the American Academy of Management, the discipline's annual jamboree, attracted no fewer than 4,500 people. Journals such as the *Harvard Business Review* and the *California Management Review* have an influence and an audience that spreads far beyond the universities that spawned them. The Graduate Management Admission Test or GMAT examination, which practically every business school in the world compels its prospective students to sit, is a huge business in its own right. Four times a year 60,000 people sit down in 700 centres in over 100 countries to try to win a ticket to study management.

The MBA's popularity is easy to explain. The typical member of Harvard Business School's class of 1974 now looks set to retire with a net worth of $8m, and the chances are that his successors will look down on him as a pauper.[2] In 1994 the median starting pay from Harvard and Stanford hit $100,000. Nowadays, the keenest recruiters, led by banks and management consultancies, dazzle the students with offers including signing bonuses of $30,000, interest-free loans, stock options, tuition reimbursements, free cars and moving allowances. Invitations to a recent reunion of Stanford graduates from the early 1990s included a request that attendees 'chip in' for a small gift from the grateful students to their *alma mater*; it was only after he had booked his air ticket that one graduate, who had foolishly taken a lowly paid job in the British civil service, realised that the chipping-in amount was $1,000 a head.

Yet, despite this bonanza for the best students from the best schools, there are doubts about how much the average MBA is worth. After all, for many students the combined costs of two years of tuition and forgone salary can come to $100,000; and the proper way to measure the gain from a business–school education is not just to take the starting salary but to compare it against what you would have earned without the MBA. One academic who constructed an economic model of the costs and benefits of going to business school, Ronald Yeaple of Rochester Business School, found that, in nearly all cases, it took several years for students to make a profit.[3] After seven years, a Harvard Business School student could claim a positive net value of nearly $150,000, but average students from five of the top twenty schools were all sitting on losses.

The third, and least well defined, part of the management industry is what might be called the guru business. There are plenty of ways for individual management thinkers to make money. The most obvious is by writing business books, which have gone from being an exotic specialism in the mid-1970s to a mainstream money-spinner today. About 2,000 business books appear each year in America, and the best of these can sell in their millions. Until the 1980s business books were a fairly obscure specialism, selling in little more than academic numbers. All this changed with the publication of *In Search of Excellence* by Tom Peters and Robert Waterman, which sold a million copies in one year and turned both its authors into celebrities. At one point in 1983 the top three slots in the *New York Times* best-seller list were all filled by business authors (who, incidentally, had all studied at Cornell University together): Tom Peters (*In Search of Excellence*), John Naisbitt (*Megatrends*) and Kenneth Blanchard (*The One-Minute Manager*). Two years later Lee Iacocca's autobiography became the best-selling business book of all time, and one of the best-selling hardbacks ever. From then on every publisher worth his or her salt set out to discover, nurture and promote talented business writers.

Nevertheless, for many management theorists, books are largely a form of advertising for even more profitable activities. Many of these involve speaking of one kind or another. Nowadays no business conference is complete without at least one guru. Not only does the author give the event an intellectual edge, but he or she will probably be the only speaker who does not try to turn his speech into a commercial for his own company. The conference also gives the audience a chance to catch up on the latest theories without having to plough through the book. The business-speaking circuit is expanding quickly. America's Conference Board alone now holds 100 events a year (double the number five years ago): that means it requires at least 2,000 speakers a year.[4] In 1996 the biggest earner on the circuit was probably Harvey MacKay, the boss of an envelope-manufacturing firm and a motivational guru best known for *Swim with the Sharks Without Being Eaten Alive*, who charged $50,000 a speech – and gave about fifty of them a year. This put MacKay on the same level as Henry Kissinger and General Colin Powell. A clutch of other gurus, including the persistently popular Tom Peters, did not charge much less. All-day seminars or workshops with individual companies can be even more remunerative.

Like the Hollywood studios, the gurus have discovered how to sell their ideas through a range of outlets, including diaries, cassettes and training camps. For example, the Tom Peters Group, three training and communication companies headquartered in Palo Alto, California, produce videos, churn out a regular newsletter and generally help to stretch his brand. One of its more recent offerings is 'The Tom Peters Business School in a Box', which comes complete with forty-two 'personal agenda cards', fourteen 'time cards' and two dice, one coloured, one white. Significantly perhaps, the 'Business School' was the work of three of his employees, and has only a foreword by Peters. Meanwhile, Peter Senge, a prophet of 'the learning organisation', seems to have introduced franchising, allowing a Taiwanese follower, Young Show-ing, to translate his books and popularise his ideas in the Chinese-speaking world.

Overpaid and over here

Dividing the management industry into consultancies, business schools and gurus implies that it is a much more precisely structured and narrowly defined affair than it in fact is. Where for instance should one include 'MBA-ware' sellers — software companies that make teach-yourself-management programmes with names such as 'Negotiator Pro' and 'ManagePro'? Or more orthodox software makers that design their products specifically to help companies implement management fads? (The rapid rise of Germany's SAP can largely be put down to its products for companies conducting re-engineering exercises.) And what about companies that take groups of executives to the African bush or to the Scottish highlands so that they can hone their leadership skills? Or the firms that specialise in counselling outsourced workers? Or the growing numbers of management psychologists — psychometrists who draw up profiles of desirable recruits, or psychiatrists who were trained to deal with suicidal teenagers but have found it more remunerative to 'facilitate' team meetings and explain to top executives how to cope with the pressure of large pay rises.

Another complication for those who want to tie down the management industry is that it is now a global affair. Not so long ago, anyone who wanted to understand management went to an American university, studied American gurus, argued about American corporations and probably joined an American consultancy. The great debates in the subject – such as the one about the relative merits of scientific and humanistic management – were almost all conducted between Americans. But in the past couple of decades the rest of the world has started to catch up.

From Bradford to Barcelona and Berlin, the cities of Europe are now littered with business schools. A few – Insead, just outside Paris, the London Business School (LBS) and Switzerland's Institute for Management Development – deserve a place in America's first division. Britons alone spent around £50m on MBA fees at 100 schools in 1994 – and around half that figure on business books. Continental Europeans, particularly the French, remain a little more suspicious but most of the leading American gurus have broken through. *In Search of Excellence* sold 100,000 copies in three years in France, and did even better in Germany, Holland, Spain and Sweden. This was quite an achievement given that the book barely mentioned Europe; in *Liberation Management*, published almost a decade later, the canny Mr Peters devoted whole chapters to ABB Asea Brown Boveri, a Swiss-Swedish Industrial giant, and Germany's medium-sized companies. Nowadays, leading North American gurus such as Gary Hamel and Henry Mintzberg spend at least part of the year in Europe (at LBS and Insead respectively).

And Europe is beginning to produce gurus of its own. There is as yet only one European guru who ranks in the first division by American standards: Britain's Charles Handy. However, a cluster of other names including John Kay (head of the Oxford Business School), Sumantra Ghoshal (LBS) and Yves Doz (Insead) are knocking on the door. There are also several areas where European gurus look as if they are ahead of their American counterparts. One example is the cultural side of managing multinationals: any big firm in Europe becomes multinational very quickly. Geert Hofstede of the Netherlands' Institute of International Culture more or less invented cultural diversity as a management subject, pointing out that attitudes towards pay and hierarchy can vary enormously from country to country. Another Dutchman, Fons Trompenaars, is one of the leading writers on corporate culture.

Indeed, in many 'soft' management areas, Europe has a stronger tradition than the more scientific-based Americans. Many gurus, for instance, are now re-examining work done on human motivation at Britain's Tavistock Institute back in the 1950s by a team of psychologists led by Elliot Jacques. And at a time when the younger American gurus seem to spend half their lives studying ever more esoteric sub-disciplines, the Europeans' comparative lack of specialisation may be an advantage. One reason why Peter Drucker has described Charles Handy as 'the most interesting management writer today' is because he sees shades of himself: both had comparatively little formal management education, both served time in the real world (Handy as an oil executive; Drucker as a banker) and both are generalists, as interested in sociology and politics as they are in management. Drucker, it should not be forgotten, was himself once a European.

With Western Europe firmly within its orbit, the management industry is now moving east and south. By introducing management theory to the former Soviet bloc, western governments and business schools hope to create a cadre of people who are familiar with the language and techniques of western management. For instance, the Stockholm School of Economics has an outlet in Riga which teaches economics and business to 100 students a year from Estonia, Latvia and Lithuania. Even in Moscow, business schools are starting to appear, although many of the graduates exhibit an almost puppy-like enthusiasm for buzzwords. One western entrepreneur recalls having to shout at his new recruit that relentlessly mouthing acronyms such as EBIT (business-school speak for 'earnings before interest and taxes') was doubly pointless: first, the entrepreneur did not know what EBIT meant; and, second, it was based on meaningless figures in the first place. Even South Africa has made a contribution with the rise of something called 'ubuntu management' which tries to blend western ideas with African traditions, such as tribal loyalty.

However, the biggest growth is in the Far East (we devote a chapter to management in developing Asia – see page 291–309). The region has long sent its bright young things to American business schools – Taiwan's government is stuffed with people with American MBAs. Now Asia is producing schools of its own, though nowhere near enough to meet the demand for places. In China, a country which is desperately short of trained managers, the China Europe International Business School plans to move from its present temporary home on the outskirts of Shanghai into a huge new campus in Pudong, the city's as-yet-unbuilt financial centre, in 1997; it will also double its annual intake to 120 students (a fair number until you consider that it already gets 4,000 applicants). Despite the fact that most of the big Asian businesses remain family-run, the consultancies have already made impressive progress. McKinsey's Indian office is the company's fastest-growing. As the younger business-school-educated generation of Asians takes over, the consultants can expect a bonanza.

Step on to any of Hong Kong's crowded trams and you will find a young Chinese puzzling over the latest offering from Tom Peters or John Naisbitt. In a mammoth pan-Asian survey of business people in 1995 roughly half of the respondents had bought a book by a western management writer in the previous two years (although it was noticeable that nearly the same proportion admitted that they had not finished reading it).[5] For many western gurus, Asian speaking tours offer much the same enticements that the musical variety do for elderly rock stars. The money is good ($25,000 a seminar), the audience large and relatively uncritical, and there is also a chance that you can find an Asian anecdote or two to spice up your performances back home. The only question is how long the western gurus will be able to survive without local competition. At present, there is only one well-known Asian guru, Kenichi Ohmae of Japan, but there are plenty of up-and-coming ones. One of the best thinkers at Insead is Chan Kim, a South Korean.

The importance of theory

Set down in these geographic terms, the management industry can look a little dismembered. The substance that not only keeps it together but also provides much of its vitality is management theory. Theory and industry feed off each other – and both grow bigger as a result. For three groups of people, the link between theory and money is particularly important: professors, consultants and managers.

Increasingly, academics are keen not just on thinking up striking new ideas, but on selling them. Once such a taste for publicity might have provoked academic ostracism. Now, with house prices in the more desirable university towns soaring, every young professor dreams of writing a best-seller; and, with even the best business schools desperately competing for students, every business-school dean encourages him. Once business school professors prided themselves on cloaking incomprehensible ideas in impenetrable prose for a tiny audience. Now the likes of Rosabeth Moss Kanter, a professor at Harvard Business School, and Jeffrey Pfeffer, a professor at Stanford Business School, write in deliberately accessible prose and allow their publishers to mount jazzy advertising campaigns, with publicity packs, book signings and endorsements by leading businessmen. Although it is difficult to condemn any management theorist who can write books in English, it is hard to imagine the same hoop-la surrounding the launch of, say, an economics textbook.

Significantly, business-school academics are setting up their own consultancies. Michael Porter is a director of Monitor, Rosabeth Moss Kanter a founder of Goodmeasure, another Boston-based consultancy. Just to show that the British can play the same game, John Kay is a founder of London Economics. Indeed, the lines between academia and commerce are often so blurred that it is hard to categorise people. Should Kenichi Ohmae, long head of McKinsey's Tokyo operation and now head of his own consultancy, who gives packed lectures at business schools around the world and edits Harvard Business School books on subjects such as globalisation, be counted as an academic or a consultant? Is a 'Chief executive officer thought summit' at the Massachusetts Institute of Technology sponsored by Price Waterhouse an academic get-together or a corporate public-relations ploy?

For consultancies, the link between new ideas and profit is even clearer. As one consultant puts it, 'customers expect you to add to their intellectual capital'. McKinsey spends $50m–100m a year on research. The *McKinsey Quarterly* (which looks as if it is trying to best the *Harvard Business Review* – and occasionally does) and the McKinsey Global Institute have long given the firm a quasi-academic glow. Virtually every other consultancy nowadays produces a magazine with a name like *Prism* or *Insights Quarterly*. One of the more flaky products, *Transformations*, from Gemini, comes with significant passages already highlighted or underlined. The most determined attempt to catch up with McKinsey has been made by Booz Allen & Hamilton, which has appointed sundry knowledge officers. It has also brought in Joel Kurtzman, a former editor of the *Harvard Business Review,* to run a new periodical, *Strategy & Business*.

Few things reflect as well on a consultancy as a best-selling business book. *Reengineering the Corporation* helped CSC Index raise its annual revenues from $70m before the book appeared to more than $160m in 1994. Arthur D. Little aims to produce at least one big book a year and offers consultants time off for writing if they can come up with a good enough proposal. *Product Juggernauts*, an excellent study of product innovation, was one result.[6] Consultancies happily arrange for such books to be serialised in magazines, advertised in newspapers and endorsed by well-known businessmen. A few of them even arrange for them to be bought in bulk – as we have already seen with *The Discipline of Market Leaders* (see page 27).

The scramble to produce the next management blockbuster reflects how competitive consulting has become. Strategic consulting used to be something of a cosy business. Now giants such as Andersen Consulting and Electronic Data Systems are pouring resources into the area. EDS has already gobbled up one of the oldest firms in the business, A.T. Kearney. Two of the leading strategic companies, Gemini and Mercer, are themselves the products of the consolidation of several smaller firms. Despite this increased pressure, there remains a clear difference between those consultancies that want to be seen as originators of the latest trend and those that, though keen on keeping up to date, are wary of becoming its slaves. The first camp includes most of the later arrivals on the scene, such as CSC Index and Gemini. By contrast, McKinsey has produced several blockbuster-books – Tom Peters, Robert Waterman and Kenichi Ohmae have all worked for the firm – but it has shied away from the sort of concerted 'this is our new idea' approach of its younger rivals. This is partly a function of size: even if the firm wanted to force a single idea down its clients' throats, it is doubtful that it could get all its partners to agree on it. But it is also because McKinsey, with its impressive array of contracts, does not need jazzy new products to act as calling cards. Interestingly, the Boston Consulting Group, which originally made its name with ideas such as growth-share management and time-based management, also takes a similar approach.

That does not mean that consultants at the more established firms are any less keen on writing books themselves. McKinsey has churned out over fifty books since 1980, compared with only two between 1960 and 1980. Despite working famously long hours, there is no shortage of consultants who are willing to sacrifice their holidays, weekends and evenings to write on management. Ever since Tom Peters transformed himself from an unknown McKinseyite (named Thomas J. Peters) to the middle manager's pin-up by publicising an internal research project, consultants have daydreamed about writing a business block-buster. At worst, a successful book can win you clients and project you up the consultancy's ranks; at best, it can allow you to launch a career as an independent consultant and speaker.

Much the same thoughts seem to be going through the minds of corporate chairmen. Nowadays, more and more retired businessmen are carving out second careers – and piling up second fortunes – as management pundits. Sir John Harvey-Jones, the amiable former boss of Britain's ICI, has starred in a television series, *Troubleshooter*, in which he wanders the world dispensing advice to other managers; he has also turned himself into one of the most familiar figures on the business lecture circuit. The days when practising bosses had time to come up with new theories may be over, but they are making ever greater efforts to influence academic opinion. Percy Barnevik, the chairman of ABB, is a regular guest at business schools, and has written the introduction to a Harvard Business School book on globalisation. The *Harvard Business Review* regularly subjects leading businessmen to searching interrogations, and has no shortage of willing victims. Anita Roddick, the founder of Britain's Body Shop, was so frustrated by her few weeks as a guest lecturer at Stanford Business School that she tried to shake up the 1995 conference of America's Academy of Management with a passionate lecture on the socially responsible company. She is also founding a New Academy of Management, a sort of new-age business school with a spot of social do-goodery thrown in.

It is tempting to damn chief executives for spending so much time chasing will-o'-the-wisp theories when they should be looking after their shareholders. However, in many cases, the chief beneficiary is the company they head. A taste for management theory allows companies to present themselves as 'go ahead' – and even gives them a chance to earn money. One way for a company to get noticed is to promote itself as a 'centre of excellence' – and charge people for watching it perform. Every year 2,400 management pilgrims trek to Springfield ReManufacturing, a diesel-engine assembler based in Missouri, to watch it practise something called 'open-book management'. The company earns $1.4m from the tours, and assorted videos, books and tapes. Other Meccas include DisneyWorld, home to a people-management seminar, and AT&T's Universal Card service centre, where guests pay $375 a day to watch the telephone giant demonstrate its skills in customer service.[7] Quite apart from the money such demonstrations earn, they also spread the word that, for instance, Motorola and Federal Express are the last thing in quality.

Another similar tactic is to promote yourself as a small business school in your own right. Companies such as Merck, 3M, Procter & Gamble, Disney, Marriott, IBM, McDonald's and Motorola in the United States, and Unipart in Britain have all dignified their in-house training programmes with the title of 'university'. As befits their new-found status, the 'faculty' members of these universities are keen on developing new ideas, not just transmitting received wisdom, in order to seem up to date.

At first sight, it is tempting to praise the breadth of the management industry. One result of having so many different sorts of people, with such different styles and perspectives, keen on contributing to management theory is that it helps to widen the audience for the discipline. There is something there for most sorts of readers, from fantasists who dream of getting rich quick to social scientists who want to understand the way organisations operate. Retired businessmen usually write in anecdotes, showing how their own careers demonstrate general business principles, while academics have a weakness for powerful analytical techniques, such as regression analysis. There is also an (expanding) cornucopia of management tools for companies to use.

On the other hand, when one adds up the management industry's various battalions – the teachers, consultants, business people, publishers, software makers etc. – a more worrying conclusion suggests itself: there is a veritable army of people who have a vested interest in hyping the gurus, and almost nobody criticising them. Even the press has, to some extent, been co-opted. Gurus regularly write articles for business magazines and newspapers. News organisations such as the *Financial Times*, *Business Week* and, yes, *The Economist*, are all expanding their conference business, turning themselves into both purveyors of management thought and critics of it. In general, we would argue that the mainstream business press is, at last, getting a little less tolerant of the gurus. Some of the management industry's more recent offerings – notably *The Discipline of Market Leaders* and *Transforming the Organisation* – were given a (deservedly) hard time by reviewers. Various columnists, such as Lucy Kellaway in the *Financial Times*, make a speciality of scurrying around the rubbish tip of daily press releases from consultancies and publishers that now gathers outside every management journalist's door, and finding some particularly absurd new fad to ridicule. However, given our vested interest, it is only fair to record that many other people reckon that the media's critical instincts are fading even further. 'How many requests do you think we receive from publications doing yet another survey of fads like re-engineering?', moans one senior consultant, who thinks that the pack mentality among journalists increases with each and every new management page or management correspondent. Journalists, he argues, are more interested in being the first to write about an apparent trend than investigating whether the trend actually works or not.

Thriving on anxiety

If all these vested interests transform the management industry into an impressive marketing machine, they do not completely explain why customers fling themselves under its wheels. What drives a man who is already working himself into an early grave to use his few spare moments to read some ill-written screed on organisational transformation? And what drives a company which is staring oblivion in the face to send key employees on expensive seminars on liberation management?

Andrzej Huczynski, a student of management gurus, argues that part of the answer lies in managers' anxiety about their status.[8] The first American business schools were built so that managers could look graduates from the great schools of law and medicine straight in the eye. Managers started to go on executive-education programmes and international conferences because that was the sort of thing that professional people did. Managers lapped up 'scientific management' because everybody who was anybody seemed to have a branch of science to support him.

Some of the most successful gurus have been shameless flatterers of managerial egos. Peter Drucker subtitled his classic *The Practice of Management*: 'a study of the most important function in American society'. 'The manager,' he argued, 'is the dynamic, life-giving element in every business.' Henry Mintzberg has repeatedly stressed the difficulty and complexity of managers' jobs, reinforcing the idea that managers are special people, grappling with intractable problems. Tom Peters tries a slightly different tactic, telling managers not just that they are important, but that they are rather wacky as well. Their wives and children may call them squares; but, listening to Tom Peters, they become crazy guys, dreaming impossible dreams and making unbelievable things happen.

The average struggling doctor or university lecturer might be surprised to discover that managers are so socially insecure. The gleaming buildings and carefully manicured lawns of business schools bespeak the arrogance of wealth. Top managers have seen their incomes increase substantially over the past decade, at a time when the income of shop-floor workers has stagnated or even declined. Surely the people who are really anxious about their status nowadays are members of the traditional élites, such as civil servants and academics? The answer is that, by most statistical measures, the managerial class is probably more secure than it used to be. But today's managers have a lot of other things to be worried about, and management theorists have become virtuosos at discovering and calming these worries.

Managers are much more fearful of the future than they have ever been before. They know that they are living through momentous changes in the global economy – the rise of Asia, the fall of household companies like IBM, the collapse of career ladders – and they do not know whether those changes will make them rich or turn them into casualties. At the most basic level, they are terrified of losing their jobs. First in the United States, then in Britain and now in Europe and Japan, companies have broken with the convention that a job in management is a job for life.

Even if they have survived the latest round of restructuring, managers still have to come to terms with radically redesigned jobs. What, after all, are they supposed to do when they 'manage'? Are they strategy setters? Or sergeant-majors in business suits? Or coaches? Or even amateur psychotherapists? In the old days of steep hierarchies and deferential workers it was all too easy: senior managers set strategy, subdivided tasks into their component parts and designed incentive schemes; their juniors supervised workers and bawled them out if they slacked. But now that computers are putting information in the hands of more and more employees and decision-making is being devolved to front-line workers, the traditional sources of managerial authority are disappearing. Some 'lean' factories have even introduced the semi-Maoist device called 360-degree assessment, whereby managers have to listen to frank reports on their personal foibles and failings from the people they are supposed to be managing.

Allan Katcher, an American psychologist, asked senior American executives what they would least want their subordinates to know about them. In nineteen out of the twenty cases the answer was the same. They feared that their subordinates would learn how inadequate they felt in their jobs. And these cowering individuals were professional managers, groomed from the first for top positions. Yet many people who end up in middling managerial positions are promoted not for their managerial skills but for their excellence in other jobs – as engineers or lawyers or editorial writers. In their former jobs, they no doubt despised management theory. Perhaps they despise it still; but as potentially dud managers they reluctantly fall under its spell. So they turn to the people who 'know', guiltily buying a book on management, then organising a conference, with, say, a consultant from McKinsey to act as a 'facilitator'.

To these anxiety-ridden men and women, management books offer a rare source of security. The most obvious beneficiaries are those fringe thinkers who concentrate on the individual rather than the organisation: hence the charm of Stephen Covey's new-age psychotherapy (*The Seven Habits of Highly Effective People*) and of motivational gurus such as Anthony Robbins. However, managerial angst has also helped more mainstream authors who provide their readers with a more general explanation of what exactly is happening to them. For instance, Charles Handy's *The Age of Unreason* addresses the disappearance of jobs for life. A follow-up, *The Empty Raincoat,* looks at the widespread feeling that life is out of balance, with some people working round the clock and others having nothing to do. Even fairly straightforward management books often come in packages designed to appeal to the nervous. Who would have guessed that *Control Your Destiny or Somebody Else Will* is actually a (fairly good) business biography of Jack Welch? One Tom Peters book begins with a quotation from Andy Grove, the boss of Intel: 'Only the paranoid survive'; another is called *Thriving on Chaos*. The ideal 'unique selling proposition' for a management book is something along the lines of: 'buy me or else you will not be among the élite who avoid being downsized out of a job or put on a short-term contract'.

Often, the gurus offer the illusion that, for all the complexities of the world, the answers are really rather straightforward, provided you let the guru be your guide. *In Search of Excellence* is full of reassurances that 'the answer is surprisingly simple, albeit ignored by most managers'.[9] To find the truth you need neither a gigantic brain nor a magic wand. Peters even argued that it was the book's relentlessly common-sensical nature that made it a best-seller: 'The absence of magic – practical common sense – turned out to be its biggest selling point'. And he called the first chapter of his subsequent book, *A Passion for Excellence*, 'A flash of the obvious'. Another way to make ideas seem simple is to translate them into formulas, such as Douglas McGregor's 'Theory X and Theory Y'. Nowadays alliterative formulas are so rampant that a reader does not know whether the 'three Cs' refers to commitment, creativity and competition, as Kenichi Ohmae preaches, or competence, connections and concepts, as Rosabeth Moss Kanter would have it.

When such charms are not soothing managers' fears, they are usually firing their ambitions. A taste for management theory can help bright young executives to steal a march on their colleagues. Being chosen to attend an expensive management seminar means that they are in favour with their immediate superiors. Attending the seminar gives them access to a trendy language and helps them to network with similarly ambitious colleagues from other companies. (It also makes a welcome break from doing any real work.) Championing an idea suggests that a manager is open to change, willing to take risks, in touch with the latest thinking.

The chance to put the fad into practice gives him much higher visibility throughout the company, tests his mettle as an agent of change, not just a stooge of the status quo, and generally increases his chances of winning promotion.

Another reason why managers are keen on management theory is defensive: what better way to defend your turf than to clothe your specialism with the dignity of scientific theory? Peter Drucker's 'management by objectives' strengthened the position of general managers.[10] 'Total quality management' reinforced the role of production chiefs. The training department is forever on the look-out for ideas that will help inflate the training budget, while the 'human resource specialists' are suckers for any theorist who argues for 'putting people first' (to borrow the title of a book by Jeffrey Pfeffer of Stanford).

The importance of being faddish

Why do managers flit from theory to theory rather than settling for one idea or, as their disappointment mounts, rejecting the whole guru business entirely? And why do management gurus keep tearing up the sacred texts and starting from scratch? The outline of an answer should already be apparent. The sheer number of would-be gurus means that there are always numerous ideas in the market place. The prevalence of fear and ambition among the consumers of management ideas means that the market is always unstable.

Arguably, the ground for the current frenzy of management fads was prepared by the professionalisation of management in America in the wake of the Second World War. This was based on the premise that there was a set of general concepts and generic principles which could be applied in all circumstances. These universal ideas weaned managers from their earlier reliance on improvised in-house management practices and prepared them to become consumers of mass-produced and mass-marketed managerial techniques.

This regimented system, which allowed for fads but was not built around them, lasted only as long as the 1980s. Suddenly, most of its fixed points were called into question. The mass-production model no longer seemed to be working. The paragons of good management – companies such as General Motors and IBM – were slipping. Ideas that had been invented outside the system – foreign notions such as 'lean production' and 'customer-supplier' partnerships – appeared to be working better. American companies now had to consult Tom Peters and Toyota rather than just the Harvard Business School and McKinsey. What might be called the velocity of management faddism increased exponentially just about everywhere. The more companies panicked the more they flitted from technique to technique in search of salvation. Of the twenty-seven fads highlighted by Richard Pascale in *Managing on the Edge* in 1990, two-thirds were spawned during the 1980s. Since then, the process has only speeded up.

And, from the management industry's viewpoint, the beauty of the system is that none of the formulas works – or, at least, they do not work as completely as the anguished or greedy buyers hope. The result is enormous profits for the gurus but confusion for their clients. 'In the past eighteen months,' one mid-western equipment manufacturer told Pascale, 'we have heard that profit is more important than revenue, quality is more important than profit, that people are more important than profit, that customers are more important than our people, that big customers are more important than our small customers, and that growth is the key to our success. No wonder our performance is inconsistent.'

If there is one thing for which the management industry deserves to be repeatedly flagellated it is its propensity to sell its ideas as permanent solutions. The longer you study management, the more convinced you become that the discipline remains an art rather than a science. With that in mind, we will now move on to deal with the ideas themselves, beginning with a look at the two best-known witch doctors: Peter Drucker and Tom Peters.

PART TWO

Prophet and Evangelist

3

PETER DRUCKER:
THE GURU'S GURU

In most areas of intellectual life nobody can quite decide on who is the top dog – sometimes because rival schools of thought have rival champions, sometimes because there are so many fine specimens to choose from. In the world of management gurus, however, there is no debate. Peter Drucker is the one management guru to whom other management gurus kowtow. He is also one of the few thinkers from any discipline who can reasonably claim to have changed the world, as the inventor of privatisation, the apostle of a new class of knowledge workers, the champion of management as a serious intellectual discipline. One South Korean businessman has even gone so far as to adopt Drucker as his Christian name in deference to the great man. This is perhaps a little extreme, even sad, but Drucker is the one management theorist who every tolerably well-educated person, however contemptuous of business or infuriated by jargon, really ought to read.

This unrivalled position has a lot to do with age and industry. Now in his late eighties, Drucker was a leading management pundit when today's management pundits were re-engineering their train sets. Since discovering the discipline back in the 1940s, he has produced an astonishing quantity of work: twenty-six books, thousands of articles, tens of thousands of lectures and goodness knows how much practical advice for managers. Not all this thought has stood the test of time; and some of Drucker's later work is a little thin, padded out with immodest references to his early work. Yet the thing which makes all this effort worthwhile is the sheer quality of his intellect. No matter how many blind alleys Drucker heads up, his relentlessly curious mind always makes the reader think. Drucker will tell you that he hates the word guru, thinking it synonymous with charlatan. But, in truth, he is the one management thinker who genuinely deserves the accolade.

The road to Drucker

Tom Peters has argued that 'no true discipline of management' existed before Drucker.[1] Yet it is increasingly fashionable to trace virtually any modern management idea back to the 'pioneers and prophets' of the early 20th century – and sometimes even further back. But, for the modern reader (let alone the modern manager), the academic squabbles over who first said what are of limited interest. Even if Cato's list of job descriptions for provincial administrators in the Roman empire is a distant ancestor of Charles Handy's theories about the workplace 2,000 years later, the logical response of every sane modern manager should be: 'So what?'

Peter Drucker, partly thanks to his own talents and partly thanks to his timing, is the first management thinker consistently to pass this relevancy test. Like his Biblical namesake, he is the rock on which the current church is founded. All the same, it is legitimate to listen for a while to the voices crying in the wilderness who preceded him.

Management, in one sense, is as old as man. Drucker himself has pointed out that 'all the great business builders – from the Medici of Renaissance Florence and the founders of the Bank of England in the late 17th century down to IBM's Thomas Watson in our day – had a clear theory of the business which informed all their actions and decisions.' One history of management has traced the craft back to the Sumerians in 5000 BC.[2] Organising either the construction of the pyramids or Julius Caesar's invasion of Britain must have called upon basic skills and talents that we might describe as management.

Sun Tzu, the author of *The Art of War*, who argued that 'the supreme act of war is to subdue an enemy without fighting' has many modern admirers including some of Hollywood's most

Machiavellian figures. Indeed, Niccolò Machiavelli (1469–1527) himself is considered by many to be the first western management theorist. The *Financial Times* once dubbed Machiavelli's *The Prince* the 16th-century equivalent of Dale Carnegie's *How to Win Friends and Influence People*.[3] Any executive exposed to corporate politics (i.e. every manager in the world) could do worse than read *The Prince* with its advice about being 'a great dissembler and pretender'.

As the industrial revolution gathered pace, management archaeologists find more significant fragments to examine, not only in economic theorists such as Adam Smith (1723–90) and Jean Baptiste Say (1767–1832), both of whom devoted many pages to the running of enterprises, but also in practitioners such as Eli Whitney (1765–1835), an American gunmaker who built his rifles from interchangeable parts and thus, arguably, invented the assembly line, and Robert Owen (1771–1858), a Scottish mill-owner who thought there was money to be made by treating workers as if they were human beings (he would not employ any child under ten years old) and thus has been deemed to be 'the pioneer of personnel management'.[4] However it was only with the introduction of mass production around the beginning of this century that business demanded the creation of a new élite of managers and a new, formal science of management theory.

The principal inspiration for this new science, in America at least, came from Frederick Winslow Taylor, an engineer who invented carbon-steel machine tools. Taylor believed that there was a single best method of organising work, and that this method could be discovered through a detailed study of the time-and-motion involved in doing each job. The stop-watch, the motion-picture camera, the slide rule and psycho-physiological tests: these were the tools of the trade of Taylor and his acolytes. The principles at the heart of scientific management were clear: break jobs down into their simplest parts; select the most suitable workers to fit the available jobs; turn those workers into specialists, each an expert in his own appointed task; arrange these specialised jobs along an assembly line; and design the right package of incentives (including bonuses and prizes) to ensure that the workers did indeed work.

In Taylor's world 'managers' were not just unthinking sergeants carrying out the owner's instructions. They played two vital roles in turning factories into 'smoothly running machines'. The first was co-ordinating the various specialised tasks (after all, the workers themselves could hardly be expected to understand how their speciality fitted into the whole); the second was monitoring and motivating the workers (who might easily weary of their tedious routine). The principle of the division of labour also applied to managers: there were specialists in accounting, recruiting and so on. At the top of the pyramid sat an élite, Taylor's version of Plato's guardians, whose job it was to design and regulate the entire system, to monitor thé behaviour of competitors, and, above all, to plan ahead.

Taylor's ideas were translated into practice remarkably quickly – particularly by Henry Ford, a self-made mechanic just like Taylor, at his new factory at Highland Park, in a suburb of Detroit. At the same time Taylorism helped to shape the curriculum at a new sort of educational institution, the business school. The first business school, Wharton, was set up at the University of Pennsylvania in 1881. The University of Chicago and the University of California both established undergraduate schools of commerce in 1899. New York University's Stern School of Business, Dartmouth's Amos Tuck School of Business Administration and Harvard's Graduate School of Business Administration followed in the next decade. The *Management Review* was founded in 1918, the American Management Association in 1925. By the end of the Great War, Arthur D. Little, originally an engineering firm, included management advice among its services. James McKinsey set up his consultancy firm in 1925.

Ironically, given Henry Ford's patronage of Taylor's ideas, one of the first results of scientific management was the growing success of General Motors, where Alfred Sloan turned himself into a professional manager, detached from the hurly-burly of the shop floor. (In contrast, Henry Ford himself was an inveterate meddler, keeping his firm in a state of near chaos.) Meanwhile, many of Taylor's disciples found their way into state and local government, and tried to apply scientific management to places like the schoolroom and the operating theatre.[5] Congress held hearings on the subject as early as 1912, giving publicity to the new idea. Herbert Hoover, an engineer by training, tried to use scientific management to make government more efficient.

But the apostles of scientific management did not have it all their own way. A rival school of theorists, who became known as the human-relations school, stressed the importance of involving workers in managerial decisions. Mary Parker Follett stressed that 'we can never wholly separate the human from the mechanical side'.[6] Elton Mayo, a psychologist based at the Harvard Business School, stressed the importance of non-economic rewards for productivity. 'So long as commerce specialises in business methods which take no account of human nature and social motives, so long may we expect strikes and sabotage to be the ordinary accompaniment of industry.'

This humanistic school of management was at its most influential in Europe, particularly in Britain, where the powerful craft unions set their faces against Taylorism and leading businessmen preferred a gentler approach. Quakers such as the Cadburys and the Rowntrees urged their fellow employers to treat their workers like human beings rather than machines. William Morris, the father of Britain's car industry, was so dismayed by the difficulties of introducing the new system that he christened it 'mess production'.[7] C.S. Myers, a psychologist, criticised scientific management for taking a simplistic view of human motives. Elliot Jacques, another psychologist, stressed the social dynamics of group behaviour and after the Second World War turned the Tavistock Institute in London into the headquarters of humanistic management.

A fair number of Europe's leading intellectuals became caught up in the struggle between scientific and humanistic management. In Germany, *avant-garde* thinkers made a cult of scientific management: Bauhaus architects like Walter Gropius and Ludwig Hilberseimer tried to marry design with scientific management;

Bertolt Brecht and Fritz Lang briefly sang the praises of the new craze. Max Weber, the father of organisational theory, studied different types of bureaucracies to see which would be the most efficient. In Britain, intellectuals usually sided with the humanists. Aldous Huxley in his book *Brave New World* (1932); English-born Charlie Chaplin in his film *Modern Times* (1936); George Orwell in his 1946 essay 'James Burnham and the Managerial Revolution' and his novel *Nineteen Eighty-four* (1949): all expressed their fear of mass production, scientific management and the reduction of the individual into a cog in a vast industrial machine.

An intellectual refugee

This then was the slightly schizophrenic discipline that Peter Drucker stumbled upon on the eve of the Second World War. Drucker pours scorn on the idea that he was the man who invented management (although there is a book about him with that title). Instead, he argues that by the mid-1930s, 'nothing had come together . . .' Nobody, as he put it, had asked the question: 'What is management?'

Drucker was born in 1909 into the Austrian upper-middle-class – and still has a slight accent to prove it. His father, a cosmopolitan government official, introduced young Drucker to Sigmund Freud. As a student he got to know such illustrious intellectuals as Karl Polanyi, an historian, and Fritz Kraemer, a military strategist. He earned a doctorate in international and public law from Frankfurt University in 1931, and published articles in German economics journals.

The process whereby a Viennese intellectual came to write about something as removed from the mainstream as management was complicated and largely accidental. Drucker spent his twenties trying to avoid Adolf Hitler and drifted between a number of jobs, including banking, consultancy, academic law and journalism. (His journalistic training included a spell as acting editor of a women's page.) He finally found a home in an American university, teaching politics, philosophy and economics.

His first book, *The End of Economic Man* (1939), concentrated on politics and economics, and warned about the Holocaust. His second book, *The Future of Industrial Man* (1942), annoyed academic critics because it mixed economics with various social sciences, arguing that companies had a social dimension as well as an economic purpose; but this bizarre idea also attracted the attention of General Motors.

The American car giant, then the biggest company in the world, invited Drucker to pen a portrait of the company, and gave him unrestricted access to GMers, from Alfred Sloan down. The result, *The Concept of the Corporation* (1946), sealed Drucker's fate. The book immediately became a best-seller, in Japan as well as America, and has been in print ever since. However, it further alienated turf-minded American academics – economists regarded it as vulgar sociology and political scientists dismissed it as economics gone mad. One reviewer hoped that 'this promising young scholar will now devote his considerable talents to a more respectable subject'.[8] Shunned by his natural homes, Drucker was forced to write about management.

Since then Drucker has either invented or influenced virtually every part of management theory (his name thus crops up in this book with infuriating frequency). However, many of the themes that have dominated his work were present in *The Concept of the Corporation*. Like all Drucker's books, *The Concept of the Corporation* is not afraid to roam: it begins with a story from China and, at different times, worries about the proportion of Victorian Englishmen who were gentlemen (a minute fraction, in Drucker's view) and the efficiency of Russian industrial management. However, the book also clearly had a central purpose: it was the first study to treat a company as a social system as well as an economic organisation. The two longest sections in the book are entitled 'The corporation as human effort' and 'The corporation as a social institution'. Drucker found the way that people worked together interesting in its own right rather than just a means to make profits.

All the same, the subject that most of Drucker's readers seized upon was decentralisation. Drucker showed how GM's decentralised structure enabled it to respond to challenges such as the transition from war to peace – and concluded that the car firm 'realised its concept of decentralisation sufficiently to obtain from it an overall pattern of behaviour and a basis for the successful solution of the most difficult concrete problems of economic life'.[9] Although Drucker made it clear that he had doubts about the value of decentralisation for organisations in general, other big American companies, such as Ford and General Electric, rushed to copy it. By the 1980s, Drucker was credited with 'moving 75–80 per cent of the Fortune 500 to radical decentralisation'.[10]

Drucker's people

Nevertheless, the two most interesting issues that come out of Drucker's dissection of the car company – and which have dominated his work ever since – are only marginally to do with decentralisation: the case for empowering workers (or 'creating the self-governing plant community' as Drucker somewhat clumsily put it at the time) and the rise of the knowledge worker (i.e. the worker whose value lies in what he has in his head not what he can do with his hands).

For all its dry academic language *The Concept of the Corporation* was essentially a passionate plea for GM to treat labour as a resource rather than just as a cost. Drucker insisted that industrial relations ought to be based on people's desire to be engaged in their job and proud of their product. He was also a stern critic of the assembly line, even though at the time it was regarded as the most advanced form of manufacturing. Criticising 'the assembly-line mentality' which believed 'that a worker was the more efficient, the more machine-like and the less human he is'[11], Drucker argued that the monotony of assembly-line production made it inefficient – partly because it slowed the line to the speed of the slowest member and partly because workers never got any job satisfaction from seeing the finished product.

This enthusiasm for self-management was ahead of its time.

Nowadays, team-manufacturing techniques such as cell-manufacturing are commonplace, and companies are handing ever more power to their workers. When Japanese car makers set up shop in Britain in the 1980s and told Geordie factory workers that they were supposed to think as well as rivet, weld and hammer, many of Britain's car bosses scoffed at the foreigners' naivety. Today every car factory in Europe imitates their methods. The tragedy for GM was that it rejected Drucker's advice about using teams in the 1940s – only to have the same lesson rammed down its throat by the Japanese in the 1970s.

A second great theme of Drucker's work has been the replacement of the old industrial proletariat with knowledge workers. The advanced world is being transformed from 'an economy of goods' to 'a knowledge economy', he argues, and management is being transformed as a result. Managers are having to learn how to engage the minds, rather than simply control the hands, of their workers. This softer approach is a direct challenge to Taylor's stop-watch theories and their fans in business. But the idea of 'a knowledge worker' (a term, incidentally, which Drucker coined in 1959) also poses questions for politicians. It suggests that a country's raw materials are really its educated workers; hence the importance of training and education. Less easily, it suggests that, rather than trying to defend dying industries against cheaper, less 'knowledgeable' workers abroad, governments should concentrate on improving the country's stock of knowledge, but otherwise keep well out of the way.

Typically, Drucker has not just confined himself to the question of how managers and governments ought to handle these new knowledge workers. He has spent much of his career looking at how the knowledge workers themselves can come to terms with this new world in which they are neither workers nor bosses. Since they, rather than their employers, control the key productive asset of modern society, brain power, they have considerably more freedom than their predecessors. Workers are free – or in the dreadful jargon that Drucker did not invent but unfortunately helped to legitimise – 'empowered' to shape their own careers, hopping from firm to firm in pursuit of the highest salary or the most interesting job. But Drucker was also quick to spot that this freedom could be destabilising as well as liberating: knowledge workers needed more training, new pension arrangements and so on.

Drucker's ideas about the changing nature of work have since inspired a whole generation of writers to look in more detail at the subject. However, as one of the most prominent, Charles Handy, admits, 'virtually everything can be traced back to Drucker'.[12] The gist of a long debate (see Chapter Seven) is that the nature of work has changed but perhaps not yet as fundamentally as Drucker predicted. Still, it is worth noting that Drucker, who started his career by turning down opportunities to become a banker, and has always enjoyed a somewhat ambivalent relationship with academia, is himself an archetypal knowledge worker.

The rational temptation

This may sound as if Drucker was just another exponent of the human-relations school of management, a 'soft' inspirer always looking for the human angle. In fact, there has always been a hard, 'Taylorist' side to his thinking.

Drucker invented one of the rational school of management's most successful products, 'management by objectives', an approach which dominated 'strategic thinking' in the post-war decades. *The Practice of Management*, published in 1954, focused on the importance of having clear objectives, both for the corporation and the manager, and of translating long-term strategy into short-term goals. In particular, Drucker believed that a firm should have an élite of general managers who would determine strategy and set objectives for more specialised managers. The structure of the firm, he argued, should follow its strategy: 'Organisation is not an end in itself, but a means to the end of business performance and business results . . . Organisation structure must be designed so as to make possible the achievement of the objectives of the business five, ten, fifteen years hence.'

Management by objectives has been under a cloud since the early 1980s. The best modern companies such as 3M and Motorola allow ideas – including ideas for long-term strategies – to emerge from the bottom of the organisation. (See Chapter Eight.) Those companies which have stuck with the imperial system of command and control – notably General Motors – have looked hopelessly inflexible. The problem is that command-and-control management cuts senior management off from the people who know both their markets and their products best: the ordinary workers. Hence the current fashion for that other great Drucker theme, handing decisions back to workers through delayering and empowerment.

On balance, management by objectives looks like a fad which will stay in the graveyard. But it leads to a bigger question. Why did the prophet of empowerment turn to such a rigid approach to management? His critics say that Drucker lost his way, faddishly endorsing two incompatible approaches to management. But it is possible to apply a more generous interpretation.

Drucker was trying – as he has done ever since – to create a balance between what was best in both the humanist and rationalist schools. Management by objectives is not incompatible with empowerment, he argued: senior managers should set general goals for their subordinates but allow them to decide how to reach them. And throughout his management-by-objectives phase Drucker continued to lay heavy emphasis on the importance of culture. He was one of the first people to realise that companies are held together by a shared vision of the future – and that it is the boss's job to come up with it.

Drucker's suspicion that, if we are to avoid both anarchy and alienation, soft ideas like empowerment need to be mixed with harder ones like management by objectives is proving prescient. Anybody who studies the collapse of Barings will find it hard to be an uncritical supporter of empowerment. But simply restoring the old system of command and control risks alienating the knowledge workers on whom the success of most companies depends. Druckerish compromise looks like the best way forward.

New worlds to management

Drucker was one of the first people to realise that good management is not confined to the United States. In the 1950s, when most people dismissed Japan as nothing more than a maker of cheap crud, Drucker became fascinated by Japan's idiosyncratic approach to management. *The Concept of the Corporation* turned him into something of a sage in Japan – a position he has never lost; and he has since extended both his influence and his interest to the rest of Asia. However, his more original insight into the scope of management is that it is not confined to business.

For Drucker, management is all-pervasive, as important for universities, churches, hospitals or charities as it is for soap-powder manufacturers. Indeed, he refused chairs at both Stanford and Harvard because both schools wanted him to confine his teaching to business case-studies, and his consulting and writing to business organisations, whereas he believes that management is not just business management but, as he puts it, 'the defining organ of all modern institutions'. In keeping with this approach, his own clients include voluntary organisations such as the American Girl Scouts as well as large companies; and the business school which Claremont founded in his honour recruits about a third of its students from outside the business world.

Drucker's enthusiasm for taking management theory to the public sector should not be mistaken as enthusiasm for government. It was Drucker who gave the world the idea of 'privatisation' – and he has always been damning about government's ability to run just about anything. In *The Age of Discontinuity* he argued that the job of governments was to govern rather than to try to do things that could be done by the private sector. Drucker's definition of things that lie outside the government's scope extends well beyond telephone companies and utilities to organisations such as universities, which even Margaret Thatcher never dared privatise. In one of his later books, *Post-Capitalist Society*, where he questions other shibboleths of shareholder capitalism, he still insists that the best way for governments to avoid depressions is to stop meddling with the economy. Warfare, Drucker has argued, is the only example of a modern government programme that has achieved its objectives.

Does he still matter?

There are plenty of other less weighty areas where Drucker either led the way or cleared the path for others. Even when criticising him, his peers approach him with reverence – almost out of relief that their much maligned industry has at least one class act. When asked which management books he has paid attention to, Bill Gates begins by replying 'Well, Drucker, of course' before going on to discuss other lesser mortals.[13] Drucker has also had the satisfaction of seeing many of his ideas put into practice. As Drucker himself has boasted, *The Concept of the Corporation* 'had an immediate impact on American business, on public-service institutions, on government agencies – and none at all on General Motors'. (If a GM manager was found with a copy of the book, Drucker noted, his career was over.) Institutions as diverse as Michigan University and the Archdiocese of New York have used the book to restructure their own organisations; it was also the first book to be prescribed for students entering Charles de Gaulle's élite Ecole Nationale d'Administration. One of Drucker's more recent fans is the Rev. Bill Hybels, senior pastor of Willow Creek Community Church in South Barrington, Illinois, and one of America's most successful 'megaministers'. He has a quotation from Peter Drucker hanging outside his office: 'What is your business? Who is our customer? What does the customer consider value?' Hybels has got to know Drucker well and regards him as nothing less than 'a wisdom figure'.[14]

Yet, even around the management industry's great totem, doubts swirl. Drucker has never enjoyed quite as much adulation from academia as he has from either guru-land or from his public. ('I have never been quite respectable in the eyes of academia,' he himself confesses.[15]) There is no single area of academic management theory which he has made his own, as Michael Porter did with strategy and Theodore Levitt did with marketing. Some academics regard him as a journalist rather than a scholar, and, twisting the knife, as a glib generaliser rather than a first-class reporter. Tom Peters recalls that he never saw Drucker's name on any reading list when he was a student at Stanford Business School.

The least persuasive criticism is that Drucker does little more than state the obvious, that his persistent themes – the rise of the knowledge worker, the importance of clear objectives, the fact that firms are social as well as economic institutions – are all too obvious to bear mentioning, let alone repeating over and over again. The trouble with this argument, as we have mentioned earlier, is that most of these observations are obvious only because Drucker has made them so. Drucker is a victim of his own success in popularising a way of looking at the world. And some of these observations, however obvious, do not seem to have got through to the managerial élite. Would America's bosses be sacking their workers with one hand, while awarding themselves huge pay rises with the other, if they understood Drucker's arguments about the social nature of firms?

Other criticisms have more force. Drucker sometimes manages to be both simplistic and obscure at the same time. He repeatedly tells us that we live in a society of organisations but fails to make clear what this means. His insistence in *Post-Capitalist Society*, that America has embraced pension-fund socialism, is more a play on words than a deep analysis of American society. He is broadly right that the real bosses are not the likes of John D. Rockefeller and J.P. Morgan, but the workers themselves, who own most of society's capital, through their pension rights, and who receive most of society's rewards, through their wages and social benefits. But wouldn't it be better to call this popular capitalism?

Drucker's work does not always keep up the same high standards. *The Concept of the Corporation* may be a model monograph, tightly argued and based on original research, but some of his later books can be rambling and repetitive, full of recycled examples. He has also become less of a distinctive voice. Although it is true that as early as 1954 he was arguing that an 'organisation structure should contain the least possible number of management levels', his enthusiasm in the 1980s for 'information-based organisations' and stripping out layers of management often failed to distinguish his voice from the baying pack following Tom Peters.

In general, he is not as good on small firms as big ones. In *The Concept of the Corporation* he asserted, flatly, that 'we know today that in modern industrial production, particularly in modern mass production, the small unit is not only inefficient, it cannot produce at all'.[16] Indeed, the book helped to launch the 'big organisation boom' that lasted for the next twenty years. Drucker has since recanted: he now believes that 'the Fortune 500 is over' and has written progressively more about the importance of entrepreneurship, including his 1985 book, *Innovation and Entrepreneurship*. (Indeed, anybody who accuses Drucker in print of being a fan of big companies is in for a long letter, chronicling his enthusiasm for decentralisation.) All the same, Drucker still seems much more at home with the giant corporations which dominated America under Eisenhower than with the small-to-medium-sized businesses that regalvanised the country under Reagan. He has written nothing of the quality of *The Concept of the Corporation* about a small company.

On the other hand, the charge that Drucker is a jack of all trades rather than a master of one tells us more about the limitations of academia than it does about Drucker's shortcomings. Remember Drucker was expelled from the ivory towers of economics and political science because his work would not fit into their narrow classifications. As for charges that he resorts to the dark art of journalism, that may be just another way of saying that he is readable. Drucker was – and still is – too idiosyncratic a figure to fit in with the turf-conscious conformists who make up modern academia.

In a business dominated by American professors and gurus with nanosecond memories Drucker is happy to range across the centuries, and use a reference to Tang-dynasty China or 17th-century Byzantium to throw a shaft of light on contemporary debates. Commenting on globalisation, for example, he points out that a larger share of manufacturing was 'multinational' before the First World War than it is today. Companies such as Fiat (founded in 1899) and Siemens (founded in 1847) produced more abroad than at home almost as soon as they got off the ground. Henry Ford, a notorious xenophobe, started his English subsidiary before he began to expand his original automobile plant in Detroit.[17]

In writing about business alliances, Drucker throws in a reference to his heroine, Jane Austen, and her obsession with dynastic alliances; in commenting on the latest bout of speculative fever on Wall Street he is soon regurgitating bits of Charles Dickens' *Little Dorrit*; and, most surprisingly of all, he illustrates an article on the rise of the knowledge-based organisation with a reference to the civil service in British India. What is more, his is not common-or-garden erudition. He quotes from Volume Three rather than Volume One of Marx's *Capital*, from Harrington rather than Locke. Among other interests, he has written two novels and held a chair in Oriental Art at Claremont Graduate School.

Drucker's is not the sort of history which can be found in the textbooks: his interest lies neither in the kings and queens of the old history, nor in the capitalists and proletarians of the new, but in managers and organisation. His heroes are the likes of Jean Bodin, who (according to Drucker at least) invented the nation state, and August Borsig, who invented the German apprenticeship system. His trademark is his ability to cut between panoramic views and striking close-ups. One moment he is churning out broad generalisations about the rise of the car industry, the next he is relating an anecdote about Henry Ford's forgotten partner. He is not afraid to predict the future as well as to generalise about the past. He has had his share of failures (remember his admiration for large companies) but his batting average is higher than most (most notably with privatisation and the collapse of the Soviet Union).

The last encyclopaedist or a management Utopian?

Arguably, Drucker is not a management theorist at all; rather a cosmopolitan intellectual in the European tradition. Drucker is one of the last of the encyclopaedists, contemptuous of the over-specialisation of modern academia, and determined to know everything about everything.

Perhaps the most interesting question to ask about Drucker is why this polymath chose management. The glib answer 'because it is important' is probably the truthful one. Discovering management had much the same effect on Drucker as discovering God (or Marx) has on lesser mortals. 'Management is the organ of institutions,' he hymns, 'the organ that converts a mob into an organisation, and human efforts into performance.'[18]

If there is a core running through Drucker's writings, it is this: at best, good management will bring economic progress and social harmony in its wake. Marx based his prediction of the imminent demise of capitalism on the 'inexorable law of the diminishing productivity of capital'; and it is because managers have succeeded in outfoxing this law, by realising that the key to improved productivity lies in working smarter rather than working longer, that the modern economy goes from success to success. The real reason, Drucker argues, why some countries made the breakthrough into sustained growth is not because they discovered new technologies but because they invented new organisations. Thus Alfred Sloan's General Motors is a more awesome creation than the combustion engine, and the hospital is a more important medical breakthrough than any new-fangled medicine.

Drucker has no illusions about how difficult management is. In *Managing in a Time of Great Change*, a collection of essays published in 1995, he focuses on three things which are making the modern manager's life hell. The first is the sheer scale of contemporary managerial change, as vertically integrated companies give way to networked organisations. The second is the frequency of managerial failure. He points out that most managers have failed to understand what it means to manage in revolutionary times, and that they spend their time tinkering with their business when they should really be rethinking the whole theory on which it is based. The third is the growing tension between business and its environment: between business's need for perpetual innovation and the community's need for stability; between the rapidly changing nature of knowledge and the limited capacity of the human mind; between business's need to compete internationally and society's interest in the common good.

Good management means doing the decent thing by both workers and consumers, not just amassing profits for bosses. 'An organisation is a human, a social, indeed a moral phenomenon,' Drucker notes, in a phrase which today's re-engineers ought to be forced to learn. Drucker has argued that the best managers are driven by the desire to create value for customers, and that the best way to do this is to treat workers as resources, capable of making a sustained and valued contribution, not just costs of production. This enthusiasm for the well-being of workers led Rosabeth Moss Kanter to compare him to Robert Owen, the 19th-century Scotsman who ordered his factory managers to show the same due care to their vital human machines as they did to the new iron and steel which they so lovingly burnished.

Is Drucker right? Moss Kanter classifies Drucker as 'a management Utopian'. Perhaps he is, but then there are worse sorts of dreamers.

4

TOM PETERS:
MANAGEMENT AS PERFORMANCE ART

To most people the term 'management guru' is synonymous with
Tom Peters. His first book, *In Search of Excellence*, co-written with
Robert Waterman, was the original management blockbuster,
selling a million copies on its first printing in 1982, going through
numerous reprintings, and turning both of its authors into
millionaires. It has now sold more than five million copies. More
books have followed. Peters pours out a constant stream of tapes,
videos, articles and, together with his army of assistants, a quirkily
readable newsletter. On the international lecture circuit Peters has
outlasted and outearned such shooting stars as Ronald Reagan,
Norman Schwarzkopf and Oliver North. Every year thousands of
middle managers gape in awe as Peters, arms flailing, brow
sweating, voice hoarse with preaching, urges them to nuke
hierarchy and learn to thrive on chaos.

An all-day Tom Peters seminar remains an event. Against a
backdrop of slides with messages such as 'The Most Important
Sentence in the English Language!?', he orders the befuddled
young watchers in suits to make mistakes and to have fun.[1] 'You
advertise for a marketing job. Luciano Benetton walks in. He's
wearing no clothes. Do you hire him?' Then he adds as an
afterthought: 'Don't worry: *he* wouldn't want to work for *you*
anyway.' One moment you are being told to learn from the
threaded needle in a complimentary sewing kit in London's Four
Seasons hotel; the next moment Peters is praising a car dealer who
put flowers rather than automobiles on his forecourt. Questions
about practicalities only push him to new extremes. 'I see no
reason why you need to spend more than six minutes every three

months in your office,' he tells the head of the Eurostar London–Paris train service. 'Get on that railroad.'

The llama factor

Peters' extraordinary prominence is not an unmixed blessing for his profession. Many people only have to read one of his columns or watch one of his television performances to have their prejudices about management theory redoubled. How can a man in his fifties parade around like that? How can a self-respecting columnist waffle on about his penchant for power-walking or his wife's Zen Buddhism? How can somebody finish a day by wishing a group of senior managers 'loud times and lots of screw-ups'? As if to taunt his critics, Peters illustrated the cover of one of his books, *The Tom Peters Seminar: Crazy Times Call for Crazy Organizations*, with a picture of himself in his boxer shorts. He also dedicated the book to his mother, 'a talker who raised a talker'. Peters' books are littered with words like 'wow', 'yikes' and 'ho-hum'. 'Prosewise, he is no Edward Gibbon', as he himself might put it.

It is worth saying at the outset that there is a lot more to Peters than that. True, he has contradicted himself spectacularly over the past decade; but that is partly because the corporate world has changed spectacularly over the past decade. True, he has a penchant for dashing off fairly flimsy newspaper columns (who else would use a guest spot in the *Financial Times* to teach readers breathing-relaxation exercises?); yet he also wrote an admirably obscure PhD thesis, and continues to churn out articles for heavy-weight (and unremunerative) academic periodicals such as the *California Management Review*. True, he is willing to rant and rave to get his point over; but he has persuaded more managers to think a little bit more carefully about what they are doing than almost anyone else alive.

Even Peters' harshest critics should be willing to concede two things in his favour. The first is that he has a remarkable talent for making a dull subject like management sound interesting. What is noticeable about all the titles of his books – *Liberation Management*,

A Passion for Excellence, Thriving on Chaos – is that they convey his fascination with his subject. The second is that he has an intimate knowledge of corporate life, not just in the United States but also in Europe and around the Pacific rim; not just in the boardroom, but in the marketing department and in the machine shop; not just in the giants like Sony and IBM but in countless small companies that nobody else seems able to track down. He cannot book into a hotel, fly in an aircraft or park his car without finding an interesting management angle. One of the best stories in *Crazy Times* is about Valerio's, an eccentric Italian restaurant he stumbled across in New Zealand which refuses to put up menus outside and frames complaints from disappointed customers.

Before becoming a management guru, Peters managed to fight in Vietnam and work for both the Pentagon and the Office of Management and Budget in Washington DC. He also picked up an MBA from Stanford Business School. But the two most important parts of his training were his first degree in engineering, and then the time he spent as a consultant with McKinsey. Peters has always retained a consultant's ability to inveigle his way into hundreds of companies and an engineer's curiosity about how things actually work.

In other words, Peters is a much more complicated and accomplished man than he first seems. All the same, if the normally peaceful herd of llamas that roam around his Vermont farm were to turn nasty and trample their owner to death, Peters would face an uncomfortable epitaph: that what he did – launching, leading and defining the current guru boom – was more significant than what he actually said, much of which was subsequently either proved wrong or contradicted by Peters himself. That judgement contains a fairly damning criticism of Peters, and we will try to substantiate it later in this chapter. But it also contains a compliment. Few of the business heroes Peters worships have changed their industry in the same way that Peters has his. In so far as the current management theory boom has a starting date, it is with the publication of *In Search of Excellence*; and in so far as it has had a presiding genius, who has kept the arguments rolling and the punters coming, it has been Tom Peters.

An excellent beginning

In the late 1970s McKinsey decided to pour a substantial amount of money into a research project on the 'excellent company'. Peters and another consultant, Jim Bennett, were chosen to review the existing literature on 'organisational effectiveness'. They concluded that the emphasis that theorists had traditionally placed on strategy and structure had gone beyond the point of diminishing returns, and that other, softer factors, such as management style and 'culture', were also crucial to success. This was relatively controversial stuff since most McKinsey men were steeped in the lore of strategy and structure. The young researchers' project only took off when three other people joined: Robert Waterman, a more experienced McKinseyite, and two business-school professors, Anthony Athos, a specialist on corporate culture, and Richard Pascale, who had for years been conducting comparative research on American and Japanese companies. Peters and Waterman decided to write up the project as a book.

Why did *In Search of Excellence* do so well? In part, because it was based on a formidable amount of evidence, at least by the far from exacting standards of management science. But it also acted as a show-case for the four main ingredients of what might be called the 'Peters phenomenon': an uncanny sense of timing, an extraordinary ability to articulate the mood of the moment, the skill to dispense practical-sounding advice, and a breathtaking talent for marketing. As Peters readily admits, the timing was 'pure luck'.[2] The book appeared in October 1982, the month that American unemployment hit 10 per cent, the first time it had broken the double digit barrier since the Great Depression. *In Search of Excellence* also came out after a glut of books on the wonders of Japanese management.

Indeed, the book seemed perfectly designed to appeal to an America that was worried about its declining competitiveness but tired of being told about the Japanese miracle. Like many other pundits, Peters and Waterman accepted that American managers bore much of the blame for their country's plight, thanks to their obsession with the short-term and their indifference to quality and service.[3] However, they argued that Americans did not have to look all the way to Japan for models of how to run excellent companies and revive national competitiveness. America, they pointed out, possessed a host of companies that were producing new products, pioneering new processes and working overtime to satisfy all their constituents – customers, employees, shareholders and the public at large.[4] Peters and Waterman thus sounded the 'morning in America' theme two years before Ronald Reagan used it to seal his re-election. And like 'the great communicator' they trumpeted the abilities of Americans, relying on their own grit and brains, to solve any problem.

> The findings from the excellent companies amount to an upbeat message. There is good news from America. Good management practice today is not resident only in Japan. But, more important, the good news comes from treating people decently and asking them to shine, and from producing things that work. Scale efficiencies give way to small units with turned-on people. Precisely planned R&D efforts aimed at big bang products are replaced by armies of dedicated champions. A numbing focus on cost gives way to an enhancing focus on quality. Hierarchy and three-piece suits give way to first names, shirtsleeves, hoop-la, and project-based flexibility. Working according to fat rule books is replaced by everyone's contributing.[5]

The book had another virtue: simplicity. For all the research that went into it, *In Search of Excellence* sometimes reads like a popular how-to book. For example, Peters and Waterman list eight easily identifiable (and memorably expressed) characteristics of excellent companies, such as 'sticking to the knitting' (i.e. concentrating on what it does best and contracting out everything else to other specialists), creating simultaneous loose-tight control systems (i.e. centralising core values but decentralising how they are achieved); and staying close to the customer. As Peter Drucker has waspishly put it, *In Search of Excellence* made management sound 'incredibly easy. All you had to do was put that book under your pillow and it will get done.'[6]

Peters and Waterman democratised management theory, turning it from a monopoly of chief executives and their boards into something that junior managers needed to master. Significantly for a business book, examples were plucked from all levels of big companies and from several small ones as well. As Drucker conceded: 'When Aunt Mary has to give that nephew of hers a high school graduation present and she gives him *In Search of Excellence*, you know that management has become part of the general culture.'[7]

That the book reached the Aunt Marys of this world was not just because it was preaching a simple, relevant message; it was largely due to Peters' final talent: marketing. He took to publicising the book with almost indecent zeal (certainly at a pace that his more laid-back collaborator, Robert Waterman, has found difficult to follow). No conference was left unaddressed, no article unwritten, no talk-show untalked. Three years later Peters could boast that between 100,000 and 200,000 people had been through his 'excellence' seminars. Where his extraordinary stamina came from remains a source of some debate even within the ranks of the gurus. Henry Mintzberg, a close friend, thinks that Peters threw himself into publicity because he was convinced that the boom would not last – something that Peters admits was probably true.

Whatever the explanation, Peters brought a new evangelical edge to the profession. He treated 'excellence' as a crusade. The truest believers were 'skunks' – innovative outsiders who worked on the fringes of companies (the name came from a famously inventive part of Lockheed, called the Skunk Works). In September 1984 Peters held his first annual Skunk Camp: 'Forty brave souls who have been going their own way met in California and swapped tales about the battles fought, the scars accumulated, and the personal and soul-satisfying experiences that have come from watching their people become winners . . .' Having this hard core of true believers matters because, as Peters is the first to admit, *In Search of Excellence* was more bought than read. Three years after its publication, Peters calculated that 5m people had bought the book; 2m–3m opened it; around 500,000 read five chapters; 100,000 read it all; 5,000 made detailed notes. As he put it 'the number with bent pages and heavy underlining is dispiritingly low'.[8]

Peters' next book, *A Passion for Excellence*, which he wrote with a new collaborator, Nancy Austin, was, from a marketing point of view, a piece of brand reinforcement. The book, he declared from the outset, was about the skunks and their battles. The message was deepened (Peters now stressed how important leadership was), but it was also simplified. The eight 'excellent' characteristics were boiled down to a triangle of virtues. The three sides of the triangle were care for customers, innovation and people. At the centre of the triangle is leadership, exercised largely by what Peters calls 'Management By Walking Around' (MBWA) – arguably his first great zany slogan. Once again, the book was peppered with intriguing examples. To emphasise the point that 'quality is not a technique', Peters and Austin cited a $250,000 industrial 'blow dryer' bought by Frank Perdue because the chicken seller reckoned that 'the most obnoxious thing in the world is the eight hairs that stick up on a typical wing when it is barbecued'. The new blow dryer fluffed up the hairs and burnt most of them off before the chicken went to the stores. 'The new technique,' Peters and Austin tell us admiringly, 'on average reduces the eight hairs to two. Frank doesn't think it is enough.'[9]

Thriving on Silicon Valley

In pop-music terms, *A Passion for Excellence* was the classic second album: it sounded a bit like the début blockbuster, but it was a neater, more professional effort. The third book needed to see the star reinvent himself. With *Thriving on Chaos*, Peters, now clad in his 'crazy times for crazy people' clothes, achieved exactly that. 'There are no excellent companies,' the book began, which must have been as much a shock for the skunks as Bob Dylan turning electric was for the folk-music community. Once again the timing was eerily perfect. *Thriving on Chaos* appeared in the same week that the stock-market crash of 1987 threatened to unleash chaos on the western economies.

In the book, Peters articulated a widespread feeling that the world was in the grip of a revolution which was running out of control, and that businesses needed to reinvent themselves if they were to have any chance of surviving. Traditional companies, he argued, were terrifyingly like East European economies: tightly controlled from the centre, grotesquely over-manned, and obsessed with long-term planning. The spread of information technology was allowing companies to by-pass middle managers (whose main role in life was to collect and control information) and hand over decision-making to the people who assembled the machines or stocked the shelves. The pace of innovation and the fickleness of consumer taste was rendering long-range planning redundant. And increased competition from poorer countries was forcing rich-world companies to slash their labour costs, either by replacing men with machines, or by inventing cleverer production processes.

Once again, Peters was attractively certain about what to do: shrink your company, get rid of your middle managers, and devolve power to the lowest possible level. And above all keep on changing. 'If you aren't reorganising, pretty substantially, once every six to twelve months,' Peters warned bosses, 'you're probably out of step with the times.' And, again, Peters made it clear that this was an attitude which even the humblest workers had to embrace. Taking the idea of the permanent revolution to its logical conclusion, he advised people to ask themselves at the end of each day, 'What exactly and precisely and explicitly is being done in my work area differently from the way it was done when I came to work in the morning.'

Thriving on Chaos spent sixty weeks on the *New York Times* best-seller list, half as long as *In Search of Excellence*, but longer than any of its successors. Peters' more recent books, such as *Liberation Management* and *The Pursuit of Wow* have repeated the anti-rationalist message of *Thriving on Chaos,* reinforcing the brand in the same way that *A Passion for Excellence* reinforced *In Search of Excellence.* In general, the arguments get ever zanier and the prose ever more high-octane. The layers of management that need to be eradicated now seem to include everything between the chief executive and the messenger boy. Peters' lists of things managers have to do now stretch for pages (there were forty-five precepts for managers of all levels in *Thriving for Chaos* alone). *Liberation Management* includes a list of maxims for modern management, including 'get fired', 'take off your shoes' and 'race yaks'.[10] He concludes *Crazy Times* with nine 'beyonds', including 'beyond change: towards the abandonment of everything' and 'beyond TQM: towards wow!'. Peters now preaches 'the sublime pleasures of modestly organised anarchy'.

Peters' later writing (it might be stretching a point to describe it as 'mature') can be read as a long hymn of praise to his adopted home, Silicon Valley. The Californian computer industry has generated an extraordinarily entrepreneurial, free-wheeling, convention-busting management style. The area sees more than 300 businesses founded every year, as scientists and entrepreneurs get a bright idea, form a company to test it on the market, and then move on, either because the idea has flopped or because the technology has changed; the result is that people and capital are recycled quickly and efficiently to take advantage of changes of fashion or breakthroughs in technology.[11] Bankruptcy is a badge of honour. As Peters puts it himself: 'Through luck I ended up in Santa Clara county – a big godawful mess populated by failures.'[12]

The inhabitants of Silicon Valley are happier in sneakers and jeans than suits and ties, and gob-smacked at the idea that people should spend their entire lives working for the same organisation. They happily hop from job to job, confident that their value lies in the quality of their ideas rather than their track record of loyalty. Such people like to work in companies which are organised around projects, and as free from bureaucracy as possible. Examine even a fairly large company, such as Intel, and soon you discover that it is less appropriate to see it as a normal company with set divisions than as a free-flowing collection of 'chip squads' – a series of ever-changing teams working on different generations of microprocessors. Valley people hop not just from job to job, but from career to career, with scientists becoming entrepreneurs, entrepreneurs becoming managers, and managers becoming venture capitalists. In other words, they thrive on chaos.

The point of Peters

All this explains why Peters is a multi-millionaire. But is he any good? Even if you accept that he knows a huge amount about companies, you could still argue that there are two potentially fatal flaws in Peters' work: first, he has got it wrong too often (two-thirds of the companies singled out as excellent in 1982 have now fallen from grace); and, second, he has contradicted himself even more often than the average politician. Add them together and the canon of Peters' work looks worryingly insubstantial and ephemeral. Hence the suspicion that what he has done is more interesting than what he has said.

This charge can partly be answered by saying that Peters writes his books for the real world, for people to use, and that the real world changes fairly quickly. Although he has not quite stooped to writing get-rich-quick books, he has always made it clear that, far from being exercises in academic analysis, his books are intended to help people prosper, or at least survive. *Thriving on Chaos* is sub-titled 'Handbook for a Management Revolution'. From this perspective – from the perspective of the manager (one is tempted to say skunk) in the field – an unfailing nose for business trends is one of Peters' strengths rather than his weaknesses, even if those trends often do not last long.

Peters' *modus operandi* is to sense where the corporate world is heading, usually correctly, and then shout it from the rooftops. *Liberation Management* is, amongst other things, a feisty guide to the latest management fads, each amply illustrated with case-studies: flexible organisations (CNN virtually reinvents itself at the start of every news day); learning organisations (Quad/Graphics insists that its employees keep on educating themselves); relentless focus on customers (Britain's Joshua Tetley pub chain offers prizes to bar staff who can recite the names and drinking habits of 100 customers). The list could go on for pages. Indeed, one of the faults of *Liberation Management* and some of Peters' later books is that it does.

In other words, criticising Peters for giving out advice that was only relevant for, say, five years, misses the point. Peters' readers need advice that they can use now. Many of the companies that Peters selected as excellent in 1982 were indeed so at the time; their decline cannot be blamed on him. What mattered from the reader's point of view back in 1982 was 'What can I learn now?' In a recent newspaper article[13], Peters regretted having dismissed two even more unconventional writers, Stephen Covey (*The Seven Habits of Highly Effective People*) and Ken Blanchard (*The One-Minute Manager*) for not being intellectual enough. Yet, the books by Covey and Blanchard, argued Peters, 'give ordinary people (like me) practical things to do this afternoon to make the world of work a little better'. Surely some part of Peters was writing about himself?

All this may get Peters off the hook for being disproved by events. However, even by the standards of one-minute managers, there have been some fairly substantial contradictions. Remember that this was the man who having launched the 'excellence movement' in 1982 was willing to claim 'excellence isn't' in 1987. All the same, the charges against him are often exaggerated. Take for instance one of the most frequently voiced objections: that, having started his career genuflecting before big companies, Peters now preaches that small is beautiful. Though *In Search of Excellence* is devoted to giant companies – and given McKinsey's exorbitant fees these were the only companies that could afford to hire its authors – it is, on closer reading, remarkably sensitive to the ills of gigantism and the advantages of staying small:

> The message from the excellent companies we reviewed was invariably the same. Small, independent new venture teams at 3M (by the hundred); small divisions at Johnson & Johnson (over 150 in a $5 billion firm); ninety PCCs at TI; the product

champion-led teams at IBM; 'bootlegging' teams at GE; small, ever-shifting segments at Digital; new boutiques monthly at Bloomingdale's . . . Small is beautiful.[14]

Such decentralisation cut down on the need for layer upon layer of middle managers. It also ensured that companies were committed to innovation and focused on their customers.[15]

Still crazy after all these years

However, there is a deeper consistency to Peters' work. Everything he has written, from *In Search of Excellence* to his latest *Crazy Times* ramblings, can be read as an extended critique of scientific management. One of his most characteristic phrases, about creating a 'technology of foolishness', came from his first book.[16] Peters is the Michel Foucault of the management world: a scourge of the rationalist tradition and a celebrant of the creative necessity of chaos and craziness.

When Peters went to business school, management was still dominated by numbers ('The only facts that many of us considered "real data" were the ones we could put numbers on'[17]). Management education celebrated the virtues of quantitative analysis, pooh-poohed 'soft-headed humanism' and unscientific intuition, and sought detached, analytical justifications for all decisions.[18] In short, it made damn sure that the 'technical jocks' were in charge.

The rationalist model found its most influential exponents in 'the whiz-kids', a group of strategic analysts who helped mastermind America's victory in the Second World War and then went on to reshape the Ford Motor Company.[19] For Peters and his generation the horrific weaknesses of this approach to management were demonstrated not just in America's ailing industries but in its hopeless foreign policy: the brightest whiz kid of them all, Robert McNamara, left the chairmanship of Ford to become secretary of state for defence, where he tried to win the Vietnam war by escalating enemy kills. The rationalist model 'is right enough to be dangerously wrong,' Peters and Waterman mused in 1982, 'and it has arguably led us seriously astray'.

In Search of Excellence advances three arguments against the rationalist model. First, the model puts too much emphasis on financial analysis, too little on motivating workers or satisfying customers. The obsession with cost persuades firms to undervalue quality and value, to patch up old products rather than invent new ones, to treat workers as costs of production rather than sources of value. The authors quote their colleague Anthony Athos approvingly: 'Good managers make meanings for people, as well as money.' Second, the rationalist model encouraged bureaucratic conformity at the expense of entrepreneurial innovations. Rationalist managers believe that big is best, because it brings economies of scale; that messiness is disastrous, because it means waste and confusion; and that planning is essential, because it allows firms to control the future. For Peters and Waterman, the best firms, such as the office products giant 3M, were almost exactly the opposite: hotbeds of experiment, happy with irrationality and chaos.[20]

Above all, the rationalist model rests on a misunderstanding of human nature. 'The central problem with the rationalist view of organising people is that people are not very rational,' the authors argue. 'To fit Taylor's old model, or today's organisational charts, man is simply designed wrong . . .'[21] Scientific managers overestimate the importance of financial rewards in motivating workers: people are much more interested in intangible things, like winning the praise of colleagues or working for an organisation which they admire. 'All the companies we interviewed,' the authors argue, 'from Boeing to McDonald's, were quite simply rich tapestries of anecdote, myth, and fairy tale.'[22]

Peters and Waterman were hardly the first people (and hardly the last, either) to draw attention to the limitations of the rationalist model of management. As we have already noted, there is a long tradition of bashing scientific management, stretching back to the human-relations school of management theorists who devoted themselves to demonstrating that man is a social animal, not just a rational calculating machine. In *The Human Side of Enterprise*, published in 1960, Douglas McGregor argued that management theory had paid too much attention to 'Theory X', which holds that workers are lazy and need to be driven by financial incentives, and not enough to 'Theory Y', which holds that, on the contrary, workers are creative and need to be given responsibility. The business press was not indifferent to the softer side of business thinking either: *Business Week* even ran a cover story on corporate culture in the late summer of 1980.[23]

Even so, Peters has taken his anti-rationalist stand to extremes hardly dreamed of by his predecessors. The world has gone bonkers, he rants, and to cope with it we must go bonkers too. It is no longer enough for managers to pay attention to the intuitive as well as the rational side of their jobs. They must go mad: throw away their slide rules, forget about climbing the career ladder, and turn themselves into zany entrepreneurs. It is no longer enough for companies to slim their headquarters and thin their middle management. Firms should use internal markets to turn their employees into mini-entrepreneurs, and external markets to make sure that they are not wasting their time doing things, like cooking and computing, that could be done better elsewhere. For Peters, 'crazy' organisations are more efficient as well as more fun than their sane rivals.

But is this really true? The real criticism of Tom Peters should focus not on whether he is consistent but whether his extreme and relentless anti-rationalism is really sensible. Peters is blind to the importance of such humdrum virtues as stability and continuity. For instance, in Peters' chaotic world there is no room for schedules or middle managers; in the real world, middle managers are often the people who hold organisations together and schedules are the framework around which most of us uncrazy people build our days. Indeed, Peters totally underestimates the extent to which even the craziest organisations (just like the best jazz musicians) need some sort of structure to thrive.

Even Peters' beloved Silicon Valley is fortunate to possess two islands of stability in Stanford University and the computer company Hewlett-Packard, both of which have trained entrepreneurs and provided them with a network of contacts. As for the relentless reconfiguration of other organisations in the area, this has not come without its costs. In *The Breakthrough Illusion* Richard Florida and Martin Kenney pointed out that 'hypermobility' can lead to waste, as research programmes are disrupted and creative individuals burn themselves out, ending their careers before they are forty. In his book on company man Anthony Sampson quoted Frank O'Mahoney, a spokesman for Apple, lamenting the company's amnesia:

> There's not much institutional memory at Apple. When we celebrated the tenth anniversary of the Macintosh it was hard to find people who remembered it. We wanted to have an Apple museum but not enough early products had been kept. The consultants seem to know more about the history of Apple than we do.[24]

Indeed, the history of Apple over the past decade might be read as a sermon on why following a crazy dream is not enough. Anarchy is a provocative idea, it is not a business strategy.

Far enough out to be interesting

Having said all this, it would be churlish not to concede that Peters-the-provocateur is on to something even if Peters-the-prophet is not. The world will, one hopes, never go as 'crazy' as Peters predicts; but it is definitely moving in his direction, as cycle times collapse, command-and-control systems buckle and the pace of innovation increases. Companies such as Apple may perish, but Silicon Valley will survive precisely because its business culture is more fluid and its companies more entrepreneurial. Middle managers may be reinvented as 'coaches' and so on, but they will never be the bureaucratic pen-pushers of old.

Peters concedes that the firms he celebrates may have got a little further ahead of the norm. *In Search of Excellence* talked about the likes of Hewlett-Packard, Johnson & Johnson and 3M. In later works, he also has case-studies on well-known firms such as ABB and Union Pacific. But alongside these sturdy beasts are more exotic creatures – including 'virtual' firms such as Verifone,

Oticon and 3.00 (yes, this is the name). Peters' ambition is to be a change agent: 'far enough out to be interesting, close enough in to be plausible'.[25]

Does he pass this test? At the lunch-break of a Tom Peters seminar two British businessmen – one in petfoods, the other in brewing – are asked privately whether the likes of Verifone, a credit-card authorisation firm which has no head office and bans the use of paper, are really relevant to their fairly stable industries. The two managers both admit that they see Peters primarily as a provocateur. But they insist that his ideas do help. Challenged, the petfood manager explains that the main effect is psychological: 'It's in the way I look at the world . . . the way I treat people.' The brewer looks stumped; then he says, 'We're just about to empower our draymen – to let them negotiate with the pubs to which they deliver. That was an idea that we got from a Peters seminar three years ago.' Three years sounds quite a long time in the 'nanosecond nineties'. The world is going in Peters' direction; just not as quickly as he hopes.

PART THREE

The Great Debates

5

RETHINKING THE COMPANY

The Shell Centre, on the south bank of the Thames in the heart of London, is a striking monument to corporate self-confidence, solid and imposing, serenely surveying all that surrounds it, including the Palace of Westminster and a dozen Whitehall departments. With its labyrinthine corridors, hundreds of meeting rooms and all-pervasive sense of bureaucratic permanence, the building has been a perfect habitat for Shell Man – as the company's employees were once mockingly-known. By tradition, Shell Man was a bureaucrat in all but name, differing from the civil servants and paper pushers who accompanied him on the daily commute from the suburbs to Waterloo Station in only one thing – the size of his pay packet. He looked forward to a lifetime of secure employment and an index-linked pension at the end of it. The company provided country-club membership not just for him but for his children. When he was posted to Asia and Africa – as he often was as part of his carefully planned progression up the company – he competed in pomp and circumstance with the British ambassador, and was not above doing a little spying on the side for his friends in the British Secret Service.

A continent away, in Washington state in America's Pacific North-west, the headquarters of Microsoft could hardly be more different. To reach the software giant you have to drive out of Seattle into the surrounding redwood forests until you come to Microsoft Way. The company has dispensed with corporate skyscrapers and awe-inspiring reception areas: instead, the visitor is confronted with groups of white buildings, as modest and low as traditional head offices are imposing. Microsoft employees look more like graduate students than successful businessmen, dressed in sweat-shirts and sneakers, sporting long hair and pony-tails. The average age is only thirty-four, and there are noticeably more women around the place than at Shell. But these Microserfs are at least as dedicated as their counterparts at Shell, often working late into the night, sustained by pizza and free Coca-Cola; and, for the most part, they are a great deal richer. Many of those who have stayed the course – and a great many have fallen by the wayside – have ended up as millionaires.

At first sight, an outsider might conclude that Royal Dutch/ Shell and Microsoft live in two separate worlds, one designed for an industry where the basic product often takes a decade of hard prospecting just to locate, the other for a business where change is measured in weeks. The outsider might add that Shell looks a bit more like the 'classical' model of a company – the sort of thing that other firms would try to copy and that, one day, Microsoft would mature into. However, rather than Microsoft evolving into Shell, it is Shell that has recently been trying to become more like Microsoft. Over the past decade the oil company has strived, amongst other things, to become both more entrepreneurial and more female. In March 1995, this Microsoftisation was speeded up when Shell announced that it was shedding 1,200 jobs in its headquarters, in an attempt to cut bureaucracy and rid itself of its 'committee culture'.

Management theory is currently dominated by an attempt to understand the seismic shift in corporate organisation that has driven Shell to become more like Microsoft. This is the starting point for five chapters on what we have dubbed 'the great debates' of modern management. In this chapter we look at the way that uncertainty has forced the modern company to question its old assumptions about size, strength and structure. In Chapter Six we look at how these new, more flexible companies try to use knowledge. In Chapters Seven and Eight we ask what this means for the leaders of companies: how should they set strategies? How should they govern themselves? And to whom are they now answerable? Finally, in Chapter Nine, we examine what all these corporate changes mean for the world of work.

The end of certainty

Over the past decade companies have been forced to rethink almost every tenet of managerial wisdom. Once companies prided themselves on the size of their headquarters and the length of their payrolls. Now they are renting out space in their head offices and cutting their corporate staff to the bone. Once companies prided themselves on 'vertical integration' – running themselves like self-contained empires with as little recourse to outsiders as possible. Now they are 'sticking to their knitting' in a different sense, focusing on their core business and contracting out everything else to independent specialists. Once they had a clear line of command and control, starting with the chairman at the top and stretching to the lowliest menial. Now they are turning themselves into 'inverted pyramids', encouraging workplace democracy and handing power to front-line workers. Once they had a clear idea of to whom they were responsible – their shareholders – and what they were supposed to be chasing – ever higher profits. Now they are being urged to think about their stakeholders, and aim to increase 'well-being' rather than just make more money.

What forces have unleashed this maelstrom? A computer scientist might say that every company in the world now has to change from the machine age to the information age. An investment banker would point to the mobility of capital. But arguably the change facing managers everywhere is best summed up in two factors both first identified by Peter Drucker: uncertainty and knowledge.

Nowadays, change is discontinuous – or, perhaps more accurately, more discontinuous than it has ever been before. If history was ever a guide to success in the commercial world, it certainly is not any longer. Industries can be upset overnight, giants felled by a single blow. In the space of five years one can go from being frightened of IBM to pitying it; in the space of a few days a bank such as Barings that has lasted for centuries can disappear. Thanks to globalisation, a company can be surprised or outwitted by competitors in countries on the other side of the world. Technology is changing so quickly that a Nintendo Game Boy now contains as much computing power as the supercomputers that used to control America's missile defence system. As a result, Niccolò Machiavelli's maxim that 'whoever desires constant success must change his conduct with the times', which once seemed like the type of thing that managers needed to think about only at the occasional corporate weekend, has become a daily challenge.

In this more frantic world, the only currency that really matters is knowledge. Brute force, huge factories, distribution networks, mineral resources, even money: all count for far less. By early 1997 the stock market valued General Motors and Ford (two companies with combined sales of more than $300 billion and a combined workforce of one million people) at about $80 billion; by contrast two 'ideas-based' companies – Microsoft and Intel – could muster combined sales of only $30 billion and just 70,000 employees, but their stock was worth three times as much as the two Detroit juggernauts. As Tom Peters puts it, 'The age of lumps is gone; the age of ephemera has just begun.' Witness the enormous value of fantasy and star quality: the $6 billion that Seagram, a drinks company, bid to enter the entertainment industry, the $2.3 billion rise in the value of shares of companies who sponsored Michael Jordan just on the rumour that he might return to basketball and the $1.3 billion fall in IBM's share price when it was announced that its chief financial officer, Jerome York, was leaving.

Globalisation only makes knowledge more important. As the price of communication drops to close to zero (it will soon be as cheap to telephone Delhi from Manhattan as it is to call the Bronx), bringing millions of cheap hands and brains into competition with western ones, the only sustainable advantage is likely to be the capacity to produce ideas. Nor is 'knowledge' just something that firms in Silicon Valley and Hollywood need to be worried about. Even metal-bashing firms like America's Chaparral Steel, a mini-mill that has repeatedly broken productivity records, have shown that brains are more important than iron ore. One of America's most admired companies is Rubbermaid – a firm that makes an endless supply of low-tech houseware and the like but does so in an outstandingly intelligent way.

Reasons to panic

Modern management theory is obsessed with 'change' of one sort or another: how to generate it; how to respond to it; how to stop being swept away by it. This is perhaps not surprising given the number of celebrated companies that have either ended up in the boneyard or at least got a good look over the fence. At one time or another over the past decade doubts have been raised about the likes of Metallgesellschaft, Daimler-Benz, Mazda, Nissan, Caterpillar, Philips, Bull, Olivetti, Du Pont, Salomon Brothers and Westinghouse. In 1993 General Motors, which more or less invented modern corporate management, lost $2.6 billion.

Rather than celebrating their size, large companies seem to be trying to hide it, imitating their smaller rivals by shrinking their headquarters, slashing layers of management and subdividing themselves into smaller, more manageable units. ABB Asea Brown Boveri, a Swiss-Swedish engineering giant, has a corporate headquarters of 171 people, and has divided itself up into 1,300 local companies, each one a separate legal entity. Percy Barnevik, the company's founder, says that he operates a 30 per cent rule: whenever he takes over a company he reduces the size of its bureaucracy by a third. Some firms have even gone the whole hog and broken themselves up into separate companies. In the early 1990s, both Courtaulds, a British textile company, and ICI, a British chemical company, divided into two; both AT&T, America's biggest telephone company, and ITT, its quintessential conglomerate, split themselves into three in 1995. 'It has become clear to me that the best way to take advantage of the incredible opportunities springing up in the communications industry is to separate into smaller, more focused enterprises,' explained Bob Allen, AT&T's boss. 'Our integrated structure worked very well for us. But it is an idea whose time has passed.' The stock market agreed: the market capitalisation of the new broken-up AT&T, like those of ITT and ICI, increased dramatically. (In ICI's case, within three years of announcing the break-up, the combined value of ICI and Zeneca was two and a half times that of the old ICI.)

Even the Germans have been forced to join in all this 'unbundling'. Since Jurgen Schrempp took over Europe's biggest company, Daimler-Benz, in May 1995 the company has been offloading businesses almost as quickly as it once went about acquiring them: in March 1996 Schrempp let Fokker, a Dutch aircraft-maker that he had advised Daimler to buy in 1993, go bankrupt. In Japan, Toyota has eliminated three of its seven layers of management and decoupled pay from titles.

This change of thinking has also had dramatic consequences for firms' sense of social responsibility. Even the most paternalistic companies, which ran themselves rather like privatised welfare states, have been forced to join the blood-letting, ruthlessly sacrificing managers as well as workers. Some IBM employees feel so misused by their once benevolent employer that they have formed 'IBM Workers United', which publishes a monthly newsletter called *The Resistor*.[1] And the cutting looks set to continue. Despite a panic about 'corporate anorexia', some American companies have recently introduced a practice known as 'pruning' – regularly cutting the workforce in order to promote the health of those who survive.

The virtues of virtuality

Management theorists have produced wildly differing diagnoses of this corporate malaise. Many of them revolve around the size of the companies concerned. In general, this is a mistake, since neither bigness nor smallness confers an inherent advantage: it depends enormously on what sort of market a company is in, what sort of product it provides and how it is structured (as we shall see, there are plenty of ways for a giant to act small and for a small company to punch beyond its weight). So why is the debate important? First, because, until relatively recently, bigness pretty much automatically was a guarantee of success: the traditional company was based on the doctrine of economies of scale. And, second, because the size debate opens up most of the other issues about the modern company.

Current management fashion has it that bigness has had its day: that the giants are being rapidly replaced by much smaller, nimbler organisations. Indeed, in its most extreme form, management gurus hold that the future lies with 'virtual' companies – small, fast-changing, amoeba-like organisations which come together to get a job done and then break apart, only to reconfigure in a different form around another project. Peter Drucker has announced that 'The Fortune 500 is over.' Tom Peters argues that 'smaller firms are gaining in almost every market'.[2] Charles Handy talks about organisations becoming corporate condominiums – temporary collections of knowledge workers. Both *Inc* magazine in America and *The Economist* in Britain have at various times been aggressive promoters of the 'small is beautiful' argument and cautioned governments for supporting dying monoliths.[3]

The prophets of virtual organisations point out that such firms have few of the fixed costs of their bigger rivals – head offices, company perks and pensions and the like – but can still use modern communication tools to imitate their global reach. From this point of view the craze for downsizing and delayering can do little more than stave off the death of the big company. In the end the only way that they will be able to compete with small companies is to join them, and break themselves up into a thousand parts.

Critics of big companies also point out that economies of scale have been falling dramatically since the 1970s. 'Lean manufacturing' and 'just-in-time production' have shifted the emphasis from size to timeliness; freer capital markets and cheaper, better communications have radically reduced barriers of entry into industries; and the spread of affluence has generated demand for customised goods and services, fragmenting mass markets into thousands of niches. At the same time, the 'diseconomies of scale' have loomed ever larger. Giant companies generate bureaucratic bloat; giant factories create shop-floor alienation; and many giant corporations fail to attract creative workers, or to make good use of them if they can get hold of them. Worse still, the standardised, homogenised products that pour out of these factories are suffering from a double squeeze: fashion-conscious customers are opting for goods that are tailored to their specific needs (or passing whims), while value-conscious ones are less and less willing to pay a premium price for a global brand.

Big is back

The average size of both companies and workplaces has certainly been falling steadily throughout the industrialised world since the late 1960s, with Europe leading the way and America struggling to catch up. But size (or the lack of it) is in itself no guarantee of failure. IBM and Daimler-Benz may have run into trouble, but other big firms such as McDonald's, Marks & Spencer and Toyota have prospered. *Fortune*'s 1997 list of America's ten most admired companies was headed by Coca-Cola, and included such stalwarts as Merck, United Postal Service, Johnson & Johnson, Pfizer and Proctor & Gamble, as well as more recent creations such as Mirage Resorts, Microsoft, Intel and Berkshire Hathaway. The most vigorous challengers to established big businesses are often other big businesses. Sears, Roebuck has lost market share in America principally to other big retailers, such as Wal-Mart, which increased its payroll by 182,000 in 1992–94.

Indeed there has recently been something of a 'big-firm' backlash. In industries such as banking, health care and media, bosses have convinced themselves that size, integration and synergy are wonderful things, and embarked on enormous mergers to prove it. Their logic looked faulty. In banking the only way to justify mergers such as Chase-Chemical and Lloyds-TSB is by cost reductions – something which is unlikely to improve the industry's already low standards in customer service. ('Why anybody thinks that they will produce a gazelle by mating two dinosaurs is beyond me,' commented Tom Peters on the Chase-Chemical tie-up.) In health care, the mergers may provide a way for the industry to cope with the new cost-consciousness of its customers; but they could also stifle the innovative parts of companies where most of the drug industry's profits come from. In entertainment, it makes more sense for a distribution channel, such as a television network, to buy shows and films from as many producers as possible, rather than just taking its parent's offerings. As for size, although a studio needs to be big enough to produce enough hits to cover the multitude of duds, nobody has yet proved that there is any gain from being as big as the new Disney-ABC combine. Certainly, its closest rival, Time Warner, is hardly an inspiring example of vertical integration.

One 1995 study by *Business Week* and Mercer Management, a consultancy, of 150 deals worth more than $500m completed in the early 1990s, found that only 17 per cent created substantial returns relative to other companies in their sectors; and 'non acquirers' – companies that did not do big takeovers – outperformed acquirers.[4] This was in line with a host of studies of takeovers in the 1980s by academics such as Michael Jensen at Harvard, most of which showed that leveraged buy-outs and mergers did create value – but mainly for shareholders in the companies that were bought. In other words buyers paid too much. Why? One delightful study, released in 1995, by Matthew Hayward and Donald Hambrick of Colombia University, found a statistical way of confirming what we all knew already: there was a link between the premiums paid by bosses and their own inflated self-esteem, which the academics measured by things such as the boss's salary relative to his peers and the acres of flattering press coverage. The moment you see any boss twiddling his golf clubs on the cover of an American business magazine alongside a headline such as 'Hurricane Jack lands on the green', sell the shares.

However, the dubious arguments for megamergers should not obscure the fact that another quieter group of big companies has proved that size can have more solid advantages. The best big firms – such as Coca-Cola, Levi Strauss, Nestlé and Philip Morris – have shown that it is possible to have the best of both worlds: the weight which comes with size and the nimbleness that used to be associated with smallness. Percy Barnevik has taken two lacklustre engineering companies, Asea and Brown Boveri, and combined them into a large world-class organisation. Jack Welch's war on bureaucracy helped to boost General Electric's stock value from $12 billion in 1980 to $130 billion in 1996.

Can small firms really stand up to competition from these new 'lean and mean' big firms? Bennett Harrison, a professor at Carnegie Mellon University in Pittsburgh, has looked at the way that small firms cluster around big ones and argued that, even if such small firms count as separate entities, their workers are in fact no less reliant on these corporate hubs than their peers working at the big firms.[5]

Far from revelling in their nimbleness, the chief preoccupation of many small firms in Silicon Valley is structuring alliances and mergers so that they can gain the necessary scale. According to Broadview Associates, an American consultancy, there were 2,913 mergers and acquisitions worth a staggering $134 billion in the world's high-tech industry in 1995 (compared with 1,861 deals worth $90.5 billion in 1994). Much the same thing is going on in another part of the world much praised for its smallness: Germany's *Mittelstand*. Some 25,000 medium-sized companies went bust in Germany in 1995. In a time of cost-cutting, small and mid-sized firms in industries such as machine tools found it harder to 'outsource' things than big companies; and they also felt that they lacked clout when it came to distributing products – particularly overseas. 'The notion of a critical company size holds true in our industry too,' admits one prominent *Mittelstand* leader.[6] In Japan, although a few upstarts have managed to steal a march on the giant *keiretsu* in businesses such as retailing, most small independent firms feel incredibly exposed, particularly because of their lack of capital. The bankruptcy in August 1995 of Nishiki Finance, one of the few banks prepared to lend to small businesses, led to the bankruptcy of over 400 companies.

The death of a model

The argument about size will no doubt continue. But if size *per se* is no more a portent of disaster than it once was of success, then it seems fair to ask whether all this talk about a corporate revolution is justified. One school of gurus takes an increasingly sceptical view of the apocalyptic visions offered by the likes of Tom Peters. Henry Mintzberg, a Canadian of contrarian bent who holds managerial chairs on both sides of the Atlantic, at McGill University and Insead, likes to point out that there is nothing new about 'turbulence': every generation believes that it is living through an unprecedented spate of corporate births and deaths.

Accept this point of view, as many managers secretly do, exaggerate it a little, and you end up reaching one of two conclusions. The first is that all you really need to do is to refine the traditional company – to make its strategies more far-seeing, its structures more elaborate, its control mechanisms more comprehensive. Indeed, many of the most successful management tools of the last couple of decades, such as the Boston Consulting Group's 'growth-share matrix', which divides markets into cash cows, stars and dogs, are intended to super-charge existing managerial systems. The alternative muddle-through solution is to keep your basic structure but to build or acquire an 'entrepreneurial' wing, crammed full of T-shirted people and computers, in order to combine the virtues of bureaucratic solidity with those of entrepreneurial zeal.

Both solutions are dangerously complacent. Nostalgia may add a glow to the post-war period but it was certainly much stabler than the 1980s and 1990s: N.C. Churchill and D.F. Muzyka, two academics at Insead, have calculated that the 'death rate' (the percentage of names that do not reappear from one year to the next) of the Fortune 500 companies was four times as high in 1990 as it was in 1970.[7] Even the best managers have found that fine-tuning traditional command-and-control systems is subject to the law of diminishing returns. Similarly, grafting an entrepreneurial wing on to a hierarchical company works only for a short time, if at all. Part of IBM's problem in the 1980s was that the comparatively free-thinking mentality of its personal-computer division never reached the other parts of the company. One of General Motors' ideas behind buying Electronic Data Systems was to absorb a little bit of the computer-service company's entrepreneurial culture; it never did.

Companies are indeed undergoing a revolution, but the explanation lies in something other than the (debatable) demise of size. A growing band of management thinkers believe that companies of all sizes are living through a transition from one corporate model based on control to another based on entrepreneurialism. The current leaders of this school are Christopher Bartlett, of Harvard Business School, and Sumantra Ghoshal, of London Business School, but its members also include Yves Doz and Chan Kim of Insead, Gary Hamel and John Stopford of London Business School and C.K. Prahalad of Michigan.

The departing ideology is Sloanism, a managerial philosophy named after Alfred Sloan, who took over as president of General Motors in 1923. Sloan's great achievement was to do for management what Henry Ford had done for labour – turn it into a reliable, efficient, machine-like process. Indeed, to a large extent, Sloan's system was supposed to be an antidote to temperamental company founders like Ford, whose irrational dislike of producing anything other than the model 'T' (he once kicked to pieces a slightly modified version) nearly bankrupted his company. Sloan wanted to invent a company that could run itself. He thus invented the modern multi-divisional firm, in which businesses are divided into a set of semi-autonomous operating units, each responsible for maintaining the market share and profits of a single business or market, and in which the heads of each division report to a group headquarters, which is responsible for setting long-term strategy and allocating capital. Although the Sloanist firm was decentralised, there was a rigid (and formal) command-and-control system. And there was even a professional class of managers to run it – the people whom sociologists once dismissed as 'organisation man'[8] and commentators now remember with growing nostalgia.[9]

Who killed Alfred Sloan?

If the 20th century is the American century, it is also Alfred Sloan's century. Sloanism inspired some of American capitalism's greatest achievements. It was also an unsurpassed way of producing standardised goods. General Motors, for example, raised its share of the American market from 18 per cent in the early 1920s, when Sloan took over, to over 45 per cent by the late 1970s, making it by far the largest car company in the world.[10]

However, for the past thirty years the Sloanist model has been under attack. As we have already seen, its noisiest critic has probably been Tom Peters. But, even if Peters had never picked up his pen, Sloanism was being undermined in the real world by four antagonists. The first was the Japanese who relentlessly inundated western markets with better, cheaper, more reliable goods, and they did this through 'lean' production, based on team-work, which involved workers in every aspect of the production process, from checking products to suggesting improvements, and so avoided both the alienation and the waste of Sloan's system (see Chapter Eleven). The second front was opened up by Michael Milken and Ivan Boesky, who, for all their faults, demonstrated that Sloanism had allowed many American firms to be hijacked by managers who were more interested in their pay and perks than in shareholder value. The third attack came from Silicon Valley where Apple's Steve Jobs *et al* have repeatedly demonstrated that you can succeed in business without growing a giant bureaucracy or even donning a suit. Meanwhile the last attack came from the re-engineers who, as we have already seen, ripped apart all the old Sloanist functional departments such as 'marketing', 'production' and 'research', and pushed workers into cross-functional teams, forcing them to use computers to bridge the gaps.

All of these things – and a hundred smaller ones – can be related back to those two awkward concepts, uncertainty and knowledge. Under pressure from them, the Sloanist system has disintegrated – or more accurately an extreme version of one of Sloan's beliefs, decentralisation, has triumphed over two of his other tenets: the importance of formal controls, and the notion that each company is a self-sufficient organisation.

Consider first the two losing parts of Sloan's formula. The most obvious has been Sloan's belief in an elaborately structured hierarchy, with the most senior managers concentrating only on long-term planning and the most junior on day-to-day problem solving. The hierarchy was a slowly moving conveyor belt, relaying information, ground into statistics and re-interpreted by middle managers, to strategy makers at the top. However, modern companies have to be driven by their customers, not their bureaucracies. Jack Welch, chairman of America's General Electric, once vilified the Sloanist company for having 'its face toward the CEO and its ass toward the customer'.

As for the data conveyor belt, markets today are so quicksilver that information that arrives late is not worth having. Rather than worrying about rationality and the importance of being 'an objective organisation, as distinguished from the type that gets lost in the subjectivity of personalities', as Sloan once put it, modern business has a craving for the instinctive. Richard Branson, for example, had the idea of setting up an airline when he spent three days trying to get through to People's Express and found the phone permanently engaged. Indeed, the idea of allotting people permanently to departments of any sort seems strange. Even if the departments are industry specific, such as 'our computer division', they can still be caught out by new markets and products which often spring up between the cracks of old industries.

Inside the walls

The next casualty is the idea of each company as a self-sufficient organisation. Sloanist firms were self-sufficient fortresses, making many of their own raw materials. Now managers are smashing down barriers – not only with suppliers but also with competitors. More than 20,000 new alliances were formed in the United States between 1987 and 1992, compared with just 750 during the 1970s, according to Booz Allen & Hamilton, a consultancy. Xerox alone has 300 alliances – fifty of them with IBM. There are now over 400 airline alliances around the world, many of them designed to get round national boundaries. Europe has also caught the alliance bug. France Télécom and Deutsche Telekom spend half their time hopping into bed with each other (and the other half trying to entice various American firms to join them).

The success rate of alliances is still very low – surveys put it at about one in five. They also have a low life expectancy, rarely lasting longer than four years. A third of the managers questioned by Booz Allen described alliances as dangerous. The same forces of change that make a company look like an ideal partner one day can turn them into a competitor the next. And even when they work, there can be problems about how to share the spoils or about how to deal with issues that have nothing to do with the way they work together in the field: the marketing alliance between KLM and Northwest Airlines is generally deemed to be the most successful in the airline industry, bringing in some $150m of extra revenue to each partner, but, despite their obvious compatibility, the two carriers have come close to divorce over non-operational issues, such as shareholder rights.

All the same, alliances are still seen by most companies as a way to gain outside expertise without having to go through the rigmarole of a full take-over. They also let you dip your toe into a new industry that you do not yet fully understand. Through corporate venturing and the like, big drug firms such as Glaxo-Wellcome and Merck now have strings of tiny cousins in the biotechnology industry with whom they have research agreements.

Another place where the old corporate wall has been breached is in the relationship between a company and its suppliers. Around the world companies are reducing the number of suppliers and forging much closer relations with those who survive, showing them sensitive information, helping them improve their procedures and including them in company bonus schemes. As part of its huge reorganisation programme, Ford 2000, the Detroit car maker hopes to halve its number of suppliers (currently 1,600); it is also handing across to them various engineering tasks it previously did in-house. The motive is partly to reduce costs; but it is also to get better performance. After all, a trusted supplier is more likely to come up with ideas for new products (as Marks & Spencer's food suppliers do) or to allocate good people to the job than a one-night stand. Ford and Chrysler have always got better performance from their suppliers than General Motors because they have promised them long-term deals. One supplier of ABB's knocked 30 per cent off its costs once it was given design responsibility.[11]

The more general thinking behind such 'connected corporations' is that, far from being the prerogative of a particular company, any product or service is the responsibility of an entire chain of firms, starting with suppliers and ending with distributors. France's Renault even got its suppliers to design the headlights, instrument panel and other parts of its Twingo car. Procter & Gamble, a consumer-goods company, and retail giant Wal-Mart have invested in a joint information system, in a bid to co-ordinate production with sales.

As with the vogue for alliances, the charms of 'supply-chain management' may have been exaggerated. It is noticeable that the Japanese manufacturers which pioneered the idea are trying to extract themselves from these marriages now that it is cheaper to source parts abroad. A host of problems can arise from inviting in as a partner a firm that may also be a competitor. Nevertheless, as Jordan Lewis, an American author who specialises in the subject, points out, it looks increasingly silly for any manager to think about his particular firm in isolation. Even if the firm is not already entwined in a cat's cradle of alliances with other firms, its own internal structure is probably beginning to resemble a network of alliances between different parts of the company.

From decentralisation to empowerment

Inviting lots of suppliers and rivals inside Sloan's fortress is a blatant attack on everything that the great man held most dear. So too is the current fashion for flattening hierarchies. However, the third way in which modern management fashion has turned against Sloan is perhaps the most cruel. Critics of Sloan have accepted one of his ideas, decentralisation, and then taken it to extremes that he would never have countenanced.

Sloan divided General Motors up into separate arms such as Buick, Pontiac and Chevrolet. Now some big companies have tried to break themselves into thousands of small firms – hoping to 'empower' the workers in the front line. The theory is that in today's frantic business world it is often better to make the wrong decision quickly than the right one slowly. (Asked what his strategy was, Bert Roberts of MCI, one of America's biggest telephone companies, replied, 'We run like mad, and then we change direction.') Some companies, such as Britain's Virgin, make a point of breaking up subsidiaries once they reach a certain size; Acer, a Taiwanese computer company, is splitting itself up into twenty-one subsidiaries, each of which it intends to float on a stock market.

As GE's Jack Welch has pointed out, each big company has to give away power to its subsidiaries until it hurts – and then give away more. For some management theorists even this level of decentralisation is inadequate. Tom Peters, for instance, thinks that companies should think about each individual worker as a small company in his or her own right. He praises the Ritz Carlton group, which has given even its lowliest bell-hops the power to spend up to $2,000 on the spot to solve a customer's problem. One of Peters' business heroes is Virginia Azuela, the housekeeper on the fourth floor of the Ritz Carlton in San Francisco, who 'owns' that floor because she makes all the decisions that involve it.

The problem with decentralisation on this sort of scale is that it can seem as if it is only one step away from anarchy. The natural reply of some Peters acolytes might be: 'Fine. Step on the gas!' On the other hand, there is a whole range of big companies, such as Procter & Gamble and McDonald's, that seem just as capable of thriving in the new chaotic world as virtual companies. And even when you look at trendier, flatter companies such as Microsoft, Intel or McKinsey, you do not find disorganisation; just organisation of a different type. Such firms may be flat but they are also more than just a collection of individuals. There is something holding them together. Now that we have disassembled the old Sloanist structure, what are the building blocks for the horizontal company?

The new building blocks: (1) core competencies

The natural inclination is to look for another formal structure – a new set of departments, divisions and teams. Unfortunately, if nothing else, the collapse of the Sloanist system has proved that there is no universal answer of that sort. Rather, management theory has tended to focus on processes – things which a horizontal company can try to stretch across its many divisions in order to define itself. These include both network-building and entrepreneurialism. But the starting point for every company is one of management theory's ugliest but most influential buzz-words: 'core competencies'.

Core competencies, as defined by Gary Hamel and C.K. Prahalad, are the skills and capabilities, codified and uncodified, that gave a company its unique flavour, and which cannot be easily imitated by a rival. It is these collections of knowledge that give companies their competitive edge. Sony's core competence in miniaturisation, for example, allows the company to make everything from the Sony Walkman to video cameras to notebook computers; Canon's core competencies in optics, imaging and microprocessor controls have allowed it to enter such seemingly diverse markets as copiers, laser printers, cameras and image scanners.

However, the whole point of core competencies is not so much what you do as what you decide not to do (and contract out to specialists). Often, selecting a core competence means excluding yourself from parts of the production process you are no good at. Canon may be good at making photocopiers but the Japanese firm buys 75 per cent of the components from outside the company. Nintendo lets others design its video games. Nike designs and sells sports shoes but does not stitch anything itself. In the semiconductor industry 'fabless' (or fabrication-less) firms, such as America's Cirrus Logic, have stuck to design; that has left room for companies such as Taiwan Semiconductor Manufacturing Corporation to sell their services as 'foundries' – manufacturers who will work to order.

In an age where Brooks Brothers contracts out its tailoring, it is fair to say that nothing is sacred when it comes to 'outsourcing'. By one estimate nearly half the production costs of large American firms at the end of the 1980s was accounted for by their small subcontractors. Even fairly small companies are hollowing themselves out so that they can concentrate on their core competencies. At the forty-two companies in the Boston area that Rosabeth Moss Kanter visited for her most recent book, *World Class: Thriving Locally in the Global Economy*, the most likely things to be outsourced were food, payroll, cleaning, building mainte- nance, mail, security, local transportation, travel arrangements, public relations, child care, training, technical writing and printing. In addition, manufacturing companies were outsourcing things such as metal fabrication, painting, die cutting and even assembly.

In general, this seems to benefit the companies concerned. A 1993 survey by Coopers & Lybrand of nearly 400 fast-growing companies showed that the 65 per cent of those that outsourced performed better than those that did not. A quick look at the car industry shows that Toyota and BMW (which buy around 75 per cent of their car parts) have done better than Ford (50 per cent) which in turn has done better than General Motors (25 per cent). Meanwhile, the outsourcing industry has grown like Topsy, fattening not only giants such as Pitney Bowes and EDS, but also countless smaller firms. Even monasteries have got in on the act. The Holy Cross Abbey in Virginia and Gethsemani Abbey in Kentucky have computerised various technical and intellectual databases, selling their services via a data-services broker called the Electronic Scriptorium.[12]

Spotting the core competencies of successful companies is rather easier than deciding what your own are. Many old- fashioned conglomerates cheat by choosing wide areas. In South Korea, when the government tried to restrict companies to a few core businesses, the *chaebol* (as the country's conglomerates are called) responded by choosing things such as technology, industry and energy. In France, water companies have somehow persuaded themselves that cable television is a natural business for them to be in, because, like water, it involves pipes and has a complicated billing system. Even in America, plenty of big diversified companies, such as Rockwell and General Electric, base their core competencies around things such as being number one or number two in an industry.

Another problem with core competencies, as Hamel and Prahalad admit, is that, if the market changes and managers get stuck in a rut, they can easily degenerate into 'core rigidities'. One common problem is complacency. Until well into the 1980s Sears' internal position papers did not even mention Wal-Mart as a competitor to be watched. Another problem is making too much of a good thing. By the mid-1990s Sony's obsession with churning out new variations on products was beginning to tire customers. Perhaps the biggest problem, however, is the basic conservatism of human nature: most people go on thinking about problems in the same sort of way, using the same old technologies and satisfying the same old customers.

The new building blocks: (2) renewal

It is dangerous therefore to treat core competencies as things set in stone. For this reason modern management theorists are always looking for ways to keep a company on its toes ('renewal' in the jargon). How does a company avoid sclerosis?

In most cases the responsibility for shaking up the company falls on the company chairman. The best leaders are often subversives who enjoy blowing up their own creations. However, this is hardly a solution that can be applied too often. The theorists have also come up with two other ways of making sure that companies stay alive. Once again these are processes that have to be infused into the whole organisation rather than just optional extras which can be bolted on to some departments.

The first of these is entrepreneurialism. Entrepreneurship, which Tom Peters once defined as 'unreasonable conviction based on inadequate evidence', was exactly the sort of thing that Sloan's system was supposed to eradicate. Yet one of the biggest problems for Sloanist companies was their conservatism: the cloistered élite in charge of innovation was too far removed from the market and too bound by conventional wisdom to see new demands. The link between entrepreneurialism and innovation is one of the things we will look at in the next chapter (see pages 134–158). But it basically means creating small units, giving them the power to try out ideas and, perhaps most important, encouraging them to make mistakes. This does not involve throwing money at them. Peters likes to point to *Inc* magazine's list of the 500 fastest-growing small firms in America in 1992: 75 per cent of these firms were started with less than $100,000 and 50 per cent with less than $50,000. Ideas factories such as 3M and Canon have long encouraged employees to 'have a go'.

The other process is networking, to make sure these entrepreneurial ideas spread throughout the company. Wal-Mart has a video link connecting all its stores to corporate headquarters and to each other: store managers frequently hold video-conferences to swap information on which products are selling and which promotions are working. At Kao, a Japanese consumer-products company, an internal information network allows everybody to find out about everything to do with the company, and its laboratories frequently fly company scientists from the other side of the world to attend meetings. Sweden's Ericsson has linked 17,000 engineers in forty research centres in twenty countries into the same network. Xerox encourages technical representatives to make videos of themselves talking about their achievements in solving tricky problems and then distributes them all over the world, just as scientists distribute research papers. Ford has an internal television network that keeps employees informed about everything from the stock prices of the world's car companies to the latest motor racing results.

Often, however, electronic networking is not enough. Managers still need to meet face to face. William Bruns, a professor at Harvard Business School, points out that it is not uncommon for senior managers in America to spend three out of every four weeks on business trips – or to have their timetable worked out twelve to fifteen months in advance in colour-coded diaries: red for Europe, blue for South America, green for the home office.

But one man's crowded schedule does not make a networked corporation. Companies such as Nestlé, Unilever and ABB constantly throw people from different parts of the organisation together in the hope that they will generate electricity. ('Technology transfer is more than just a piece of kit,' remarks one senior Unilever figure.) Wal-Mart uses its private air force to ferry store managers to its headquarters in Bentonville, Arkansas. Most companies get their money's worth from seemingly extravagant arrangements such as regular retreats for senior managers and global get-togethers for the marketing department. Motorola even sent workers from Singapore and Florida to a mountain resort to help them get on better.

If nothing else networking means getting rid of exclusive departments – encouraging what Jack Welch calls boundary-less behaviour: 'Every time you meet somebody, you're looking for a better and newer and bigger idea. You are open to ideas from anywhere.'[13] The importance of ideas and knowledge to corporate success means that everybody must be willing to share the fruits of their thinking. At Verifone there is a saying: 'Share, or screw you.'

Culture as glue

Core competencies, renewal, networking and entrepreneurialism: a cynic might say that this sounds like a fairly vague list around which to build a company. And the cynic would be right. Indeed, rather than trying to construct a horizontal company out of these building blocks, it might be intellectually more honest to argue that the perfect post-Sloanist company is almost structureless. All that holds it together is its culture – that intangible thing that inspires employees to be self-disciplined and allows managers and their workers (to use two outdated terms) to trust each other. In fact as we shall now see, culture is not as ephemeral as it sounds.

Arguing that the most successful companies are those with the strongest corporate cultures is something of a self-fulfilling prophecy. Most managers dream of working for a company in which most of the employees know instinctively what they should do. However, a few do exist. At Johnson & Johnson, for instance, the 'Credo' – a sort of formalised mission statement – is emblazoned in the company's factories throughout the world; the Credo has not only helped keep an increasingly diverse company together but it is also credited with guiding the company's principled response to the Tylenol crisis, when a lunatic laced some of the company's Tylenol tablets with cyanide.

In most cases the company's culture cannot be captured in some anodyne mission statement. At Nordstrom, an American retailer, the entire employee manual amounts to one piece of paper saying 'Use your good judgement in all situations', but everybody who works at the retailer is obsessed with customer services. Similarly, when people at Hewlett–Packard talk about something called 'the HP way' they are not referring to a rule book. In *Built to Last: Successful Habits of Visionary Companies* Jerry Porras and James Collins argued that the most successful companies have stuck to certain core values – a sort of cultural version of core competencies. Thus, though its empire now stretches from theme parks to network television, Disney has basically stood by its core values of wholesomeness and making people happy. IBM stumbled because it paid less attention to its core value (customer service) than to a business strategy (dominating mainframe computers). Back at HP, Bill Hewlett and David Packard refused to take on big government contracts because they thought it would force them to adopt a hire-and-fire mentality, which would destroy the respect for the individual that is part of the HP way.

Corporate culture is not something that just appears. Companies – and bosses in particular – have to work at it. It is noticeable that many of today's business heroes, such as Richard Branson of Virgin, Anita Roddick of the Body Shop or Herb Kelleher of Southwest Airlines, are particularly talented at generating enthusiasm – and even passion – among their staff. But even 'inspirational' leadership involves perspiration too. Roddick spends much of her time meeting her employees; she has installed bulletin boards, faxes and video-recorders in each of her 700 shops. Senior managers everywhere are spending more time on what Goran Lidahl, ABB's executive vice-president, calls 'human engineering': getting to know workers.

However, the most obvious place for companies to perpetuate their culture is in recruitment and training. One aim of modern corporate education is to encourage self-discipline (which in the ideal post-Sloanist organisation is supposed to replace authority from above). Throughout the 1980s Ingvar Kamprad, the founder of Ikea, led week-long training sessions for hand-picked managers on the company's history, culture and values. Andersen Consulting, a management consultancy, has such a thorough training programme that its employees are often mocked as 'Andersen Androids'. The Androids start off with six weeks of intensive training that resembles nothing so much as an army boot camp, with eighty-hour weeks and a strict dress code. In their first five years with the company they receive about 1,000 hours of formal training. On being recruited each 'Android' is assigned to a 'counselling partner' who meets him every six months to discuss his performance.

However, self-discipline only operates when people trust one another. Even before Francis Fukuyama turned 'trust' into a talking point, management theorists had been putting ever more emphasis on the concept – and rightly so. Junior managers will obey their seniors in these much looser organisations only if they feel that their seniors have the company's best interests at heart; and senior managers will hand power over to their juniors only if they feel that they can trust them. Chan Kim, a professor at Insead, and his colleague Renée Mauborgne, have demonstrated on the basis of a survey of 3,500 companies and follow-up interviews with ten leading companies that trust flourishes only if top management builds fairness ('procedural justice', in their terms) into the heart of the firm. Senior managers must go to great lengths to ensure that decisions are fair, and are seen to be fair, particularly in sprawling companies, where lines of control are vague and suspicion of political in-fighting is rife.

But it is stable?

Today's business-school academics are perhaps a little hard on Alfred Sloan. Always worried that his ideas would be misused by bores and bureaucrats, Sloan was not quite the advocate of machine-like obedience that people now imagine. He argued that managers should see themselves as the workers' servants rather than their masters, and tried to encourage intellectual independence. On being told that one of GM's top committees was in complete agreement on a subject, he proposed postponing the meeting until people had cultivated independent opinions.[14]

If Sloan was presented with the post-Sloanist company, he could with reason point to at least three protruding faultlines in the model that has replaced his. The first is the enormous importance it ascribes to charismatic leaders. As we shall see later (see Chapter Eight) the modern boss is seriously overworked. Companies are also having to confront problems that Sloanism banished: the risk that an all-powerful boss will gently go off the rails, and the problem of finding an equally charismatic successor. Two companies that have popped up repeatedly in this chapter, ABB and General Electric, have both been built up by charismatic monarchs whose reigns are now ending. The fact that powerful leaders have a habit of grooming second-rate people to succeed them (one only has to look at Margaret Thatcher) means that succession crises are likely to become an ever more important part of the corporate scene.

The second problem is that, as companies grow ever more complicated, the job of managers becomes ever more ill-defined. Once managers could simply tell their subordinates what to do. Now people have to report laterally as well as vertically, across borders as well as within countries, and they have to do so in conditions of mounting ambiguity, where competitors are suddenly allies and where the supplier you used to boot around is now given a bigger office than yours in the same factory. Now you might be made 'team leader' of a group which has thrown German researchers alongside Californian designers.

However, Sloan's biggest concern would probably have been

over the area of control. Companies are finding that the shift from formal to informal management structures is rife with risks. The weakening of formal structures has clearly led to some spectacular disasters. The Baring family lost its bank because the management over-empowered an individual, Nick Leeson. General Electric lost a small fortune at Kidder Peabody and Daiwa, a Japanese bank, was kicked out of America for much the same reason. In Hollywood, Japan's Sony did what you were supposed to with creative knowledge workers: it gave them billions of dollars and oodles of trust — and got kicked in the face. One senior figure at Unilever blames its Persil Power fiasco (when it produced a stronger version of its detergent which had the side-effect of damaging clothes) partly on handing responsibility to a self-governing team.

In theory all these external sources of control are supposed to be replaced by 'trust' and 'self-discipline'. Even if he had found these words palatable, Sloan would have pointed out that their effectiveness as controlling agents has been dramatically reduced by all the other things modern management is up to. The system that has replaced his own is fraught with contradictions.

The popularity of downsizing and delayering means that nobody can be sure of their long-term futures. The fluidity of alliances means that friends are rapidly transformed into enemies. The emphasis on speed means that people have less time to develop long-term trusting relationships. Pressure of time and money is forcing companies to compress training courses in which people meet each other. The arrival of multicultural companies means that people can no longer rely on shared backgrounds and tacit understanding to bind them together. Worst of all, many managers are expected to act as willing participants in their own destruction. Company bosses are asked to transform themselves from local barons into loyal lieutenants, and middle managers are being told to develop systems that will make middle management unnecessary.

These contradictions are already forcing some firms to reintroduce some of the command and control modern gurus despise. It is noticeable that some of the companies that made a great fuss about being democratic to the outside world are also amongst the most hierarchical. Park your car in somebody else's space outside a Hollywood studio and you will soon discover that all the Armani casual wear disguises a rigid class system. When on tour the Rolling Stones have seventeen grades of security pass. Even at Microsoft, there is one automatic form of control: everything of any value goes through Bill Gates' office.

This is a correcting impulse rather than a reversal. Even if modern 'informal' companies are somewhat less robust than their Sloanist predecessors, there seems little doubt that they are the organisational form of the future. Once again, you have to return to those old concepts: uncertainty and, particularly, knowledge. Companies used to think that their most precious resource was capital and a small élite was all that was needed to allocate that capital and boss around workers. 'How come when I want a pair of hands I get a human being as well,' Henry Ford once famously remarked. Now firms realise that their most important asset is knowledge. The trouble with knowledge is that it is so much more difficult to manage than capital: fixed in the heads of pesky employees, rather than stored in the bank, and infuriatingly volatile and short-lived to boot.

It is to the subject of managing knowledge that we must now turn.

6

KNOWLEDGE, LEARNING
AND INNOVATION

South Korea's capital city is a fairly dismal place at the best of times, a mess of building sites, standard-issue tower blocks and poky corner shops, all touting ginseng and shiny 'hand-made' suits. But in the depths of winter Seoul can be positively hellish. Freezing winds chill the bones; icy pavements make walking all but impossible. You spend much of your time scrambling for a taxi to take you from one well-heated hotel to another. The only consolation is that the bars are well-stocked with whisky, and the locals, who revel in the title 'the Irish of Asia', encourage you to drink late into the night.

So it was a strange city for Steven Spielberg and Jeffrey Katzenberg, two of Los Angeles's wealthier inhabitants, neither of whom is famed for his whisky consumption, to have chosen to visit for four days in November 1995. Even odder perhaps was the two moguls' choice of host: Cheil Food and Chemicals, one of Korea's stodgiest companies, better known for making things like seaweed soup than films.

This unusual rendezvous came about because Cheil had invested $300m in DreamWorks, the film studio founded by Spielberg, Katzenberg and David Geffen. The investment gives Cheil an 11 per cent stake in DreamWorks and makes it the single largest outside investor after Paul Allen, the co-founder of Microsoft. The deal was masterminded by Miky Lee, a grand-daughter of the founder of Samsung, one of Korea's most powerful companies, and head of Cheil's new multimedia division, Lee Entertainment. In return for its investment, Cheil got the rights to distribute DreamWorks' products throughout much of Asia, a seat on DreamWorks' five-member executive committee for Ms Lee, and a chance to draw on DreamWorks' expertise for Cheil's new film studio, J-Com. Cheil is also forming several joint ventures with Raymond Chow, a Hong Kong film tycoon, to distribute western and Asian films in Asia, and to build large numbers of multiplex cinemas. 'Five years from now,' a spokesman for Cheil predicts, 'we'll be the first major multimedia entertainment group in Asia.'

What is going on here? Part of the explanation lies in family politics. Cheil's boss, Jay Lee (Miky's brother), had expected that he would eventually inherit the top job at Samsung from his grandfather. But his branch of the family was passed over, receiving the group's food and chemical business as a consolation prize. He severed Cheil's connections with Samsung in 1993 and then set about getting his revenge. Seeing that DreamWorks had already rebuffed an offer by Samsung to invest $800m in the new Hollywood studio, Cheil's success in securing the partnership was a notable coup. Cheil rammed home its triumph over Samsung by festooning all Seoul's leading hotels with banners welcoming DreamWorks, and putting on a banquet more suited to Henry VIII than the scrawny visitors from Tinseltown.

But there was a deeper, more strategic reason for the alliance: the younger Lees sincerely believe that Cheil has to become 'a knowledge company'. Like many of their generation, Miky and Jay Lee are cosmopolitan Americanophiles. (The latter, who is something of a new-age manager by Korean standards, makes a point of wandering unannounced into mid-level meetings, and has put the company cafeteria on the top floor of its headquarters, a position normally reserved for the chairman's office.) Korean firms have always been adept at buying know-how from the West. Miky Lee points out that her grandfather started in the flour business and ended up in semiconductors. Now she thinks it is time to import the latest western industry, multimedia, adding that the sort of management skills that can be learned from managing film companies – the ability to weave networks and create vivid images – will be increasingly useful in managing the food and chemical businesses.

On one level it is easy to poke fun at the Lees. There are no synergies between food and films (other than the fact that cinemas are a good place to sell hot-dogs and popcorn). South Korea, with a language which is spoken by only 46m people and a native film industry which is one of the weakest on the continent, looks an unlikely Hollywood of Asia. Cheil is staffing its multimedia division with stolid company men who cut their teeth selling food products and expect to spend the rest of their life with the company – hardly the right sort of culture for the networking, deal-a-minute world of multimedia.

However, although their solution may be a little wacky, the Lees' diagnosis is surely right: that we are in the middle of the transition to an information age, in which the most important resources are not physical but intellectual; and that, given the difficulty of making this transition, it is best to start early.

Knowing me, knowing you

As we have already seen, knowledge – alongside uncertainty – has forced companies to change their structure dramatically. But managers' problems with knowledge go much deeper than that. Not only do they have to learn how to husband knowledge – to 'grow' it as they once grew their capital – but they also need to learn how to handle the people who possess it. For the modern masters of the universe are the gilded few who have had the good fortune to be born bright – lawyers, scientists, stockbrokers, skilled mechanics, indeed anyone who can make connections and generate ideas more rapidly and imaginatively than his peers. Nor can the problem of 'knowledge' be solved just by throwing money at technology. In the 1980s General Motors ploughed nearly $80 billion into new factories and equipment to reduce its dependence on its troublesome workers; its productivity gains were minuscule. By contrast Ford, which concentrated on knocking down barriers between the boardroom and the shop floor, accelerated noticeably.

This presents a problem for management theory. Most firms are used to measuring relatively simple things such as the amount of stock in their warehouses or their income flows. But how do you measure something which you cannot even define, like knowledge? Traditional managerial systems have been developed to persuade bored people to keep their noses to the grindstone. But how do you manage people who keep the company's most valuable resources in their heads, who answer back as a matter of principle, and who would rather move to a competitor than tolerate a boring job? To manage something you need to be able to understand it. But what is knowledge? How do you define it, locate it and measure it? How do you encourage knowledge to grow? How do you turn abstract theory into winning products?

These questions are the stuff of some of today's most lively management debates. They have also prompted some of the most pretentious answers. Consultancies, for instance, have talked about successful companies trying to maximise not profit but the 'self respect' of their employees. Nevertheless, it is also clear that, for all the hot air and contradictions, management theory now has fairly sensible things to say on the two central issues: how do you make your company into a place where knowledge is encouraged ('a learning organisation')? And how do you turn that knowledge into new products ('innovation')?

The beginning of wisdom

It is debatable when exactly 'knowledge' became so important. After all, back in Henry Ford's time, many of the assets of his company were not physical things such as his factories, but the accumulated skills of his workers. However, if intellectual capital was more important then than people cared to admit, it is now paramount. In more and more cases, the ratio of a company's market value to the book value of its fixed assets is reaching double figures. Even in fairly boring manufacturing companies, three-quarters of the value-added comes from different forms of knowledge, according to one calculation by James Brian Quinn of the Tuck School of Business at Dartmouth.[1]

As we have seen already the first person to notice the rise of the knowledge-based society was the ever-prescient Peter Drucker. However, from the 1960s onwards management thinkers have been producing detailed academic research on how individuals and organisations learn. Three decades ago Herbert Simon, a professor of computer science at Carnegie Mellon University in Pittsburgh, and a Nobel prize winner in economics, used computers to simulate and analyse the way that organisations reach decisions. Chris Argyris, a psychologist based at Harvard Business School, argued that failure is a better teacher than success. Success can only generate what Argyris calls 'single loop' learning (I did X and it worked); failure, on the other hand, can generate 'double-loop learning', in which people question the assumptions behind their failures as well as the failures themselves. Walter Wriston, former chairman of Citibank, puts the same point rather more succinctly: 'Good judgement is the result of experience, and experience is the result of bad judgement.'

Such thinking was not confined to universities. Royal Dutch/ Shell pioneered the use of 'planning as learning' in the 1970s. The firm's scenario planning division, invented by Pierre Wack and headed for many years by Arie De Geus, acted as a sort of think tank, in which managers used various versions of the future to test their assumptions about their company, their competitors and the market. The 'total quality' movement indirectly promoted learning by encouraging workers to monitor their own progress and solve their own problems, rather than simply deferring to managers.

Indeed, by the mid-1980s, 'learning' and 'knowledge' had both become buzzwords that conferred instant modernity on the user. Even General Motors got in on the act. One of the features of its innovative Saturn division, announced in 1985, was to be 'a learning laboratory' built right next door to Saturn's factory in Spring Hill, Tennessee. Called the Workplace Development Centre, it included a complete mock-up of an assembly line, where engineers and workers, working together, can videotape what they do and study it at their leisure.

By this stage mainstream gurus had begun to follow where Simon and Argyris had led. Shoshana Zuboff, a professor at Harvard Business School, argued that, in the age of the smart machine, 'learning is the new form of labour . . . the heart of productive activity'. Others warned that those who depended on brawn would be impoverished and marginalised. Robert Reich, then a Harvard professor, who went on to become Bill Clinton's first labour secretary, predicted growing tension between knowledge workers (whom he rather pretentiously dubbed 'symbolic analysts') and manual workers, the first group able to take advantage of globalisation, the second stuck in parochial poverty. Rosabeth Moss Kanter, also from Harvard, argued that, in a knowledge-based society, companies would have to share more power with their employees.

All this means that it is hard to find anybody in the business world who thinks that knowledge is a luxury. By the same token, most people seem to know broadly what a learning organisation should be able to do: many quote the example of the Honda motorcycle managers who went to America on a mission to sell big bikes but found that the Californians they met were much more impressed by the small 50cc Hondas the managers were using to visit their prospective customers: despite having invested a lot of time and money in the big bikes, Honda switched to the small ones – and made a fortune. Other frequently cited examples are firms such as 3M and Rubbermaid that have reputations for being ideas factories. However, management writers have pointed out that too many companies think of a learning organisation as a product rather than as a process (which is a more accurate way of envisaging it).[2] And the managers who can explain how you create a learning organisation are few and far between.

Peter Senge and the fifth discipline

From this point of view, it does not help that the management thinker who is most widely known as a prophet of the 'learning organisation' is one of the hardest to pin down: Peter Senge, head of the Center for Organisational Learning at the Massachusetts Institute of Technology, and the author of the best-selling *The Fifth Discipline*. Senge argues, in brief, that people who are keen to learn should embrace five disciplines: they should put aside their old 'mental models', learn to be open with others ('personal mastery'), understand how their organisation really works ('systems thinking'), agree on a 'shared vision' and then work together to achieve a common purpose ('team learning').

Senge argues that managers will be able to make the leap from the machine age, with its narrow, compartmentalised view of jobs, to the information age, only if they undergo a 'personal transformation', which leaves them at once more open to their fellow men and better equipped to understand the world as a coherent system. And he provides a set of mental tools designed to help people to make the leap, emotionally as well as intellectually. One tool, intended to improve communication, is 'the container' – an imaginary receptacle into which all the participants in a meeting place their fears and frustrations. As the container fills up, the meeting begins to achieve real results, unhampered by 'negative' feelings. Another tool, intended to break down preconceptions, is the 'ladder of inference'. To climb the ladder people need to stop making decisions on the basis of prejudice and start doing so on the basis of empirical observation, instead. A third tool is meditation. Senge recommends that, after a particularly stressful meeting, executives should all sit down together and meditate, in an attempt to communicate with their inner selves. The most powerful tool of all, however, is 'systems thinking', which teaches us how to 'see' underlying structures driving behaviour.

To be frank, it is difficult to see why *The Fifth Discipline* proved such a huge success. Not only is the book hard to understand, but at the time of its publication, dozens of other consultants were arguing that the West was in the middle of a 'paradigm shift' from an industrial to a knowledge-based economy, and that the knowledge-based economy needed a 'new man', equipped with new ways of thinking. By his own admission, Senge drew his inspiration from a number of 'extraordinary people' such as Jay Forrester, who supervised his PhD thesis on systems dynamics, and Chris Argyris. Systems dynamics was particularly important to Senge because it taught him to look at things as parts of a system rather than just as independent entities – hence his insistence that all his five disciplines are of equal importance.

Senge's personal contribution to the subject of learning has been twofold. The first has been to give all this thinking a fashionable new-age slant. (Senge is a devotee of Zen.) The second has been to give learning a practical edge which had been missing from the academic discussion. Although much of Senge's own thinking sounds like psychobabble Senge took his ideas to companies and persuaded them to adopt them. In 1994 Senge and a group of consultants published *The Fifth Discipline Fieldbook*, a collection of case-studies and essays that provided illustrations of how his ideas worked at companies such as Ford, Federal Express and Intel – and is, in general, a much more helpful book than its predecessor. His research centre started in 1990, has eighteen corporate sponsors, including AT&T, Ford, Motorola and Federal Express. Each pays $80,000 a year to try out ideas that might help organisations learn. He has set up his own consulting and training firm, Innovation Associates, which was recently bought by Arthur D. Little. He is also connected with the Learning Circle, a sort of club for devotees of 'learning organisations'.

If they are lucky, these devotees will be invited to one of Senge's regular management retreats. Usually held in a rural backwater, they take place to a background of tinkling piano music or beating drums (depending on the time of day) and involve outdoor events at which people bond through shared physical suffering. The object of all this activity is to overcome the fragmentation of modern society and appreciate the world as a connected system. Senge thinks that the West is suffering from an advanced case of fragmentation – education has dissolved into a collection of banal facts and government has disintegrated into a battle of special interests – and nowhere is the harmful effect of all this fragmentation more evident than in management. Marketing departments are at war with manufacturing, front-line managers with corporate headquarters, workers with bosses. The object of the management guru, according to Senge, is to make this fragmented world whole once again.

Well now we know . . .

What is knowledge?

Given his long list of satisfied corporate clients, it is hard not to believe that Senge is better at putting his ideas into practice than he is at explaining them on paper or indeed at conferences. ('This isn't management; it's abstract art,' one infuriated *Mittelstand* businessman confessed after attending a packed-out Senge speech in Switzerland.) Fortunately, for those who find Senge's new-age thinking a little fuzzy, the past couple of years has seen a succession of much more weighty books on how companies create and use knowledge, including *Competing for the Future* by Gary Hamel and C.K. Prahalad, *Wellsprings of Knowledge* by Dorothy Leonard-Barton, a professor at Harvard Business School, and *The Knowledge Creating Company* by Japanese management theorists Ikujiro Nonaka and Hirotaka Takeuchi.

Any discussion of the learning organisation begins with what sort of knowledge it wants to cultivate. Almost immediately, this brings us back to the subject of core competencies – the skills and traditions that give the firm its competitive advantage. Although we have already discussed core competencies in the previous chapter, it is worth emphasising that core competencies revolve around learning. Core competencies inevitably reside in the heads of the firm's employees – which is what, if anything, all this saccharine talk about 'people being a company's most precious resource' really means. Divide up any core competence and you find three things: public knowledge, industry-specific knowledge and firm-specific knowledge.[3]

This underscores a fundamental point about the sort of knowledge a learning organisation wants to gather. From a learning organisation's point of view, the collected degrees and qualifications of workers represent only part of its knowledge base. Knowledge and competencies also reside in various traditions of collective behaviour – even in the physical layout and databases of a factory.[4] Increasingly, theorists are studying 'tacit knowledge' – the informal, occupational lore generated by workers grappling with everyday problems and passed on in cafeterias, not the official rules written down in company manuals and transmitted in compulsory training sessions.

The leaders in this respect may be the Japanese. Visit a Japanese factory and you will see plenty of employees communicating without actually talking. Nonaka and Takeuchi argue that Japanese firms are past masters at tapping into the tacit insights and hunches of the mass of employees. Indeed, one reason why Japanese companies have been more reluctant than western ones to get rid of middle managers is because they acknowledge the vital role played by middle managers in bringing different sorts of tacit knowledge together. They are, in effect, the real 'knowledge engineers' of the knowledge-creating company, according to Nonaka and Takeuchi.

Sucking in ideas . . .

The hallmark of a learning organisation is that it keeps on adding to this treasure trove of knowledge. There are two ways in which it can do this: sucking in ideas from outside its frontiers, and making sure that they circulate inside the company.

Learning organisations, almost by definition, should scour the world for ideas which might be adapted to suit their particular ends.[5] It is surprising how much commercially valuable knowledge exists in the public domain; and more and more of it is being generated every day. Japanese firms post researchers abroad for years on end and send representatives to an extraordinary number of conferences. (Any visitor to a scientific conference will be familiar with the Japanese delegate in the front row carefully photographing each and every slide.[6]) Japanese companies have established research laboratories as close as possible to American universities: Hitachi's Chemical Research Centre even shares premises with the University of California at Irvine.

Although this sounds a little bit sneaky, the ability to absorb knowledge from outside is becoming an ever more important source of competitive advantage now that even the biggest firms admit that research is too expensive for them to finance on their own: already, once-lavish research facilities like AT&T's Bell Labs and Xerox's Palo Alto Research Center face a future of contracting resources or collective funding.

In many cases this means forming institutional relationships with firms that would normally be regarded as enemies. Ford and Chrysler have formed a dozen consortia dealing with things such as dummies for crashes and electric batteries. The Power PC chip was developed by IBM, Motorola and Apple. These arrangements have proved so popular that the United States Department of Justice calculated that the country had 325 different research consortia by the early 1990s. But perhaps an even better way of encouraging an organisation to share information and gaining access to another company's 'core competencies' is to go into business together, through alliances, joint ventures or even mergers. In the car industry, for example, joint ventures between American and Japanese firms, such as Chrysler's with Mitsubishi and Ford's with Mazda, are one reason why the American firms have all but eliminated the once yawning productivity gap between themselves and the Japanese.

In Detroit's case, the reason for forming alliances was simply to build better cars – and the choice of a partner was fairly obvious. But in technological industries, where the boundaries between many businesses are collapsing, firms often form alliances or joint ventures just to keep in touch with industries that may become their future. This often means hopping into bed with companies from industries that you never considered compatible. For instance, Electronic Data Services (EDS), whose basic business of servicing customers' mainframe computers is looking ever more elderly, has pushed into interactive media through innumerable alliances: with Spectradyne, to provide movies in hotel rooms; with Video Lottery Technologies, to provide gambling; with USTravel, to dispense tickets from automated machines for everything from flights to Broadway shows; and with USWest and France Télécom to provide home banking.

... and making sure they circulate

Sucking in ideas from the outside world is no good if they get stuck as soon as they penetrate the firm. For organisations really to be learning ones they have to make sure that knowledge ricochets around their systems like a ball in a pinball machine. This is actually a twofold task: first you have to build networks to shunt formal information from one end of your company to the other; and second, you have to look for barriers to tacit knowledge – and remove them.

Virtually any company-wide information system, no matter how mundane, will help a company to share information. Most big companies now use Lotus Notes or a similar groupware program. Now management consultancies have started to set up special learning networks with names such as 'Knowledge On-Line' or 'Knowledge Xchange' which allow consultants to pool expertise, swap ideas and consult a library of case-studies.

However, machines can only do so much. Hence the fashion for appointing knowledge officers and 'mentors' – senior workers whose job, like that of the fag masters at old-fashioned British public schools, is to watch over the progress of younger workers. Dorothy Leonard-Barton points out that some companies now look for people who possess what she calls 'T-shaped' skills – deep expertise in one discipline (the stem of the 'T') combined with a sufficient intellectual range to relate that expertise to lots of other areas of corporate activity (the crossbar).[7]

Setting up formal networks for knowledge to travel around makes sense. (Perhaps the biggest advantage is that the information that has been input by consultant X or nerd Y stays in the system long after he or she has left the company.) Nevertheless, what knowledge workers need most to prosper is not structure but freedom – and many more opportunities to keep their minds sharp and their skills up to date. Many software companies have started to organise themselves like universities. Microsoft calls its headquarters in Redmond, Washington, a campus. In his heyday, Steve Jobs, the founder of Apple, cultivated the style of a professor at an alternative university, conducting free-flowing arguments with his sneakered staff. Imagination, a British design company, boasts an in-house restaurant and bar, where employees hang around and socialise after work, in much the same spirit as students do in college bars.

Bold experimentation

The other characteristic of a 'learning organisation' is a passion for experiment – and a willingness to fail. Experiments allow companies to broaden their portfolio of products – a key to long-term survival in periods of great uncertainty. They also help them to shake up established ways of doing things, thus preventing core competences from degenerating into core rigidities. Recently many such experiments have been grand 'top-down' ones in which senior managers have tried to change the direction of the entire company by, for instance, taking over other firms. However, on the whole, it is much better for bosses to take a back seat: to encourage a culture where experiments are frequent.

Fairly marginal projects can sometimes end up changing the entire nature of the company. Hewlett-Packard pioneered the pocket-calculator business because one of the firm's co-founders, Bill Hewlett, wanted an 'electronic slide rule' for his own use. Corning broke into the fibre-optics business because some of its researchers had the idea of introducing an impurity into glass, making its inner core more refractive than its outer layer and thus better able to transmit light. Most successful innovations seem to happen in the office furthest away from the corporate headquarters.

From this perspective, one of the chief faults among would-be learning organisations is the habit of suppressing or even punishing unsuccessful innovations. In science, failed experiments can be as instructive as successful ones; most business organisations, on the other hand, are poor at acknowledging failure, and so incapable of learning from it. This bias towards success may have a generally dulling effect on the learning ability of most organisations (remember Chris Argyris's conclusions). Learning organisations should not only be willing to admit their mistakes, they should be prepared to promote them. This is something that creative industries understand better than manufacturing ones. Steve Ross, who built up Warner Bros, had a policy that 'people get fired who do not make mistakes'.

Another way to experiment is to be bold not only in promoting people who have failed but also in recruiting people who might fail in the future or who are not 'one of us'. Tom Peters likes to describe visiting a typical corporate retreat (either at Palm Springs or Palm Beach), having read yet another long description of how the company wants to become a learning organisation, but still finds itself turning out too many me-too products. The moment he walks into the seminar, he discovers the reason why: '150 people, 147 of whom will be white, male and around forty-eight years old and 144 will be wearing lime-green polyester golf-trousers'.

The jibe carries a serious point. The secret of managing knowledge workers, like the secret of making a martini, lies in the mixing. The group which produced Hitachi's high-capacity computer disk drive included nuclear engineers and chemical engineers as well as computer scientists. In its search for what its director, Gerald Hirshberg, has called 'creative abrasion', Nissan Design International deliberately hires people in contrasting pairs, balancing, say, nerds with hippies.[8] It even encourages workers to display a colour chart of their 'personalysis' on their desk so that managers can mix and match staff more easily.[9]

Much of Microsoft's success stems from its recruitment policy. Microsoft cultivates relations with leading professors so that it can spot talent as early as possible. It also targets people with what it calls 'bandwidth' (i.e. those who show a breadth of interest) and it looks out for 'cross-overs' – people whose academic background might have been in something like music but who have invested a lot of time mastering computers. After that, it throws together super-logical 'bit heads' with artistically sensitive designers. As one insider describes it, 'Designers are invariably female, are talkative, live in lofts, have vegetarian diets and wear found objects in their ears. Developers are invariably male, eat fast food and don't talk except to say, "Not True".'[10]

But will all this create a learning organisation? The answer is 'not for long'. No matter how many weirdos an organisation recruits, no matter how much it forgets, no matter how knowledgeable its chief knowledge officers are or how 'T'-shaped their skills, most companies will still find it a hard target. Even if a company keeps its eyes and ears open, forms alliances with the most unexpected partners and routinely executes one in three directors, the chances are that it will still find it manages 'knowledge' less effectively than it hoped.

The reason for this is simple: learning is hard – and organisations can suffer from learning disabilities, just like individuals. Even when a company appears to have mastered one challenge, technology or its competitors throw up another one. There is no magic single answer that enables a company to become a learning organisation. The management theorists, however, do seem to be showing managers the right places to look for answers. Much the same can be said when it comes to innovation, the area where all this accumulated knowledge and learning should bubble to the surface.

The challenge of innovation

Most management theorists now agree that the ability to produce good new products is not just a matter of luck and prayer. It can be planned, managed and taught, just like any other aspect of a company's work. The art of innovation, management theory tells us, is really a series of balancing acts – be obsessive about developing new products, but make sure that they fit into your long-term vision; build new products in self-governing teams but set those teams demanding targets; listen to, but do not follow, what your customers say; and so on. If mastered, these habits can make the art of generating a stream of new products a little closer to a science.

The first problem to do with innovation is to decide what you want out of it. For Japan's Sony and Rubbermaid, an American household goods maker, winning means product proliferation. 'Our objective,' says Wolf Schmitt, chairman of Rubbermaid, 'is to bury competitors in such a profusion of products that they can't copy us.' Sony realised that it could not prevent its Walkman from being copied. So it flooded the market with different types of Walkman – 170 different models by 1989 alone. Speed is also essential for clothes companies: after all, many Hong Kong tailors can get copies of the latest Paris fashions on the backs of their customers faster than the Paris fashion houses that dreamed up the ideas.

For a car manufacturer such as Toyota or a specialist retailer such as Ikea, success means offering value for money: a minivan or a sofa will sell if it offers the best quality within that price range. For lift companies like Otis and Westinghouse it means outstanding after-sales service: indeed, nowadays, lift companies make most of their money out of servicing their products, not building them. For Intel, a chip maker, the goal is continual technological improvement, or as its chief executive, Andy Grove, puts it, perhaps more clumsily, 'Double machine performance at every price point every year.'[11] Even as Intel launched the 486 chip in 1989, a new team was at work on the fifth generation chip, the Pentium; and by the time the Pentium appeared another team had already started on the P-7, the seventh generation chip.

Their aims may be different, but most innovative companies share one thing: an obsession with what they produce.[12] The character in the film *The Graduate* who keeps talking to Dustin Hoffman about plastics may not have been a particularly interesting man but he was arguably ahead of his times in his devotion to what he produced. The product is the glue which keeps the company together, the subject which dominates the corridor gossip. Companies can instil this obsession in different ways. Rubbermaid instructs rival business teams to get as many new products to market as possible. The teams meet to discuss their plans and compare their performance at an annual company-wide product fair. American computer company Hewlett-Packard links the pay of some managers to the number of new products they introduce. Merck, a pharmaceutical company, prods its research staff to win governmental approval for one major therapeutic drug each year. Many Japanese companies set themselves the task of outperforming their most feared rivals – an attitude vividly captured in Sony's 'BMW' slogan: 'Beat Matsush-ita Whatsoever'.

In many of the best companies the chairman is responsible for creating a culture of obsession: an obsessive himself, he recruits other obsessives and encourages them to devote their lives to their products. Sony's Akio Morita kept prototypes in his pocket and demonstrated them to hapless visitors. Rubbermaid's Wolf Schmitt confesses that he is 'probably the biggest pain to our people in sending out notes with ideas and clippings. I'm probably on every mailing list in the world because I buy a lot of products I find in catalogues. I send them to people to stimulate new ideas.'[13] Microsoft's two founders, Bill Gates and Paul Allen, used to sleep under their computer terminals as adolescents, so as to be able to get back to the machines as soon as they woke up. For decades some of Gillette's male employees have come to work unshaven so that they can try out new razors – a different one on each side of the face.

However, an obsession without a target can end up as wasted energy. Hence the importance of vision. Vision, which might be dubbed the modern version of strategy, is something we talk about more broadly in a later chapter (see pages 159–80). But for the purposes of innovation, vision is the idea of how the market will look (or could be made to look) in the future which inspires and focuses workers. This sounds a little airy-fairy, but it is a formidable weapon. Japan's Canon saw a vision of a future in which photocopiers were small, cheap and ubiquitous, and persisted in producing its personal copier against all outside advice. Ted Arison decided that the cruise-ship business did not need to be the traditional mixture of deck quoits and dinner at the Captain's table – and set up Carnival Cruise Lines to prove it. In 1995, Carnival made net profits of $451 million and carried 1.5m passengers. One reason why IBM, which spent $6 billion on R&D, was beaten to the punch by Steve Jobs and Steve Wozniak working from a California garage is because Apple's founders had a dream of a computer for 'every man, woman and child in America'.

It's a team game

Teams – particularly ones that span functional and even national boundaries – can be vital for innovation. Organising people into teams is one of the best techniques for getting them to focus on the matter in hand. The first people to make this discovery were the Japanese. Firms such as Canon and Sharp made a habit of setting rival teams to work on the same project and asking one team to design the successor to a project which is still on the drawing board. Nowadays, teams are regarded as *de rigueur* just about everywhere – and firms lay on special facilities to encourage them. Sun Microsystems offers laundry and dry cleaning services to members of teams who work round the clock. One of Ford's facilities contains a barber shop, a laundry and several restaurants.

Perhaps the most valuable aspect of this team-based approach is that it cuts down on the wastage created by dividing firms into functional fiefs. Under the old system, designers designed things without worrying about whether they could be made. Fundamental engineering errors were often discovered only after months or even years of work. This was one reason why when it came to building the 777, Boeing formed some 200 'design-build' teams, forcing engineers, designers and even customers to use the same computers. Not only were mistakes spotted sooner but Boeing's huge factory seemed slightly smaller ('it was no longer a case of air conditioning over here, finance over there and manufacturing over there,' remembers one engineer).

Even when companies do not divide people into teams, they can still gain from persuading them to team up in less formal ways. Silicon Graphics provides white boards in the (spacious) cafeterias in its Hong Kong research centre so that its staff can exchange ideas whilst they eat. One of Glaxo-Wellcome's facilities in Cambridge, England, is designed so as to force researchers to talk to each other: all the chemicals are kept in a common store; newspapers and journals are put in people's rooms so that others have to ask to borrow them.

Devolving power to teams sounds all fine and dandy. But just as obsession has to be directed by visions, so teams have to be given strict goals (if not strict instructions on how to get there). Perhaps the most widely studied ideas factory in the world is 3M, whose portfolio of 60,000 products includes everything from stationery to reflecting road signs. The company, which registered 543 patents in 1994, does plenty of anarchical things such as encouraging people to spend 15 per cent of their time 'bootlegging', working on their own inventions. But it also demands that 30 per cent of annual revenues should come from products less than four years old. And the targets are being tightened. 3M's eventual goal is for 10 per cent of revenues to come from products that are less than a year old.[14]

Other companies are similarly exacting. Microsoft grades its employees' productivity: 'They review your progress twice a year, with marks from one to five,' a Microsoftie told Anthony Sampson. 'Four means exceptional; one means you're out.' Many leading companies, including Motorola and Ford, 'benchmark' their skills at producing products against their rivals and against other market leaders. Analog Devices, a Massachusetts-based manufacturer of integrated circuits, publishes figures on how long it takes for each business unit to halve its product development time or defect rates. Japan's Toshiba tracks both the technical and managerial accomplishments of its employees. Hewlett-Packard produces graphs measuring the contribution of each team member in terms of time and money.

Japanese companies seem to be particularly demanding. Ikujiro Nonaka and Hirotaka Takeuchi quote an executive at Honda on the process: 'It's like putting the team members on the second floor, removing the ladder, and telling them to jump or else. I believe creativity is born by pushing people against the wall and pressurising them almost to the extreme . . .'

The customer is almost king

The next area where an innovative company has to strike a balance is with its customers. A survey of innovation conducted by Arthur D. Little showed that the greatest number of good ideas comes from customers, not marketing, sales or top management.

Once again the Japanese have led the way. A favourite approach is 'product churning': putting hundreds of different products on the market and then backing the ones that the consumers prefer. About a thousand new soft drinks are brought out every year in Japan but only a handful survive more than a year. Sony puts realistic-looking mock-ups of new products in its showroom in Tokyo's Ginza district and watches the reaction of shoppers.

This technique of turning consumers into co-developers has now been copied in the West. Boeing involved eight airlines in planning and designing its twin-engine 777; British Airways alone obtained more than 200 changes to the aircraft's basic specifications. Other companies have invented clever ways of involving customers too. A laboratory run by Hewlett-Packard in Bristol sent its researchers to hospital emergency rooms so that they could see how doctors could use the company's mobile-communications gear. Epson, which makes small printers, asks its young development engineers to spend six months in the field, as salespeople, and six months in the service department. Harley-Davidson's boss spends more than half his time hanging around with his customers – in stores, at motorcycle rallies and burning up the freeway. Xerox has even employed anthropologists to observe people using its photocopying machines.[15]

But companies can take deference to their customers too far. Customers are usually immensely conservative, wanting better, cheaper versions of what they already have rather than innovative products. No customer could have come up with 3M's Post-it notes; indeed they showed little appetite for them when they first appeared – just as they initially scorned both the fax machine and CNN. Chrysler pushed through its Minivan despite research showing that customers thought it was strange looking because the company correctly bet that they would like it once they got used to it. If Compaq had listened to its mainframe-loving customers, it would never have entered the market for PC-network servers. As Hajime Mitarai, Canon's president, once explained to *Forbes*: 'We *are* crazy . . . We should do something when people say it is crazy. If people say something is "good", it means that someone else is already doing it.'[16]

Perhaps the most worrying indictment of the modern 'system' of innovation is that it seems to produce a proliferation of similar products rather than startling new ones. There are now close to 30,000 new food products launched each year in American supermarkets, yet, from soap to coffee, most of the brand leaders date back to the turn of the century. When products have woken up markets such as Snapple in soft drinks or Ben & Jerry's in ice cream they have tended to come from small 'counter-cultural' firms. 3M's recent history has seen a string of advances such as the 'Scotch Brite Never Rust Wool Soap Pad', but not another 'Post-it'. One reason why Unilever committed itself so wholeheartedly to the ill-fated Persil Power detergent was that it thought it had uncovered an all too rare technological edge over Procter & Gamble.

During the 1980s, gurus such as Kenichi Ohmae used to scold American companies for always chasing 'home runs' in innovation, whilst Japanese firms, through their doctrine of continual improvement, notched up a succession of singles. Now that Sony and Matsushita are watching the more innovative parts of the consumer electronics industry migrate to Silicon Valley, people are reassessing this idea. 'Incrementalism is innovation's worse enemy,' argues Nicholas Negroponte, the high priest of multimedia.[17] Tom Peters points out, correctly, that too many cars look the same: you can't tell the difference between the Nissans, the Hondas and the Toyotas, and now that quality is very close to perfect (when did the last new car you bought break down?) people are increasingly likely to choose things on the basis of style. If there is one area in which all Peters' predictions about craziness, ephemera and consistent change are likely to pay off, it is innovation.

A kindergarten or a barracks?

As the debate about innovation shows, one of the biggest issues in any company nowadays is control. Most management theorists have followed Peter Drucker's lead and argued that the new knowledge-based economy is doing what Marx and Mao tried to do and failed: shifting power from 'the bosses' to 'the workers'. The reality is a little more depressing.

It is certainly true that employers who behave in a high-handed manner will soon find that they go out of business for lack of talent. Employees who feel unhappy can simply take their brains to another employer – or else set up on their own. As Gary Hamel has written: 'In the knowledge economy the only employees that are worth having are those with many other choices of employment. The most capable knowledge workers are less inclined to think of themselves as sought-after faculty members. It's not HQ any more, it's the corporate campus . . . Beavis and Butthead are not the only ones who have a problem with authority – try winning the fealty of a whip-smart thirty-two-year-old bond trader or brand manager on the basis of raw, positional authority.'[18]

The most successful knowledge workers can indeed dictate terms to their employers – or else set up as freelances or consultants if they get the urge. 'If I want to change jobs,' a leading computer engineer told Anthony Sampson, 'I just turn my car into a different driveway.'[19] Companies woo intellectual stars in much the same way as sports teams woo sports stars: the announcement that a star researcher or columnist is moving to a rival can be enough to depress a company's share price, and set off a wholesale migration of talent into the bargain. Witness what happened at Saatchi & Saatchi, where shareholders drove out the eponymous brothers – and then watched them set up a new agency that lured away many of the old firm's clients.

Nor is it just a case of a few talented individuals being given a soft time. Companies everywhere are having to treat workers of all sorts with more respect than they used to. Yesterday's 'hired hands' have become today's 'associates' or 'colleagues'. More firms encourage employees to use company facilities to work on their own projects. More and more companies give their employees sabbaticals to write books or just recharge their batteries. (*The Economist* is fortunately one of these, or this book might never have been written.)

As the word 'empowerment' implies, bosses have had to hand

over power to people lower down the chain. Companies have to market membership just as aggressively as they market products and services – and perhaps more so. The best employers go out of their way to earn the loyalty of their workers by looking after their welfare (particularly their educational welfare) and providing them with opportunities to put their knowledge to work.

For all that, the 'knowledge economy' is not going to be the workers' nirvana many people envisage. As we have already seen, companies owe their success to a whole host of things other than the combined IQs of their employees: their underlying values, their managerial systems, their traditional routines, their custom- ised factories and their local traditions; in other words, their organisational memories, laboriously built up over their corporate life-times. Some of the most valuable knowledge is highly company specific: you need to join the company in order to acquire it (because it is only passed on to initiates, rather like Masonic lore) and you need to remain part of the company if you want to use it (because it only makes sense when it is combined with the skills of your fellow employees).

Learning organisations are successful precisely because they are so good at generating knowledge in ways that others cannot imitate. Successful companies recruit people when they are young and impressionable and devote a lot of effort to turning these raw recruits into company men and women, sending them on in- house training courses (Motorola, Disney and numerous other companies have their own 'universities'), influencing the way they speak and dress and encouraging them to spend their time with other company people. The training programmes for high- flyers will often last for years and involve moving them from job to job and from country to country in order to give them an overall view of how the company operates.

Companies can put heavy emphasis on knowledge while still leaving their employees with no doubt where the real power lies. Wal-Mart, that has been repeatedly praised by management theorists as a model learning organisation, gets its new recruits to raise their right hand and swear that 'Every time a customer comes within ten feet of me, I will smile, look him in the eye, and greet him. So help me Sam.' Until recently IBM expected all its employees to wear a white shirt and sober tie. People who work for Nordstrom, a retail chain, happily refer to themselves as 'Nordies' and start every day by chanting 'We want to do it for Nordstrom'.

Indeed, for many workers, perhaps even most, the fundamental division in modern society will not be between capital and labour but between insiders and outsiders – between those who, as part of knowledge-intensive companies, have a chance to sharpen their intellects and hone their skills, and those who are left out in the cold. This is particularly bad news for two sorts of people. The first is people who leave school or university in the middle of a recession, and who are judged too old when the next round of hiring comes along. They will find that no amount of government-sponsored training or general education can make up for the lack of company-specific skills. The second group is middle-aged workers who become victims of the fashion for downsizing or delayering, whose skills and values have been so finely tuned by their previous employer that, however hard they try, they cannot fit in elsewhere.

Does a model exist to show how a knowledge-based economy might work? There are worse places to look than Hollywood. It may stick in the gullet to think of, say, Sylvester Stallone as a knowledge worker, but the star system already provides a model for how the most talented people in other industries may one day strike deals with their employers. From being contract workers bound to studios, actors have become free agents. The studios are no longer vertically integrated companies owning everything that they produce. Rather, every film is made by a complex alliance with the studio acting as no more than the banker: virtually all the important parts of a film, such as casting, special effects and the producer's chair, are contracted out. And yet the other moral to be drawn from Hollywood is that the studios have survived. They may not be able to push around Stallone, but the vast majority of entertainment workers cross the studios at their peril. The studios' web of production deals and alliances continually creates and disperses more knowledge. They are learning organisations *par excellence*; but they have given away power only where they have had to.

7

STRATEGY:
FROM PLANNING TO VISION

In the witch doctor's world one thing is prized above all others: the ability to predict and control the future. In the old days, soothsayers donned strange clothes, performed exotic gyrations and sacrificed unfortunate animals. In return, tribal chiefs put luxurious huts and a mind-boggling supply of young virgins at their disposal. Naturally enough, the witch doctors did everything possible to protect the secrets of soothsaying from the curious gaze of outsiders or the critical questions of cynics.

Management theorists may not dress up in feathered head dresses or pore over the entrails of dead animals – at least not in public. But in their bid to predict and control the future they have developed plenty of exotic-sounding techniques, such as SBUs, PIMs, PPBSs and 3x3 matrices (to name only the most comprehensible); and they have kept those techniques as mysterious as possible, protected from the prying eyes of laymen by complicated mathematics and labyrinthine diagrams. One business-school student recalls attending a fifteen-part course on 'strategy' (for that is what we are talking about) given by one of the leading names in the field: 'I learned a great deal about military history and Confucian metaphors. But the only practical advice that we were given was that every company should send teams of people from different disciplines to country hotels every year to think about the future.'

Indeed, in terms of clarity, strategy has become an ever more obtuse art. For most of this century 'strategic planning' was regarded as the very kernel of management thought; indeed it often had a department devoted to it. Planning – a neat, definite, military concept – was adapted and refined into what seemed to be an ever more precise science. However, since the 1980s strategic planning – like many other management nostrums – has been discredited. In uncertain times, when few businesses feel happy predicting their next month's profits, the idea of five-year plans strikes many managers as a little, well, socialist. Yet the appeal of having some goal to aim for – even a less attainable, more ephemeral one – remains. Strategy has thus been recast in several ways, most prominently as 'vision'. The question at the heart of this chapter is whether this is really an improvement.

Building the planning machine

The organisation that was most susceptible to the claim that management theory can confer control over the future was the multi-divisional firm that achieved its finest flowering in America in the 1960s and 1970s. Technically, the credit for putting planning at the centre of corporate life should probably go to writers such as Igor Ansoff and Alfred Chandler, who both, in their different ways, spent the 1950s and 1960s insisting that all companies needed an overall corporate strategy.[1] However, the trail had already been blazed by a familiar duo – Frederick Taylor and Alfred Sloan. By separating the performance of a task from its co-ordination, Taylor prepared the way for the arrival of a new class of professional strategic planners. At Sloan's General Motors managers sitting in the corporate headquarters were responsible for crafting long-term strategy for the entire organisation.[2]

Arguably, managers' fascination with planning goes even deeper than Sloan and Taylor. Pick up virtually any book about strategy, and you are confronted with a string of military metaphors about the importance of 'reconnaissance' or 'good intelligence'. If nothing else, managers have always fancied themselves as an officer class. Strategy is what separates them from the sergeants. The planning department was as close as many of them came to an officers' mess. Indeed in America there was an explicit military connection. The American army embraced planning with a rare fervour in Vietnam: one of the architects of America's policy of 'strategic bombing' had been an architect of strategic planning at Ford in the 1950s, Robert McNamara. Meanwhile, in France, strategic planners tried to run the whole country, public as well as private.

By the early 1960s, planning was still a fairly simple process.[3] It usually involved three stages: designing a blueprint, setting out a company's or a division's future; then agreeing on it; and finally implementing that plan. Each part of the process, which in total took around a year, had its own dedicated workers. Ideas were the province of the planning department. Agreement was left to senior management and the board. Implementation was the job of the other managers who had been specially trained for this role (at places like General Electric's Crotonville centre) and were issued with weighty manuals (such as GE's famous 'blue books') to tell them how to fulfil the task. The function of an organisation in the eyes of Ansoff was to implement strategy: everything – its structure, its hierarchy – followed from the plan.

Flattered by the success of their brain child, management theorists tried to turn planning into a rigorous and sophisticated science. The academics decomposed strategy-making into its constituent parts: mission, objectives, external analysis, internal analysis and so on. Confronted with objections to the rigmarole, they simply made the strategy-making process even more complicated: George Steiner (a management theorist, not the renaissance man) took almost 800 pages to explain the rudiments of planning in *Top Management Planning*, published in 1969.[4] Ten years later in *Strategic Planning* (tellingly sub-titled *What Every Manager Must Know*) Steiner even introduced a new phase, the 'plan to plan'.[5]

By the end of the 1960s, firms such as General Electric found that they needed at least three levels of strategy-makers: first the managers of particular products or divisions, then a layer of 'strategic business units' that looked after several related areas of business, and finally a layer of corporate strategists who acted as 'portfolio planners' deciding how to allocate the company's resources between the various strategic business units. Tools that helped planners through this maze were soon all the rage. GE itself developed an 'industry-attractiveness-business-position matrix', but the most successful aid was the Boston Consulting Group's 'growth-share matrix', which classified businesses into cash cows, stars, question marks and dogs. The aim of all these devices was the same: to tell managers whether to invest, harvest or divest, depending on where their business fell on the chart.[6] By 1979, 45 per cent of the Fortune 500 companies were using some form of portfolio planning.[7]

Porter the planner

All this complexity might have been tolerable, had the strategy gurus agreed on what they were trying to do. But they did not. The biggest split was between the Harvard Business School, which emphasised case-studies and argued that each problem had a particular solution, and the Boston Consulting Group, which always tried to provide a universal explanation of the way that companies operated: BCG believed that successfully identifying your business, as, say, a cash cow, was as useful to a coffin maker as to an advertising agency.

It looked for a while as if these disputes might be solved by Michael Porter, who churned out a series of books on corporate strategy during the 1980s, before turning his attention to globalisation (see pages 251–5). Porter brought to the subject the intellectual vigour of somebody who has both an MBA from Harvard's Business School and a PhD from the economics faculty that sits glowering at HBS across the River Charles; however, he is not known for his brevity.

In his first book *Competitive Strategy*, published in 1980, Porter tried to plot a middle way between the two approaches, arguing that there were both individual and general lessons to be learned about strategy: thus he studied individual companies but set them in the context of their relevant industries, and he outlined 'generic strategies' but emphasised that different firms must choose different paths to success. In his next book, *Competitive Advantage*, published five years later, Porter became more prescriptive, outlining generic strategies that firms could take. Before deciding on what strategy to pick, he argued, a firm needed to do a lot of homework. This included analysing the 'five competitive forces' which determine an industry's attractiveness (potential entrants, buyers, suppliers, substitutes and competitors), and deciding what sort of industry it was (growing or declining, ripening or mature, and so on). Porter also argued that a company should think of itself not as a single unit but as a 'value chain' of discrete activities (designing, producing, marketing etc.).

This love of analysis explains why Porter became something of a god to planners. Porter's work does not lend itself to one-line summaries, yet, underneath all his lists and copious examples, there is arguably a fairly simple message. The essence of strategy is really about making a choice between two different ways of competing. One choice is market differentiation, competing on the basis of value added to customers, so that people will pay a premium to cover higher costs. The other choice is cost-based leadership, offering products or services at the lowest cost. Though quality and service is never irrelevant, reducing cost is the major focus of the second sort of organisation; and vice versa for the first. Porter's data showed that firms with a clear strategy performed better than those that either lacked a clear strategy or that consciously tried to follow both paths (i.e. lead the way in price and quality).

Why the planning machine stalled

All this was marvellous for Porter, whose big, square books on strategy remain set texts in many business schools. But it was not enough to rescue the idea of planning from collapse. For even as Porter was refining his ideas, the Japanese car companies were demolishing his arguments, beating the Americans at both cost and quality. The result was that planning quickly went out of fashion.

Not only did the Japanese manage to combine things that Porter thought were incompatible, they did so without bothering to prepare strategic plans. The American addiction to corporate planning struck Japanese thinkers such as Kenichi Ohmae as a private-sector version of the Soviet addiction to central planning, with the same disastrous impact on innovation and enterprise. Nor did the attacks on strategic planning just come from overseas. Even in the Harvard Business School, frustration with planning had been growing. Robert Hayes pointed out that many line managers found strategic planning an impediment to good management.[8] Amir Bhide noted that two-thirds of the founders of fast-growing companies he had interviewed had started their companies with either back-of-the-envelope business plans or no business plans at all.[9]

Indeed, nowadays strategic planning is as fashionable as the kipper tie. Companies have shifted their attention from planning the future to getting the most out of the present through disciplines like re-engineering. 'Doing more with less' has become the way to get ahead. Many companies have disbanded their strategy departments entirely; and some strategic consultancies, starved of work, have had to mug up on re-engineering. One leading management thinker, Henry Mintzberg, has even written a lengthy but excellent obituary called *The Rise and Fall of Strategic Planning*.

So what exactly is wrong with strategy and planning? The charge sheet is a long one, but essentially divides into two complaints: practical difficulties and theoretical impossibilities. Top of the list of difficulties is the fact that strategic planning never really amounts to strategic thinking. Instead it becomes an annual ritual in which representatives of each department try to grab whatever resources are being doled out. That not only leads to fights (the marketing strategy contradicts the manufacturing strategy); it also means that the company's strategy often takes no account of the inter-departmental connections that can lead the way to the markets of the future.

Strategic planning soon becomes a numbers game. The real substance of General Electric's round of meetings was about making the numbers add up rather than discussing its future. And in this world, where increasing a department's budget by 1 per cent in real terms is seen as a drastic move, incrementalism is king. True, IBM's planners did gradually allocate more money to the company's personal-computer division, but they never grasped how radically their industry had changed. One reason why Rupert Murdoch has consistently beaten the world's other media giants to the punch is because he relies on instinct rather than committees.

Paradoxically, when a company's planners do decide (usually too late) to do something, they often blunder into a big acquisition or diversification which proves anything but strategic. Think of Westinghouse's decision to enter the financial-services business in the late 1980s or AT&T's attempt to break into the computer business with its acquisition of NCR, or any of Daimler-Benz's catastrophic forays into aerospace and electronic goods.

Fine, you might argue, but surely all this proves is that strategy can be poorly executed. But planning can frequently be a pointless activity even in the hands of the most talented managers imaginable. Strategic planning is usually hopelessly conservative, projecting current practices into the future. This conservatism may have been appropriate in, say, America in the 1950s (though many would dispute that) but it has no place in a business world where the environment can change radically and where the greatest source of competitive advantage is not really 'cost' or 'quality' but 'creativity'. After all, planning preserves existing categories of thought, whereas creativity blows them apart.

Even the best planners can get things completely wrong. Consider two fairly predictable industries. Five years ago, most western financial institutions were still terrified that Japan's banks would take over their business, and drew up complicated strategies and briefing documents on how to cope with the Japanisation of their markets. Today the same banks and securities houses are still worried about Tokyo's bankers – but only because they might go bust. Similarly, for most of the past decade British Airways has been obsessed with stopping American carriers such as United and Delta from establishing competing 'fortress hubs' at Heathrow. Now Virgin Atlantic – an upstart founded by a man whom BA refused to take seriously because he didn't wear a tie – is BA's chief competitor on the Atlantic route. Nor have United, Delta and American been that clever: they spent most of the past decade fighting each other whilst small airlines such as Southwest stole their customers. And, remember, both airlines and banking are highly regulated, capital-intensive businesses. Who would want to be a strategic planner at an Internet pioneer such as Netscape?

The second objection follows on from the first: that statistics are by no means as reliable as the planners believe. (Indeed, planners tend to resemble the Lilliputian tailors in Jonathan Swift's *Gulliver's Travels*, who measure Gulliver with a quadrant and sextant, perform a set of complex computations, and return several days later with a suit of clothes 'very ill made'.) Far from being objective and trustworthy, statistics are often based on flimsy data and shaped by the prejudices of those who collect them. Even in the late 1980s the CIA's planners argued that the Soviet Union possessed one of the world's biggest economies – despite the fact that any Moscow taxi driver could have told them this was nonsense. Henry Mintzberg has repeatedly pointed out that the most important knowledge in any organisation is not what is written down in formal reports and expressed in statistics but what is exchanged in informal conversations, with customers, suppliers and other workers.[10]

The last objection is that strategic planning separates thinking from doing. The strategy-makers – a tiny élite – think; the workers – everybody else – act. Strategists lack the detailed knowledge of organisations needed to make informed decisions. And the front-line workers who possess that intimate knowledge are too far removed from strategy-making to have any impact. If all the guff about learning organisations and so on means anything at all, it is that a company's strategic intelligence involves all its workers; it is not just the preserve of a small group of planners.

Growth is back

Strategy is clearly in trouble. But the announcement of its death is somewhat exaggerated. The past few years have seen more and more managers pining for the halcyon days of strategic thinking, if not quite strategic planning.

To a large extent this is a reaction against re-engineering (see

Chapter One). Managers have started to realise that restructuring is not in itself a strategy, but a means of dealing with the failure of earlier strategies. More often than not, downsizing leads not to long-term growth but to yet more downsizing, and the obsession with the short-term leads not to organisational mastery but to drift and panic. The urgent drives out the important and the fleetingly fashionable distracts attention from the real opportunity. Driven to produce short-term profits, managers forget to ask if their industry has a long-term future; determined to squeeze more out of less, they fail to spot new markets or invent new products.

In *Grow to be Great: Breaking the Downsizing Cycle* two consultants from Mercer Management, Dwight Gertz and João Baptista, looked at some 1,000 American companies and found that only 7 per cent of the best performing ones in 1988–93 had cut costs in the previous five-year period. Companies that invested in growth were rewarded with a compound 15 per cent annual rise in their share price; those who invested in cost savings saw only an 11 per cent rise.

The real successes of American business of the past decade are not those companies such as General Electric and Xerox that have completed heroically bloody turnarounds, but those which never went in the wrong direction in the first place – and kept on growing. Venerable old Hewlett-Packard, for instance, has quadrupled in size. By mid-1995 even those companies that had cut back hard realised that future profits would come from growth. 'Union Pacific used to have 80,000 employees. Today we have fewer than 50,000,' Drew Lewis, the company's chief executive, declared to *Strategy & Business*, a periodical. 'There is still room to cut costs, but we're not going anywhere unless we grow our revenues through improved services and satisfactory margins.'[11] And as bosses' thoughts have turned to growth, their time horizons have lengthened. In late 1995 Brian Dickie, a consultant at Booz, Allen & Hamilton, estimated that his clients' 'strategic focus' had lengthened considerably to around seven years ('on earlier occasions eighteen months was not unusual').

With 'growth' suddenly back in fashion, management theorists have reinvestigated strategy – and reached two general conclusions. The first one is that, for all its faults, planning was not an unmitigated disaster. For instance, in the previous chapter, we mentioned a system of scenario planning pioneered by Royal Dutch/Shell. This was meant to be more of a learning exercise than an attempt to make accurate predictions. However, by asking a succession of 'what if' questions, scenario planning gave the oil company a better understanding of its strengths and weaknesses. It also produced some fairly accurate predictions: Shell was the only major oil company to predict the 1973 oil crisis and to have a ready-made strategy for coping with it.

The other more general conclusion is that, even if they have ditched planning, the most successful companies remain intensely interested in thinking about the future. Microsoft has an Advanced Technology Group, Toshiba boasts a Lifestyle Research Institute and Yamaha has a 'listening post' in London, chock full of all the latest musical gadgetry, which it makes available to Europe's most talented musicians. The most adventurous companies are indulging in what Disney calls 'imagineering'. Electronic Data Services hired Disney alumni to help the company put together an exhibit demonstrating how information technology would reshape people's lives. Some leading businessmen, including Olivier Lecerf, former head of Lafarge, a large cement manufacturer, and Frank Carruba, the chief technology officer of Philips, have started taking sabbaticals in order to reflect on the future.[12]

Management consultancies have also started to develop new techniques for thinking ahead. Arthur D. Little encourages its clients to imagine a future in which a particular technology – virtual reality, say – has become commonplace.[13] Children spend their time in VR playgrounds; clothes buyers 'try' clothes on in VR mirrors before asking for them to be made; students tour the world looking for the best VR classroom. The clients have to think about what all this means for their own business. They also have to 'write a history of the future' in order to see what technological breakthroughs and regulatory changes are needed to make this possible. The consultancy argues that this technique provides a way of thinking about the future without either extrapolating from the present or indulging in the pseudo-science of prediction: the point, a little like Shell's scenario planning, is simply to ask 'What if . . . ?'

The importance of science fiction

But can all this futuristic thought be translated into a strategy without falling back on the (generally bad) idea of planning? The answer according to many theorists is to come up with a strategic vision – something that provides a company with a sense of mission without entailing the costs and constraints of central planning. Visions, according to their advocates, define a few outstanding goals around which companies can organise their resources; and they help to inspire the workforce to pursue common aims: think of the way that John F. Kennedy used his vision of putting a man on the moon within the next decade to galvanise America's space programme; or Apple's dream of a computer for every man, woman and child in America. Microsoft's clearly articulated dream of 'owning the desktop', which dates back to the early 1980s, has helped it to dominate first operating systems, then applications software and now seems to be pushing it towards the Internet. Sun Microsystems has stuck by its idea that 'the network is the computer' for almost a decade.

Nor are visions confined to sneakered entrepreneurs. In Japan even the dowdiest managers spend some of their time gazing into crystal balls. Ever since he published *The Mind of the Strategist* in 1982 Kenichi Ohmae has been pointing out that Japanese companies organise themselves around common visions – visions, moreover, that emerge from a continual process of negotiation, rather than from the mind of a single domineering leader.

Perhaps the only creature more admired in American business during the 1980s than the generic Japanese manager was Jack Welch. Welch, too, has an obsession with visions.[14] When he dispensed with all GE's strategic-planning apparatus, he set a fairly simple goal instead: 'Be one or two in an industry – or else get out.' This was easy to understand but hardly an inspiring vision.

For much of the early 1980s all that GE's workers knew about strategy was the pain of Neutron Jack announcing yet more redundancies. Welch's first attempt at a loftier theme – trying to persuade GE's staff that they owned the business – flopped. He had a little more success with his idea that GE was like a 'business engine', but his message really got through only in late 1988 when he launched 'Work-Out' – an empowerment programme that began with whole series of meetings where GEers could air their grievances.

Once Welch's new vision caught on ideas started coming from the very middle managers who had been most hostile to him. For years Welch returned every month to 'The Pit' – the amphitheatre at GE's Management Development Center in Crotonville where Work-Out was conceived – to deliver a sermon on Work-Out to employees. Already – like all the best visions – it has acquired its own language. 'Low-hanging fruit' for instance are easy-to-make savings in factories; a 'python' is an entwining bureaucracy. Now Welch has changed his message again, and dreams of turning GE into a 'boundaryless organisation'. 'Companies need overarching themes to create change,' Welch has argued. 'If it's just somebody pushing a gimmick or a programme, without an overarching theme, you can't get through the wall.'[15]

All this has been enough to turn dreaming up visions into a management industry in its own right. Virtually every firm now has a mission statement that purports to articulate its view of the future. An increasing number of companies assemble 'vision task forces'. Even bosses who took the same dismissive attitude to 'the vision thing' as George Bush have had to knuckle under. Lou Gerstner came into IBM declaring that the one thing that the computer giant did not need was another vision; by 1995 he had begun mumbling about 'building a networked future'.

Even accountants now feel the urge to dream. In 1994 Arthur Andersen's auditing arm, which five years earlier had embarked on a project called Vision 2000, decided it was time for a fresh message called (cringingly) Creating Our Future. The vision task force was made up of 100 people – seventy-five partners and twenty-five young high-flyers; it met in Chicago, Lisbon, Berlin and Singapore, and the 'visionaries' chattered away on-line between these gatherings. Arthur Andersen also consulted clients, such as Jack Welch, and gurus, such as Charles Handy.

Having played around with highly speculative propositions such as 'By 2005 Arthur Andersen has become the biggest law firm in the world', the dreamer-accountants decided that the company's aim should be to change from auditing the books of its clients to auditing their business. To meet this more consultative role, the accountants came up with one equation and one slogan. The equation was $K=(P+I)S$, where 'K' was knowledge, 'P' our people, 'I' information and 'S' the power of sharing. The slogan was that Andersen should become 'The World's Greatest Place to do Great Work'. Although this must surely count as the most cheesy battlecry in history, Andersen's accountants swear that the process has helped redirect their company – and that five years is too long to wait for another dream; 'visioning has to be an ongoing process'.

The new synthesis

Can visions really be fleshed out into meaty strategies? To generalise slightly, academics have tended to split into two groups. The first group wants to push the subject of strategy into more ephemeral fields. John Kao, a professor at the Harvard Business School (and a successful entrepreneur in his own right), argues that the chief strategic aim of a company should be to encourage creativity. In the old days planners used to hand out sheet music with exact descriptions of what each person should play; now strategy, according to Kao, is like jazz. The strategists should set the overall direction, but let individuals improvise. This creative approach is proving so popular that one 'paper' at the 1995 American Management Association consisted of a bunch of jazz musicians, jamming for all they were worth.

A second group of thinkers still hearken after a more disciplined, Porterish approach. For instance, in *Foundations of Corporate Success* John Kay, a British economist turned management theorist, took on an approach almost as complicated as

Porter's. Kay argues that strategy should be built around identifying each firm's strength in four fields: its reputation (which can include brands), its ability to innovate, its strategic assets (such as a drug patent or a government-sanctioned monopoly) and its 'architecture', by which he means the network of relationships within and outside a firm (he is particularly keen on Marks & Spencer's supplier network). Kay offers an excellent analysis of why particular firms have succeeded, but he remains adamant that each firm's position is different, and that there are no generic answers to strategic success. This may well be an intellectually rigorous approach, but it is hardly designed to win him readers.

The book that has had the biggest impact in strategy, *Competing for the Future*, published in September 1994 by Gary Hamel and C.K. Prahalad, combines elements of both approaches. Prahalad has helped turn his employer, the University of Michigan Business School, into one of the foremost centres of thinking on business strategy in America; Hamel is arguably the brightest (and, according to his peers, the richest) business thinker of his generation. In 1997 he launched a new consultancy called Strategos. But *Competing for the Future*'s success also owed something to the marketing savvy of the book's publisher, Harvard Business School Press, which spent $75,000 marketing the book, secured serialisation in *Fortune*, one of America's most widely read business magazines, and sent the authors on a national tour to publicise their ideas.

The central claim of *Competing for the Future* is that the most important form of competition is the battle to create and dominate emerging opportunities, and that the whole of traditional strategic thinking, from the role of senior managers to the nature of strategy itself, needs to be rethought in the light of this insight. Traditional strategists looked upon companies as a collection of products and business units; Hamel and Prahalad look upon them as a collection of skills. Traditional strategists tried to position their organisation as cleverly as possible in existing markets; Hamel and Prahalad argue that a company should try to reinvent its whole industry by following a vision.

For Hamel and Prahalad, Motorola's greatest asset is its vision of a 'wireless' world in which telephone numbers are assigned to people rather than places and everybody has a portable phone. The best way of dealing with an increasingly uncertain world is not to take refuge in short-termism but to imagine what the market will be like ten or more years hence and then try desperately to get there. The winners can reap benefits in numerous ways: by establishing a monopoly, however briefly, of a particular product (as Chrysler did with minivans and Sony with the Walkman); by setting standards or owning intellectual property rights (as Matsushita has done with VCRs and Microsoft with DOS); by establishing the rules of the game (as Wal-Mart did with out-of-town hypermarkets). As for the losers, they are consigned to a perpetual cycle of downsizing.

One obvious riposte to this argument is that visionary companies may earn the applause of management theorists but it is the plodders who come after them who make the real money. Why not let the leaders make all the investments and take all the risks and then simply copy or buy their product, just like Bill Gates did? Until recently most academic research tended to hint that 'first movers' had a big advantage (by one count nineteen of the twenty-five firms that were market leaders in various consumer products in 1923 were still on top sixty years later). However, such surveys often tend to deal only with surviving companies and surviving brands. For instance everybody (including Procter & Gamble) tends to believe that P&G invented the disposable nappy business when it launched Pampers in 1961. In fact another brand, the inelegantly named and now defunct Chux, had already been going for a quarter of a century, though it had concentrated on wealthy households and people who were travelling. Pampers were not new; they were just cheaper and aimed at a wider market. The same thing happened in video-recorders when an American firm, Ampex, pioneered the product in 1956 but was swept out of the way twenty years later by cheaper models from Japanese manufacturers such as Matsushita and Sony. Gerard Tellis of the University of California and Peter Golder of New York University's Stern School of Business have completed a detailed study of over fifty different markets, which looks at the brands that have perished as well as those that survived: it found that the pioneers are leaders in only one in ten of the markets, and, on average, the current leaders entered the market thirteen years after the 'first mover'.[16]

On balance this sort of research challenges but does not invalidate Hamel and Prahalad's argument. In many cases the follower's product was sufficiently different that it could almost count as a new one. And even if some copiers may have won in the past, it does not look like a tempting strategy for the future. The problem with copying the leaders is that there are dozens of other companies that are trying to do the same thing, on ever narrower profit margins. In most branded-goods businesses nearly all the profits are chewed up by the leading two products. Besides, following companies not only have to imitate a product; they also have to copy the core competencies that helped produce the product. Having let Japanese competitors take the lead in camcorders, Philips and Zenith have simply found it impossible to catch up; much the same has happened to Japanese producers themselves in cellular phones where they are still chasing Motorola, Ericsson and Nokia.

An alternative line of attack on Hamel and Prahalad is that visions don't mean a fig if you don't have the resources to back them up. An entire school of management thinkers support something called the 'resource-based theory of the firm', which argues that what really matters is the physical firepower a company brings to the battle. In fact, physical resources are becoming a less and less important source of competitive advantage. All the money and accumulated brain power in the world will not save a company if it fails to think carefully about where it will be a decade hence. IBM spent $6 billion a year on research and development but failed to see that the market was shifting from mainframes to personal computers: as late as 1991 a third of its R&D budget was spent on 'big iron'. Returning to cellular telephones, all Matsushita and Sony's clout have not stopped tiny Nokia running rings around them.

Stretch yourself

Besides, Hamel and Prahalad are more than just airy-fairy futurologists. They insist that companies should first spend money on thinking about the future (as Microsoft, Toshiba, Yamaha, Disney, Motorola and EDS do); and that firms need what Hamel and Prahalad call a 'strategic architecture' – a sense of what benefits they want to deliver to their customers and what delivery mechanisms they should use to deliver those benefits. Two concepts are crucial to strategic architecture.

The first is 'stretch' – trying for huge gains without telling people how to get there. Traditional planning departments were preoccupied with engineering a tight fit between goals and resources; Hamel and Prahalad argue that strategy is about 'stretch' – about using your vision of the future to inspire workers to go that little bit further. This sort of ambition and sense of purpose is most common in start-ups. (Tracy Kidder's gripping account of Data General, *The Soul of a New Machine*, shows how managers can happily impose eighty-hour working weeks and impossible deadlines if they can inspire their workers with a vision of greatness.) But big firms have also pulled off the same trick, especially in Japan. Toshiba told its employees to design a new VCR using half the number of parts and taking half the time to make and at half the cost. As an admiring Jack Welch has pointed out: 'Nobody in Japan asks "How much productivity can you get?" as if it were a finite element.'

On the other hand, there seems to be a very thin line between stretching employees and destroying them. It is noticeable that when chief executives set their own targets (for instance, the 'strike price' at which their share options become profitable) they rarely stretch themselves. Steve Kerr, General Electric's Learning Officer, warned *Fortune* in November 1995 that the discipline can be destructive. 'To meet stretch targets, people use the one resource that is not constrained, which is their personal time. I think that's immoral . . . I'm seeing all around this country people working evenings, working Saturdays, working Sundays to achieve stretch targets.'

Hamel and Prahalad's other concept is our old friend 'core competencies'. For Hamel and Prahalad, defining your core competencies is the first step in designing a strategy. If you know what you are good at – logistics management in the case of Federal Express – you can then choose something to aim at, like 'on-time delivery'. Competencies also form the basis for the modern equivalent of portfolio management: if you know what you are good at, you will venture only into new areas where your core skills can be applied to create new products, and buy only companies that can add substantially to your portfolio of skills.

As we have already seen, one problem with core competencies is that they can easily become just as unbending as five-year plans. What is even clearer about core competencies is that they are not the only answer. Some of the world's most admired companies – such as ABB Asea Brown Boveri and America's General Electric – have followed deliberate 'multibusiness' strategies. Three British academics, Andrew Campbell, Michael Goold and Marcus Alexander, have argued that strategy should be based on the 'parenting' skills of the holding company rather than any links between the skills of its subsidiaries.[17] In its heyday, Britain's Hanson spotted mature businesses that were being appallingly managed and then subjected them to fierce financial management. A good parent knows when to get out of a particular line of business as well as when to get in. In 1995, 3M decided to get out of the tape business, even though it was profitable and fitted in quite nicely with its other subsidiaries. The skills of 3M's senior managers lie in nurturing vigorous technical businesses: it would have been a bad parent for a business in which efficiency was becoming more important than technology.

One could argue that the distinction between core competencies and parenting is often one of semantics: one man's parenting skill is another's core competence. On the face of it, 'economic value added' or 'market value added' is a radically different approach, since it is based on the efficiency with which a company uses its capital rather than any abstract ideas about synergy. Under EVA a company judges whether something is worth doing by taking the net operating profit from that business and then deducting the cost of the capital deployed to make that profit; MVA, which has been championed by a New York consulting firm, Stern Stewart, basically calculates the amount of money shareholders have invested in a business – and then subtracts that sum from its market value.

The idea is to encourage managers and even shop-floor workers to think like shareholders. Britain's ICI has sent some 1,000 managers on a course designed to persuade them to 'pull levers which create shareholder value', which has forced factory bosses to learn about beta factors and free cash flow. Roberto Goizueta, who under the MVA formula is America's most successful boss having added $59 billion to Coca-Cola's value (narrowly beating Jack Welch who added $52 billion to GE's), has always used his own pocket version of EVA that his grandfather taught him: 'You borrow money at a certain rate and invest it at a higher rate and pocket the difference.' It is this formula that led Goizueta into Hollywood (Coke briefly owned Columbia Pictures). More successfully, it has guided Coca-Cola's strategy of concentrating on its soft-drinks business; as long as Coke can continue to earn returns of 30 per cent and borrow money at 10 per cent, its strategy will stay the same.

Interestingly, the discipline is also spreading to areas where shareholders have less weight. Veba, a huge German utility, used an EVA system to restructure itself into a mere fifty pieces. Led by the Mitsubishi Corporation, leading Japanese companies are taking a much harder, more mathematical line to portfolio management, judging the performance of their divisions by their return on equity.

All the same, core competencies and economic value added are not as incompatible as they seem at first blush. It turns out that the best way for companies to improve their returns to shareholders is to focus on their core businesses. Researchers at J.P. Morgan, an investment bank, have constructed an index measuring a company's focus on a scale of 1–100. American companies that 'clarified' their businesses outperformed the market by 11 per cent in the following two years; firms that diversified underperformed by about 4 per cent. Institutional investors would prefer to do their own diversification by buying a range of shares in different specialists rather than investing in a conglomerate. And focused firms are usually easier to manage than diversified firms. It is this sort of gainful clarity that AT&T was pursuing when it split itself up into three separate businesses in 1996.

Competing for the past

Competing for the Future is probably as close to required reading as any management book in the 1990s. But, for all its virtues, *Competing for the Future* is not free of two of the maladies afflicting management theory.

The first is the discipline's enthusiasm for pulling companies in opposite directions. It would be nice to think that Hamel and Prahalad's concept of 'stretch' sits nicely with all those other theories about 'empowerment' and 'trust': one imagines a team of cheery souls setting off together in search of their dream watched over by a kindly father figure. In practice, for most workers, 'stretch' means being told to work themselves into the ground in pursuit of an unattainable goal – something that most people would describe as hell.

The second problem is the industry's propensity for reinventing the wheel. In 1960, Theodore Levitt, a professor at Harvard Business School, wrote an article called 'Marketing Myopia', which argued that companies should define themselves in terms of their broad orientation rather than their specific products. This led to a great deal of guff as railroads redefined themselves as 'transportation companies' and oil refineries reclassified themselves as 'energy processors' and began to think about buying other mineral companies. But it did not produce much clarity of thinking, and the fashion eventually faded.

Supporters of *Competing for the Future* would argue that it is a much more complicated, more sophisticated approach than Levitt's. However, that does not make modern core competencies any easier to find than their 1960s equivalent. In both financial services and the jumble of industries that pass for multimedia, companies are having trouble deciding which businesses match their skills. Are banks really in the same industry as stockbrokers and insurers? Would a newspaper baron's skills be more useful in Hollywood or in electronic publishing, or neither? Even when companies have to make a move, they can often go in the wrong direction. Henry Mintzberg points out that if horse-drawn carriage companies had decided, at the turn of the century, that they needed to start thinking of themselves as transport companies and moved into cars, they would probably have still been wiped out by the likes of Ford, because they had no expertise in making combustion engines; instead they would have been better advised to capitalise on their operating skills, such as making wooden toys for children or turning out horse whips for the flagellation market.[18]

In the end, all strategy is gambling on the future. Visions – no less than plans – are only as good as those who make them. Even the dumbest lottery player can work out that companies that predict the future correctly do better than those that do not. Hamel and Prahalad hardly strengthen their argument by focusing on companies which have bet on a possible future and won (Canon, Motorola, Microsoft etc.) rather than companies which have made the same bet and lost. Apple lost to Microsoft because all the vision in the world cannot make up for lack of more mundane business skills. One of the company's misfortunes was that the man who was brought in to bring a bit more mundane professionalism to the company, John Sculley, spent too much of his time musing on the long-term future of the industry.[19] As chairman of General Motors in 1981–90, Roger Smith did everything right in Hamel and Prahalad's terms, dreaming of making GM 'the car company of the twenty-first century' and spending billions to improve the company's technological skills, but he still saw his company's share of the domestic market fall from 46 per cent to 35 per cent.

Nor is 'poor visioning' confined to a perennial loser like GM. Texas Instruments tried to exploit the core competencies it had developed in its semiconductor business in areas such as calculators, watches and home computers. But its managers lacked the necessary experience in managing such consumer-oriented businesses. The Saatchi brothers, who it should not be forgotten had revolutionised the advertising industry, decided that banking and consultancy were also people businesses that would respond to the same management techniques. Airlines, on the whole, have made a hash of running hotels, even though it seemed sensible to combine the two.

Looking forward, it is easy to see quite a few visions ending in tears. Some of the richest people in Hollywood are about to lose spectacular amounts of money on multimedia, thanks to a combination of overwhelming greed and overheated imagination. America's two most successful software billionaires have diametrically opposite visions of how their industry will develop. Larry Ellison of Oracle believes that the personal computer will give way to cheap, easy to use network terminals, which will be able to pull down information from a central database. To Bill Gates this is just 'the latest in a string of misconceived visions that Larry has been coming up with'; his own vision remains centred on the PC.[20] Doubtless, in ten years' time some son-of-Hamel and son-of-Prahalad will write a book saying that vision was correct, and make it seem an easy choice; today, any normal mortal confronted by Gates and Ellison is reminded of the old jibe: 'Two men say they're Jesus; one of them must be wrong.'

8

STORM IN THE BOARDROOM

The annual general meeting of British Gas in May 1995 was an unusual affair. Not only did it attract some 4,000 shareholders – a record; it was also a tale of two Cedrics. The first was Cedric Brown, then the chief executive of the privatised utility, a slightly worthy and anonymous man who had suddenly found himself dubbed by the tabloids 'the most hated man in Britain' for awarding himself a pay packet of £492,000; the second was a pig, also called Cedric, who had marked himself out to his owner by being the greediest in his sty. Whilst the human Cedric tried to keep order in the hall, his swinish namesake sat outside, guzzling potato peelings from overflowing troughs labelled 'share options'.

Perhaps Brown only had himself to blame. However, he is only one of several bosses around the world to suffer the wrath of the outside world. Outsiders – politicians, economists, pension funds, even individual shareholders – have begun asking painful questions: Who owns a company? Who is accountable for running it? What responsibility does a company have to the community, to the environment, to equal opportunities? These questions – particularly those concerning corporate governance and ethics – used to be something of a side-show. Now they are discussed at every board meeting.

Meanwhile, within companies, insiders have not proven themselves any less heretical, posing disturbing questions about the nature and conduct of leadership. Apply the question 'Who?' to virtually any unsolved problem of management theory – as in 'Who will choose the company's vision?' or 'Who will unleash the organisation's entrepreneurs?' – and the answer is nearly always 'the chief executive'. Indeed, this unfortunate soul's responsibilities have grown all the greater the flatter organisations have become and the more empowered and uppity their 'intrapaneurs' feel. 'No institution can possibly survive,' Peter Drucker once argued, 'if it needs geniuses or supermen to manage it. It must be organised in such a way as to be able to get along under a leadership of perfectly normal human beings.' One might have thought that, after nearly a century, management theory would have removed some of the superhuman element from leadership. Instead, the latest managerial fashions have done the opposite, and imposed ever more onerous responsibilities on the head of the organisation.

So how should the leader lead? Read a few books on leadership and you are quickly confronted with a set of contradictory conclusions. The first implies that leadership is fairly easy to pick up: it involves no more than setting clear goals, being honest with your employees, saying 'We' not 'I', and so on. The alternative conclusion is that leadership is so damned esoteric and instinctive that it is a gift that only a few are born with: no number of weekends character-building in Wales or enlightened mission statements is going to turn Joe Public into Jack Welch.

This debate is management's equivalent of psychology's nature-versus-nurture debate. The notable scarcity of leaders who can change organisations, and the unorthodox ways in which those few people persuade others to follow them, is a powerful argument on the side of nature. Nevertheless, some thinkers insist that leadership can be taught – a view that harkens back to the military idea that men can be trained to do anything. Which school of thought will prevail? Those readers whose appetite for words of wisdom from the gurus must be slaked immediately can jump ahead to the next section of this chapter. For those who can tolerate a small diversion for scene setting, it may be useful to begin our examination of leadership by having a quick look at the standing of the modern boss, and the strangely unproductive relationship between the current generation of superbosses and management theory.

The mind of the practitioner

For most of this century, successful bosses tended to occupy two entirely negative roles in the public imagination. In one role, they were evil capitalists who tried to make money by any means possible, who sewed up markets and who ganged up against the little guy. This was the many-headed serpent Rockefeller that appeared in newspaper cartoons and the William Randolph Hearst who Orson Welles lampooned in *Citizen Kane*. Alternatively, business people were just, well, boring-suited company men like Jack Lemmon in *The Apartment*. 'The office' was a byword for tediousness. During the 1960s, both images were taken to extremes: businessmen were either crooks, fixated by money and bent on destroying the environment if not the whole world (remember *Goldfinger*), or just ridiculously tedious (remember the role of the 'plastics' bore in *The Graduate*).

Anti-business sentiment has not disappeared entirely: Pat Buchanan managed to fire some of the embers in the 1996 presidential campaign. On the other hand most liberal parties, such as America's Democrats and Britain's Labour party, have never seemed more pro-business. Modern entrepreneurs, particularly computer-industry ones such as Bill Gates and Steve Jobs, are regarded as surprisingly 'cool' even though their business practices are sometimes just as ruthless as John D. Rockefeller's. Even in Britain – a place with an endemic, grievously damaging anti-trade culture (the best-known entrepreneurs on British television are Arthur Daley and Delboy Trotter, both small-time London crooks who peddle things like Korean scent) – it is noticeable how Richard Branson of Virgin has begun to compete against the likes of Mother Teresa, the Pope and the Archbishop of Canterbury as a role model in opinion polls. In America's 1992 presidential election, a businessman, Ross Perot, at one stage was ahead of both George Bush and Bill Clinton in the opinion polls: there are still people in Washington who believe that the former boss of Electronic Data Systems could have won if he had proved a less eccentric campaigner. Four years later, despite a public backlash against Big Business and downsizing, another eccentric businessman, Steve Forbes, also made a mark. At lower levels of government, American voters have found managerial competence – or at least the appearance of it – an irresistible asset. In the aftermath of the riots, Los Angeles turned to Richard Riordan, a businessman schooled in the real world, to reorganise the scarred city.

This phenomenon may be principally a reflection of voters' frustration with modern professional politicians. But it also seems to represent a craving for management, for efficiency, for the type of leadership that has been tested in the private sector. Indeed, much more revealing than the list of those businessmen who have run is the increasingly long 'What if?' list of those bosses who could mount a political challenge if they wanted to. Would America at the last election rather have chosen between Bill Clinton and Bob Dole – or between Jack Welch and Bill Gates? Would Britain rather choose between John Major, Paddy Ashdown and Tony Blair – or between Lord Hanson, Sir John Harvey-Jones and Richard Branson? In Finland, would any politician willingly campaign against Jorma Ollila of Nokia, or in Ireland against Tony O'Reilly of Heinz?

We deal elsewhere with the lengthy list of politicians trying to introduce management theory to the public sector (see Chapter Thirteen). However, it is clear that 'mismanagement' has become the new global political insult. Even in bombed-out Beirut you can find a billboard for a 'total quality management' conference standing proudly next door to a cluster of yellow Hezbollah banners. Hence it is not entirely surprising that those who can manage are more appreciated.

Given the weight of public expectations, one might have expected business people to be great generators of new management theories. The reality is more disappointing. In the early days of management, men such as the gun-maker Eli Whitney and the mill-owner Robert Owen were both businessmen and management thinkers. As we have already seen, two of the most important thinkers of the early 20th century were businessmen: Henry Ford and Alfred Sloan. Over at IBM, the company's founder, Thomas Watson, helped define what customer service meant. 'The beliefs that mould great organisations,' his son (and successor as head of IBM) Thomas Watson Junior once wrote, 'frequently grow out of the character, the experience and the convictions of a single person.'

In Japan people still look to businessmen for theories about business, as we shall see in Chapter Eleven. In Korea Lee Kun Hee, the boss of Samsung, has invented a 'new management philosophy' which can roughly be described as one part Californian new-ageism and two parts Korean autocracy. Another example of a modern boss is Ricardo Semler, a Brazilian businessman and author, who has taken his family firm, a pump and propeller making company called Semco, to extremes of empowerment that even Tom Peters at his most wowish has not dreamed of. Semco used to be the sort of place where even visits to the lavatory were timed. Now workers choose their own bosses; a third of them select their own pay.

However, in Europe and America, theorist-bosses are rare on the ground. ABB Asea Brown Boveri's Percy Barnevik may be an exception (see Chapter Ten). Most practising bosses like to be seen as being *au fait* with the latest thinking, but do not have time to put pen to paper. It is also very difficult to be original. When Noel Tichy, a respected professor at Michigan School of Business, recently claimed that the 20th century had produced 'only two business leaders who will be remembered for their ideas: Alfred Sloan of General Motors and Jack Welch of General Electric' many readers' first instinct may have been to question whether Welch really counted rather than to add alternatives.[1] Despite his near divine status in American management, Welch's management theory is arguably more anecdotal than revolutionary. Yes, he empowered workers, but so did a lot of other people. His maxims – 'Don't manage, lead', 'Control your own destiny or somebody else will' – are punchy rather than profound. Massive though Welch's achievement is, it cannot be compared with Sloan's.

Meanwhile, bosses are often reluctant to ascribe their success to the gurus. There are exceptions such as David Packard who said in *The HP Way* that 'no other operating policy has contributed more to Hewlett-Packard's success than management by objectives', and then goes on to quote Drucker enthusiastically.[2] But most managers claim that it is all their own work. Barnevik likes to point out that everybody agrees on what makes for a good company, from empowerment to decentralisation. The tricky part is putting these ideas into practice, and no theory can tell you how to do that. Bill Gates admits to an admiration for Peter Drucker but otherwise treats the genre with suspicion. He points out that in the early 1980s most management writers were enthusing about IBM at just the same time that he, as a young entrepreneur, was discovering that the giant had feet of clay.[3]

Gates's own book *The Road Ahead* has virtually nothing to say about management; it is about information technology. Indeed, most books by (or about) bosses are not, strictly speaking, works of management theory. Instead, they tend to fall into one of three categories. The first might be described as 'tips from the top'. One of the first business best-sellers was *Think and Grow Rich* by Napoleon Hill.[4] Although subsequent writers have cast doubts on Hill's ability to tell the truth, the author always claimed that the book began when, as a cub reporter, he was sent to interview Andrew Carnegie in 1908, and the steel baron suggested that he interview other business leaders to find the secret of their success. In the end Hill collared over 500 people, including Rockefeller, Ford, Eastman, and Woolworth: the result, published in 1937, has since sold seven million copies.

A more recent 'tips from the top' book is Mark McCormack's *What They Don't Teach You at Harvard Business School*. McCormack runs a successful sports-promotion business – a trade he revolutionised. Yet any reader looking in it for some Druckerish insight on how to transform a services industry will come away frustrated. Rather it is an apparently random list of thoughts, most of them illustrated by a couple of anecdotes featuring its name-dropping author: be punctual, listen 'aggressively', 'once you've sold, shut up'. Having introduced us to the idea of time-management by saying that he is one of the best time-managers around, McCormack gives hints on how to save those seconds, such as knowing which elevators are the quickest in a building you visit frequently, or, if you are arriving by plane at an airport, getting your driver to pick you up at the less crowded departures gate.[5]

By contrast, the other great manager-writer of the 1980s, Lee Iacocca, belongs to the 'I did it my way' school. His tome, modestly titled *Iacocca*, is probably better remembered for the line 'Henry Ford made my kids suffer, and for that I'll never forgive him' than for any management insight.[6] A chapter near the end of the book, called 'The key to management', reduces the skills of his trade to three essentials: have quarterly meetings with your executives, be decisive, and concentrate on people rather than information. Indeed the whole point of the book seems to be that Iacocca has a unique collection of non-transferable skills.

It is worth adding that other writers, who have since taken a cooler look at the Iacocca myth, have depicted the car baron as somebody who spent too much time hunting subsidies and promoting himself, and too little building better cars.[7] Nevertheless, there are genuinely successful bosses whose achievements seem to be built on unique, non-transferable business skills. Read any biography of Rupert Murdoch, and one of the most lasting impressions is that 'none of this can work without him'. Nearly all News Corporation's most successful gambles have been personal hunches of Murdoch; it is hard to imagine his successor inheriting his management style.

Yet that does not mean that the careers of either Murdoch or Iacocca are alien to management theory. News Corp's history could be rewritten as a case-study in globalisation – a subject about which Murdoch can talk as fluently as any guru (particularly when he is raising money). Scratch away at Iacocca's time at Chrysler and you will find plenty of Japanese management techniques – particularly ones concerning customer service and lean production. Indeed, it was arguably Iacocca's failure to do such things more thoroughly that meant that the American car giant had to be re-rescued by his successors.

The last category of manager-books, 'the fixer', is close to the spirit of the Perot campaign: that a good manager can draw on his experience and his instinct rather than any great theory to fix problems. The prime example of the fixer is Sir John Harvey-Jones. After a long and fairly successful spell as chairman of ICI (and also a stint as chairman of *The Economist*), he discovered a second life as the star of *Troubleshooter* – a popular BBC series in which Sir John visited companies and tried to fix them. Although Sir John is not afraid to invoke gurus (particularly in later books such as *Managing to Survive*), his approach is that of a pragmatist. Indeed his whole brand, from his kipper tie to his elderly footballer haircut, is that of a man who will give it to you straight. Which he does. Sir John's advice tends to be along the lines of 'You should sell this factory', or 'You should stop making these', rather than 'You should re-engineer this business'. There is plenty for any manager to learn from *Troubleshooter* – more than you will find in most management books written by theorists – but once again it does not offer a blueprint in the same way that, say, Alfred Sloan did.

The general separation of theory from practice is, arguably, a reflection of the maturity of management theory. To use a parallel from economics, people expect their finance ministers to know their way around monetarism and Keynesianism; they do not expect them to spend their spare time experimenting with complicated new formulas on blackboards. In the end, however, there is no getting away from the fact that the relationship between great managers and management theory is not always a warm one. One reason for this ambivalent relationship is that management theory has done relatively little to help most bosses in their jobs.

That leadership thing

Imagine that the long-awaited day has come. Your talent is finally appreciated and you are made chief executive. Sit yourself down behind your big mahogany desk, take a puff of your cigar, and consider how management theory is going to help you do your job. Soon two things become obvious.

The first is that even within the wayward, word-spattering world of management theory, no subject has produced more waffle than leadership. By one count there are 130 different definitions of leadership. 'Never have so many laboured for so long to say so little,' argued Warren Bennis and Burt Nanus in *Leaders: The Strategies for Taking Charge*. 'Time and again the old military analogies are rolled out from Alexander the Great to Nelson, Montgomery and in due course no doubt General Norman Schwarzkopf,' Carol Kennedy complained in 1994. 'Business leadership is evidently harder to recognise and define than the "follow me" qualities on a battlefield.'[8] To borrow one of these military metaphors, writing about leadership is a little like invading Russia. Even writers of Drucker's class tend to run into deep snow.

This hurts all the more because the other obvious thing to any new boss is that management fashion has made the top job immensely more difficult. Part of the problem is structural: there are fewer layers of management between top and bottom. Many head offices now contain fewer than 100 people, and decisions have to be taken ever more quickly. By late 1995 Jack Welch of General Electric and Roberto Goizueta of Coca-Cola, who were both appointed at the beginning of the 1980s, agreed that their jobs were 'three times as fast'.[9] Yet the other side of the problem is that the modern boss is no longer supposed to be bossy. Leadership is no longer about issuing instructions but about releasing other people's energies. In Charles Handy's Federalist model of the company, 'The centre does not run the corporation except in times of war or its equivalent.'

The changing nature of companies has been the subject of the past four chapters. But it is worth – at least briefly – looking at the rise of the new, chaotic knowledge-based organisation from the boss's point of view. Although Alfred Sloan partly built his system in order to cage unruly bosses like Henry Ford, it was a structure most bosses felt happy with. It had firm rules. The boss's job was threefold: to set the strategy, design a structure and install effective controls. Many of the management fads in the 1960s and 1970s – particularly management by objectives – gave bosses a good excuse to stick with Sloan's model rather than to question it. Setting an objective for a manager was after all just another way of determining the 'strategy' part of Sloan's model. If the business world appeared to be moving faster, then that just meant that strategies, structures and controls had to be that little bit more complicated and comprehensive. Now, wearily, the bosses seem to have admitted defeat: '[The Sloanist model] was right for the 1970s,' argues Jack Welch, 'a growing handicap in the 1980s and it would have been a ticket to the bone yard in the 1990s.'

No one wants to end up in the boneyard, of course, and it is hard to find any modern boss who has a bad word to say about empowerment. But should we believe them? Recent management literature on leadership has tended to praise people such as Jean Kvasnica, a Hewlett-Packard manager who has led several successful projects by getting out of the way, or Jaguar's North American managers, who, after a troubled restructuring, actually put the most difficult people in charge of employee involvement groups – again with successful results. However, most bosses would have sent Kvasnica to the company doctor and fired the troublemakers at Jaguar. It is hard to tell which Jack Welch is the more genuine: the one who preached the virtues of empowering General Electric's employees; or the one who went ballistic when his 'empowered' traders at Kidder Peabody ran up huge losses. In reality, most bosses would much rather see themselves as generals at the head of an army, rather than as the teacher–facilitators that gurus such as Peter Senge would like them to be. Lord Sheppard of Britain's Grand Metropolitan once described his own style as 'management by a light grip on the throat'.

To make things worse, at many companies this freedom means freedom to criticise the boss. In Britain companies such as BP, British Telecom, BMW and even the English rugby union team have experimented with '360-degree feedback' – letting the workers tell the bosses what they think of them. In some cases, the answers are given directly, in other (usually more successful) cases the answers are filtered anonymously through a third party who then tells the boss the good or bad news.

However, bosses' problems with 'learning organisations' are not purely ones of ego. Bringing out the best in others (particularly thousands of others) is more difficult than just absorbing information and sending out commands. As we have already seen, it is devilishly difficult to devise a structure that allows people to come up with new ideas whilst at the same time giving an organisation a common purpose. All the current talk about the importance of being a coach rather than a general tends to forget how difficult being a coach is. 'Managing is like holding a dove in your hand,' Tommy Lasorda, the long-running coach of the Los Angeles Dodgers, has argued. 'Squeeze too tight, you kill it. Open your hand too much, you let it go.'[10]

Nature versus nurture

Whatever their problems with empowerment, bosses are clearly putting more emphasis on the 'leadership' part of their job, and less on the purely 'managerial' part. The difference between the two was set out by Warren Bennis in a famous but lengthy list ('The manager maintains, the leader develops. The manager focuses on systems and structure, the leader focuses on people. The manager relies on control; the leader inspires trust . . .').[11] However, elucidating the difference between managers and leaders is not the same as finding a way to turn the former into the latter. Can leadership be taught?

Recently companies have set about trying to develop leadership in a systematic way, aiming perhaps not so much to teach leadership as to hone it. Unsurprisingly one of the leaders in making 'the soft stuff hard' is Hewlett-Packard, a firm which has always mixed the two (it used to make calculators but lives in free-wheeling Silicon Valley).[12] HP measures people's leadership potential against a list of twenty-six characteristics: it then sends staff on a coaching course. Each January some 80,000 people at General Electric fill in internal résumé forms. GE monitors people's 'boundarylessness' on a one-to-five scale (you score low points for blocking ideas travelling around the company). It also has a formal process called 'Session C', matching managers to jobs, which occupies a whole month of Welch's time every year.

All the same, leadership training remains an imprecise and wasteful business. To find twenty-five leaders likely to run its big operations, PepsiCo trained some 100 people. At one time Bank of America tracked the progress of 1,000 potential leaders; six years later more than 80 per cent of them had left. And sometimes even the best-regarded training systems can turn out to be flawed. In the early 1980s, IBM was thought of as being the ideal cradle to develop leaders; today, it is dismissed as a graveyard of corporate bureaucrats.

Indeed it is possible to argue that even the combined powers of nature and nurture are not enough: like Napoleon's generals, modern leaders need to be lucky – particularly when it comes to timing. One of America's most widely admired bosses, Lawrence Bossidy of Allied Signal, was asked how a single person can change a large organisation; he replied by enunciating the 'burning platform' theory of change. 'When the roustabouts are standing on the offshore oil rig and the foreman yells "jump into the water", not only won't they jump, but also they won't feel too kindly towards the foreman. There may be sharks in the water. They'll jump only when they see the flames shooting up from the platform. Chrysler's platform was visibly burning; the company changed. IBM's platform was not visibly burning; it didn't.'[13] In other words, a boss's ability to change companies depends more on the state of the company than on the boss's character.

Out of the box thinking

It is still possible to say three things about leadership. The first is that vision is crucial. In order to change organisations, it helps to be identified with a particular set of ideas or values. The point is not that the vision should be right or even particularly profound, but that it should be a rallying point for a diverse group of people. In some cases, the theory does not even have to be spelled out. What Richard Branson has actually said about Virgin has been fairly flaccid; what really matters is that he stands for a certain way of doing things.

The second is that the gulf between 'transactional leadership' and 'transformational leadership' has widened. These two terms were devised, ironically, by an unsuccessful politician, James McGregor Burns, who was an adviser to John F. Kennedy and then ran for Congress. Transactional leaders, he decided, were ones who dealt with their followers on a tit-for-tat basis: you give me your vote, I will get you a job. A transformational leader is somebody who spots some profound need that the follower had not realised existed and sets out to answer it. This latter approach engenders far greater loyalty. This echoes some sociologists who point to the potency of 'normative' organisational power: where people do what you want them to do because they share the same values rather than because they are responding to sticks and carrots.

The final point about modern business leadership is more of a hunch: that being a maverick is a decided advantage – and becoming more so. 'Out of the box thinking', as the jargon goes, has become more valuable now that many companies can do the basic things perfectly well and mundane products can be copied instantaneously. In a world in which most bosses are doing the same things – flattening their command structures, turning their workers into entrepreneurs – it is often the quirky who stand out, attracting better employees and dreaming up more exciting products. Fewer and fewer bright business-school graduates want to join big companies – unless those big companies are themselves mavericks like Microsoft and Virgin. In 1989, 70 per cent of Stanford's MBA graduates joined big companies; in 1994, only 50 per cent did.

Talk to Bill Gates, Rupert Murdoch or Richard Branson and the first impression you get is of relentless curiosity. Yet most leadership programmes concentrate on the nuts and bolts of management, and most managers are depressingly narrow sorts of people (as a glance at the hobbies listed in any Business Who's Who demonstrates). Some inspirational managers have made a point of encouraging young high-flyers to broaden their minds. Yotaro Kobayashi, Fuji Xerox's boss, was surprised when, as an up-and-coming manager, he was sent off by his hero, Joe Wilson, to the Aspen Institute in Colorado to learn about Plato and Aristotle; Kobayashi has now set up a similar centre in Japan, in an attempt to encourage Japan's ultra-conformist businessmen to broaden their minds. Tom Peters takes the same message to thousands of middle managers when he encourages them to throw away their management books and read novels – or even race yaks.

Another maverick asset that current management structures do little to instil is the experience of failure. Welch was first noticed at General Electric in the 1960s because he ran a plastics plant that blew up. As a young entrepreneur, Richard Branson spent a night in a police cell after smuggling records into Britain from France. Rupert Murdoch nearly went bust on several occasions at the begining of the 1990s. Babe Ruth may have been best known for his home runs, but he also set a record for strike-outs. However, thanks to those flatter management structures, the chance of having one of these constructive experiences of failure is limited.

So where does that leave the modern boss? The simple answer is: overworked. He (or she) faces a far more complex challenge than his predecessors: one where he is expected to give away power while keeping some form of control, and tap the creative talents of his employees while creating a common culture within the company. He has to spend far more time meeting and motivating those irritating knowledge workers, who are now spread across an increasingly wide range of countries. And on top of all this, he has to be a maverick who may have failed in the past and knows his Aristotle as well as his Drucker. It is hardly surprising that the executive search market is growing at 15 per cent a year, and that it is now normal for bosses to be divorced or married to their secretaries.

In other words management theory seems to have flunked Drucker's challenge: to come up with an institution that does not need to be led 'by geniuses or supermen'. Far from easing the job of a leader, management theory seems to have made it more difficult – in fact, well nigh impossible. Even the hallowed excuse of looking back to great leaders of the past seems increasingly self-defeating. Would Winston Churchill have been a good 'teacher leader' in a multicultural corporation? Would Alexander the

Great have been prepared to let squadrons of T-shirted knowledge workers disappear to follow their own ideas for a couple of years?

Unaccountable, sexist and under siege

Although management theorists have piled all these responsibilities on the boss and the boardroom, they have, until recently, been less keen on making such a top-heavy structure accountable. This is a serious flaw. To call in Drucker once again: 'Any government, whether that of a company or of a nation, degenerates into mediocrity and malperformance if it is not clearly accountable for results and not clearly accountable to someone.'[14] It cannot be entirely coincidental that, although virtually every other part of the company has been redesigned, re-engineered and reinvented, the gurus and consultants have left the people who have sanctioned these revolutions well alone. No witch doctor ever advanced his career by suggesting a change of ruling family.

According to the old joke, a company's board is like 'the parsley on the fish' – there for ornamental purposes rather than anything more substantial. Even accepting this description, most boards no longer make a particularly appetising garnish. In 1970 *Management Today* looked at the composition of the boardrooms of 200 big British companies. In 1995 the magazine repeated the exercise with 2,000 companies.[15] After a quarter of a century of radical economic and social change the typical inhabitant of the British boardroom remains an Oxbridge-educated male in his early fifties. Only 3.7 per cent of the directors were women – and many of these held non-executive posts. The most obvious sign of change was that pay packets in the boardrooms of FTSE-100 companies had risen three-fold in real terms (to £248,000) in a period when average wages were up only 50 per cent.

Nor is Britain particularly politically incorrect or greedy. White men constitute 43 per cent of America's work force, but hold 95 per cent of its senior management positions. The only area in which women have done well – middle management jobs such as assistant vice presidents and office managers – is the one that has been hit hardest by re-engineering. America's only prominent female chief executive, Loida Lewis of Beatrice, a food and retailing conglomerate, got the job only because she inherited a large shareholding from her late husband. In France, the senior layers of management are even more deftly snapped up by the 'Enarques' who have come from the tiny civil-service school, ENA. In 1993, almost half the bosses of France's 125 largest companies were former civil servants.

This exclusiveness matters. America's WASP élite lacks the range of experience to deal with an increasingly multicultural home market, let alone to mastermind the conquest of world markets. France has bred an élite which is good at certain types of management, such as long-range planning or big infrastructure projects, but out of its depth in fast-moving industries such as computers. Worse, the very similarity between the middle-aged, blue-suited, white-shirted men who are directors and chief executives around the world increases the 'parsley effect'. Indeed it stifles thought at the top of companies. The homogeneity of America's senior managers makes a nonsense of high-falutin' plans to divide companies into autonomous, competing units. It also means that companies get out of touch with their consumers. Surveys have shown that, even when it comes to fairly chunky products such as cars or life insurance, the decision about what to buy is now often – if not mostly – made by a woman. There are very few female directors of car companies or insurers – and no prominent chief executives.

Shareholders at the gate

The chief pressure on boards to change their ways has come not from the gurus, but from the emergence of a new class of shareholders-rights activists. These include individuals such as Robert Monks, a genial American who once took out a full-page advertisement about Sears in the *Wall Street Journal* under the title 'Non-performing assets' and Ekkehard Wenger, a German economics professor who specialises in causing grief at annual meetings and who defends his often unsubtle style by quoting

Schiller. 'One must tell the Germans the truth as coarsely as possible.'

However, most of the clout has come from institutions such as the California Public Employees Retirement System (Calpers), the state-workers pension fund which has taken a vigorous approach to its portfolio, building up big blocks of shares in companies and then trying to force them to change. In America pension-fund managers and other fiduciary organisations are obliged to vote at annual general meetings. But they have also been spurred into action by the way that boss-friendly states in America, such as Delaware, allow lumbering giants such as Time Warner to choose lower take-over offers or adopt things like 'poison pills' and 'golden parachutes' which make take-overs more expensive for acquirers and protect the board's own salaries.

General shareholder pressure has led to a spate of public inquiries, including the Cadbury and Greenbury reports in Britain and the Vienot report in France. A string of studies has shown that interventionist shareholders, such as Calpers and Warren Buffett, have got better returns on their investments. And in America, at least, angry shareholders have succeeded in booting out some of the worst performing bosses including the chief executives of Eastman Kodak, General Motors, Kmart, Morrison Knudsen, Apple and WR Grace. They have also forced directors to get their act together by suing them. There were 347 suits filed against directors by shareholders in America in 1994; the average pay out was $7.7m.

The list of grievances

There are three chief areas where boards and bosses in most countries carry on in an unaccountable way: executive pay, succession and non-executive directors. The one that sticks in the gullet most is executive pay. By virtually any measure directors in general – and bosses in particular – have been paying themselves generously. In 1995 the 'winner' in America was Laurence Coss of Green Tree Financial, a consumer-finance company, who was paid 328 times the $200,000 salary of Bill Clinton. Between 1990 and 1995, the average American chief executive's pay rose 92 per cent to $3.75 million; over the same period corporate profits rose 75 per cent and workers pay 16 per cent (to $26,652 in 1995).[16] Shares authorised for management equity now account for 10 per cent of the outstanding shares of America's biggest 200 firms. But the real problem is not so much one of scale as of performance. Most of the high-pay deals come from share-option deals that reward bosses generously if they succeed, but balk at punishing them if they fall. Although Disney shareholders have been happy to pay the company's chairman, Michael Eisner, hundreds of millions of dollars in salary, many of them expressed outrage in 1997 at the $90m pay-off awarded to Michael Ovitz, who served only eighteen far-from-successful months as the company's president.

Similar one-way bets are now common for other senior managers, too. The 'value sharing' deal that tempted Jerry York, IBM's chief financial officer, to the same post at Kirk Kerkorian's Tracinda Corporation in 1995 was worth $25m. A survey by *CFO* magazine concluded that 'although more CFOs are taking risks with their compensation, only a few are sharing downside risk as well as upside reward with their shareholders'.[17] One of the most interesting parts of the Barings scandal was the pyramid of bonuses constructed on top of Nick Leeson's performance. The trader himself was on a £420,000 bonus; those above him got much more.

The problem with pay is that, although it annoys some shareholders intensely, one man's undeserved million-dollar salary in a multi-billion-dollar company is seldom a big enough issue to persuade shareholders to revolt — particularly when the financial world itself is hardly known for parsimony when it comes to pay cheques. At British Gas's shareholder meeting the institutions actually voted in favour of the besieged Cedric Brown. Critics of the boardroom have consequently concentrated on getting bosses to reveal more about what they are paid and why, hoping to shame them into good behaviour.

Most bosses still regard it as their privilege to choose their successor. The abuse is worst in continental Europe: in France, for example, it is still normal for the stewardship of a large company to pass from one Enarque to another with barely a word to the company's owners. The two General Electrics – America's GE and Britain's GEC – have both dithered over the choice of a new boss. But what can be done about bosses, like GEC's Lord Weinstock, who have simply held on to power too long? So far the most radical solution has come from John Kay of the London Business School who has pleaded for fixed terms for bosses on the grounds that authoritarian structures are 'insidiously corrupting' for all but the most remarkable men and women.

A better solution would be to force the board to do its job and represent shareholders' interests. Non-executive directors and, particularly, non-executive chairmen are a vital part of this process; after all, a chief executive who is also chairman is a bit like a student who marks his own exam papers. In Britain, in the wake of the Cadbury report in December 1992, over 80 per cent of the country's biggest companies have a non-executive chairman. In America, power has shifted slightly towards the non-executive members of the board who are now taking their jobs much more seriously. There are now even 'director schools' such as the Directors College at Stanford Law School. Three-quarters of the 1,000 directors quizzed by Korn/Ferry, a head-hunter, in 1995 said that their boards had clear objectives for measuring the performance of CEOs; two-thirds had formal annual reviews. The coup at General Motors that got rid of Robert Stempel in 1992 was organised by a group of non-executive directors led by John Smale who then became non-executive chairman.

This is not to say that non-executive directors are infallible. Many of the same names keep popping up on the boards of companies associated with lousy performance and poor corporate governance. In 1995 Lilyan Affinito, a retired manager of a sewing-pattern company, earned $300,000 a year from sitting on the boards of the likes of Kmart and Tambrands.[18] Such directors have a habit of emerging unscathed from the worst corporate wrecks. It was also John Smale who persuaded Stempel's successor Jack Smith to offer José Ignacio López de Arriortúa the job as head of North American operations because his cost-cutting had such a big effect on the car giant's bottom line. (López then hightailed off to Volkswagen.) And, in December 1995, Smale handed back the chairmanship to Smith, making it clear that, like many other directors in America, he regarded splitting the two posts as an emergency procedure.

However unhappy they may be, American shareholders can at least thank God that they do not have to deal with French firms. In 1966 a law allowed French companies to adopt a two-tier German-style supervisory board. Less than one in fifty have bothered to do so. Despite evidence of poor management at Suez, Air France and Crédit Lyonnais, French companies have resisted attempts to divide the président from the directeur général. The idea of collective board responsibility is not enshrined in French law. In a 1994 survey of independent directors in France over half said that they did not have enough information to exercise control over bosses.[19] 'In the Anglo-Saxon model there is a very strong degree of control exercised by the market,' Jean Peyrelevade, chairman of Crédit Lyonnais, has pointed out. 'The French market is too weak to fulfil that role.'[20] Even when members of France's narrow business élite do fall out, the boss can usually shrug off the challenge. When Jacques Calvet, the head of Peugeot, threatened to resign as a director of Générale des Eaux over the selection of a new chief executive, Guy Dejounay, the water utility's boss, ignored him, and Calvet stayed anyway.

A question of ethics

Interestingly, the French bosses caught in the corruption scandals of the mid-1990s (known locally as *les affaires*) were usually charged with '*abus des biens sociaux*' – abuse of corporate funds. This underscores the general link between ethics and corporate governance. For companies no less than débutantes, a good name is easy to lose and very hard to rebuild. The study of corporate ethics is one of the fastest-growing areas in management theory.

Royal Dutch/Shell's hard-earned image as a kinder, gentler sort of oil company, conscious of its social responsibilities and fashionably multicultural, was quickly destroyed in 1995 – first by its attempt to dump the Brent Spar oil rig in the North Sea (the correct decision, as it happened, though poorly explained) and then by its association with the Nigerian government which executed Ken Sarowiwa, a poet who had caused a fuss in his country by investigating the oil giant's environmental record.

Shell's dilemma may strike many as extreme. But nowadays companies can end up in the headlines for milder things. In October 1995, Bausch & Lomb was the subject of a cover story in *Business Week* headlined 'Blind Ambition' which argued that in its go-getting quest for profits the company had jumped over certain commercial niceties such as selling its supposedly exclusive Ray-ban glasses to grey-market distributors. The issue dominated the company's subsequent board meetings. Politicians have also discovered that companies are easy to embarrass. In 1995 Robert Reich, America's labour secretary, made a point of taking journalists to a Californian sweatshop, recently raided by the police, to show them goods bound for retailers such as Montgomery Ward and Dayton Hudson.

Nowadays, a company's board has to think about a different sort of accountability. Many of the assets they are charged with looking after are intangible ones – notably the firm's reputation. In an environment where more and more consumers in the developed world make commercial decisions on 'non-commercial' grounds, Milton Friedman's maxim that a company's only responsibility is to make money legally looks ever less defensible. A firm that does not break the law but is seen as socially irresponsible has a tough time. By the same token, companies such as Levi Strauss, Johnson & Johnson, Body Shop and Ben & Jerry's have all prospered from their 'ethical' reputations.

There are two problems with ethics from a management theorist's point of view. The first is that, like motherhood and apple pie, nobody is against ethics. There are over 500 courses in 'Ethics' at American business schools (one even sends its students off to a monastery). By 1995 around two-thirds of American companies had formal codes of ethics, a third had ethics offices or ombudsmen.

The second problem is more serious: there is a yawning gap

between what people say and what they do. One of the prime examples of this is a series of recent whistle-blower cases, in which managers who tried to report alleged 'unethical' behaviour were hounded out of their jobs. (In one case involving Archer Daniels Midland the sacked whistle-blower was even pilloried by a preacher in the American agribusiness company's home town.) Few firms are prepared to go as far as Ben & Jerry's and allow outsiders to publish audits of their performance. Even ethical firms have trouble sticking to their own high standards. In January 1995 Johnson & Johnson, which had earlier earned plaudits for its honest behaviour over the Tylenol scandal (when a lunatic laced its painkillers with cyanide) had to pay out $7.5m in fines and costs after admitting that a subsidiary had shredded documents relating to a federal investigation.

In some cases the lapses are more to do with image than with substance – though that can be damaging enough. Body Shop was forced to rephrase a claim that its products were not tested on animals after it was revealed that some of the ingredients that went into its cosmetics had been tested on animals by other firms in the past. However, there is also evidence that many firms only have a skin-deep approach to ethics. One survey of young managers by Joseph Badaracco of Harvard Business School and Allen Webb of McKinsey found that most of them thought that 'over-investing' in ethics was not the way to get ahead: only a third of the young managers thought that their companies would respect whistle-blowers.[21] Like many other theorists, Badaracco and Webb believe that responsibility lies with the board: first to set up firm ethical codes with clear sanctions; and second to set a good example themselves.

But on whose behalf are these directors acting? So far in this chapter, the general presumption has been shareholders. But an increasingly noisy group of theorists argue that the modern firm is 'accountable' to a wider group of people – including its local community and its workers. Who, in the end, should own a company?

That stakeholder thing

'It is time we killed a myth,' Charles Handy has declared. 'The myth that it is the shareholders who run the business, and that it is for them that we all work.'[22] Britain's leading management theorist argues that shareholder capitalism was designed for an era when the owners of a business were also its managers. Nowadays, most individual shareholders are punters rather than owners, swapping between companies as if they were race-goers picking horses. By dint of their size, pension funds take a slightly longer-term view, but, according to Handy, their role is more akin to that of financiers rather than owners. At the first whiff of a take-over, they usually sell out. Besides, argues Handy, shareholder capitalism is basically a 'machine-age model', designed for the days when the chief asset of a firm was its property; now that the value in most companies resides in the heads of its employees it is not appropriate 'for anonymous outsiders to own or trade collections of people'.

Corporate governance, in Handy's eyes, is essentially a political problem; it should thus be settled in a political way through some kind of separation of powers, so that the executive part (i.e. the managers) is separated from the legislative part (the shareholders) whilst 'a judiciary' of accountants and other observers sets the rules. Rather than being formal corporations, companies should be 'membership communities' – the members being anyone, from workers to customers, who have a stake in the enterprise. Money should still be raised through shares, Handy argues, and the shares should still entitle shareholders to some say in the way the company is run – but they should not entitle them to fire its board or sell the company over the heads of its employees. Shareholders with, say, a 1 per cent stake in a company would get membership rights.

There are several equally strong traditions of corporate governance around the world, and almost all of them are now under fire in their own countries. In the interests of simplicity, we will concentrate on the two most discussed models: the American system, which is similar to the British one, and the German one, which is broadly similar to that in Japan and others in continental Europe.

Under the American system, a great deal of power ultimately rests with the shareholders. Take-overs are relatively common and shareholders can also pester directors through 'proxy' resolutions by which they force 'their' managers to do this or that. By contrast, the German model gives a much greater voice to stakeholders – particularly banks and workers. Germany has a two-tier board system in which the managerial board is monitored by a supervisory board. Under a 1976 law shareholders' representatives (nearly always banks) and workers have equal power on the supervisory board – but the chairman (usually chosen by the shareholders) has the casting vote.

Both systems have changed over time more than their adherents like to admit. Many Wall Streeters would argue that the stakeholder-shareholder debate in America was settled earlier this century when the Dodge Brothers sued Henry Ford for keeping back too much profit from the car company in which they all had shareholdings, and the Michigan Supreme Court ruled that 'A business corporation is organised and carried on primarily for the profit of the stockholders.' But it is clear that the modern American company – particularly the multi-business conglomerate – barely resembles the original joint-stock companies of the 19th century. Rather than being one family's property, a company has become a lot of people's investment.

Peter Drucker's original solution to this problem, back in the 1950s, was to argue that a company's management was a trustee, accountable to no single group of shareholders or stakeholders. This sounded like a comfortable solution. But, as Drucker admits, American bosses did pretty much what they wanted until the 1980s. The 1980s take-over boom saw a fierce restatement of shareholders' rights with the owners often selling off the company from under the managers' feet. Now, there is a great deal of talk in America about 'maximising shareholder value', but this will not wash either, according to Drucker, because it forces the company to be managed for the shortest term. 'Long-term results,' argues Drucker, 'cannot be gained by piling short-term results on short-term results.'[23]

Moreover, like Handy, Drucker has doubts about whether this

is a sensible way to inspire knowledge workers: 'An engineer will not be motivated to make a speculator rich.' Drucker is more enthusiastic about shareholders' rights than Handy, but he still believes that some kind of formal separation of powers is necessary to give managers room to manage. He thinks that there should be some sort of formal 'business audit', which would allow long-term owners to set the managers public performance targets, and then let them get on with it.

The sort of criticisms that Drucker and, particularly, Handy have been voicing for some time have now reached the political mainstream. In 1995 Will Hutton, the editor of the *Observer*, had a surprise best-seller in Britain with *The State We're In*, a polemic which blames shareholder capitalism for Britain's presumed social ills, and argues that the solution lies in stakeholding. In early 1996 Tony Blair, the leader of the Labour party, also declared himself a believer in a 'stakeholder society' – though he was tantalisingly vague about what the phrase meant. In private briefings, he made it clear that his thinking was influenced not by Hutton but by John Kay of the London Business School, another prominent advocate of stakeholder values.

In his State of the Union Address at the start of 1996 Bill Clinton asked American firms to put 'long-term prosperity above short-term gain'. Robert Reich, his then labour secretary and a long-term admirer of stakeholder societies such as Germany, wrote an article in the *New York Times* accusing companies of abandoning their responsibilities to communities and employees. In the old days, Reich argued, gentlemanly capitalists took care to balance the interests of shareholders, employees and the public at large; in the age of 'electronic capitalism' footloose investors simply look for the lowest wages and the laxest regulations. His solution is to encourage firms to maintain jobs and neighbourhoods through tax penalties.

The German question

But have the advocates of stakeholding proved their case? So far the stakeholder lobby in both Britain and America has been much better at pointing to the inadequacies of shareholder capitalism than at coming up with robust-sounding systems of their own.

Much of their argument relies on gazing admiringly at Germany (or Japan) and deciding that their impressive performance since the war 'proves' the case for stakeholder capitalism. This does not hold water. First, there are plenty of other things that explain Germany and Japan's 'success', such as the strength of their education systems and their long-established manufacturing skills. And, second, that success looks more questionable now that the Japanese and German economies have stumbled.

Many of the peculiarities in the German system owe more to circumstance than to deliberate strategy. Very few German companies are quoted: the country's stock-market capitalisation amounts to less than a third of its GDP. The German stock-market is much less liquid than its counterparts in London and New York, making it difficult for German investors to trade out of their shares. And many of those investors are banks.

This system is changing, partly because financial deregulation is creating a new, more critical class of fund manager, but mostly because it has not worked very well. A supervisory board stuffed full of bankers did little to prevent Daimler-Benz's woeful diversification in the 1980s or Metallgesellschaft's disastrous flirtation with oil futures. Bankers and shareholders have different priorities: shareholders want the company to make as big a profit as possible, whereas bankers are content if it makes enough profit to pay off its loans. Employees too have different priorities from shareholders. Inviting workers into the boardroom is surely one reason why Germany's manufacturers are now battling with high wages and comparatively low productivity.

Stakeholder capitalism looks even less impressive when it comes to dealing with knowledge workers. So far cruel old shareholder capitalism has proved a far more effective nursery for the industries of the future. Silicon Valley is in California not the Ruhr. Germany can muster only three software companies of any significance: Software AG, SAP and Siemens. Indeed, an interesting game to play with any advocate of stakeholder capitalism who starts prattling on about emancipating knowledge workers is to ask him or her to name German high-technology firms that do not begin with 'S'.

Gekko versus Blair

An alternative argument in favour of stakeholder capitalism is that there is really no contradiction between stakeholders' interests and those of shareholders. Indeed, a stakeholding approach is in the best long-term interest of shareholders. Robert Waterman reckons that 'corporate cultures that tend to put three constituencies – shareholders, customers and employees – on the same plane, as opposed to putting shareholders first, are perversely the ones that do best for shareholders'.[24] 'You're accountable to more than one constituency,' John Kotter at Harvard has warned bosses.

This sounds like a temptingly fluffy compromise. After all, in most normal circumstances the interests of various stakeholding groups coincide with those of the shareholders. Contented workers deliver better services; contented customers make for a profitable company. It is indeed in shareholders' interests to treat workers – particularly knowledge ones – well. However, treating all the constituencies as equals does not work when times get tough. The lack of clear accountability makes it difficult for managers to make tough decisions – as both the Germans and Japanese have recently discovered.

For most of the post-war era, the economies of Germany and Japan boomed, and the interests of the various shareholders coincided. But in the mid-1990s the decisions became more pressing, and managers' habit of fudging or delaying them more damaging. The result was that companies kept on workers who might be better employed elsewhere, and in both countries the economy failed to move into higher value-added industries and services. By contrast, Anglo-Saxon capitalism, with its clearer lines of authority and constant pressure from the stock market to perform, forced managers to take unpalatable decisions. The downsizing and restructuring that followed may have been painful but they increased economic efficiency.

This defence of shareholding may sound horribly complacent. What about all those fat cats paying themselves gigantic salaries? And what about the golden parachutes that allow these weighty felines to get rich out of failure? In fact, the best way to deal with the anxieties that have given rise to the recent stakeholder debate is to give more power to shareholders, not less. Study almost any corporate disaster – from the collapse of Maxwell Communications to the decision by Japanese firms to overpay for American property in the 1980s – and you find a board acting without anybody looking over its shoulder.

As Matthew Bishop concluded in a survey of Corporate Governance in *The Economist* in 1994, 'Few if any woes have stemmed from too much shareholder interference.' An ideal system, argued Bishop, would do three things. 'It would, first, give a boss enough freedom to manage well. It would ensure that he used that freedom to manage the firm in the interests of shareholders. And if somebody else could do a better job it would let him.'[25] The key concept, from an economist's point of view, is contestability – the ability for shareholders to be able to change managers if they are not doing a good job. The best way to solve the problem of corporate governance is to create a market in it.

Nobody can deny that shareholders are sometimes a little quick to sell out in take-overs, but that does not obscure the fact that the biggest losers in most take-overs are usually the shareholders in the acquiring company. When the shareholders in Saatchi & Saatchi finally rose up and booted Maurice Saatchi out at the end of 1994, they may well have made a tactical mistake (Saatchi founded a rival agency which then won many of his previous employer's clients) but the real reason why 'old Saatchi' reached its parlous state was that the Saatchi brothers had blown their shareholders' money on an acquisition spree.

It may not be a popular way to end a section on stakeholders and shareholders, but perhaps the last word should belong to Gordon Gekko – the fictional raider in *Wall Street*. His 'greed is good' speech to a group of shareholders is every liberal's nightmare. But it also contained the following passage:

Now in the days of the free market when our country was a top industrial power there was accountability. The Carnegies, the Mellons, the men who built this great industrial empire made sure it was, because it was their money at stake. Today management has no stake in the company. Altogether those men sitting up there own less than three per cent of the company. You own the company, that's right, you, the stockholders, and you are being royally screwed by these bureaucrats with their stock lunches, their hunting and fishing trips, their corporate jets and their golden parachutes.

Trying to change shareholder capitalism into stakeholder capitalism assumes that the former has been given a chance to work, and has failed. Most of the evidence suggests it has not.

9

THE FUTURE OF WORK

The first thing you notice when you visit Yasuyuki Nambu, the boss of Pasona, Japan's biggest manpower-services agency, is the photographs. There are lots of them, covering the walls from floor to ceiling, and they all feature Nambu posing with the world's best-known politicians: Margaret Thatcher (several times), Ronald Reagan, Bill Clinton, and Mikhail Gorbachev. (Asked how he got to know Prince Charles, another featured friend, Nambu replies that Ronald Reagan introduced the two of them.) Indeed, the whole office is, by Japanese standards, an ostentatious affair: the colours bold and bright, the secretaries (of whom there are an impressive number) all strikingly pretty and impeccably dressed.

The Japanese establishment might have been able to forgive Nambu all these things – even perhaps the scarlet shorts he wears to cycle to work – if he had chosen a different career and founded a different sort of company. In a country in which the ideal is to become a salariman, chained for life to some big, safe corporation, Nambu is an entrepreneur. He started his first company, a Buddhist-style kindergarten, when he was still at university, employing his fellow students as teachers. Noticing that Japan was full of bored mothers, who had nothing to do all day, and frustrated companies with too few staff to meet surges in demand, he then went on to start Japan's first temporary worker agency: the Pasona Group. The business grew rapidly: by late 1995 it had 120,000 employees and Nambu had become a multimillionaire.

Nambu's wealth is a striking reminder of how much 'work' has changed. Even the Japanese, it seems, no longer want to spend their lives doing the bidding of a single employer; and employers can no longer afford to keep people on the books regardless of how much value they are adding. Part-time and temporary workers already make up more than a quarter of Japan's workforce.

To the Japanese establishment temporary workers spell anarchy. The Ministry of Labour has blocked Nambu's relatively innocuous scheme to help move middle managers from big firms, that are trying to slim, to smaller ones, that would like to expand but cannot afford to pay much, by getting the big companies to subsidise the smaller ones' wage bills. The ministry also allows temps to work in only sixteen categories of jobs. Those 'protected' by the current rules include nurses, telephone marketers, receptionists and even janitors – in other words, the stalwarts of manpower agencies in the rest of the world.

Nambu clearly relishes his status as an outsider, and showers visitors with press cuttings about his struggles with the Japanese bureaucracy. But he also takes the establishment's criticisms seriously enough to be determined to rebut them at length. Japanese firms will have no chance succeeding in an increasingly cut-throat world unless they get rid of their hidebound business practices, he argues. And the move towards temporary work will not necessarily produce anarchy, so long as it is handled correctly. Nambu prides himself on Pasona's success with the younger generation – he has even set up a junior executive board, elected from the younger employees, to generate ideas and offer him advice. Every year, on the anniversary of the company's creation, he holds a 'challenge day', when all employees are encouraged to suggest new ideas.

Nambu's biggest concern is ensuring that temporary workers feel that they belong to Pasona. The senior managers have desks on a raised platform in the middle of the company's giant open-plan office, so that they meet the temps when they come to collect their pay-checks. He sends out thirty or more 'herograms' a day: hand-written notes that express his appreciation for outstanding work. Much of the top floor is taken up with a stylish café where workers can socialise, and a health centre, where they can get a check-up or a $3 massage. Temporary work does not mean going unappreciated or being left out in the cold, argues Nambu. His temps can feel just as needed and secure as any salariman; indeed, they have the advantage that they can go when they want to. They are not just chattels.

The end of your job?

Nambu is just one participant, albeit a rather gaudy one, in a world-wide debate about the changing nature of work. If Freud was right, and work, like love, is a prime source of self esteem, then most modern managers have been on a psychological assault course. Sacking surplus shop-floor workers has always been a managerial chore. Now it is the managers themselves who are getting the sack. Having been celebrated for much of the post-war period as the visible hand which made capitalism so successful, they are now often dismissed as so much unnecessary flab. Indeed, many theorists argue that something even more profound and frightening is upon them: the job itself – their unit of power, the place where they manage others – is facing extinction.

In an article called 'The Temping of America', *Time* magazine warned on 29 March 1993 that 'America has entered the age of the contingent or temporary worker, of the consultant and subcontractor, of the just-in-time workforce – fluid, flexible, disposable. This is the future. Its message is this: You are On Your Own.'[1] A year later, in a cover story entitled 'The End of the Job', *Fortune* was even more pessimistic. 'What is disappearing is not just a certain number of jobs – or jobs in certain industries or jobs in some parts of the country or even jobs in America as a whole. What is disappearing is the very thing itself: the job. That much sought-after, much maligned social entity, is vanishing like a species that has outlived its evolutionary time.'[2]

The *Fortune* article was an extract from a book called *Jobshift: How to Prosper in a Workplace Without Jobs* by William Bridges, which argues that the traditional job has become a fixed, artificial solution to a fluid problem. Before the late eighteenth century, Bridges points out, 'job' referred to an undertaking rather than a fixed position (people were 'job-doctors'); soon, he reckons, it will return to that original meaning. And *Jobshift* is positively optimistic compared with *The End of Work*, by Jeremy Rifkin, which predicts a future of mass unemployment and social unrest.

> In the past when new technologies have replaced workers in a given sector, new sectors have always emerged to absorb the displaced labourers. Today all three of the traditional sectors of the economy – agriculture, manufacturing and services – are experiencing technological displacement, forcing millions on to the unemployment rolls. The only expanding sector is the knowledge sector, made up of a small elite of entrepreneurs, scientists, technicians, computer programmers, professionals, educators and consultants. While this sector is growing it is not expected to absorb more than a fraction of the hundreds of millions [of jobs] eliminated in the next several decades.[3]

Politicians have discussed 'the future of work' at G7 meetings. Writing papers on the subject is a growth industry in both Brussels and Washington. Throughout the rich world, increased anxiety at the workplace has been blamed for 'voteless recoveries' where economies improve but people still feel miserable. The idea that the basic laws of employment are being turned upside down has encouraged mavericks such as Sir James Goldsmith and Pat Buchanan to raise protectionist banners, calling for barriers to be erected to protect jobs.

A cynic might argue that, as far as the poor are concerned, jobs have always been 'nasty, brutish and short'. What is different about the current furore is that it has affected the managerial class. There is now a tidal wave of middle-class angst about the information age. A precis might go something like this: thirty years ago, most managers had a reasonable chance of building a safe career. You went to work for a company like GM, GE, ICI or some other acronym, and stayed there for around forty years, doing progressively less work. Getting older meant getting a bigger office, more power, a better title. Today, downsizing, outsourcing, subcontracting, 'the home-office movement' and so on are all turning people into temporary workers. Even famously paternal middle-class organisations such as the BBC and IBM have dispensed with the idea of a job for life. This has come as a blow for a generation who idled away their university years reading about how demographic shortages and technology would mean that we would all work fewer hours for more pay.

Is all this really true? Or has a subject that rightfully deserves contemplation been whipped up into one that incites paranoia? The more mundane truth is that jobs are not so much coming to an end as changing. Yes, some aspects of the transition to a knowledge society (which is what we are really talking about) will be painful; but most should be beneficial. Above all, the victims, such as they are, will increasingly be the poor and the uneducated – not managers who pore over books about the future of work.

The age of Putney

The best place to begin any discussion about the future of work is a large, elegant flat in Putney, a prosperous suburb in West London and the home of Britain's best known guru. Charles Handy stands out from most of the other writers about work not only because he has been saying relatively quietly for quite some time what many of them are now screaming from the hilltops, but also because some of his prophecies have been proved right. His forecast a decade ago that fewer than half the workforce would be in 'proper' full-time jobs by the turn of the century has just about come true in Western Europe; in America the proportion of people who are unemployed, self-employed or on short-term contracts is currently about 35 per cent.

Technology and competition, Handy has argued, are ushering in a new era, in which 'work is something you do rather than something you go to'. Companies will survive, but in a much diminished state. The core of a company (which he has at various times likened to the centre of a doughnut and the heart of a shamrock) will be staffed by a small squad of entrepreneurs and bureaucrats, and governed by the 'half by two by three' rule of corporate fitness: half as many people will be paid twice as much for doing three times as much work. Two sorts of people will try to sell their services to this inner ring. The first will be the general, unskilled 'somebodies' (as in 'somebody can do that'). The second class will be 'portfolio people' – knowledge workers who have assembled a portfolio of skills that they can sell to a variety of different companies. It will not be unusual for somebody to be a portfolio worker in their twenties, then join the core of an organisation, then return to being a portfolio worker in his or her 'troisième age'. Indeed, one of Handy's recurring themes is that workers will carry on working much longer (albeit on a part-time basis), partly to earn more money and partly to give themselves something to do.

Handy's diagnosis may be harsh, but his prescriptions are usually fairly soft – arguably too soft. He believes that the pursuit of profit is not everything and that companies should change their ownership structure to give stakeholders, such as workers and customers, more power in relation to shareholders. Training, education and the importance of voluntary work remain persistent Handy themes.

Handy may be better at provoking thought than prescribing solutions (a fault or virtue that he shares with Drucker). But it is worth noting that his philosophy is rooted in at least one reality: his own. Should we be surprised that the prophet of the portfolio worker and the troisième age is himself a man in his mid-sixties who 'sells' his services to a variety of clients (including the London Business School and several charities), drifts between Putney, the English countryside and Tuscany, and spends only six months a year working on his own projects? Certainly, the idea that there is more to life than profit is easier to take from a thinker who limits himself to around a dozen high-paying 'cabarets' a year and does the rest of his speaking assignments either free or for charity. In many ways the questions about the future of work are not just about whether Handy's prediction is correct, let alone his answers, but also about just how typical he is of his audience.

What is not changing

Any manager who thinks that there is something new about technology threatening jobs should read George Eliot's *Middlemarch*. As the railway moved ever closer to the Victorian market town, panic mounted about what the new technology would mean for its inhabitants. But was it justified? Certainly, the railway changed people's lives dramatically, but it did not necessarily do so for the worse. For every stagecoach driver the iron horse put out of work, it would have created many other jobs not only on the railway itself but in businesses and shops that were now connected to the outside world. Even if some of these changes would have been painful, in the longer run jobs would surely have been safer in a town such as Middlemarch that was connected to the railway than in those that were not.

There are three reasons for believing that this optimistic version of history will repeat itself: one rooted in basic market economics and two in (slightly more suspect) statistics. They do not disprove the 'end of work' theorists, but they do suggest that their ideas should be taken with a pinch of salt.

Ever since the Luddites rose up and smashed their looms in the early 19th century, market economics has had an unbroken record of disproving warnings about new technology.[4] Over the past two centuries countless jobs have been pushed aside by machines, but more have been created on the way. The pessimists counter by claiming that the computer – or, more accurately, the computer-plus-telephone – will have a far wider effect than machines like the Spinning Jenny that so annoyed the Luddites. By some calculations three out of four jobs in the industrialised world are the sort of repetitive ones that might be automated. There is something in this: many economists reckon that there may be a short delay whilst the labour market invents new jobs. It is hard to imagine a displaced 'railroad engineer' (the biggest predicted job decline in America) rapidly picking up work as a home health aide (the biggest increase).[5]

But this is a quibble over timing. So far, at least, there seem to be far more similarities than differences between this wave of technological change and previous ones. Calling for protectionist measures not only looks impracticable (how on earth do Goldsmith and Buchanan imagine that they will keep out cheap third world products and technology anyway?), it is also counter-productive: putting up barriers against technology only means that you end up like the towns in Victorian England that were not connected to the railway.

The two sets of statistics should also be of some comfort to our worried manager (though neither is conclusive). The first indicate that, although managers are now more likely to lose their jobs than before, they are also much more likely to find them. In America 'managerial and professional' jobs now make up the biggest slice of the workforce – and the sector is growing fast. In Britain, a study published in 1995 by the University of Warwick's Institute for Employment Research found that, despite a decade dominated by headlines about downsizing, 1.35 million new managerial jobs were created in Britain in 1981–94; it also forecasted that there will be another 630,000 new managerial posts by 2001, bringing the total up to 4.9m people or 18.5 per cent of the employed labour force. As usual, the losers are the poor and the unskilled.[6]

The standard retort to statistics like this is that it is simply a matter of labelling: in factories, team leaders and work supervisors are now managers; in the high street, a video-store attendant can often be a manager too. This point is a fair one, but it does not completely invalidate the statistics. For example, the researchers at Warwick were adamant that, even allowing for this trend, the number of managers 'is going to grow hand over fist'.

The second set of statistics that the worried manager ought to bear in mind suggests that – so far – the job for life is not becoming any rarer. The proportion of Americans who stayed in the same job for more than eight years hardly changed at all between 1971 and 1991; indeed the average length of time middle-aged Americans spend with one employer has actually edged up from a little over six years in 1966 to just over seven years in 1991. Similar figures can be found in most other countries.

Once again, it would be unwise to read too much into this set of statistics. There are doubts about whether the numbers include all temporary workers, and the most recent figures date back only as far as the early 1990s, before the full effects of downsizing had been felt. And if you dig into the figures, you can find signs of change: there has been an increase in the number of people who have retired (or been pushed out) at the age of fifty-five or earlier. And the overall figures can hide considerable turbulence within companies as employees get switched around all over the place.

The 'end of work' school has relied on a caricature of the traditional job as an inflexible eight-hour block dedicated to doing one thing. The truth is that jobs – particularly managerial ones – have always involved doing 'a bit of this' and 'a bit of that'. People endlessly cover for each other as a result of holidays and illnesses. Projects are assigned on the basis of whoever comes through the door next. Reading a breathless description of how, say, CNN is 'a virtual organisation' where people are assigned to projects, regardless of experience, one tends to forget that news organisations have always been chaotic places in which nature writers are sometimes sent off to cover the latest war in Abyssinia. If Lord Beaverbrook wandered into CNN, he would be bemused by the gadgets and nonplussed by the absence of alcohol, but he would recognise a world in which the big story dominates everybody's lives, and in which editors throw people at stories regardless of their previous experience.

Nevertheless, the statistics (not to mention economics) imply that the managerial Armageddon is a little further off than some have feared, and that work is changing less radically than many people have claimed. The 'job', a little like other maligned institutions, such as the company and even the city, is not going to disappear in the immediate future. In twenty years' time, you will still be able to walk into any office and discover a group of greying employees gathered around a decaffeinated coffee machine bitching about their superiors, discussing who is sleeping with whom and complaining about the aforementioned coffee machine.

Listen to Bangalore

All this clearly means that the management theorists have exaggerated their case when they talk about 'the end of the job'. Indeed, the more honest among them admit as much. That does not mean that the workplace is not changing.

Any western trade unionist who visited the dusty office in Bangalore belonging to Wipro Infotech, an Indian software firm, would risk a heart attack – and not just because of the lengthy climb up four flights of steps. Despite the noise, and the beggars outside, all three forces of change – technology, communication and global competition – are on display. Here are Indian hands and brains doing the work that western ones used to – redesigning General Electric's internal software system – and doing so for a fifth of what it would cost in the West. After the Indian engineers have finished, their product will be transmitted to America via the satellite on the building's roof. In other corners of India there are people doing back-office work for companies such as Swissair and even people studying video screens, acting as security guards for premises in America.

Nor does our trade unionist have to take a flight to be amazed or terrified. The countryside of western Europe and America is being repopulated by a new kind of worker. Visit an old smithy in Exmoor and you will discover a company making expensive microscopes with computer-controlled manipulators out of components from as far afield as Japan and America, and for customers in eighty countries.[7]

It is understandable that people should get dreamy about the possible impact of all these things. Here is Handy:

Our world is about to see a change as significant as the technological event which, in many ways, launched Europe into a new age 600 years ago when the printing press was invented and developed. For the first time then people were able to read the Bible in their own language in their own home in their own time . . . They could now make up their own minds about right and wrong, God and devil. As a result, the authority of the Church crumbled, and with it the authority of most institutions. Individual freedom led to creativity, which led to the Renaissance . . . The television set and the telephone, with the computer at the end of it, the wired and unwired world which we now contemplate, are the modern equivalents of the printing press. When Motorola achieves its dream of a personal number for each of us at birth, then a telephone will truly belong to a person not a place. Insignificant as that sounds, it means that the office will become as unnecessary as the churches became.[8]

Once again, it is easy to quibble with Handy over details: 500 years after Gutenberg, churches remain 'necessary' for many people, including Handy. Yet the world of work is clearly changing, if not quite as much as some people claim. The undercurrents upsetting the old order – and troubling managers in particular – can be crudely divided into three questions. Where do we work? Whom do we work for? And what do we do?

Ring me at home

Handy's argument that work will be something we do rather than the place where we go is slowly becoming true. Around 43m Americans do some portion of their work at home – a figure that is 75 per cent higher than in 1988. Twelve million of these are full-timers. In many cases the force for change is demography as much as technology or high office prices: everywhere women are accounting for a larger share of both the fully employed workforce and the part-time one. According to the researchers at Warwick University, 46 per cent of Britain's employed labour-force in 2001 will be female. They also predict that by then there will be an extra 1.3m part-time jobs and the number of self-employed will rise by 436,000 to 3.7m or 14 per cent of the total employed labour force. All these sorts of workers tend to do some of their work at home. America's AT&T has guessed that by the end of the decade one in every two working Americans will do at least some of their work from home.

In America and many parts of Europe there is a growing 'SoHo' movement, which either stands for Small Office/Home Office or Single Operator/Home Office, according to taste. One in three American homes already has a computer; some 40 per cent of these have modems allowing their computers to talk to the outside world. Nowadays virtually every salesman or woman has a portable telephone. Within five years it is highly likely that most modems will be cellular, meaning that a salesperson visiting a client does not even have to find a phone-jack to download the latest sales information. Enthusiasts claim that not only is working at home more convenient – especially for women – but it is also more efficient. Numerous studies have shown that people in office jobs spend half their time working by themselves. By some calculations, a worker's productivity rises by 15–20 per cent if he or she stays at home.

Is this true? The best argument for the efficiency of staying at home is usually the inefficiency of going to work. One study of 90,000 managers by Booz Allen & Hamilton found that people waste a quarter of their time at work. Add up the hours spent in pointless meetings, commuting and hanging around the coffee machine and you should find this is an underestimate. Plenty of companies have allowed people to stay at home and found that productivity improved. In one experiment, Compaq, an American computer maker, gave all its sales people personal computers connected to its main network (so that they had instant access to all the latest information and prices) and told them to work from home. Not only did Compaq save on office space; it also found it could get by with two-thirds of the original sales force, largely because each salesman sold six times as many computers. At *The Economist*, it is noticeable that all but the laziest foreign correspondents are more productive than their London counterparts: one reason why is that they gain roughly a day a week in terms of meetings that they do not have to attend.

But is working at home really such a charmed, productive life? In many countries it is either impossible or complicated for home-office workers to claim their full expenses against tax. In Japan, Toshiba, an electronics group, has begun to experiment with letting software researchers stay at home. But most houses in Japan are too small for people to live in comfortably, let alone work there too; and telephone costs can make the whole exercise punitively expensive. Indeed, the motives of those replying to surveys look a little suspect. If you were a mother with three small children, would you not claim that working at home was more productive? Anecdotal evidence suggests that many of the home-office fanatics are loners with formidable powers of concentration. Most 'normal' workers, particularly managers, worry that being at home means being out of the loop. In any normal home there are plenty of distractions, ranging from cricket matches on the television to sex, that are not usually available in the office (try sitting at home and writing a book, particularly on management).

The supporters of the SoHo movement are also a little selective with their examples. They make a great fuss about the number of young companies that have sprung from domestic surroundings, such as Apple and Mrs. Field's Cookies. But this is hardly a new trend. Companies as big as Disney and Ford both started as home-based businesses. Similarly, the growing implication that just about any type of worker can now work at home is nonsense. Time after time the same groups of home workers pop up – management consultants, writers and so on; in other words, the sort of people who write management books. Such portfolio workers are thin on the ground. As John Kay, a British guru who also flits between various comfortable careers, observed when reviewing one of Handy's books, 'There is Charles Handy, and me, but not many others.'[9]

It's a temp's world

Temporary workers are not a new phenomenon, particularly in Europe, but they are becoming more common. A report in October 1995 by Britain's Institute of Management found that nearly nine in ten British companies used part-time and tempo-rary workers (a rise of 15 per cent and 8 per cent over the previous year). In the period 1990–95, the number of temporary workers in Britain increased by 350,000 at the same time as the overall workforce declined by 750,000. And an increasing proportion of these temporary workers were working in factories.

In America, part-timers, leased employees and the self-employed now account for one-quarter of the workforce. America's biggest private employer is no longer General Motors but Manpower, a temporary agency with 600,000 people on its books. There are now about 6,000 temporary companies in America – double the figure ten years ago. Even in Japan, that temple of lifetime employment, heretics such as Yasuyuki Nambu are appearing in unprecedented numbers despite the highly regulated system. 'You can work at the place of your choice at the time you like and the job you like,' says Nambu, 'without being bound to one company.'[10]

From an employer's point of view, Nambu's optimism about the virtues of temporary work may be justified. Enthusiasts in America talk about there being 'a contingency spot market.'[11] In *Jobshift*, William Bridges gives the example of Home Corporation, a Montgomery, Alabama firm that owns apartment complexes, which decided to lease its entire 500-strong property management staff from a temporary agency called Action Staffing.[12] Temporary workers do not need the same benefits as full-timers; and they are much easier to lay off. Blue Cross/Blue Shield of Rhode Island cut its workforce by 40 per cent over five years without having to sack one 'real' worker. A report published in October 1995 by Reed Personnel Services, a British employment agency, indicated that demand for temporary staff was at an all-time high, but warned that too many employers were short-changing temps when it came to holidays, training, sick-pay and so on.

This sort of problem explains why the 'corporate condominiums' and 'virtual corporations' that so excite Handy, Drucker and Peters may be some time in coming. Far from being invigorated by the choice now open to them, most temporary workers feel insecure – and their work shows it. There are plenty of examples of quality declining when temporary workers are brought in. At one condom factory the managers could tell when the temporary workers had arrived by the number of faulty products tripping off the end of the assembly line. Surveys have shown that roughly 60 per cent of the people in the contingency labour force would rather have full-time jobs.

Small is fragile

Ask anybody who they work for nowadays, and the answer is likely to be 'a small company'. As we have explained elsewhere (see Chapter Five, 'Rethinking the Company'), fascination with size is no more revealing in management theory than it is in other areas of life. However, regardless of the relative merits of big and small companies, nowadays you are more likely to work for a smaller company – and that company is more likely to go bust.

Of the twenty-one million business enterprises in the United States only 14,000 have more than 500 employees.[13] Even in economies where small firms seem less numerous they are still often the prime source for new jobs. For instance, in semi-socialist Sweden, where 70 per cent of the country's manufacturing employees toil for big companies like Volvo, the only type of company to add jobs in 1985–92 employed fewer than twenty people. However, small companies remain fragile creatures. Studies of employment growth in states such as California have pointed to the importance of 'gazelle' companies: firms, not necessarily new ones but usually fairly small ones, that suddenly leap forwards but can also trip up. Californians are both more likely to be sacked and more likely to be hired than those in most other states. A similar story emerges if you look at industries instead of regions. Some 60 per cent of high-tech start-ups die before their fifth birthday.

Working in the midst of all this creative destruction may not be to everybody's taste but it appears to attract the best and the brightest. In *The New Rules: How to Succeed in Today's Post-Corporate World*, John Kotter tracked 115 members of the Harvard Business School's Class of 74.[14] Only 23 per cent of them were employed by companies with more than 10,000 people. Most worked for companies with fewer than 1,000 employees – and 40 per cent of them claimed to be entrepreneurs. By 1991, those employed at the smaller businesses were paid an average of

$450,000 – twice as much as their slowcoach cousins stuck at the bigger firms.

Even employees who work for big companies are not free from this sort of uncertainty. As we have already seen, the most successful big companies such as Rubbermaid and Hewlett-Packard have become more entrepreneurial, pushing decision-making down the ranks and restructuring themselves around teams. The difference nowadays between working for one part of a large federated engineering group, such as ABB Asea Brown Boveri, and working for a small company, such as one of the network of small clothing suppliers clustered around Benetton in Northern Italy, is becoming ever harder to tell. In the old days, if a subsidiary asked for more independence it would probably be told to go to hell; nowadays it is more likely to be encouraged with lots of warming talk about the need to 'create villages within our cities'.

This has an effect on the way that people work. Even in a big company, people can no longer afford to see a career as a ladder leading straight from the humblest office to the boardroom. Rather it has become a series of islands connected by causeways, loosely governed by a small floating flagship. In many ways hopping from one corner of General Electric to another can be just as terrifying as leaving one Silicon Valley start-up and going to another.

What we do

Whether a manager's job is at a big firm or a small one, a striking number of things about that job are changing – from whom the manager bosses about, to what hours they work, to whether they have an office, or even a desk. This explains why managerial insecurity runs much deeper than mere fear of losing a job.

As ever fewer people take on ever more tasks, conventional job descriptions have to be thrown out of the window. Suddenly managers are being told what to do by people they once considered their juniors, and are having to share information that was once exclusively theirs. Managers often have to supervise not only temporary workers but also people who work for other companies. Call up your computer department and someone from Electronic Data Systems or Computer Services Corporation may come to fix your problem; ring down to the mailroom and you may be talking to a Pitney Bowes postman. Even if you shout at somebody on the assembly line, they might turn out to be a subcontractor's representative. Ten out of the 120 employees at Walters Hexagon, a small British company which supplies different types of screws and fasteners, are 'engineering envoys' who sit in its customers' factories and ferry goods from its delivery people to the correct department of their customers.[15]

Managers are even losing those traditional symbols of their status, their offices and desks. The trendiest companies are introducing 'hotdesking' and 'just-in-time desks'. There are plenty of high-flown justifications for this trend. Getting rid of desks reduces clutter and allows companies to make more imaginative use of their space. (The Finnish office of Digital Equipment, a big American computer company, has used the space created by getting rid of individual cubicles to build a sauna which can be used to entertain clients.) It reduces preoccupation with status and hierarchy. And it forces workers to get on the road. Gemini refuses to give its consultants their own desks because it wants them to spend most of their time with their clients rather than hanging around the office.

But it is hard to escape from the suspicion that the real reason for this fashion is cost. By changing its person-to-desk ratio from two:one to twelve:one, Digital Equipment's British arm saved £3.5m a year. As Charles Handy points out, people are much less efficient at using office space than machines. Our mechanical cousins can work for a full 168 hours a week; we rarely get beyond sixty. Worse, an increasing number of us are not even in the office during the hours when we could be there. Franklin Becker, director of the International Workplace Studies Programme at Cornell University (and the only professor proud of not having his own desk), argues that 'about 70 per cent of the people who work in management consultancy, sales and customer service are usually not at their desks'.[16]

However, it is not clear whether all this hotdesking is popular with employees. Herman Miller, an American furniture-design company, gives its employees carts in which they can carry around their belongings so that they can personalise their workstation when they work at it. Similarly, the current vogue for open-plan 'networking' offices can deprive people of places where they can have time for themselves to think. At one part of Asda, a British supermarket chain, employees who want space to themselves have to wear red caps.

This might seem disorientating enough for any manager. Yet at hip technology companies such as Intel and Microsoft managers have to get used to being a member of a temporary taskforce rather than the leader of a permanent division: there are often no precise physical locations or job titles ('You won't last long at Microsoft if your job is just a job'). And the pace is different. Rather than working a regular nine to five day, the project tends to build to a pizzas-at-midnight, you-can't-see-your-children crescendo, followed by a holiday after it is all over.

Arguably, a career built around creative bursts is much closer to that in the pre-industrial age. In *Jobshift*, Bridges illustrates the shift from the pre-job world to the world of jobs and then on to the dejobbed world by looking at long-distance transport in each of his three ages. In the 18th century, the pre-job vehicle was the ship, where there was little permanent employment (you were hired for each voyage). At sea, although the day was divided into watches, most tasks were accomplished by people clubbing together (e.g. pulling down the sails). Although the boat's owner was usually a landlubbing merchant, almost all the practical decisions had to be left to the captain. In the next age came the railway which required far more organisation. Schedules and prices were set by head office. Workers had specific jobs (conductors did not shovel coal). The airliner, to Bridges, is a transitional vehicle. To begin with it conformed to the world of jobs. Now young carriers are stealing a march on their older peers by letting their staff do a variety of jobs (at Southwest Airlines, the pilots or 'team leaders' help people with their baggage). That leaves the space shuttle as Bridges' example of the dejobbed future, where, although each crew-member has his own speciality, the most important skills tend to be team ones.

Men in the middle

Bridges is straining the analogy a little with the space shuttle. Most companies are still very much at the airliner stage – and likely to remain so for some time (after all, Southwest does not let its baggage handlers fly the aircraft). Although many companies have reorganised a little along project-based lines, few have gone as far as Microsoft or Intel. Besides, there is something of a backlash in favour of a more structured approach to work. Nothing typifies this correction more than the attitude towards middle managers.

Until recently the attitude of most companies to middle managers was similar to that of Stalin towards the Kulaks. Middle managers were the bureaucratic class of time servers who sat awkwardly between the shop-floor and the factory, who impeded the swift flow of information, and who accounted for a fifth of all the jobs lost in America since 1988. 'Middle management as we know it will simply disappear,' Michael Hammer, one of the inventors of re-engineering, declared. Tom Peters put it more simply: 'Their goose is cooked.'

Yet fashions change. By the mid-1990s, theorists had begun to talk of middle managers bringing a 'mid-level' perspective to a company's work. They are the sergeants: the only people who know enough about the shopfloor and customer to be able to tell strategic thinkers in the upper ranks how their ideas can be put into practice. Steven Floyd of the University of Connecticut and Bill Wooldridge of the University of Massachusetts, who studied management at twenty American firms, claim that companies that gave middle managers a say in forming strategy performed better.[17] Far from being barriers to innovation in big companies, middle managers are often champions of it: they are the only people who know how to get things done in big organisations. Francis Westley of McGill University points out that middle managers are also skilled networkers, forever making informal alliances with colleagues from other companies.[18] And middle management is a valuable part of the career ladder: it gives workers at the bottom something to aim for, and it provides a few years of training for high-fliers to get their balance.

The question is not whether to have middle managers, but how to use them without letting them indulge their weaknesses for hierarchy-building and paperwork. Some firms such as Digital and 3M have tried to turn middle managers into entrepreneurs whose job is to invent good ideas and persuade senior managers to back them. In Japan, a place which has long looked on middle managers more kindly than the West, Honda developed its Civic car by giving middle managers a general goal (make it youth friendly and fuel-efficient) and letting them do the rest.

The result of all this talk is that even big companies which pride themselves on being lean have been forced to reinvent middle managers – albeit under titles such as 'facilitators', 'boundary spanners', 'process managers' and 'employee coaches'. As with most other things to do with the modern workplace, big companies are changing – but not by as much as the pessimists predict.

Enslaved or empowered?

Accept that work is changing (at least, a little) and you are immediately plunged into two fierce debates. The first revolves around the question of whether the new work culture liberates or enslaves the working man or woman. Does it tip the balance in favour of the employer or the employee? Are we going to live more fulfilled lives or are we destined to be racked by anxiety? The second debate, which tends to be greatly coloured by the diagnosis of the first, turns to prescription. What should be done to make jobs more liberating experiences? What should a manager demand from his or her employer?

Read Tom Peters and you come away with the impression that the personal computer will perform much the same role for managers that William Wilberforce did for slaves. Managers, he suggests, are on the verge of a new, empowered age. 'Forget loyalty. Or at least loyalty to one's corporation. Try loyalty to your Rolodex – your network – instead.'[19] To work nowadays, argues Peters, is to résumé (yes, he does turn yet another noun into a verb): everybody should become an independent contractor or think of themselves as one. 'Powerlessness is a state of mind,' declares Peters.

By contrast, many other gurus reckon that 'powerless' is exactly what most managers are. The most downbeat are the 'end of work' crowd. A gloomy prognostication of the future of work (and a corresponding need to regulate the market which will cause this distress) has already become a staple of left-wing politics everywhere. Both America's labour secretary, Robert Reich, and Tony Blair, the leader of Britain's Labour Party, have talked about the rise of 'the anxious class', most of whom hold jobs but are justifiably uneasy about their lack of security and fearful of their children's future.

A third group of people, including Charles Handy, seem to hop from one side of the fence to the other, sometimes celebrating those who have the necessary skills and knowledge to flourish in the new economy, sometimes sympathising with those who will be left behind. Rosabeth Moss Kanter for instance divides people into 'New Cosmopolitans' rich in the 3Cs ('concepts, competence and connections') and 'Locals' – her equivalent of Handy's 'portfolio workers' and 'somebodies'.

The idea that there is a growing division is something virtually everybody can agree on. Where the pessimists are wrong is in assuming that most people in the western world fit into the losing camp. There is a big, and growing, group of workers who should gain from the technology that makes it ever easier for people to set up on their own. You do not have to be one of John Kotter's Harvard MBAs to seize the opportunities of the modern economy. Wander around a Denver suburb or even a Cotswold village and you will find plenty of moderately qualified people working for themselves – and usually being paid more for it. A quarter of the small American businesses surveyed by *Business Week* in October 1995 rated 'a lack of qualified workers' as one of their three biggest problems (a proportion that has risen annually). As for those who remain inside big companies, flatter management structures mean that bright people can now bound to the top more easily.

That said, there is also a class of people who are doomed to lose out from the changes in the workplace. This group certainly includes some managers who are down on their luck: for example, the middle-aged manager, delayered out of a job, who is now more expensive to rehire than a fresh young college graduate. However, as we have seen already, there does not appear, in the aggregate, to be a shortage of managerial jobs. For instance most people read *Executive Blues: Down and Out in Corporate America*, an autobiography of a manager called G.J. Meyer coming to terms with unemployment, as a primary example of a new sort of 'work-horror' genre ('In Edvard Munch's *The Scream*, a solitary empty-eyed figure stands in a roadway clutching its head, mouth open wide,' proclaims the self-pitying author. 'I hope that's not what I look like as I walk the streets of Manhattan . . .') However, at the end of *Executive Blues* the author has to admit that he has found 'a job that I like very much with a company that I like very much on the outskirts of Cleveland'.

The real losers are the unskilled poor, who are now more likely to spend their lives drifting between short-term jobs, or perhaps dropping out of formal work entirely. In 1995, 46 per cent of Europe's unemployed had been out of work for longer than a year. As Jeremy Rifkin has pointed out, when an early wave of automation began taking its toll in America's manufacturing sector in the 1950s, the hardest hit were unskilled workers – particularly blacks. By 1964 black unemployment had reached 12 per cent, against a previous post-war high of 8.5 per cent. By contrast white unemployment crawled up from 4.6 per cent to 5.9 per cent.[20] The same appears to be happening again. Virtually everywhere, 'the inequality gap' between the rich and poor has widened.

The paranoid manager

This suggests that managers should be worried about the poor and not themselves. However, the winners and losers in this new world of work should be judged in psychological as well as material terms. Here managers fare less well. For all the talk of empowerment, most are scared and anxious creatures. Any number of factors could account for this insecurity: the recent waves of downsizing; the fact that managers are conservative people who tend to dislike change, even if it is beneficial, and like hierarchies, even if they are restrictive; the practical difficulties of being a portfolio worker (try arranging a mortgage if you are only on a short-term contract); even, perhaps, the relentless propaganda about the end of 'the job for life'.

The chief contribution to this psychological unease is probably overwork. One of the developing world's biggest problems (and one for which management theory should take part of the blame) is that modern economies seem to combine rising unemployment with longer working hours for those in jobs. On balance, Handy's rule (about half the number of people being paid twice as much to do three times as much work) looks something of an exaggeration; but, even if they are only working one-and-a-half times as hard as they used to, most workers feel shattered. In *The Overworked American*, Juliet Schor, an economist at Harvard, calculated that her countrymen spent the equivalent of four weeks more a year on the job in 1989 than in 1969. The average American now works fifty-two hours a week — forty-six hours in the office and a further six at home. Commuting times have grown longer; and holidays shorter. Work-related ailments, such as repetitive strain injury, are on the rise. According to one study by MIT, depression costs the American economy $47 billion a year. In Japan, where by some calculations people work 400 hours a year longer than most Europeans, they even have a word, *kaoroshi*, for death from overwork.

Managers are nearly always the hardest-working. Once again, management fashion is partly responsible. Delayering reduces the number of managers available to do jobs. Re-engineering forces managers to take charge of a whole process: suddenly you are no longer just another R&D manager; instead you are in charge of an entire 'new product development' process, responsible for people from sales and production as well as your familiar team of white-coated scientists. If a company reduces the number of job specifications from 1,300 to thirty-two – as did one electronics firm visited by Rosabeth Moss Kanter – then you are bound to increase a manager's workload. Indeed, each manager at the company now looks after twenty-four workers rather than just twelve.

To add to these psychological strains, the fashion for long hours has gone hand in hand with the fashion for flexibility. Workers often devote themselves to their companies almost to the exclusion of their social lives. Poring over reports takes the place of hobbies; networking on the telephone takes over from normal socialising. People disrupt their family lives in order to take foreign postings. They also make many of their strongest friendships at work. But then suddenly the firm is re-engineered and they become surplus to requirements. The thing which has filled their days and given their life purpose is taken away from them. The overworked company man suddenly becomes just another anomic citizen.

One day this may change. Companies may employ more people and work them less hard. Employees may agree to work strange shifts in exchange for working fewer hours and getting paid the same. A few companies, including Hewlett-Packard, have certainly experimented along these lines. But most companies would rather work their existing workforce to the bone and reward them accordingly. A study of British Telecom managers by Britain's Society of Telecom Executives showed, perhaps unsurprisingly, that those who worked fifty to sixty hours a week were much more likely to get one of the top two grades in their annual reviews than those who did not. Indeed, the whole system of incentive pay is geared towards persuading staff generally – and managers in particular – to work ever harder.

In other words the new work order is not producing 'the

unemployed manager'; rather the paranoid manager. The probabilities remain firmly in his favour (it is still predominantly 'his'
rather than 'her'): he will keep his job; even if he loses it he will
be re-employed fairly quickly; he has more opportunities than
ever before to decide where he wants to work; he will probably
be given more power earlier; he should be worried about his
unskilled colleagues rather than himself. It is not the probabilities
that have unhinged him, but the possibilities: the possibility that
he could be one of the minority of managers who get sacked and
are not employed again; the possibility that technology will
replace his job rather than just make it easier. As he commutes
back to his home in Pasadena or Sevenoaks, the paranoid manager
does not find the idea that his new neighbour is a consultant who
works from home and earns more money than he does
encouraging but frightening. And his own company plays on this
insecurity by telling him that he will only be paid more if he
works harder. What can be done to make him feel more secure?

The new moral contract

The social contract between man and society has been a mainstay
of philosophical debate for centuries. Management theory's
equivalent is the dispute over the responsibilities a company owes
to its workers. Some people talk about 'a new moral contract'
between employer and employee. But what does a company owe
its workers? Management theory has thrown up a number of
answers, varying from 'nothing except a good pay packet' to
'employability' to 'a stake in the company'.

For many bosses employee-employer relations can be brought
down to a single word: pay. Not only is this what most workers
want to talk about; there is often a clear trade-off between job
security and the size of a pay packet. Nobody pities a bond trader
who accumulates several million dollars in a few years before
being sacked. Indeed, many people go into the bond trading
business with exactly that aim. Nowadays, even the most
humdrum jobs can be 'incentivised'. Roughly six out of ten

American companies have some broad-based system which tries to reward their employees in line with performance.

Pay is an attractive solution, particularly to economists fascinated by risk-return models. But it is not a complete solution. One of the most irritating things about middle-class angst is that it often springs from exactly the same sort of people who decided to go into, say, marketing rather than teaching because they thought that the latter was too 'safe' and badly paid. Moreover, incentive pay remains a blunt tool, particularly lower down any organisation. Indeed, in many cases, incentive pay tends to increase paranoia rather than soothe it. If a group of people do extremely well and are rewarded 96 per cent of their possible bonus, the likely response of the recipients will be that somebody has stolen 4 per cent of what they deserved.

So something more is needed. Does the promise of 'a job for life' fit the bill? There are still a fair number of companies that reap the rewards from offering workers secure employment. For instance, before a 'jobs for life' pledge was introduced at a British Range Rover factory in the early 1990s, barely 11 per cent of the employees bothered to enter an annual 'suggestions' competition because they were worried that improved efficiency might cost them their jobs; afterwards the proportion rose to 84 per cent. One proposal alone saved the company £100m – enough presumably to employ one or two surplus workers. Japanese and German companies have long looked at this trade-off and reached a similar conclusion, keeping jobs at home long after strict economic logic would have despatched them abroad.

The problem, as both the Japanese and the Germans have recently discovered, is that such promises are often not sustainable. In 1995 Sony reached a landmark when it reluctantly had to stop making televisions for export in Japan. Over the past five years Mercedes-Benz and BMW have relentlessly increased production outside Germany, always assuring their expensive German staff that the new cars are for export only. One day, perhaps, Range Rover too will regret its promise. Its current range of models may be successful, but it is impossible to guarantee that the same thing will be true in 2010. A 'jobs for life' pledge in retail banking or computer-production is not worth the paper it is printed upon.

Employed or employable?

At first sight, the concept of 'lifetime employability' looks like a poor substitute. For instance when IBM's director of employee relations announced in the mid-1990s that 'unconditional lifetime employment is no longer the name of the game; instead it's lifelong employability', he was only acknowledging reality. After all, Big Blue had laid off 175,000 people since 1986. But it is surely better to tell workers the truth than to offer them a job for life and leave them unprepared for any other employment.

At Apple, John Sculley offered staff a 'new loyalty' pledge: 'Look, Apple can't promise you a job for life. Not even for five or ten years. Maybe not even for a couple of years. But what Apple can – and does – promise is that, whether you're aboard for three months, six months, six years, or, unlikely as it may be, sixteen years, you will be constantly learning, constantly challenged. At the end you will be demonstrably better positioned in the local or global labour market than you would have been had you not spent time with us.'

'Training' is a word often invoked by companies which talk about employability. Raychem, an industrial products company based in Silicon Valley, has made it clear that none of its employees has a guaranteed job for life, but it has guaranteed the opportunity to learn. The firm even has an in-house careers centre to help employees get new jobs either in other parts of the company or outside the firm.[21] Ford offers up to $3,100 a year to each employee to spend on approved courses. Andersen Consulting spends 7 per cent of its gross revenues on training, and the average employee spends 135 hours each year in a classroom. ISS, a Danish cleaning contractor, sends all its employees on a short course before giving them their mops and brushes; it even has a cleaning university in Copenhagen.

One would imagine that being 'for' training is a little bit like being 'against' wife-beating: that there are plenty of good reasons for a company that does not care a fig about the emotional state of its staff, let alone their long-term employability, to invest in their education. However, examples of companies equipping managers and workers for life are rare. American companies spend the equivalent of only around 1.4 per cent of their payroll on educating their workers.

Such statistics are always seized on by the training industry to goad employers and governments into providing more courses. However, knowledge, on its own, is not quite the guarantee of employability that some people suppose, for a good deal of knowledge is specific to the company you work for. The fact that at McDonald's you know the finance director really well does not help you much if you move to Burger King. And much knowledge is job specific, not company specific. If you are employed by General Electric's television arm, NBC, it is doubtful that your Rolodex will be much help if you are moved to its turbine-making division. Even when the jobs are more similar, it can often take people time to settle in. Many a Unilever brand manager who has been good at selling ice cream has flopped when it came to flogging fish fingers.

By the same token, it is not always in the company's interest to move people around just to improve their employability: it can destroy their main value to that particular employer (their knowledge) and their sense of being a team. Employability is as much the employee's responsibility as the employer's.

Unions and stakeholders

Naturally, a knowledge worker is in a stronger position to expand his Rolodex and renew his education if he has some power over his employer. In theory, companies are 'empowering' workers just about everywhere. (MIT reckons that 80 per cent of employers in America participate in some kind of responsibility or empowerment programme.) Yet many workers want structures as well as words. The traditional response to powerlessness has been to band together in unions. However, from Japan to Scotland unions have, in general, been in retreat. Only around one in ten of America's private-sector workers belongs to a union. Even in Scandinavia, where union membership has held up reasonably well, young people are only half as likely to join unions as their parents. Worse, there are doubts about whether unions for knowledge workers make sense.[22] The battle lines are not fixed ones where the opposing sides are divided by class and money. Unions tend to be male, manufacturing-oriented and good at negotiating with similar dinosaurs such as General Motors, not small multimedia companies. Most of the knowledge worker's problems are to do with contracts, empowerment, employability, parental leave and part-time work.

Put bluntly, unions have changed far less than companies. Ironically, the solution to the unions' problems may be sitting in their own history books. Most unions grew out of ancient guilds of craftsmen. If they could put the clock back they would do much better. From this point of view the Writers' Guild of America, the union for Hollywood's 8,000 scriptwriters, is interesting. The guild is still regarded by many studio chiefs as a hotbed of communism. It has also had its share of pointless strikes. However, its basic structure is oriented towards providing services for a set of individuals rather than one uniform mob. As well as negotiating fixed minimum rates with the studios for different sorts of scripts, the Guild also offers its knowledge workers pension and health plans and legal advice. Its lawyers have already drawn up standard contracts for multimedia programmers.

There are similar signs of more enlightened unions springing up in other places such as Italy and even Britain. But an increasing number of theorists believe that there will be no new moral contract between employers and employees without some kind of structural change. In most cases this means a change in the corporate governance of the firm to give stakeholders such as employees more power at the expense of shareholders. Whether that is justified on any grounds is a subject we examined sceptically in the previous chapter (see pages 203–9). However, it is worth noting that, so far at least, the changes in the way that people work do not in themselves seem to warrant changing shareholder capitalism. For a start one has to compare the dearth

238

of knowledge industries in 'kind' stakeholder Germany with the flowering of them in 'cruel' shareholder America.

Indeed, the fuss about the iniquities of shareholder capitalism is the last (and perhaps most dangerous) of all the panics arising about the future of work. Like 'the job' and 'the middle manager', and all the other supposedly doomed characters in the plot, the company will live on – perhaps in a slightly different shape but still manifestly the same thing. Reading much of the literature about the future of the workplace one is reminded of those books in the 1960s that used to forecast an end-of-the-century future where we would all begin each day by clambering into an all-in-one, omnipurpose suit and taking a single breakfast pill. In fact shirts, skirts and ties still remain (albeit in different fashions and fabrics to the 1960s); so does breakfast, although we now eat muesli with semi-skimmed milk rather than cornflakes with cream.

The most horrifying thing about 'the future of work' may be just how similar it will be.

PART FOUR

The World in their Hands

WHAT DOES GLOBALISATION MEAN?

Europe has produced worryingly few management superstars. But one person who unquestionably fits the bill is Percy Barnevik, the chairman of ABB Asea Brown Boveri, an electrical engineering giant. A tall, bearded and fast-talking Swede, with the restless manner of a man over-endowed with energy, Barnevik has won almost every honour which his profession can bestow, from 'emerging markets CEO of the year' to (twice) boss of 'Europe's most respected company'. His name is dropped by the management panjandrums at places like the *Harvard Business Review* almost as frequently as that of Jack Welch of America's General Electric. And the gap is closing fast. 'Our greatest rival is no longer GE,' confesses one Japanese competitor. 'The one we have to be most on guard against is ABB.'

For once, the hyperbole is largely warranted. There are several reasons to praise Barnevik. One is that he has shown how a company can be big and small at the same time: ABB consists of 1,300 separate companies divided into 5,000 profit centres. He has also pioneered such fashionable practices as internal benchmarking, centres of excellence and corporate parenting. But perhaps his foremost quality is his understanding of globalisation.

Conventional wisdom has it that a more integrated world will be a more homogeneous one. Barnevik's view is more subtle. He argues that purely national companies have little chance of thriving as governments deregulate and as the cost of travel and information plummets. But he stresses that companies need to keep deep roots in local markets, because markets will continue to differ. His answer is what he calls a 'multicultural multinational' – a cosmopolitan conglomerate diverse enough to respond to local tastes but united enough to amount to more than the sum of its parts.

In 1988 Barnevik fashioned ABB from two century-old companies: ASEA, the Swedish engineering group that he ran from 1980, and Brown Boveri, an equally proud Swiss competitor. Since then, the company has been involved in more than 100 acquisitions and joint ventures, expanding into Eastern Europe and Asia, and adding (after many lay-offs) 18,000 workers in forty countries.

Barnevik has put a lot of thought into how to bind this disparate empire together. He forces all employees to read his 'bible', a short booklet on the company's aims and values. He made English his firm's official language, although only a third of the employees speak it as their mother tongue (Barnevik himself has a noticeable Swedish accent). He moved ABB's headquarters to Zurich so that the merger would not look like a Swedish take-over. But he keeps the headquarters staff small (currently 171 people from nineteen countries) in order to avoid the impression that ABB is now a Swiss company. In making cuts, he has ensured that the burden is spread fairly evenly. Indeed, the most common criticism is that he treats his native Sweden rather too harshly; he once needed a bodyguard there to protect him from angry former employees.

ABB's multiculturalism relies on an élite cadre of 500 global managers, a praetorian guard that Barnevik selects carefully, paying particular attention to the cultural sensitivity of its members, and to their spouses' willingness to move from place to place quickly. Worth more than their weight in gold, according to Barnevik, their job is to knit the organisation together and to transfer expertise around the world. Another co-ordinating device is Abacus, an information system that is open to all the company's employees. Abacus collects data on each of the company's 5,000 profit centres and compares their performance with budgets and forecasts in both the local currency and American dollars. The company also uses it to spread best practice, sending out a league table of the relative performance of various divisions in ABB and encouraging the worst performers to learn lessons from the best.

In the end, however, a lot of ABB's corporate glue comes

down to Barnevik's own relentlessness. ABBers around the world speak reverently about his ability to get by on four hours' sleep a night and his familiarity with every nook and cranny of the organisation. In January 1997, in an apparent attempt to see his wife slightly more often, Barnevik yielded the chief executiveship of ABB to another Swede, Goran Lindahl. However, Barnevik retains the chairmanship of ABB and seems to spend as much time as ever in a corporate jet. Whoever runs ABB, its history so far seems to illustrate one of the paradoxes of modern management: that the more a company tries to devolve power, the more it relies on a strong leader.

Barnevik argues that the thinking behind ABB is little more than common sense. Who in their right mind, he asks, would not want to be both global and local? And who on earth could think that you can triumph globally by trampling on local differences? The only tricky thing, he argues, is managing such a complicated organisation. But Barnevik undersells himself. The multicultural multinational is in fact the most sophisticated solution to emerge from one of management theory's most enduring debates: globalisation.

An idea whose time has come

Of all the words in the management guru's lexicon, none is used with quite so much relish as 'globalisation'. Go into the business section of any bookshop and you will see the word emblazoned on almost every other book; talk to the chairman of any big company and, before long, you will find that it starts dominating the conversation. That position is not unwarranted. Globalisation – and how to deal with it – is now the leading concern (some would say the *raison d'être*) of nearly every big multinational company: it affects where they have their offices and factories, what they make and who they employ. It is also a growing concern for thousands of smaller firms. Even in a domestic market as big as America's 20 per cent of the firms with fewer than 500 people exported some good or service in 1994 – and the proportion is growing quickly.[1]

The past decade has witnessed huge strides towards integrating the world economy. Governments have progressively lowered trade barriers both internationally, through the Uruguay round of the GATT, and within regions, through the European Union, the North American Free Trade Area, and Latin America's Mercosur. Governments everywhere now regard global companies not as predators to be avoided but as sources of investment, advice and above all jobs. Even the Chinese government, which once promised to wipe these running dogs of capitalism from the surface of the earth, now invites them to set up factories. Over the past decade, foreign direct investment around the world has been growing four times as fast as world output and three times faster than world trade. Roughly a third of trade flows are payments within individual companies, reflecting the way that most companies have production systems that stretch around the world. According to the United Nations there are close to 40,000 'transnational' companies, three times the figure twenty-five years ago: together they control about a third of all private-sector assets and their combined output in 1993 was $5.5 trillion – almost as much as America's.

More telling perhaps than the statistics is the change in attitudes. In the old days, globalisation was about a big company lazily rolling out a product across the world; now Microsoft can launch a relatively sophisticated product, such as Windows 95, simultaneously from Shanghai to San Diego. For many managers, the business lounge of their local international airport is more familiar than their own sitting room. Meanwhile, even those people who manage to avoid this sort of life spend ever more of their day talking to suppliers, customers and colleagues in foreign places. You can send a message on the Internet as easily to Cairo as to Canada.

The idea that the world is getting smaller sounds a simple one. Yet management theory has complicated it in two ways. The first problem is definition. Despite its ubiquity in management books, 'globalisation' has no single meaning. One moment, globalisation can refer to a world-wide marketing campaign, the next to some kind of organisational matrix, then to the irrelevance of national frontiers, and so on. Globalisation is not a coherent idea, rather a fuzzy feeling. This might matter less were the second problem not one of exaggeration. For the three ideas that people have most often plucked out of this cloud – that globalisation would usher in an era of standardised 'global' products; that big, global companies would triumph; and that geography would not matter – have all been shown to be myths.

The three myths of globalisation

The best modern starting point for this debate is 'The Globalisation of Markets', an article in the *Harvard Business Review* in 1983 by Theodore Levitt. Levitt, Harvard's most respected marketing guru, put forward an extreme, though admirably coherent, view of what globalisation meant: he argued that technology was producing 'a new commercial reality – the emergence of global markets on a previously unimagined scale of magnitude'. The world would be dominated by standardised products and universally appealing brands such as Coca–Cola. Christians and Muslims, went Levitt's reasoning, may worship different gods, but they still have to wash their hair – and want the best product to do the job. Global companies which ignored 'superficial' regional and national differences and exploited economies of scale by selling the same things in the same way everywhere would soon push out of the way not only small local companies but also the old sort of multinational company that spent all its time trying to be 'respectful' of local quirks and peccadillos. 'The earth is round,' argued Levitt, 'but, for most purposes, it's sensible to treat it as flat.'

This future – where gigantic firms run by global managers bestrode Levitt's flattened world like so many colossi and entertained global fantasies such as putting a soft drink within an arm's reach of every man, woman and child on the planet – was exactly the sort of thing that many managers had dreamed about for years. After all, what was the point of being a big company if not to defy geography? One of the classic books on multinationals was called *Sovereignty at Bay* (by Philip Vernon, published in 1971). Aurelio Peccei, a director of Fiat, once claimed that the multinational corporation 'is the most powerful agent for the internationalisation of society'. Carl Gerstacker, sometime chairman of Dow Chemical, confessed: 'I have long dreamed of buying an island owned by no nation and of establishing the world headquarters of the Dow company on the truly neutral ground of such an island, beholden to no nation or society.'

This has not happened. The idea that you can sell identical products nearly everywhere in the same way has been thoroughly rubbished. True, there are a few big-ticket items – jumbo jets, for instance – where there is global market, though anybody who visits Boeing's factory in Seattle will be given a long lecture about the way that every aircraft is made differently in order to satisfy its customers. True, also, there are a few niche products that appeal to broadly the same people in the same way around the world: one invariably cited by harassed globalists in interviews is *The Economist*. However, in the broad consumer market, survey after survey has shown that there are only a few truly global brands, such as Coca-Cola, McDonald's and Marlboro, and even this select handful certainly do not mean the same thing in, say, Beijing (where they are all status symbols), as they do in Baltimore.

Indeed, a close look at Coca-Cola's strategy shows that, for all the ubiquitous 'Always Coca-Cola' advertisements, the Atlanta company exploits rather than ignores national differences. It uses independent local bottlers to get its products to local markets. It also tweaks the product's recipe from country to country – and sometimes within them. In Japan, the southern Japanese like their Coca-Cola slightly sweeter than people in Tokyo, and the company obliges. And when it comes to selling other drinks, Coke adopts a very local strategy. Two-thirds of Coca-Cola's Japanese products are made specifically for the local market: Georgia Coffee, for example, can be seen everywhere in Tokyo but is unknown in Coca-Cola's Georgia home.

Indeed, virtually every global brand has had to make concessions to local taste in order to achieve its ubiquity. In Japan, McDonald's stumbled until it allowed a local entrepreneur to set up small stores in the centre of Tokyo, rather than the large suburban stores favoured by the parent company; he also used local meat, which is much fattier than that favoured in America, and even changed Ronald to Donald McDonald to accommodate the local difficulty with Rs. McDonald's hamburgers come with optional Teriyaki sauce in Japan (just as they come with chilli peppers in Mexico). Coke's old rival, PepsiCo, also adjusts both its recipe and its message from country to country. For instance, in Shanghai it has had to dispense with Cindy Crawford's charms (because the locals do not know who she is) and it has had to rename '7-Up' (because in the local dialect, the phrase means 'death through drinking'). Often products can jump one border easily but have difficulties with a second: Mickey Mouse and company hurdled successfully into Tokyo's Disneyland but stumbled initially in Paris.

Indeed, in recent years, marketing has become obsessed with segmenting customers rather than bundling them together. Back in 1983 Levitt wrote as if he assumed that America was one market. Since then, marketing to 'hyphenated Americans' (such as Asian-Americans) has been a booming business. It makes sense when selling, say, a jeep to approach a farmer in Kansas, who might actually use it, in a totally different way from a Hollywood 'urban cowboy', who will only pose in it. And information technology is driving marketing into ever more particular areas, using data culled from checkout scanners and credit-card receipts to pick out ever smaller groups of people, who are then 'targeted' with direct mail and tailored products.

Arguably, the firm that took Levitt's advice most seriously was a British advertising agency, Saatchi & Saatchi. Converted by the article in the *Harvard Business Review*, the Saatchi brothers – who invited Levitt on to their board – went on a headlong quest for expansion, proclaiming 'To be big is good; to be good is better; to be both is best'. This suited a few of Saatchi's clients, notably British Airways, which ended up with a 'global' slogan: 'The world's favourite airline'. But many customers wanted to have a wider spread of local agencies, and complained that Saatchi was just offering them dots on the map. Shareholders fared even worse, as the agency dramatically over-reached itself. Its share price fell to a fiftieth of its previous level and the Saatchi brothers were eventually pushed out in early 1995.

Indeed, in the years since Levitt wrote his article it has often been small companies rather than big ones that have gained most from globalisation. We cover management's debate about size in more detail elsewhere (see Chapter Five, 'Rethinking the Company'). However, it is clear that far from allowing a handful of giant firms to carve up the world between them, globalisation has subjected these firms to humbling competition. The lowering of trade barriers, the spread of deregulation and the plummeting cost of transport and communication means that you no longer need to be a gigantic multinational organisation in order to treat the whole world as your marketplace. In many places the value of two of the traditional multinational's prime resources – its carefully cultivated relationships with government and expensively accumulated knowledge of local regulatory quirks – has disappeared. Microsoft and Swatch both manage to sell software and watches around the world although they keep most of their employees in Seattle and Switzerland.

Other developments have allowed smaller companies to muscle in on the big multinationals' territory. The deregulation of the capital markets has allowed more small companies to borrow serious money. Thanks to the spread of manufacturing techniques, such as just-in-time production and lean manufacturing, multinationals no longer have a monopoly of managerial wisdom, while an epidemic of pirating, reverse engineering and other forms of industrial theft means that they no longer even enjoy a monopoly of their own ideas. And the plummeting price of information technology has allowed smaller companies to engage in the sort of information-dependent innovation that was once the preserve of the giants.

Gurus such as Peter Drucker make much of the fact that the exporters who led America, Britain and Germany out of their recent recessions were all small companies – often specialists. Drucker likes to use the example of one of his neighbours in California who makes special medical beepers for hospitals.[2] Drucker has long since given up being amazed by the places where the man sells his equipment, but his neighbour assures him that it is a fairly risk-free job. Ever since a nasty experience with a sterling devaluation in the 1960s, the man has billed his clients in dollars, eliminating the exchange risk. 'What about the language and the culture?' Drucker once asked his friend after he had returned from installing a new system in Osaka. 'I don't need to understand Japan,' the man replied. 'I understand hospitals.'

Meanwhile, closer inspection reveals that multinationals are often much less multinational than they seem. Many multinationals migrate only as far as their local regions. American firms invest in Central and South America, the Japanese in a handful of Asian countries, and European firms in other European countries. An obvious reason for this is that it is easier to deal with people who are just a short flight away. Another is ties of language and culture. The Japanese, for example, are much happier dealing with the informal alliances and extended company networks of South-East Asia than are the Europeans. If anything, modern management techniques are reinforcing this trend towards regionalisation: the fashion for minimising stocks and delivering supplies on a need-to-use basis means that suppliers need to be located as close as possible to their clients.

How much does geography matter?

The chief protagonists in the wider debate about the importance of geography have been Kenichi Ohmae, a Japanese consultant, and Michael Porter, a professor at Harvard Business School. Both take a more subtle position than Levitt did, but Ohmae comes closer to Levitt's vision of a more homogenised world. Perhaps an enthusiasm for borderlessness should not be surprising in a Japanese man who was educated in America, married an American wife and is given to American vices such as motorcycle riding. Indeed, Ohmae flaunts his global status. His reputation in America is largely based on his ability to explain Japan in terms people from Detroit, Denver and Dallas can understand (the *Financial Times* once unkindly compared him to Benihana of

Tokyo, a restaurant chain that sells westernised Japanese food). Meanwhile in Tokyo, where he used to work for McKinsey, Ohmae is seen as the apostle of all things western – such as cleaner politics and free trade.

Ohmae's books do contain interesting examples of how 'global' firms have become insiders. For instance, Ohmae explains how sales of Barbie dolls improved in Japan only when the size of Barbie's breasts were reduced and her blonde hair replaced with brown. Nevertheless, as the titles of books such as *The Borderless World* suggest, Ohmae believes that, in the end, firms with what he calls 'an Anchorage Perspective' (named after the Alaskan city which is exactly seven hours away from Tokyo, New York and Düsseldorf) will win. He has long argued that a firm needs to be in each of the increasingly similar triad economies – America, Japan and Europe. Ohmae's most recent book, *The End of the Nation State*, introduces yet another variant on the globalisation theme. Today's engines of growth, he argues, are not 'dysfunctional' nation states but 'natural economic zones' that cross national boundaries such as Hong Kong-South China or Tijuana-San Diego.

Put the trans-border entities identified by Ohmae together with superstates such as the European Union and the cyberstate created by the Internet and you begin to have a case for the decline of the nation state that sounds plausible. It is not. Globalisation is certainly forcing national governments to be less insular and more interdependent. It is also (thank God) teaching people more about each other. But there are still clear divisions. The defeat of communism has not left any shortage of things for nations to quarrel about – whether it be Islam, Asian values or fishing policies. And throughout most of the world there are recognisable nations that want to stay in their traditional shapes. True, countries have handed over some economic power to trade organisations, but, the European Union aside, they have shown very few signs of wanting to yield political sovereignty. And whilst Western Europe may be coming together, Eastern Europe has broken up.

As Michael Porter, a professor at the Harvard Business School, has argued, this matters to companies as well as politicians, for firms owe a remarkable amount of what makes them tick to their local origins. In *The Competitive Advantage of Nations*, Porter argued that different countries (and regions) have different competitive strengths: the Germans excel at high-quality engineering and chemicals, the Japanese at miniaturisation and electronics, the British at pop music and publishing, the Americans at films and computers. A German engineering firm will not necessarily become any better at engineering if it becomes less Germanic and more global, or a Californian software company if it becomes less Californian; indeed, it needs to retain its local roots if it is to find good recruits and suppliers or, more importantly, to remain in daily contact with challenging competitors.

Alfred Marshall, one of the founders of modern economics, once remarked, in an analysis of steel-making in Sheffield, that certain skills seemed to be 'in the air' in some regions. Some of these centres of excellence are familiar: Silicon Valley in computing, the Prato region of northern Italy in fashion and design, Hollywood in film-making. In an increasingly mobile world, such places represent stubbornly immobile resources: their skills are too bound up with the local culture to be easily copied elsewhere. Nobody has yet tried to build a cheaper Hollywood.

Far from contemptuously ignoring these geographic irritations, multinationals now bow down before them. Witness the number of Japanese electronics firms that have an outpost in Silicon Valley; witness too the way that firms that already have roots in centres of excellence are digging deeper, supporting schools, funding charities and so on. John Stopford of the London Business School argues that firms should hand across what he calls their 'world product mandates' to affiliates which are located in the right areas. Thus America's Du Pont has moved its electronics-related businesses to Japan, Germany's Siemens has moved its air-traffic management business to Britain, and South Korea's Hyundai its personal-computer business to the United States. A few small companies have gone the whole hog and uprooted themselves entirely. TomTec Imaging Systems is a German company with a turnover of $21m that is the world leader in one small, highly technological part of the medical ultrasound market. In 1993, conscious of the fact that many of its customers were in America, it upped sticks from its base near Munich and transplanted itself in Boulder, Colorado.[3]

Becoming an insider means more than just buying a few assets – however expensive they might be. On the face of it Sony and Matsushita did the right thing by buying into the entertainment industry's 'centre of excellence' – Hollywood. However both Japanese companies were utterly confused by the industry, particularly by its reliance on 'ears' or 'eyes' who could predict if an artist would sell or a film would be successful. As a result the Japanese vacillated between giving their spendthrift employees much too free a hand (for a time, the Hollywood hills were jammed with builders' trucks and delivery vehicles winding their way up to the rapidly expanding homes of Japanese-paid moguls) and then suddenly clamping down. One reason why MCA's long-time chairman, Lew Wasserman, rebelled against Matsushita in 1995 was that the Japanese company would not let the studio expand in areas such as music and multimedia. Bertelsmann, a staid German publishing company that bought several American music and book-publishing groups, has done better than the Japanese but has not had an easy time of it – not least because its executives annoyed American managers by conducting private conversations in German during meetings.

However, the best reason for thinking like an insider, not just a citizen of Anchorage (not one of the world's wealthier cities), is simply that you sell more products. Remember Coca-Cola and McDonald's efforts to go native in Japan. Or look at how Switzerland's Nestlé has built itself into the biggest foreign food firm in Japan by offering Japanese families products such as packaged cereals that taste like seaweed. By contrast, America's car makers made no concessions to the fact that the Japanese prefer small cars, and drive on the left-hand side of the road – something that George Bush's ludicrous trip to Tokyo in 1992, when he and a group of car company executives tried to force Japan to open its markets, did little to change.

The transnational corporation

By now it should be pretty clear that globalisation does not entail a lot of things which are popularly associated with it – the triumph of monolithic companies, the eclipse of local differences, or the omnipresence of global products. But this does not mean that globalisation is meaningless. After all, the things that gave the idea such power are real enough – falling trade barriers, the ability to move ideas, people and money around the globe with ever increasing speed. Globalisation may not make much sense as a business strategy but as a phenomenon it still presents both problems and opportunities to companies of all sizes.

In particular, a firm that can manufacture its products globally, making use of the different cultures rather than trampling all over them, looks a very powerful one. Such a company might act as an arbitrageur between various local centres of excellence, putting, for instance, Italian designers in touch with Japanese experts in miniaturisation, and then combining these various local skills with whatever global resources it can get access to.

By the mid-1990s, there were signs that this subtler, geographi-cally sensitive version of globalisation had a lot going for it. The question, as ever, was how you construct a company to take advantage of it. The two best answers so far are 'the transnational corporation', a phrase coined jointly by Christopher Bartlett of Harvard Business School and Sumantra Ghoshal of London Business School, and 'the multicultural multinational', epitomised by Barnevik's ABB. These unlovely sounding organisations both involve playing around with the matrix systems that lie at the heart of most multinationals, where most people report to both a geographic boss (such as the country manager) and a product manager (the head of the global car division).

The transnational corporation is a tidying-up process. For most of this century big companies were loose affiliations of national firms that happened to share the same name. Companies such as

Ford and Unilever originally dealt with the problems of high tariffs, prohibitive transport costs and stringent local-content rules by making clones of themselves in all the countries where they operated, with their own head offices, design facilities and production plants. This was extremely expensive at the best of times. At one point, Ford had two 'Escorts' on the road which had been designed and built entirely separately. Now that tariffs are much lower, many of these things can be integrated into a global system without necessarily destroying the company's local feel.

Recently, there has been a trend towards companies giving national subsidiaries responsibility for global products or global functions, partly to disperse decision-making throughout the organisation and partly to capture local expertise. For instance, Nestlé has put the headquarters of its pasta business in Italy, and Johnson & Johnson has given its German subsidiary a world-wide mandate for tampons. Meanwhile at IBM, Lou Gerstner has set up fourteen broad global product groups which have taken power away from the company's once all-powerful national chieftains.

The most ambitious attempt to build a transnational company is the 'Ford 2000' plan that began in January 1995. The American car maker had edged towards building 'world cars' over the previous decade, with different parts of its empire collaborating on design. But its chairman, Alex Trotman, decided it could go further: under Ford 2000, the company abolished a score of separate national units in Europe and North America and replaced them with five product teams, some of them headquartered in Europe. Trotman admits the project has been made possible only by the sort of technology that allows people in different locations to work on the same project: visit Ford's design centre in Dearborn, Michigan, and you will hear Germanic voices booming out of loudspeakers, as engineers on both sides of the Atlantic haggle over the shapes appearing on the screens in front of them. By developing one common small-car chassis and cutting the overall development time from thirty-seven months to twenty-four by 1999, Ford hopes to cut its product development costs (currently $8 billion a year) by 30 per cent. Meanwhile, by setting up a world-wide purchasing system and weeding out suppliers, Trotman hopes to knock $700 off the cost of manufacturing each vehicle.

Surely this sort of integration is just globalisation by another name? The difference is that transnational companies are much more particular about which products they think they can market across borders, and far more sensitive in the way that they do it. For instance, Ford 2000 is not a global programme: it applies only to North America and Europe. It also deals only with smaller cars, and, although the chassis may now be the same, the styling and marketing remain very much in the hands of local managers. Indeed, confronted by a geographic difference, a transnational company usually retreats. General Electric is only one of several companies to break with policies of dividing operations into global product lines by setting up a regional headquarters in Asia. In China, multinationals are learning quickly that Beijing likes to deal with just one local boss who can speak for all the company's product lines: hence the rush to set up 'China centres'.

Sometimes this sensitivity makes for some fairly confusing corporate history – as Unilever's Western European food operations show. In the early 1990s, as part of a plan codenamed 'Beethoven', the Anglo-Dutch giant centralised its food operations in preparation for the 1992 Single Market.[4] Then it realised that it had gone too far, so it handed back some marketing powers to its national chieftains. But it continued to centralise production. By 1996 20 per cent of Unilever's ice-cream production in Europe was sold across borders, seven times the proportion in 1992; with factories being consolidated rapidly (and ruthlessly) the aim was to reach 35 per cent by 1999. Unilever also divided its food business in each country in Europe into two product-based units (basically, frozen and non-frozen). This 'market locally but produce regionally' strategy might seem relatively simple but there was also a separate 'masterplan'. This dictated that the company should try to expand in some products (particularly, ice cream and margarine) and in some markets (Latin America and Asia), though not necessarily in both at the same time. Analysts expect Niall FitzGerald, Unilever's new British chairman from

August 1996, to push through another bout of centralisation – though that, doubtless, will be followed by more fits of localisation.

Reasons to be global

This to-ing and fro-ing prompts a more fundamental question: why bother? The reason is the belief that a properly co-ordinated multinational company can devote far more resources to any particular product than either a national company or an old-fashioned multinational. In some industries, such as jet aircraft and semiconductors, companies have always needed to sell their products globally to recoup their investments. Now the cost of innovation has sky-rocketed in a whole range of businesses. In the 1960s, Siemens had to capture only half of the German market to amortise the cost of developing an electromechanical switch; soon it will have to capture 20 per cent of the global market. Hollywood used to think only about the American box office; nowadays it would go bust without foreign markets.

Although McDonald's insists that it is a chain of local restaurants staffed by local people and often owned by them, it also centralises some things to cut costs. Its global team of specialists can now erect a new McDonald's restaurant out of modular parts in as little as eleven days, cutting the cost of building the restaurants by a third. A global purchasing team has saved the company $200m a year by cutting back on the number of its suppliers. Ikea, an international furniture company, has a specialised team to set up new stores. The team plans the building, supervises its construction, masterminds the launch, operates the store and trains the local team; after a year it hands over to the locals and heads off to do the same thing somewhere else in the world.

A good 'big firm' like McDonald's or Ikea can use the same basic advertising ploy to sell its product around the globe. OC&C Strategy, a London-based consultancy, has calculated that the advertising and promotion costs needed to convince a customer to try out a new product are, on average, 36 per cent less for a 'recognised' brand than for an unfamiliar one. The cost of developing an international brand in Europe, Japan and the United States has been put as high as $1 billion. A big multinational can also afford to experiment (if a product or a strategy fails in Sweden, then so be it).

By themselves, such economies of scale count for little, as the first failed round of globalisation proved; but, if they can be subsumed into a network that mixes and matches knowledge from around the world, they become much more potent. The United Nations Conference on Trade and Development, which keeps watch on transnational companies, distinguishes between two different types of integration, simple and complex. In simple integration, companies keep their most sophisticated operations in their home country, but contract out other production to the developing world. This tends to suit smaller multinationals. Nike, the American sportswear maker, does all its product development and marketing in its home town in Oregon, but sub-contracts production to forty other locations, mostly in Asia. Whenever the wages in the host country get too high, the firm simply shifts production to a cheaper country. Japan's Mabuchi Motors, which makes the tiny wheels which drive things like cameras and windscreen wipers, has moved all its routine production offshore, much of it to China's Guangdong province, but it has kept all its most valuable activities at home.

In complex integration, companies locate all their activities according to the logic of the market. They also disperse decision-making throughout their organisations rather than keeping it in head office. Their hallmark is the endless flow of information in all directions, horizontally as well as vertically. Xerox, an office equipment maker, is a good example of this evolution. In the early 1980s, Xerox was really just a coalition of national affiliates, such as Britain's Rank Xerox and Japan's Fuji Xerox: each firm did virtually everything itself. But competition from cheaper, more flexible Japanese companies such as Canon forced Xerox to integrate its activities. Xerox has introduced global product-development teams and centralised procurement, reducing the number of suppliers from 5,000 to 400. But it has also made it clear that it is a union of equals where all the parts are expected to come up with ideas.

Reinventing companies to make better use of knowledge is always difficult (see Chapter Seven), but doing so across borders is particularly fraught. Occasionally, transnational companies have had to deal with wholesale revolts by corporate barons, as IBM did in Italy. After the failures of the 1980s, companies have grown more cautious about imposing globalisation plans from above. Trotman admits that for much of 1994 Ford was run by 'the second team' because he forced senior managers to spend most of their time working out how they were going to implement Ford 2000. The firm's headquarters in Dearborn boasts a huge board, signed by all its senior managers expressing their commitment to Ford 2000.

And yet it can still be a hard slog. Despite Trotman's care and commitment, changing Ford's culture will probably take a decade. At Monsanto, another big American company that is trying to reorganise, senior staff refer to 'centralisation' as 'the C-word'. In 1995 Royal Dutch/Shell, a group that has always thrived on decentralisation, also moved to a hierarchy based around product-groups. This seemed certain to produce productivity gains, but insiders worried that these would be wiped out by 'softer' losses – such as the company's famous 'Shell Man' culture. There is a risk, one former director admitted, of 'the baby being thrown out with the bath water'.

The multicultural multinational

All this seems to underline a fundamental point: that, when it comes to globalisation, a company's people are more important than its products. Indeed, this is arguably the main reason why small firms, such as Peter Drucker's 'friend who knows hospitals', have so far generally done so much better than big global firms. Look at virtually any failed globalisation strategy and you will find that the company's staff did not go along with it. For instance, no matter how often the Saatchi brothers told their award-winning London agency to recommend their New York one, the copywriters and account executives in Charlotte Street regarded their Manhattan branch as a second-division outfit – and sometimes told their clients so. Nor are admen particularly extreme. The words 'not invented here' could appear on the graves of most globalisation strategies.

Yet, if multinational firms often represent the worst of all worlds, they also hold out – tantalisingly – the promise one day of representing the best of most. For their current weakness should also be their greatest strength: their variety. A multinational has access to a much larger pool of management talent than a small firm; it is also exposed to a wider range of stimuli, about such things as consumer needs, technological changes and competitors' moves. If a multinational does not use that knowledge, then it might as well close its subsidiaries and hire subcontractors; but if it exploits that multiculturalism the effect should be electric. It is this holy grail that Barnevik has pursued at ABB.

Nevertheless, the hunt for the multicultural multinational begins with a health warning. In many cases a firm's most valuable resource is its internal culture, the more distinctive the better. Visiting one of the world's great companies is rather like visiting a cult: people have their local heroes (the founder, the current chairman and one or two others), their local war stories (how the founder hit upon his winning idea) and even their local language. The 'HP way' is as Californian as decaffeinated coffee. Ford's workers seem to have nicknames for everything in their Dearborn headquarters.

However, there are two reasons why most multinationals should not be put off by the health warning. The first is still largely theoretical: multiculturalism should work for companies just as it does for countries. From Hong Kong to California, there has been one sure-fire way to inject some vitality into your economy: immigration. One reason why America's economy pulled ahead of Europe's and Japan's in the 1980s was that it opened itself up to foreign investment and foreign brainpower. Japanese know-how and competition helped to revitalise America's rust belt. Surely individual companies can gain from introducing alien cultures into their midst?

This seems likely given the fact that even imported knowledge of the most mundane sort can be a potent weapon. For example, a French company, Danone, has rapidly become the biggest biscuit firm in Asia by importing 'biscuit technology' to make biscuits that do not crumble. One of Philips' most successful recent products, an up-market large-screen television, was pushed into production only when the Dutch firm's head office received a desperate memo from Jack Lau, head of its marketing team in Hong Kong, highlighting the dramatic increase in demand for such products in the region. Philips is now moving more and more of its electronics business to South-East Asia, which is arguably the world's most creative and competitive electronics market.

The other reason why most big companies will become more multicultural is practical: they have no choice. The three pioneers of multiculturalism – Shell, Unilever and ABB – were all the products of mixed marriages. 'We were used to pushing together Dutch and English people; adding other varieties was fairly easy,' points out one Shell man, noting that there are forty nationalities in the company's head office. In Europe, nowadays, the single market is making miscegenation the rule rather than the exception. Already some 150,000 Britons work for German companies; many argue that they get the best of both worlds.

Japanese companies, according to Tadahiro Sekimoto, the chairman of NEC, a giant electronics group, used to practise what he calls 'radial globalisation' in which overseas offices were tied to the head office at the centre.[5] In the future, the norm is likely to become 'an organic network that links all overseas branches'. Management, he believes, must become more 'holonic', 'where each part acts independently but when viewed from the whole all is in balance'. To attain this state of harmony, the vital ingredient is a company's own corporate culture. 'In this age of globalisation, corporate culture has become the fifth management asset that stands on a par with labour, material, capital and information.' Even in Asia, Japanese firms have discovered that treating locals as 'dumb terminals' is self-defeating. Korea's *chaebol* may also be forced to reach the same conclusion: they have feuded with

German employees over works councils, and there have been rumours of fist fights between locals and their militaristic superiors.

In America, the pressure for a more multicultural future is coming not only from globalisation but also from domestic demographics. By 2000 white males will make up only 45 per cent of America's workforce. In 1993, a sales manager for Avon Products in Atlanta spotted an influx of Korean and Vietnamese immigrants, so she quickly recruited a squadron of Asian ladies to sell cosmetics. Avon cleaned up. It now has a 'multicultural participation council' to encourage diversity amongst employees. Sales at Sears stores sited close to Hispanic areas have risen since the firm recruited Spanish-speaking workers. AT&T has built support among recent immigrants with its Language Line, offering translations in 140 languages.

There are a few signs that such intermingled American firms do better abroad. Avon, for instance, has been very successful in both China and South America. More generally, globalisation gives these hyphenated Americans another use. Witness the rush to find ABCs (American-born Chinese) to send to China. Worried about the image of the 'ugly American', unable to speak any languages and brutally insensitive to cultural differences, companies have begun to put pressure on American business schools to become more international – to recruit their staff and students from as many countries as possible.

One result of this new sensitivity has been a dramatic turnaround in the image of multinationals. In the bad old days, when Vietnam protesters used to chant 'We won't fight for Texaco', the word multinational was synonymous with firms such as Harold Geneen's ITT, which tried to subvert the Chilean government and spent millions of dollars on illegal activities in Indonesia, Iran and Italy (to name only the countries beginning with 'I'). Nowadays, multinationals have a cleaner, greener image. They queue to endorse worthy international agreements such as the International Chamber of Commerce's Business Charter for Sustainable Development. More surprisingly, they usually stick to them – partly because a single global standard is easier to follow and partly because it usually makes life more difficult for their poorer local competitors.

The people test

Every multinational is happy to have a better image. But images are fragile things. In early 1996 Ford faced a rumpus in Europe when it emerged that it had doctored a British advertisement showing workers from its Dagenham factory so that when the ad appeared in Poland all the black faces were replaced by white ones. Ironically, the American car maker's excuse, though mocked in the British press and received with horror in Dagenham, would make sense to students of multicultural multinationals: it claimed it was being sensitive, adapting a global campaign to local tastes (there are not many black faces in Poland).

This bizarre episode shows how hard it is for companies to keep up their multicultural reputation. But even harder than keeping up appearances is making a reality of the idea. The real test of multiculturalism – not to mention the only lasting source of profits from it – is how you use your own people. One good place to look is the boardroom. After all, by appointing only a handful of foreign faces, a company can send a clear message that the top positions are not reserved for locals only. At first sight, big companies seem to have done pretty well. Who would have guessed twenty years ago that Ford would be run by a Scot (Alex Trotman), L'Oréal by a Welshman (Lindsay Owen Jones), Heinz by an Irishman (Tony O' Reilly) and McKinsey by an Indian (Rajat Gupta)?

Yet when you look beneath the surface of many multinationals you discover that they are still stubbornly ethnocentric. For all Sekimoto's talk of holonic management, Japanese firms remain the worst offenders, but American firms are also guilty. The proportion of foreign-born board members in America's biggest firms was the same in 1991 as in 1981, 2.1 per cent, according to Susan Schneider, a professor at Insead.[6] Look further down the organisation and you find suspicions of national favouritism abound. Ford Assembly Operations, for example, is known as 'For Americans Only' by European staff. In 1995 the International Consortium for Executive Development Research, based in Lexington, Massachusetts, asked 1,500 managers from twelve large companies to rank their abilities in thirty-four different categories: 'cultivating a global mindset' finished last.

Given these difficulties, it is not surprising that few multinationals make the most out of cultural mixing. After all, there is nothing particularly multicultural about letting American brains boss around Asian hands, as Nike does. What you want to see being produced abroad is not just sneakers but ideas. According to a study by John Cantwell, an economist at Britain's Reading University, only 9 per cent of the patents issued to American multinationals in the 1980s were for work done by overseas companies. For European firms the ratio was 30 per cent – though the chances are that most of those ideas came from other European countries.

The most powerful force for change is technology – or, to be more accurate, information. Video-conferencing, software programs such as Lotus Notes and now the 'Intranet' of on-line company networks all allow different people from different places to work on the same ideas. At its most extreme, this can mean letting German and American designers haggle on line about the same engine part (as already happens at Ford). One of the best ways of using information technology is to spread 'best practice' around the company. Many companies have star plants, like Motorola's pager plant in Florida, which they encourage everybody else to beat.

However, technology will only do so much. In the end, 'multicultural multinationals' require an enormous amount of human effort as well. Nestlé sets up periodic internal conferences, arranging regular short-term visits and rotating key personnel between its various technical and research centres. Richard Branson invites Virgin employees and Virgin Atlantic's most frequent travellers (together with their families) to chaotic summer picnics at his house. All the same, much of the burden falls on that old war-horse: the 'ex-pat' manager. This is not ideal.

Ex-pats are horrendously expensive, costing more than double what it takes to employ a local, and increasingly hard to get hold of – particularly if the job being offered is in Beijing or Karachi rather than London or Paris. Their flexibility has also been undermined by sexual equality: the rise of the dual-career couple means that a firm often has to uproot two people to send one somewhere. However, without an international officer class of some sort, centrifugal forces take over.

The battle ahead

Can such multicultural organisations outwit people such as Peter Drucker's friend 'who understands hospitals' or a firm using sub-contractors around the world? The answer is that it is too early to say. As David De Pury, ABB's co-chairman, put it in 1994: 'There are very few multicultural multinationals; the truly global multicultural company does not yet exist.' For every new internal information system that helps one of the monster companies to become more human and flexible, there is an Internet site that allows small entrepreneurs to swap ideas about their industries.

All that can be said with certainty are two things: first, that even though globalisation and geography may be intractable problems, they are ones that every company of any size has to face up to; and, second, that this new knowledge-based, multicultural version of globalisation stands a far better chance of working with geography than its predecessor stood of vanquishing it. That is why the endless peregrination of Percy Barnevik, and his successors, may just be worthwhile.

THE ART OF JAPANESE MANAGEMENT

In the West, paternalist companies used to be in the habit of building company towns. In Japan, Toyota has built a company city. Two hours south-west of Tokyo, by bullet train, Toyota City is proof, if any is needed, of the continuing might of Japanese manufacturing. Home to ten gigantic car plants, which churn out three million vehicles a year, the city dominates the life of the entire region. The surrounding towns exist for the sole purpose of producing parts for Toyota City's factories. It is rare to see one of the city's 350,000 inhabitants without a Toyota badge somewhere on his jacket or baseball cap. The whole place is, in effect, a gigantic machine, forever grinding out Toyota products.

But it is the way the machine does the grinding, rather than its awesome size, that has captured the attention of the world – and also changed it. This is a place where manufacturers of all races still come to gawk. It is also one of the few factories that can be classed as a successful showcase for applied management theory.

At first sight, this seems a strange claim. Life inside Toyota City's factories seems much like life in car factories the world over – the usual mix of clattering robots, blowtorch-wielding welders and, of course, assembly lines. But look a little closer and important differences emerge. The armies of workers who clog the aisles around western assembly lines are missing. Almost everybody on Toyota's shop floor is busy adding value. Missing, too, are the shelf-loads of inventory that are common in the West. Toyota's workers have only about an hour's worth of inventory to hand, conveniently stored on shoulder-high shelves next to their workstations. A constant flow of traffic – bicycles, small trucks and even unmanned carts, playing high-pitched electronic tunes to warn you of their presence – deliver material to workers so that they can lay their hands 'just in time' on whatever they need without keeping expensive supplies of spares.

Yet, amidst all this haste, each worker has the power to bring the assembly line to a halt, pulling a wire above his head if he (there are no women to be seen) spots a fault. And the news of the fault is immediately flashed on to one of the many electronic boards suspended above the ceiling that also tell everybody how many cars have been made and how near the line is to hitting its target. Indeed, the general air is of competitive collaboration, with each team vying to be the most efficient. One young man displays a tool he invented a couple of years ago to make it easier to insert the steering column into its shaft. The tool is now used in Toyota's factories around the world. A second worker shows off another invention (this time from another factory): a mobile chair, suspended from the ceiling, which allows him to dart in and out of the passing cars without having to clamber all over them. The management puts an unusual amount of emphasis on the workers' comfort. Robots do the back-breaking work of lifting rather than the skilled work of welding. The cars are suspended above the ground so that the workers can insert parts without bending down. Spare parts are stored at eye-level for the same reason.

It is worth bearing Toyota City in mind when you talk to Japan's gloomy business people. For most of the 1990s all they have been able to talk about is the high yen's crippling effect on exporters and the recession which followed the bursting of the bubble economy. A fairly typical conversation in November 1995 with the president of the Keidanren, one of Japan's leading employers' organisations, produced a long catalogue of complaints. Japan's companies were too fat, its employees too cosseted, its population too conformist, its interest groups too powerful, moaned the president. To revive its flagging fortunes, the country needed to deregulate its industries, get rid of lifetime employment and become more entrepreneurial.

All of this is true, of course. But we should not forget just how powerful much of the Japanese economy remains. In 1996 Japan was the world's second biggest economy, after the United States, and the third biggest exporter, after the United States and Germany. Japan created 3.2 million jobs during the recession of the early 1990s, and its unemployment rate in mid-1997 was only 3.3 per cent. Japan's GNP rose from 55 per cent of that of the United States in 1989 to 63 per cent in 1996, in current exchange rates. And the country owes a lot of its success to the way that companies like Toyota have out-managed their rivals.

This chapter will start by looking at one of the few incontrovertible examples of management theory being used to the good: the way that Japan's revolutionary manufacturing system – lean production – helped to transform shop floors throughout the world. We will also look at the Japanese approach to strategy and continuous improvement, both of which once seemed so unstoppable. Next, we will look at the reasons why Japanese industry has run into trouble, and at the ways in which the country's businessmen are trying to learn from western management thinkers. And then we will end by asking what Japan can still teach the West.

The allure of quality

It might seem far-fetched to argue that Japan's post-war growth has anything to do with management theory. After all, the average salaryman, relaxing after a ten-hour day over yakitori and sake, hardly spends his time talking about Drucker-San and Peters-San. Indeed, critics of management theory happily point out that Japan has only a few business schools, none of them very prestigious, and that, thirty years after arriving, western consultancies are still struggling to make ends meet. Indeed, it is because they do not have to pay the consultancies' inflated fees, the argument goes, that companies have more money to devote to 'real' investment; and because they are not tempted to follow the latest management fashions that they can develop a coherent, long-term strategy.

The sceptics are right in one respect. Japan has so far produced only one first-division guru of its own, Kenichi Ohmae (though a generation of young pretenders is emerging). Many of the 'gurus' who appear in this chapter are business people rather than professors. Nevertheless, those businessmen have thought about management just as broadly as Drucker, Peters *et al*; and their names are no less associated with theories of how to run businesses.

Moreover, in their central criticism, the sceptics are simply wrong. Japan owes a huge debt to management theory – in particular to a group of American theorists whose ideas inspired the Japanese to come up with 'lean production'. In the best study of that revolution, *The Machine that Changed the World*, James Womack, Daniel Jones and Daniel Roos present their conclusions in no uncertain terms: 'Lean production is a superior way for humans to make things. It provides better products in wider variety at lower cost. Equally important, it provides more challenging and fulfilling work for employees at every level, from the factory to headquarters.'[1]

Lean production was inspired by a set of American theories about quality that Japanese businesses first discovered during the post-war American occupation. In a nutshell, these ideas focused on the importance of getting things right first time rather than spending a lot of energy checking them afterwards – an obvious enough sounding notion but one that went against the grain of the standard corporate model of the time, which assumed that quality was something you checked after you had built your motor car (indeed, you had a quality department to do it).

Even today Japanese managers still speak of Joseph Juran and W. Edwards Deming in the same hushed tones that people normally reserve for a deity. Since 1950 an annual Deming Prize, including a medal bearing the face of the great man, has been awarded for excellence in manufacturing, and prize-winners are featured on Japanese television. Having been more or less ignored in America in the early 1950s, Deming and his friends were given the red-carpet treatment in Japan. Whenever they lectured in Japan, the halls were packed to the gods with engineers and production managers. Whatever they wrote was immediately translated into Japanese and devoured by managers the length and breadth of the country.

The Japanese realised that their goods were hopelessly shoddy by international standards; and they were also awe-struck by the might of the American economy and the sheer profusion of American products. So American gurus who were willing to visit Japan and talk about quality were manna from heaven. Even so, there were specific reasons why Deming's ideas seemed so attractive in Japan. Businesses in a grotesquely over-crowded country do not have the space to keep large quantities of inventory hanging around for months. After the war, Japan could not afford to waste precious (imported) raw materials on throw-away products or crummy machinery. Japan also lacked the migrant workers who provided Henry Ford with his factory fodder; and a surge of industrial unrest made it clear that Japanese workers were no longer willing to be treated as mere costs of production. Perhaps only a nation which loves sushi could have such an instinctive understanding of 'just-in-time' delivery.

The lean, mean machine

The original ideas might have come from across the Pacific, but it was two Japanese, Kiichiro Toyoda, boss of Toyota, and Taiichi Ohno, his right-hand man, who transformed these theories into a new system of production. They did so by turning themselves into management theorists – visiting American factories for months on end during the 1950s and studying mass production to see what made it so successful and how it could be bettered. They found the system rife with *muda* – a Japanese term that encompasses wasted effort, wasted material and wasted time. Nobody except the assembly worker was adding much value, they noticed, and the emphasis on keeping the line running at all times meant that errors multiplied endlessly.[2]

The two eventually put all the pieces together to create an entirely new system of production – dubbed the 'Toyota manufacturing system' by Toyota and 'lean production' by almost everybody else. Its genius was to shift the focus of manufacturing from economies of scale to 'economies of time'. It did this in three ways. The first was by making every employee a quality checker, responsible for spotting errors as they happened and correcting them immediately. Instead of installing a quality department as its American rivals did, Toyota gave workers the right to stop the production line as soon as they saw errors – hence all those cords hanging along the production line.

The second improvement came from introducing 'just-in-time' production. In the rest of the world, manufacturers made their components 'just in case' they were needed. They filled bins, pallets and warehouses with days' or even weeks' worth of costly parts, which gathered dust until they were finally needed. The Japanese started making components 'just-in-time', with parts arriving just as they were needed on the production line.

The third way to save time was 'demand pull'. Components in western factories were traditionally delivered by 'supply push' arrangements, with goods piling up when they were not needed. With 'demand pull' they are made to order. At Toyota, a *kanban*, or card, is attached to every box of supplies describing its contents. Returning the card to the supplier automatically reorders a further shipment. The 'demand pull' system even extends to the customer. Instead of relying on customers to wander into their local Toyota dealership and express a preference for a particular car, Toyota has an army of door-to-door car salesmen. The theory is that customers will tell these salesmen what sort of car they want and the factory will then make their car to order.

This procedure challenges the entire basis of mass production, which was (and in many parts of the world still is) the dominant manufacturing philosophy. Mass production depends on two things, economies of scale and specialisation. Workers, it is supposed, need to become more and more specialised in order to do their job more efficiently. And factories need to grow bigger and bigger to achieve economies of scale. However, as the Japanese realised, this system also entails two costs.

The first is the inability of a classic mass-production system to respond to rapid changes in demand. Mass producers tend to be much keener on keeping standardised designs in production than in experimenting with new products, partly because of the heavy costs of changing the production line and partly because their specialised workers are happiest with what they know. A change in fashion may mean that the factory has to close down for months as machines are recalibrated and workers retrained. It may also force producers to throw away huge quantities of expensively stored but now obsolete inventory. By the time it is capable of mass producing the new product the demand may have changed once again.

The second cost is an unacceptably high rate of faulty products. Large batches make it difficult to detect defects. This means that a defective part may not reveal itself until the finished car finally breaks down. It is easier for the next person on the assembly line to check a small batch. And a worker making only a small batch is more likely to feel like a craftsman, and less like a cog in a huge machine. The trouble with mass production is that it usually achieves its economies of scale by reducing jobs to drudgery. By contrast, lean production continues to engage at least some of the intellectual gifts of the workers. The worker can see the impact of his workmanship – good or bad – on the company's manufacturing process. Pats on the back from his colleagues result from a job well done, scowls from a job skimped.

Lean producers ram home this concept of responsibility by making everybody aware not only of what they are doing but how well they are doing it. One way to do this is 'quality circles' – talking shops at which people sit around discussing their performance and everybody becomes a quality inspector. Another Japanese trait is to provide continuous information to the workers: hence the lighted electronic displays that are visible at every workstation in Toyota's factories.

Lean production also involved rethinking the boundaries of the firm – in particular its relationship with its suppliers. In the West, companies have been through two stages. First, they tried to make virtually all the car themselves, setting up their own parts-making divisions. When the fashion turned against such 'vertical integration' western companies then opted for a second system based on competing suppliers. They provided a large number of suppliers with a detailed drawing of what they wanted and then offered a one-year contract to the supplier who could come up with the best price.

The classic form of Japanese supply-chain management, again pioneered by Toyota, works in a different way. The suppliers can be formally separate companies, or they can be members of the same *keiretsu* (a group of companies linked by cross-shareholdings). In either case, the parent company treats them as partners rather than playing them off against each other. The suppliers provide the goods 'just-in-time' in return for long-term relationships with the main manufacturers. Companies cement these relationships by sending mid-career managers to high-level positions in supplier companies or other members of a *keiretsu*. This means all parts of the supply chain can pool resources and also share information – thus once again cutting down on time-wasting. Even today Toyota can still design and build a car twice as fast as an American-owned factory in Detroit.

Kenichi Ohmae, *kaizen* and consensus

If lean production represents the core of 'the Japanese miracle', there are two other ingredients which, until relatively recently, were also considered indispensable parts of it: the doctrine of continuous improvement – or *kaizen*; and the value of consensus, especially when applied to long-term strategic thinking. A good way to look at both is through the work of Kenichi Ohmae.

Ohmae is now best known inside Japan for his attempt to set up a new political party. But he began to write the books which made his name in the rest of the world while working as a consultant for McKinsey. Like most gurus, Ohmae has been happy to pontificate on almost any subject within the realms of politics and economics. (In an interview with one of the authors he repeatedly compared himself with Margaret Thatcher.) In some ways this diversity fits a bilingual, Harley Davidson-riding polymath, who could have been, amongst other things, a nuclear engineer. All the same, Ohmae's main contribution to management theory can be summed up in two words: Japan and globalisation.

We discussed Ohmae's contribution to globalisation in the last chapter. But it is his knowledge of Japan that established his reputation. For most of the past quarter century, outsiders, particularly American business people, have been fascinated and frightened by Japan. Ohmae has explained it to them – showering his books with good insider examples of how Japanese companies work and usually criticising American firms in the process. Even in his later 'global' books, nearly all the memorable examples, such as the invention of a heated loo-seat with an electronically controlled bidet, come from Japan. And the best chapters tend to deal with subjects such as how to set up alliances in Japan.

Ohmae writes about innovation particularly well. By Japanese standards, he has a high appreciation of the maverick. He favours splitting a research budget into three equal parts: one for routine research (catching up with competitors, trying to make your own products cheaper), one for long-range strategic research, and one for wild-card projects. However, Ohmae has generally tended to exalt the Japanese way of producing new products through continuous improvement.

Innovation, argues Ohmae, is useless unless it adds value for consumers. He tends to pour scorn on big R&D projects, such as high-definition television, and revels in meeting challenges incrementally, particularly in mundane fields. Can you make a better coffee machine – i.e. not just one with lots of fancy gadgets but one that makes better coffee? Yes, we discover, if you add a water purifier, because the taste of coffee depends as much on the quality of the water as it does on how you percolate the beans. Can you make a better camera? Yes, if you get it to do the focusing for you (i.e. remove the human error that ruins most pictures) and include an automatic flash.

A strategy of churning out products with lots of minuscule improvements fits in quite nicely with lean production. After all, one advantage of a flexible assembly line is that it can be altered quite easily in order to incorporate a new insight and include a new innovation. It also means that you can smother your market with new versions of the same old thing. One classic example of this process was the Sony Walkman, which comes in hundreds of different shapes and sizes. Japanese firms such as Sharp and Canon have often jumped ahead by mixing different sorts of technology, such as photography and office machines. Matsushita tests its latest camcorders in one of Tokyo's rather more downmarket shopping districts to see what the punters make of them. If sales are sluggish, the products are withdrawn. One way in which Japanese car makers have generally outfoxed their rivals is by rapidly updating their model range and adding extras such as vanity mirrors and intermittent windscreen wipers. By contrast, American and European manufacturers have seemed obsessed with a 'one big solution' approach to research – the legacy, some argue, of the Apollo project.

The trick of Japanese management is to marry this relentless incrementalism to a long-term strategy based on consensus. Ohmae points out that, whereas western firms modelled themselves on the military, with their clear lines of command and rigid distinction between the officers (who do the thinking) and the rest, Japanese firms are rooted in village communes.[3] 'Grossly oversimplifying,' Ohmae writes, 'one could say, that in Japan every member of the village is equal and a generalist.' Rather than issuing orders from on high, Japanese companies prefer to put their emphasis on *nemawashi* (consensus building) and *ringi* (shared decision-making). The hope is that every decision will spring from tireless discussion, with managers obliged to gain the enthusiastic support of their workers.

This emphasis on communal decision-making means that the Japanese have an idiosyncratic approach to leadership. Where American bosses are brash and bullying, their Japanese counterparts are modest and retiring; and where Americans live to make decisions, the Japanese prefer to let decisions make themselves. They like to compare leadership to air – necessary for life but invisible and insubstantial. They rise up the corporate ranks by out-conforming their colleagues, religiously putting the group before the individual, and, having reached the top job, lead by consensus rather than command. It is not unusual for leaders to sit in silence throughout much of a meeting, while their underlings debate the pros and cons of policy. The art of leadership is to divine the will of the group, not to electrify the organisation with your charisma.

It also means that they have an idiosyncratic approach to forming long-term strategy. In the West strategy has traditionally been clear and definite, drawn up by professional strategists and written down in formal plans. In Japan, on the other hand, it is a much looser affair, generated by the whole organisation and expressed in terms of visions and missions rather than precise plans. To the western mind, producing plans like this is a recipe for disaster. But, according to Ohmae, the Japanese can do it because it fits in with their general approach to employment. The system of lifetime employment means that core workers identify with the long-term future of the company. The habit of rotating people between different departments means that they soon come to think like strategists. And the convention that everybody must start on the shop floor means that senior managers know what is going on in the guts of their organisations.

The sun also sets

The success of lean production, consensus and *kaizen* was extraordinary. By the early 1980s Japanese firms were beating the Americans ragged in everything from price to quality, and the skies of the Pacific were black with aircraft carrying managers to Japan to study companies like Sony and Toyota. Bookshops were full of books with titles such as *The Art of Japanese Management* and *The Intelligent Person's Guide to Kaizen*. In the late 1980s, Americans watched impotently as Japanese companies bought Rockefeller Plaza, Columbia Pictures, Pebble Beach golf course and other American totems. In *Rising Sun*, a thriller about corporate skulduggery in Los Angeles, Michael Crichton even paid Japanese managers the ultimate compliment of demonising them. Americans seemed obsessed by two racist stereotypes of the Japanese: they were either clever little Asians producing ever smarter gadgets, or fiendish strategists cunningly working together towards the same unstated goal. Management books – even those by Ohmae – only reinforced these myths.

Yet by the mid-1990s all those books on the secrets of Japanese management were yellowing in second-hand bookshops; and Ohmae was becoming better known as a critic of Japan rather than as an apologist for it. What had changed was not just that Japan's firms were struggling against a prolonged recession and an expensive currency, crippling though these were. The prevailing wisdom was that western companies had learned everything they needed to know about Japanese management; now it was the Japanese who would have to learn from the West.

There is no doubt that the West – and America in particular – has caught up quickly. Three decades after he had been spurned in his own country, Deming was rediscovered in June 1980, thanks to an NBC television documentary, *If Japan Can, Why Can't We?*. The day after the programme was shown, Deming's phone started ringing, and he spent the rest of his life until he died in 1993 giving seminars and being fêted by American bosses and politicians. In America, 'total quality management' was the most influential fad of the 1980s. In 1987 the American government created an equivalent of Japan's Deming prize, the Baldridge. One of the most successful adopters, Motorola, claimed that, in 1987–92, 'TQM' added $3.2 billion to the company's bottom line.[4] In 1989, the Japanese even acknowledged America's conversion to quality by decorating an American company, Florida Light and Power, with the Deming Prize.

Western manufacturers have also learned the secrets of 'lean production', largely by forming joint ventures with Japanese companies. Ford purchased 24.5 per cent of Mazda in 1979, giving Ford's senior managers full access to Mazda's main production complex in Hiroshima (Ford now owns a controlling 33 per cent stake).[5] General Motors formed a joint venture with Toyota in California, transforming one of its most unproductive, strike-ridden plants into a model of productivity. The ease with which Japanese 'transplant' plants put down roots in North America and Britain proved that lean production was not something which could flourish only on Japanese soil.

And some westerners improved on what they learned. Companies such as Marks & Spencer, Motorola and Chrysler have formed close links with their suppliers without subjecting themselves to the rigidities that have often bedevilled Japan's *keiretsu* system. 'The traditional *keiretsu* are no longer the model of best practice,' says Jordan Lewis, an expert on producer–supplier links. 'For this, one has to look to the West.'[6] To some extent, the role of master and apprentice has been reversed: even Toyota has had to turn to Ford to discover how to improve the relations between its engineers and its shop-floor workers and to Chrysler to learn about 'value engineering' – a new way to speed up car production by using more interchangeable components in different models.

All too Japanese

Having given away its secrets, Japan, many argue, retains exclusive rights only to those things that nobody else wants. The system of lifetime employment has kept Japanese companies horribly fat, while the weakness of shareholders has allowed some firms to remain hopelessly unfocused. The country's white-collar sector is only two-thirds as efficient as its equivalent in Europe and America. Japan's over-regulated economy discourages innovation and imposes high costs on businesses, such as exorbitant fuel and telecoms charges. In 'creative' industries, such as software and multimedia, which are booming in the West, Japan is way behind, isolated by language and hampered by a conformist educational system. Japan's universities are sleepy finishing schools, not vital sources of innovation; and Japan's banks are reluctant to invest in unproved companies.

What gives these criticisms added bite is that they are being made by Japanese as well as Americans. If Japan is to survive in the computer business, argues Mochio Umeda, a consultant with Arthur D. Little and a representative of the domestic art of Japan-bashing, management will have to give up 'its parochialism, its perverse egalitarianism, its in-group orientation and its tendency to suppress individuality and creativity'. The more sophisticated Japanese managers are stocking their libraries with western management books and littering their conversations with words like 'downsizing' and 're-engineering'.

The Japanese are also beginning to question two of their mooted strengths: *kaizen* and consensus. Whilst Japanese companies have carried on churning out ever smarter versions of the same thing, industry-changing products have tended to be made elsewhere. Sony and Matsushita devoted their energies to making more and more complicated Walkmans, but American firms were inventing the real breakthroughs in consumer electronics, such as the personal computer and the cellular telephone. By the mid-1990s, despite their extra wing mirrors, Japanese cars were all beginning to look the same. Indeed, the extra wing mirrors were cluttering up production. What was needed were simpler, bolder designs.

Meanwhile, the emphasis of consensus has made managing foreigners difficult. Japan's multinationals traditionally concentrated on exporting rather than investing abroad, partly because they felt that their manufacturing system was so Japanese that it could not survive on foreign soil. Now, thanks to the high yen, fears of protectionism abroad and globalisation, they have no choice. The Nomura Research Institute has predicted that, by 1998, almost 40 per cent of the production of Japan's five biggest electronics groups will be offshore. In 1994 Toyota produced 48 per cent of its cars overseas; by 1998 that portion will be around 65 per cent.

As we have already said, the basic lean-production system has actually been relatively easy to export. However, merely getting people to manufacture things efficiently is often not enough. Clever multinationals have been able to engage their foreign workers' brains as well as their hands (see Chapter Ten on Globalisation). Japanese salarymen have famously found it impossible to manage hairy artistic types: witness Sony's and Matsushita's nightmare in Hollywood. But the cultural insensitivity of many Japanese managers can even make it difficult to manage humble production workers. Sanyo Electric provoked an angry strike in Indonesia when it refused to allow thirty-three female assembly-line workers to wear traditional Muslim dress, citing safety reasons.[7]

Western employees in Japanese banks complain that there is a two-tiered management system – a dummy one in the host country and a real one between the Japanese management and their bosses in Tokyo. They are forever making decisions, they murmur, only to have them countermanded by a telex from Tokyo. In 1991, the Lantos Committee on the employment practices of Japanese-owned companies in the United States listened to a litany of complaints: that a handful of Japanese made all the most important decisions, in collusion with head office; that a 'rice-paper ceiling' stood between the non-Japanese and serious promotion; that the Japanese discriminated on the grounds of race and sex; and that the Japanese were unwilling to listen to ideas from foreigners. Consensus, it seems, is only consensual if you are Japanese.

Whilst the rice-paper ceiling has deterred foreigners from working for Japanese firms, xenophobia has also put able Japanese off working abroad. Fearing that a spell away from headquarters may handicap them in the promotion race many salarymen refer to 'overseas banishment'. Mothers often stay at home so that children can continue in Japanese schools, an arrangement that imposes huge strains on families. Those children who spend any length of time abroad run the risk of being ostracised at school and accused of 'smelling of butter'.

Japan's dithering over innovation and internationalisation seems to reflect a failure not just of particular business leaders, but of Japan's whole approach to leadership. All that stuff about consensus was all very well when Japan's economy was growing by 10 per cent a year. But a flat economy is testing bosses' ability to make hard choices. They have to get rid of surplus workers (or at least retire them early) and decide which line of business to focus on. Competition from tightly managed western companies means that Japanese companies need to be able to make decisions quickly. Japan's increasing involvement with the rest of the world, through joint ventures and overseas operations, means that

Japanese managers can no longer rely on a decision-making process which is only comprehensible to their fellow Japanese.

East meets West: the remix

Anybody who considers writing off Japanese management should always remember two things. First, that the country remains the world's leading centre of manufacturing excellence. And, second, that Japanese businesses have a genius for turning adversity into advantage. Japan's lack of natural resources encouraged the government to invest heavily in education. Two oil shocks and several steep rises in the yen have acted as powerful spurs to innovation. Several times before, Japanese car imports to the United States have dropped following steep rises in the yen; each time, Toyota City has found new ways to make lean production even leaner and come back to humble Detroit again.

However, this time the process is different because, for the first time in thirty years, the Japanese are not just trying to improve their own management models, but to merge them with western ones. One important thinker in this respect is Yotaro Kobayashi, the boss of Fuji Xerox, who is something of a hero to the younger generation of Japanese managers and who has spent much of the past decade insisting to his peers that his country's idea of consensual leadership needs to change.

Kobayashi, who graduated from the Wharton Business School in America and has spent years as head of a joint venture with an American company, argues that Japanese bosses must learn how to make tough decisions, and how to 'market' them, both within their firms and to the world at large, so that employees and outsiders can see the logic of unpalatable decisions. He also believes that Japanese managers need a dose of western-style professionalism. Leaders should be carefully trained, not just allowed to emerge from the ranks. He encourages Fuji Xerox's rising middle managers to take responsibility for strategic decisions. He also likes to send a few on American MBA courses – though he is careful not to give the impression that the firm is being turned into an American colony.

Kobayashi wants to introduce a streak of rebelliousness into the salaryman's soul: Japanese managers ought to challenge their business models rather than just endlessly improve them. Kobayashi's own career was much influenced by a visit to the Aspen Institute in the United States, which puts on mind-broadening seminars for business leaders. He now has his own version in Japan where business people sit and listen to philosophers as well as people such as Peter Drucker, and debate issues ranging from the environment to management.

A dignified retreat

Is Kobayashi just a voice crying in the wilderness? Consider two areas where Japanese management has been slow to change: lifetime employment and multicultural management.

At first sight, Japanese companies have tried hard to hang on to the idea of a 'job for life', doing anything to find new jobs for redundant personnel. In Honda it is even possible to find male managers serving coffee in place of the traditional 'office ladies'.[8] To save having to sack people, companies are cutting back on bonuses, preventing workers from doing so much overtime, and freezing recruitment. Nissan used to take on between 1,500 and 2,000 new recruits a year; it hired only fifty-five in 1995. Nowadays, Japanese graduates anxiously study the age-profiles of companies, which are published annually, to see if they have any chance of a career.

Yet there is movement. Western-style assessment procedures are creeping into big Japanese firms, and jobs are not as safe as they used to be. Despite their loyalty to the concept of 'lifetime employment', firms are redefining what they mean by the phrase, arguing that it applies only to a proportion of workers, and whittling down that proportion as far as they can. Japanese banks have introduced a system of 'up or out': those who do not make the grade by the age of forty are sent away to run local banks. Toyota has taken to moving fifty-year-old managers from supervisory jobs to 'individual work'. And a few are introducing 'voluntary' early retirement for their lifetime employees. Nissan cut its workforce by 5,000 in 1993–95, with the majority of the losses falling on white-collar workers. Toshiba, an electronics company, reduced the size of its headquarters staff by 30 per cent between 1992 and 1997, delegating more power to front-line workers as it did so. ('Small, simple, speedy, strategic' is its latest motto.) Toyota claims to be reducing its white-collar workforce by 20 per cent though the secret of this reduction seems to be shuffling people between departments.

As for the problem of dealing with foreign staff, the best Japanese companies have certainly begun to talk like 'multicultural multinationals'. NEC, a big electronics company, is putting all its products 'into a global perspective in order to determine the most appropriate locations for design, manufacturing and sales'.[9] Matsushita, once one of the keenest defenders of its home base, has now decided that it is a 'multi-local' and talks about being a 'global network manager'.[10] Nissan is keen on creating a 'global team spirit' and talks about using the entire world as a 'knowledge base'.

There are signs that this is more than just talk. More blue-chip Japanese companies are bringing foreign managers to Japan. Toyota now holds shareholder meetings outside Japan. Toshiba is reorganising every bit of its work, from accounting to technology management, on a world-wide basis, partly to get rid of duplication but also partly because there is no longer any such thing as a purely Japanese business problem. The Japanese are also establishing global networks, in which people from 'third countries' act as missionaries for Japanese management. Toshiba sends Thais to its plant in Malaysia, which has been operating for twenty years, in order to introduce them to Japanese production techniques.

The two-way flow of ideas is already producing results. Both Canon and Toshiba, for example, have produced breakthroughs in audio technology by setting up laboratories in Britain. Honda rebounded from a bad patch in the late 1980s with the Honda Accord, a car which it designed partly by organising a contest between studios in Japan, the United States and Europe to see who could come up with the best design.[11] The company also moved sixty American production engineers and their families to Japan for two years.

One of the leaders of the multicultural approach (and another ally of Kobayashi and Ohmae) has been Minoru Makihara. Makihara was born in London, educated at Harvard University, spent twenty-two years serving abroad, and speaks perfect English. He is so at home in the United States that his two children work for American companies and he is known by a nickname, Ben. In 1992 he was drafted in from abroad (an unusual move in a Japanese company) to become president of Mitsubishi Corporation, the biggest of Japan's dozen or so trading companies – or *soga sosha*.

In the past, a trading house could survive as an importer-exporter, acting as an agent for foreigners in Japan and for Japanese firms abroad. However, as markets open up, this role is dying. Mitsubishi's future, if it has one, is as a more proactive global deal-maker, using its contacts and its people to set up things like power stations and cable television networks around the world. Ever since Makihara's surprise appointment, he has tried to force his colleagues – not always successfully – to think in the same way that he does. One of his first moves was to ask all his senior managers to write him letters of resignation (so that he could use them if necessary); he also fines them if they address him as 'president'.

Makihara has tried to promote non-Japanese employees in the company. And like Kobayashi, he is a keen supporter of letting western thinkers into the company. But it is a hard slog. Western employees in Mitsubishi complain that they are on short-term contracts, while their Japanese colleagues have a job for life.

For the moment, people like Kobayashi, Makihara and Ohmae remain the exceptions rather than the rule. But they have three things going for them. First, Japan's economy is becoming ever more global. Second, their strongest supporters are amongst the younger, more flexible generation of Japanese managers, who were bred on Disney and Nintendo, and are now coming to the fore. And, finally, they are offering something new. Japanese management can change without merely becoming western.

What Japan can still teach the West

Two of the greatest problems facing managers everywhere are cutting costs and managing knowledge. As we have seen, these are both fields where western firms have been making most of the running. Nevertheless, these are also both areas where Japanese managers can still teach the West a trick or two.

On the cost-cutting side, western companies are wearying of brutalist management fads such as re-engineering, downsizing and delayering. So far, Japanese companies have been noticeably more successful than their western peers at controlling costs without tearing out the innovative heart of a company. This is not just a matter of having sacked fewer people. Japanese firms have encouraged the entire workforce to help in reaching cost-reduction targets. In many companies the walls are decorated with posters showing progress in cost control. At Topcon, an optical company, for example, the slogan is: 'The budget is God'.

Something which has undoubtedly helped this communal spirit is the approach of senior managers. In the West, executive salaries have risen relentlessly in recent years, almost regardless of the performance of the company or the riskiness of the business. A popular backlash against this threatens to create a political climate which is much less friendly towards business. But in Japan companies believe that, when the going gets tough, bosses should be the first people to sacrifice their bonuses and salaries, before they start restructuring the rest of the company.

Similarly, the Japanese reluctance to sack middle managers willy-nilly may also rebound in their favour. Yes, Japanese firms have often been slow to separate the wheat from the chaff. But in Japanese eyes, the middle manager is not just an expendable link in the chain of command but a possessor of a valuable perspective on a company's business. In particular, they knot together two visions – the strategic view of senior managers and the detailed operational view of front-line workers.

As for suppliers, there seems little doubt that big Japanese companies treat them more roughly than they used to (and much more roughly than their own employees). There is even a name for the new trend – *shitauke ijime,* or 'sub-contractor bullying'. Small and mid-size businesses shed nearly two million jobs in 1989–94, with many businesses going under. Otaku, in the east of Tokyo, once a bustling area of tiny workshops, is now a shadow of its former self, as business after business has been squeezed to death. 'We just sweat and sweat until we're all skin and bones,' one of Matsushita's sub-contractors told the *Wall Street Journal.* 'Sub-contractors like us are becoming weaker, while assemblers like Matsushita are amassing strength.' On the other hand, what was remarkable about the *Journal*'s story was that it *was* a story. In Europe or America, suppliers are used to being battered. In Japan they have usually been protected.

The other area where the Japanese can help western firms – how to manage knowledge – may sound strange, given that leadership in so many knowledge-intensive industries, from software to entertainment, belongs to America. Nevertheless, a new generation of Japanese management thinkers, particularly Ikujiro Nonaka and Hirotaka Takeuchi of Hitotsubashi University, argue that the Japanese still have certain advantages. Nonaka and Takeuchi start by admitting that western companies are well ahead of the Japanese in managing the sort of formal, explicit knowledge which can be faxed or e-mailed. (At Microsoft, front-line employees receive an average of fifty e-mail messages a day and Bill Gates receives 200; at many of the best Japanese companies e-mail has still not been installed.) But, argue Nonaka and Takeuchi, the Japanese are better at managing tacit knowledge – the informal occupational lore, which is generated by workers grappling with everyday problems and passed on in cafeterias.

This skill allows companies to tap into the insights of the bulk of their employees, and ensures that one man's hunch can become an entire firm's competitive advantage. The most important trick is to encourage workers to spend as much time as possible together, informal as well as formal. Companies routinely divide workers into teams, often expecting them to stick with the same colleagues for years on end. New recruits work closely with 'mentors' or 'team leaders', learning far more from them than they do from formal training courses. After-work drinking sessions and country-hotel weekends play an important part in promoting informal understanding. Some companies talk of 'nommunication', a word that is made up of the Japanese word for drinking (*nomu*) and communication.[12] Honda and Canon both make frequent use of 'brainstorming camps' – informal meetings in country inns in which project-development teams (and anybody else who wants to contribute) work intensively on a project, but also drink sake, share meals and even bathe together in hot springs.

These sessions are useful not only for promoting trust between workers, but also for sparking bright ideas. It was at one of these sessions that a team from Canon, trying to make a mini-photocopier, hit upon the solution to a problem that had troubled them for months: what to do about the expense of repairing the drum. After a morning puzzling over this problem, the team leader sent out for some beer. As they drank the beer, the conversation turned to the question of how much it costs to make a disposable can. This sparked off an idea: why not equip the photocopier with a disposable can-shaped drum.[13]

If you are used to looking for sources of informal knowledge inside your company you can do it outside too. The head of a team at Matsushita trying to develop an automatic bread-maker reasoned that the best bread came from the Osaka International Hotel. So she apprenticed herself to the head baker and watched the way he worked. After weeks of study, she realised that the secret of making perfect bread was not just kneading the dough, but also twisting it. She made certain that her machine could imitate this combination of movements.

The point about tacit knowledge is that it is always there: a company does not have to create it but rather remove barriers to it flowing around the place. Kao, a chemicals and cosmetics company, holds all its meetings in the open, allowing anybody to drop in if they feel like it. Half the floor space on the executive floor is given over to a 'decision-making room'. Kao's quarterly R&D conference regularly attracts some 1,800 people (out of a workforce of 7,000). The company also encourages customers to phone in with suggestions and complaints, and receives some 50,000 calls a year. It also set up a computer network which gives all employees, however lowly, access to all but the most sensitive personal information. Even the president's expense account is on public view.

One problem with implicit knowledge is that it is difficult to transfer across borders even when people share the same language. (As any Englishman who has lived in California will tell you, irony barely travels across the Atlantic and has never crossed the Rockies.) As we have already seen, Japanese companies have been fairly lousy at extracting ideas from their foreign subsidiaries. Yet, they have also been fairly capable teachers – particularly when it comes to teaching tacit knowledge about manufacturing. In places as far apart as Wales and Tennessee, local workers are using 'Japanese' methods to produce Toyotas and Nissans for their domestic markets, and can often give plants in Japan a run for their money when it comes to quality and efficiency.

Turning Japanese

Although ideas like tacit knowledge might sound a little vague and Confucian at the moment, western managers would be foolish to ignore them. In some ways the world is becoming more like Japan, not less so. Even the most successful western companies can no longer dominate entire markets in the way that General Motors or IBM once did; they are also finding that they have ever less time to make money out of a new product. By contrast, the best Japanese firms are used to over-crowded markets and instant imitation. Japan has nine car companies compared with America's three. Nothing remains secret in Japan for long: word leaks out at school re-unions and through meetings with suppliers. Japanese firms have always lived in a world of what some management thinkers call 'hyper-competition'.

This is no time to go back to the crude Japan worship of the early 1980s, with 'quality circles', morning callisthenics and thrice-yearly pilgrimages to Toyota City. Japanese companies are too bloated, and too weak at the type of 'out of the box' thinking that seems to characterise America's most inventive companies. But they are clearly learning fast, under the tutelage of men like Kobayashi and Ohmae; and there are some things that they do much better than their rivals in the West. As westerners have learned in the past, it is always worth keeping at least one eye on the East.

12

A NEW MODEL IN ASIA?

Anybody who doubts how much China has changed should spend an afternoon eavesdropping on interviews for a twenty-month MBA course at the China Europe International Business School.[1] The school, hidden in Shanghai's sprawling industrial suburbs, claims to be the fastest-growing in the world. Although the course costs $4,000 (or nearly twice the average Chinese annual income) its sixty-five places attract 4,000 applicants. Most of the interviewees are in their mid-twenties and exhibit a drive that would make the average Harvard MBA blush. Asked 'What are your weaknesses?', one replies 'I am too successful.' Several of the young entrepreneurs have applied to CEIBS before and been rejected for their poor English; despite apparently working from dawn to dusk, they have still found the energy to cram in night-time language courses. Many of the best candidates are women: one, a tiny bird-like figure who works for a local textiles company, bosses around the panel of professors in a way that Margaret Thatcher's cabinet ministers would have found familiar.

However, the most memorable candidate is a tall young man – call him 'Deng'. He explains that his career has been carefully divided into three stages, each suited to make the most out of modern China. The first was university, where Deng, being the cleverest, finished top of his class. The next stage was a prized job at a foreign-trade organisation, chosen for its 'complicated' work; pushed to explain what he means, Deng says that there is a lot of corruption, though (a momentary sign of self-doubt as he fingers an expensive watch) obviously nothing that involved Deng. Now he wants to go to a business school teaching western ideas: 'China needs managers more than anything else.'

Deng is on to a sure thing. By 1996 there were some 80,000 foreign joint ventures in China. If each requires four managers, then even this small sector of the Chinese economy needs nearly a quarter of a million managers. By contrast, China currently produces a mere 300 MBAs a year. Even adding in those Chinese students who study overseas and the ABCs (or American born Chinese) that some western firms have tried, usually unsuccessfully, to import, there is a dramatic gulf between demand and supply. Salaries for managers in Shanghai rose ten times in the four years from 1992; the turnover rate for managerial jobs in some foreign joint ventures is about 30 per cent a year.

Chaotic China's thirst for management may be an extreme. example. However, even in hyper-organised Singapore, Nanyang Technological University, which can offer only 125 places on its MBA course, has taken to selling prospecti at $25 each to put off students: it still gets 900 applications. McKinsey's fastest-growing practice is in India. Elsewhere, most of McKinsey's clients like to keep quiet about the fact that they have called in consultants; in India McKinsey has to plead with its clients not to buy advertising space to proclaim the fact that they have secured its services. Open an Asian newspaper and, where you might have expected a full-page advertisement foretelling the imminent arrival of the Rolling Stones, you find instead a similar spread announcing that 'The world's most competitive man', Michael Porter, is on his way. On the other hand, in a continent where newsagents actually put publications with names like *Supply Chain Management News* on top of *Time* and *Playboy*, then an evening with Porter seems quite an event.

Why Asia matters

All this implies that, from the perspective of western management theorists, non-Japanese Asia is simply just another, slightly over-enthusiastic pupil waiting to be taught. In fact, developing Asia has management ideas of its own, and, over the next decade, these ideas will have an enormously powerful effect on management theory. The comparison to bear in mind (even if it is one that, in the end, looks unlikely to be fully realised) is with Japan. When Japanese cars and radios first began to appear in America, American managers presumed that Toyota and Sony were beating them just because they had access to cheaper labour or because Japanese employees worked harder. The reality, as we saw in the last chapter, was that the Americans were being out-managed, and they soon found themselves copying things like lean production.

Nowadays, American bosses are grumbling about cheap imports from the likes of Thailand, China, India and South Korea. Are they in for another surprise? The glib answer is 'not of the same scale'. On the whole, developing Asia still has more to learn from established western management theory than the other way round. And even if Asian companies do push all before them, it will not be due to sticking to some easily imitable set text, such as Toyota's manuals. The new management 'theories' that are emerging in non-Japanese Asia are instinctive rather than intellectual.

Yet the region demands attention on at least two scores. The first, general reason is the sheer power of its economies, and the opportunities that they are throwing up. According to the World Bank, the world's fastest-growing country in 1985–94 was Thailand (which sped along at an annual rate of 8.2 per cent), followed by South Korea (7.8 per cent) and then China and Singapore (both on 6.9 per cent). Developing Asia is now slowing down a little and opening up its domestic markets, which makes it something of a cockpit of competing capitalisms, with a dozen or so different sorts of companies battling away: these include not only readily recognisable beasts, such as western and Japanese multinationals, but also less familiar local creatures, ranging from China's state-owned companies to South Korea's *chaebol*.

This brings us to the second, particular reason why developing Asia demands attention: the business networks created by the overseas Chinese. Although these owe little to western management ideas, they have so far managed to trounce all-comers in many of the world's most vibrant markets. As we shall see, the strength of the overseas-Chinese empires has a lot to do with history and connections. However, in other respects, such as their ability to build entrepreneurial networks, they are as 'modern' as any other on the planet. Indeed, from some angles, the best of them offer a glimpse of how the loose 'virtual' companies so beloved of western management gurus might turn out.

Why focus on the overseas-Chinese companies – and not, say, South Korea's *chaebol*? After all, many more westerners have heard of Samsung, Hyundai and Daewoo than they have of Robert Kuok or Li Ka-shing. There are also many more case studies. The answer – and this, once again, is a generalisation – is that the other management structures in developing Asia look like pale (or refined) versions of ones we have already looked at in this book. For instance, the *chaebol* are impressive enough, but structurally they resemble Japan's *keiretsu*. Indeed, the South Koreans have even followed the Japanese into the same industries – cars and electronics. Similarly, the big Indian businesses, now emerging from several decades of protected markets, follow a sort of bureaucratic version of western management theory: this may change – India is the one country in Asia which is stocked full of trained managers – but, as yet, nobody is looking to India for ideas.

By contrast, the entrepreneurial 'bamboo network' of family businesses created by the overseas Chinese is not just another interesting variant, but a fully-fledged alternative model – and one which looks intriguingly powerful. Most westerners already know that Taiwan, Hong Kong and Singapore are all full of entrepreneurial Chinese. Now they are beginning to realise just how powerful this sort of capitalism is. In the Philippines, the overseas Chinese make up only 1 per cent of the country's population but control over half the stockmarket. In Indonesia, the equivalent proportions are 4 per cent and 75 per cent, in Malaysia 32 per cent and 60 per cent. Hellmut Schütte, a management professor at Insead's Euro-Asia Centre, reckoned that by 1996 the 51 million overseas Chinese controlled an economy worth $700 billion – roughly the same size as the 1.2 billion mainlanders.

These paragons of capitalism are desperately hard to pin down. No single Chinese family firm appears in the world's 100 biggest by market capitalisation; yet there are probably at least twenty families which are worth $5 billion or more (America, by contrast, can muster only ten). Like commercial icebergs, most Chinese families exhibit only a small portion of themselves to the outside world. For instance, in early 1996 Robert Kuok, a Malaysian Chinese who is probably the most powerful of all overseas Chinese, controlled the Shangri-La hotel chain (market capitalisation: $3 billion) and the *South China Morning Post* ($1.1 billion), but most of his assets in China, Hong Kong and around the Pacific Rim were squirrelled away in a network of private companies. In November 1995, the *Singapore Business Times* calculated that the seven biggest investors on the Kuala Lumpur Stock Exchange were all ethnic Chinese. The richest of them, a gambling magnate called Lim Goh Tong, owned $5.2 billion-worth of shares in Kuala Lumpur alone. Previous estimates of his total wealth by *Forbes*, *Asiaweek* and others had put his total wealth at barely half that figure.

This lack of information extends to management theorists. So far there are only a handful of thinkers who know much at all about Chinese family capitalism: Gordon Redding at Hong Kong University is the leader; Henri-Claude de Bettignies, who teaches a course in Asian business at both Stanford and Insead, is another much mentioned name. The most comprehensive book on the overseas Chinese so far was put together by the East Asia Analytical Unit of Australia's Department of Foreign Affairs.[2] Already research teams from the Harvard Business School are working hard to catch up. Most of the existing work encourages the idea that the overseas Chinese exhibit all the networking and entrepreneurial skills that western companies lack, such as 'trust' and 'flexibility': they can be big or small, local or regional according to need, using their ready-made network of allies to dart in and out of markets. One of the more recent books about the overseas Chinese, *Lords of the Rim* (1995) by Sterling Seagrave, begins with a quotation from Sun Tzu: 'Be so subtle that you are invisible. Be so mysterious that you are intangible. Then you will control your rival's fate.'

Is the management model invented by the overseas Chinese really that good?

All in the family

Consider a typical tale of Chinese family capitalism. In 1994 Richard Savage, a Singaporean businessman, met some officials from North Korea. He passed on these contacts to his brother, Ronald, who works at Loxley, a Thai firm controlled by the Lamsam family. Loxley's business lines include, amongst other things, environmental engineering, brewing, electrical appliances, power plants, health food, chemicals, cellular telephones, entertainment, property and six computer companies. North Korea was assigned to Boonyakit Tansakul, a younger western-educated member of the family. In October 1995, following a successful dinner where senior members of the Lamsam family met various North Korean politicians, Loxley won a controversial contract to build an international telephone system for North Korea's new Rajin Sombong free-trade zone. By early 1996, although Lamsam had yet to see a dollar out of the hermit kingdom, Boonyakit was convinced that within a decade Rajin Sombong would become the 'Singapore of the North'.

Such entrepreneurial chutzpah is typical of overseas-Chinese capitalism. Its roots lie in the families that migrated from various mainland provinces – usually coastal ones such as Guandong, Fujian or Hainan – around 100 years ago. As with Jewish entrepreneurs, family ties have been hardened by persecution. It is only thirty years since the last anti-Chinese pogrom in Indonesia; Malaysia's twenty-six-year-old New Economic Policy favours ethnic Malays over ethnic Chinese. 'It is not greed that drives the overseas Chinese,' argues Simon Murray, who used to run Li Ka-shing's empire in Hong Kong. 'It is fear – and the yearning for the protection that money will give you.'

In this insecure world, clans have proved almost as important as families. In most cases the funds to start businesses came from fellow clan members. Even today, a fair chunk of South-East Asia's food business is controlled by Chinese who speak the same regional dialect. One Cantonese banker confesses that he still has to make a point of spending twice as long on the telephone to non-Cantonese clients to reassure them that he is not discriminating against them. The long-standing informal alliance between the two richest men in Malaysia and Indonesia, Robert Kuok and Liem Sioe Liong, owes much to the fact that they are both Hokkien Chinese, as are two other allies, Khoo Kay Peng (who founded Malayan United Industries) and Mochtar Riady (who set up Indonesia's Lippo group).

Chinese managers like to boast that, in contrast to their legalistic western peers, their businesses are based around negotiating relationships not contracts. The chief assets of an overseas-Chinese business are usually its *guanxi* (or connections). In a time when many western management theorists are exalting the importance of 'tacit knowledge', 'supplier-provider relationships' and the like, this makes the overseas Chinese look refreshingly modern. In fact, many of the most important *guanxi* are political ones. In the late 1940s Liem Sioe Liong, the founder of the Salim Group, was working for his uncle's peanut-oil business in Central Java when he struck up a friendship with a local army quartermaster who went on to become President Suharto. Bangkokers joke that the Charoen Pokphand group, which is controlled by the Sophonpanich family, has employed so many Thai politicians that it could hold a cabinet meeting.

The idea of loose entrepreneurial networks based around 'trust' is the sort of thing that tends to make researchers from Harvard go all gooey – often to the amusement of the networkers themselves ('I can't think of an organisation where in-fighting is more rife,' says one well connected Chinese businesswoman). In truth, most overseas-Chinese firms only work because they are centralised dictatorships: the head of the family makes nearly all the decisions. This helps in businesses such as property, where one handshake can buy a building. It also allows firms to change direction quickly. In Hong Kong industries making wigs, flowers and radios have sprung up, profited and then disappeared.

In China, such nimble-footed network building has brought

quick rewards once again. The overseas Chinese account for half the foreign direct investment in China. By 1996, Charoen Pokphand, which first entered the mainland in 1979, could claim revenues of $3 billion there. It owned some eighty agribusiness companies in China, stretching all the way from breeder farms to chicken-fast-food shops, not to mention other businesses like beer, property and motorcycles. How on earth could a food company get hold of a motorcycle plant when most of the western car industry is clamouring to get into China? The answer, as usual, is through *guanxi*. Charoen then bought the skills it needed by forming an alliance with Honda just as it has done in retailing (with Holland's Makro) and telecoms (with America's Nynex).

Unexportable

But how strong really is Chinese family management? The answer is that, on a small scale, it is as good as anything the West has to offer. Up to a certain size, Chinese management can cope with virtually any problem, particularly in the fast-growing markets where it is based. Indeed, the hallmark of such companies is their flexibility, which often puts western companies to shame. True, many of the healthiest businesses in Europe and America are small family-owned ones too, but they tend to operate in only one industry and only one country. The glory of the bamboo network is that it tends to spread across a variety of companies and industries, seizing opportunities as they present themselves.

But, once the companies begin to reach the same size as western multinationals, the comparison with foreign companies is less flattering. Unlike the Japanese and the Koreans, the overseas Chinese have had precious little success outside Asia. Most simply have not tried. Those who have, such as Li Ka-shing, have often run into trouble (although in the mid-1990s he finally found a winner with Orange, a British cellular telephone network). Henri-Claude de Bettignies, a professor at Insead, says that he advises Asian companies to learn how to manage across cultures first: 'You cannot be an amateur in America or Europe,' he says flatly.

For critics of Chinese capitalism, the failures outside Asia mean that people should cast a more critical eye over the successes at home. Their first charge is that most overseas Chinese fortunes have not come from out-managing their opponents but from gambling in a casino where nobody could lose: Asian property. This charge rings particularly true in Hong Kong where several Cathay-Pacific pilots are now multimillionaires because they bought a small flat in the (then hardly exclusive) Mid-Levels in the 1970s. Most of the local billionaires, including Li Ka-shing, have made most of their money from bricks and mortar. But easy pickings from property may be a little harder to come by in the future. Offices in booming Asian cities are now more expensive than offices in the West. Also Hong Kong's unique position as the only gateway into China (and one with a limited supply of land) is ebbing away. Already several western companies have leapfrogged straight into Beijing or Shanghai, ignoring the established practice of setting up a base camp in Hong Kong.

By itself, the charge that the overseas Chinese are just overgrown property magnates is not convincing: although property is usually their main business, they have also been successful in plenty of other fields. But the accusation does lead the way to other, less blunt criticisms. Trevor MacMurray, a consultant at McKinsey, argues that too many overseas Chinese businesses are 'structurers' as opposed to 'builders', meaning that they chase after franchises of one sort or another (e.g. running the Philippines' long-distance telephone system or the Macao ferry) rather than trying to create internationally competitive products or services. As many of the more profitable franchises are being worn down by deregulation and competition, the firms' weaknesses as builders will be exposed.

In most overseas Chinese businesses, manufacturing still means applying cheap hands to borrowed technology. Gordon Redding, a professor at Hong Kong University, argues that the problem is as much to do with organisation as ideas. An old-style family company is constitutionally incapable of building something like

Toyota's Lexus, he argues, because sophisticated car making requires both co-ordination and decentralisation as well as bosses who trust their employees. 'You need to have departments, such as marketing, production and design, rather than just vague areas given to Number-one son.'

Another growing weakness is people. Few bright managers want to work for an organisation where they can never become the chairman, and where career ladders tend to be vague. Too often respect for authority (and age) means that criticising the boss is unacceptable. One survey in Hong Kong found that Chinese professionals preferred to work for western and Japanese managers (anybody in fact who is not Chinese). Another survey, this time of 1,000 executives around the world by Britain's Cranfield School of Management, found that those working for Hong Kong businesses felt most out of line with their companies' thinking.

Why Jimmy Lai is half right

Add up all these problems and some argue that overseas-Chinese capitalism belongs to the past not the future. As evidence they cite the progress made by many western companies in most of Asia's consumer-goods markets. One of these cynics is Jimmy Lai, Hong Kong's best-known publisher. He argues that: '*Guanxi* are dead. They were important as long as business meant striking deals with only a few politicians or relations. They count for nothing in consumer markets. You have to make good products or offer good services. In fact connections, particularly corrupt ones, will count against you soon – even in China.' He gives the example of one well-known Hong Kong businessman and his connections with the Chinese leadership. All those connections, argues Lai, depended on Deng Xiaoping, who died in early 1997.

Lai's own career shows he is half right. As the founder of the enormously successful Giordano, the first Asian retailing chain where staff deliberately said 'good morning' to customers, and as the publisher of *Apple*, one of Hong Kong's two fastest-growing publications, Lai is living proof that giving the people what they

A New Model in Asia?

want is a sure way to make money in modern Asia. However, Lai has also been forced to sell off his stake in Giordano because he criticised the Chinese government in his newspapers, and he needs round-the-clock protection against Hong Kong triads whom he has also offended. As for the well-known businessman whom Lai criticises, his contacts in Beijing seem to go considerably deeper than the Deng family.

Overseas-Chinese companies, no less than any other sort, are the product of their environment; and as that environment changes, so do they. 'We have never had big home markets,' explains Raymond Ch'ien, who admits that Lam Soon, his Hong Kong food company, like many of its peers, had to change the way it did business when it went into the mainland. Virtually every big family group is experimenting in one way or another with importing western ideas. The question is how committed they are to change. The most common response has been to pack off all the children to Harvard and Stanford. Unfortunately, when these young MBAs return, their first response is usually to rush off and do deals rather than try to build or reorganise businesses.

Another slightly panicky reaction has been to recruit more managers, particularly western-trained managers. Virtually all the general managers at Robert Kuok's Shangri-La hotel chain are westerners (as are several of his closest advisers). But this enthusiasm for management often needs to be taken with a pinch of salt. Usually the western adviser's role is not dissimilar to the (non-Italian) 'consiglieri' in the Godfather films: a useful administrator but the first person to be excluded when the family does anything important. Outside investors too are treated like second-class citizens. Even though family stakes in public companies are seldom more than 40 per cent, they usually act as if they own the whole thing. Board meetings often last only fifteen minutes, and assets are brazenly shuffled between private and public companies. This will gradually change as Asian companies issue more capital (some $36 billion of new shares were issued in 1995) but there is considerable resistance. Transparency, like branding and human-resource departments, is regarded as 'un-Asian'.

Full of western promise

The idea that management theory is somehow 'un-Asian' is twaddle. There is little, for instance, that any western carrier can teach Singapore Airlines about service or marketing, even though the airline has a distinctly Asian character. But then Singapore Airlines, unlike most Chinese family companies, has a marketing department, an advertising budget and several sophisticated training programmes. In early 1996 David Li, the chief executive of the Bank of East Asia, one of Hong Kong's biggest banks, warned against Asian business people assuming that there was a uniquely Asian way of doing business. He pointed out that Confucius (a name usually invoked rapidly in any argument about Asian business) actually had no time at all for merchants. Rewarding employees well or building up a core of professional managers, argued Li, is not 'western'; it is simply good management.

That does not mean that western management theories can be daubed on to eastern structures willy-nilly. For instance, in the West, 'business-process re-engineering' has been used as a way to cut unnecessary flab in mature industries. In markets growing as quickly as Asia's, a little slack is often necessary. Nevertheless a 'kinder' version of re-engineering seems to have worked extremely well in Asia. Both Thai Farmers Bank (which, like Loxley, is controlled by the Lamsam family) and the Bank of East Asia claim enormous rises in productivity from embracing the fad – though neither has sacked anybody in the process.

A similar gradual approach also looks appropriate when it comes to concentrating on core competencies. As we have seen, outside Asia, companies do best if they build up scale and expertise in one or two specialist areas. Within Asia, diversification has not yet proved a weakness: after all, in a country like Thailand where nobody has any telecoms experience, why shouldn't a chicken-food company like Charoen Pokphand grab a licence? Indeed, it has often made sense for families to diversify their risks. In some fast-developing countries such as China and Vietnam this scatter-gun approach may still yield dividends. But, in general, companies that want to be internationally competitive will have to focus on a few core businesses.

The hereditary defect

There is one final compelling reason why even those Chinese entrepreneurs who never want to leave Asia need to reorganise their management: succession. At present, due to their inability to separate ownership from management, all Chinese companies wobble when command passes from one generation to another. In some cases empires have actually been split up: for instance Sir Y.K. Pao, a Hong Kong billionaire, divided his empire so that it could be run by his four sons-in-law. In others fights have broken out. In 1992 the Soeryadjaya family lost control of Astra, Indonesia's second biggest firm, because of enormous losses at Bank Summa, which had been run by one of the sons. Until 1995, Winston Wang looked certain to inherit Formosa Plastics, Taiwan's biggest industrial company; then, following reports of an extra-marital affair, he appeared to have fallen out with his father, Wang Yung-ching.

One old Chinese proverb says that wealth never survives the third generation. But succession is a problem for family businesses everywhere. The difference is that, outside Asia, successful family businesses – Mars, Ford, Sainsbury and so on – have turned into dynastic corporations, where there are clear divisions between the family and the firm, so that the competence of the children is less of an issue.

One set of companies that has just begun to grapple with this problem are Korea's *chaebol*. In 1996, Hyundai broke with tradition by announcing plans to bring in outside directors; it is also trying to promote non-family members inside the company. An example closer to home, albeit one that some overseas Chinese may find difficult to stomach, is the British Hongs or trading houses – Jardine Matheson and, particularly, the Swire group. The latter's interests are as wide as any Chinese business, stretching from Cathay Pacific, a Hong Kong airline, to Coca-Cola factories in China and Volvo dealerships in Taiwan. It also relies on *guanxi:* the family's connection with Rong Yiren, China's vice president, stretches back to the 1950s. But there are also two clear differences. First, unlike Chinese companies, Swire has an officer class of around 120 managers which gives the group some cohesiveness. And second, there is a relatively clear gap between John Swire & Sons, the family's London holding company, and Swire Pacific, a publicly quoted company based in Asia. This is mimicked in management where Swire's *taipan* in Hong Kong, Peter Sutch, is a non-family member.

Shih who must be obeyed

The temptation with overseas-Chinese management is to ignore Swire and the *chaebol* and simply leave it how it is: to conclude that the overseas Chinese have come up with an extremely sophisticated way of running small companies, but that they will never mature into large worldbeaters in the same way that, say, Honda and Toyota have. And where is the harm in that? The real strength of overseas-Chinese management lies in its ability to keep on building these networks of fast-moving small companies and their capacity to cope with uncertainty. Providing the stodgy old empires do not get too much in the way, this looks like a recipe for prosperity. As long as there are Chinese business people who believe a small Godforsaken piece of North Korea can become 'the Singapore of the North', Chinese capitalism does not need management theory.

However, a few Chinese companies have begun to mix western ideas with Asian ones to create something new and relatively exciting. Consider two fairly dingy offices, one in Taipei, one of the world's most hideous cities; the other in Kowloon, the overcrowded finger of land which is still considered the wrong side of the harbour by those who live in Hong Kong Island.

The first belongs to Stan Shih. Not even his friends would describe Shih as a snappy dresser, and his office feels like a 1970s Holiday Inn suite. Nevertheless, Shih is the brains behind one of the world's most interesting companies. Like many Taiwanese technology companies, the Acer group first appeared in the 1980s as an equipment manufacturer, making computer parts for better known western and Japanese companies. By 1996, it still made computers for Hitachi and components for a host of other big technology companies. But Acer had also become the seventh biggest personal computer maker in its own right, and was planning an assault on the consumer-electronics market as well. Shih was confidently predicting that Acer's revenues, which rose by three-quarters to $5.7 billion in 1995, would reach $15 billion by the end of the decade.

A visit to Acer's main factory in the Hsinchu Science Park, Taiwan's technology showcase, seems at first to confirm every westerner's prejudice that all people like Shih do is unite cheap Asian hands with western technology. To your left sit hundreds of imported young Filipinas assembling Apple Powerbooks; to your right emerges a robot transporting integrated circuits and playing a noisy electronic version of 'Camptown Races'. There is a little in this prejudice, but not much. As the Filipinas prove, Shih is just as short of cheap labour as anybody else. Besides, the real point about Acer is that it is not just a component supplier to the likes of Compaq: it is also a competitor. And its manufacturing organisation is world class. Acer has clearly passed Gordon Redding's Lexus test – as Redding admits.

That is because Shih's achievement has as much to do with management and organisation as it does with technology. Shih's philosophy has been coloured by two experiences. The first was working in the 1970s for an old-style family technology company, which collapsed, he says, for two reasons: first, it was extremely difficult to criticise any decisions made by the family even when they were obviously wrong; and second, much of the money the company made was siphoned off into the family's private companies. Shih's wife has always helped him at Acer, but he remains adamant that his children will not join him there. The second experience was a crisis at Acer in the late 1980s caused by the head office forcing different businesses to follow just one central strategy of expansion. Shih, who tendered his resignation at the time, has since tried to decentralise power in a way that few

Chinese families (or American chief executives) would countenance.

Acer is split up into a network of different companies, all with their own bosses, personnel systems and salary structures. (By 1996 only two had stock-market listings; Shih plans to list nineteen more by 2000.) When goods pass from one division to another they do so at market prices, and no division is under any obligation to use the others' services. Shih's own role is to organise the headquarters, which employs eighty people: its revenues come from dividends, and from charging the other groups for its legal and accounting services. Shih insists that he would not object if any division left the group. His only stipulation would be that the departing company could not 'fly the flag' – i.e. carry the Acer name.

In other words, Shih has taken all the best things from the Chinese family business – speed, entrepreneurialism, networking – and institutionalised them into a meritocratic system. In so doing, he has created something that would seem fresh even if it was based in San Jose instead of Taipei. Indeed, Shih's federation of small independent firms could be the answer to the problems of western companies. For instance, it looks unlikely that IBM's businesses will ever develop personalities of their own as long as they are just divisions. But if Big Blue was divided up in the same way that Acer has been, some of that hidden talent might emerge.

Interestingly, the signs are that other entrepreneurial Asian technology companies are taking the same tack as Acer. The networks of small specialist exporters that populate places like Hsinchu Park and Bangalore (India's 'Silicon plateau') tend to take the same pick-and-match attitude to western and Asian management styles. One reason why is that most of their founders once worked for western companies. For instance, another Hsinchu-Park company, Microelectronics Technology Inc, a pioneer in satellite communication, was founded by Patrick Wang, an exile from Hewlett-Packard; while Morris Chang, the founder of Taiwan Semiconductor Manufacturing Corporation, the world's biggest chip foundry, worked at Texas Instruments for twenty-five years. TSMC employs fifty engineers who have had more than ten years' experience in the United States. Twenty-six of its managers have been to business school (ten of them in America). 'It's like working for an American company,' argues Donald Brooks, TSMC's president.

Kowloon rising

Arguably, all this proves is that, if you want to survive in a business as global as the high-technology industry, you have to embrace some western management ideas. However, our second dingy office from Kowloon shows that western management ideas can also be applied to that oldest of Chinese family businesses, the old-style trading house. And once again the result is a hybrid.

The office in this case belongs to William Fung – and to be fair it is slightly smarter than Shih's. Pride of place is given to a picture of Fung's class at Harvard Business School – an institution his brother, Victor, also attended. Indeed, it was shortly after they left the school in the 1970s when they were both working in America, that the Fung brothers were summoned back to Hong Kong by their mother, who was worried about their father's health. In the best Chinese style the brothers were ordered to take over the management of Li & Fung, a trading house founded in Canton in 1906 by their grandfather Fung Pak-liu. Trading houses are no more than that; they act as middle-men for importers and exporters, taking a cut along the way.

The two brothers began by examining their family business as if it was a business-school case-study. Their first two decisions, both of which their father acceded to, were that the company should give up employing all their cousins; and that it should float on the stock market, not so much to raise cash as to bring in outside advisers and to give the cousins a chance to sell out. The idea was to make the business as transparent as possible. The Fung brothers also toyed with introducing another western idea – sacking people to cut costs. This time, their father stopped them, persuading them that this would make recruiting other staff difficult.

Li & Fung has redefined the role of a trader as 'a network manager'. It specialises in labour-intensive industries, such as toys, shoes and handbags. In all these businesses the assembly part of production tends to move to wherever hands are cheapest: bags that used to be sewn together in Malaysia are now made in China and may one day move to India. However the other characteristic of the Fung businesses is that many of the components are made in different parts of Asia. Show William Fung your briefcase and he will explain that the leather was probably tanned in Korea, the metal studs (that you had never noticed before) came from Japan, and so on. Li & Fung makes nothing itself: instead its core competence, as Fung puts it, is to act as a 'value-chain co-ordinator', linking the different arms together, designing products, finding customers and sometimes finance.

In 1995 Li & Fung bought the Hong Kong trading arm of Inchcape, an old British company, for HK$475m – a deal which doubled Li & Fung's sales to HK$12 billion. The Fung brothers egg on their managers with performance-pay structures; and staff are encouraged to criticise their managers. Nevertheless, for all the American business-school pictures on the office walls, Li & Fung is still identifiably a Chinese company. It survives by doing deals; and, even if it is no longer run as a family employment centre, it is still run by two family members, whose word, in the end, is law.

Coming to a town near you

If nothing else, our quick look at management in developing Asia shows that management theory remains a living science: at a time when many things in the West have a sense of *déjà vu*, developing Asia has thrown up new questions and perhaps the glimmer of new answers. Over the next decade, western management readers will hear much more about companies such as Li & Fung and Acer – and about overseas Chinese companies in general. The basic struggle that the overseas Chinese face – how to achieve a balance between organisation and entrepreneurialism – is exactly the same as that which most big western (and Japanese) companies face. The intriguing difference is that whilst big western firms are trying to craft entrepreneurial skills onto organisational ones, most developing Asian companies are starting from the other way round. As this chapter has made clear, we think that on balance the overseas Chinese have more to learn than they have to teach. Yet, there is also a strong feeling of 'Back to the Future'. When Tom Peters orders tired American managers to obliterate every structure in sight, the sort of virtual company he envisages is not that far from those actually already on display in (supposedly backward) Asia.

How important is the overseas-Chinese model? It is hard to imagine it sweeping across the West in the same way that 'Japanese' ideas, such as lean production and quality, did. Indeed, in the immediate future the reverse seems likely to come true: even in their home markets overseas-Chinese companies will have to change as Asia's economy slows down a little and more western companies begin to compete. Research and development, marketing, branding, command structures – in other words the sort of things that most people refer to as management – will all become more important. On the other hand, there is plainly something there. Overseas-Chinese business cannot just be written off as a fortuitous mixture of hard work and connections. Even if what might be called 'the overseas-Chinese model' ends up being subsumed into the western one, it will still bring something with it. The new hybrids that are emerging, such as Acer and Li & Fung, are genuine mixtures of two traditions.

All this leaves 'Deng', the young ambitious student at CEIBS with whom we began this chapter, supremely well placed. Providing that Beijing's politicians do not interfere, he should have the best of all worlds: an entrepreneurial nature, a knack for making contacts (remember that expensive watch), and a grasp of management ideas. Visit any big Chinese family company and you see organisations in need of management. That does not mean that Deng needs to re-engineer every company he works for. But there will be room to reorganise their manufacturing and to set up organisational structures that allow workers a clearer career. In Hong Kong, Shanghai or Bangkok the words 'Human Resources Department' no longer sound like a terrible offence to the English language; they sound like progress. Deng will follow in their wake.

PART FIVE

New Frontiers

MANAGING LEVIATHAN:
THE PUBLIC SECTOR

'Of course you have to be a quality organisation nowadays – but that's not enough. We are re-engineering all the key processes and empowering the front-line people so that we can perform for our customers . . .' Any journalist sitting down to lunch with William Bratton, the former commissioner of the New York Police Department from 1994 to early 1996, and expecting to discover the truth about the Mafia or heroin smuggling was in for a disappointment. Bratton treated his job at the NYPD as a management crusade, equating reduced crime with profits and the general public with customers. 'We've already had some interest from Harvard about a case-study,' he enthused at one point; at another he described the executive breakfasts where the likes of Jack Welch of General Electric and Ralph Larsen of Johnson & Johnson discussed management with Bratton's officers.[1]

Bratton's penchant for management theory dated back to his previous job in Boston where he used to pop in to lectures at the Harvard Business School. When he took over the NYPD job in January 1994 he made a great fuss about introducing the sort of basic office-computer technology that most companies would have taken for granted. However, his biggest changes were to do with organisation and accountability. Bratton devolved power to his eighty-six precinct commanders, and set them demanding performance targets. This was unusual enough in itself; but what made the move particularly noteworthy was the sort of perform-ance targets he set, which were all to do with preventing crime rather than just reacting to it. Bratton made it clear that he was less interested in the 'response time' to an emergency call than why the call had been made in the first place. The 'profits' he sought were the general well-being of all New Yorkers, which he measured not just in terms of the crime rate but also in terms of things like the number of businesses setting up in the city.

Every week, Bratton summoned the commanders to an early-morning meeting and examined the statistics for each precinct that all his new computers were generating. At one such meeting in 1995, Captain Michael Gabriel was hauled over the coals because murders in his Brooklyn precinct were up 62 per cent when those in the rest of the city were down 32 per cent. The centre of the murders was a single street in which forty-four shops were fronts for drug-dealing. Gabriel had only managed to close down nine. He was told to put more pressure on securing court orders.[2]

In Bratton's two years in command, crime fell sharply. Indeed, in 1995 some 1,000 fewer New Yorkers were murdered than in 1990. Bratton's crime-busting efforts attracted the interest of government officials from countries as far afield as Saudi Arabia and South Africa. Yet many New Yorkers argued that other changes – such as the police force being increased by 7,000 – must have had an effect too. They also pointed out that Bratton's re-engineering exercise had much less success in reducing corruption within his force. Quibbles perhaps; but what really exposes the gap between Bratton's rhetoric and reality is a comparison with other attempts to put management theory into practice. By the standards of most corporate re-engineering exercises, the NYPD's experience was so mild that it barely qualifies for the name. Bratton did not change the number of precincts; nor did he contract out many parts of the NYPD. Although Bratton sacked a few poor performers, he did not motivate the good ones with performance pay.

This is not so much a criticism of Bratton as a demonstration of the difference between the private sector and the public sector. Examine Bratton's 'failures' and you usually discover that he has been frustrated either by the law or by politics. For instance, he could not bring in cheap outsiders to do the NYPD's paperwork partly because there are strict rules about what work has to be carried out by police officers and partly because Bratton's real customer was Rudy Giuliani, the mayor of New York, who had no wish to offend the city's powerful police unions – and who is believed to have given Bratton his marching orders in 1996. In other words, for all the talk about 'profits' and 'customers', management theory does not fit.

A soldier's prayer

Bratton is not the only public servant to have fallen in love with management theory in the past few years. In America, on becoming Speaker of the House of Representatives, following the Republicans' triumph in the November 1994 elections, Newt Gingrich supplied his troops with a reading list. As well as the usual suspects, such as de Tocqueville's *Democracy in America*, the list included Peter Drucker and Alvin and Heidi Toffler (see page 356). Not to be outdone, President Clinton spent his holiday holed up in Camp David with two motivational gurus, Anthony Robbins and Stephen Covey. Al Gore can barely open his mouth without talking about reinventing some part of government. This enthusiasm has been copied around the world, from Sweden to Singapore, and embraced by socialists as well as conservatives. In October 1995 Tony Blair, the leader of Britain's Labour party (who went on to become prime minister in 1997), sent his entire shadow cabinet to Templeton College, Oxford, to spend a weekend learning about management theory.

Indeed, it is hard to walk down any corridor of power nowadays without hearing a new and hideous language – 'managing by objectives', 'outsourcing non-core functions', 'negotiating performance measures' and the rest of it. Even generals and admirals are 'downsizing their human resources' and 'benchmarking their competitors'. 'Of course this benchmarking is only a rough guide,' admits one Pentagon bureaucrat. 'The ultimate benchmarking exercise is war.' Given that several thousand Red Army officers have already attended a management course at Minsk, the gurus will have the comfort of knowing that, should the world's two foremost military powers go to war, they will be doing so in their language.

But is this enthusiasm for management theory 'a good idea'?

Like most such questions, it depends on your expectations. Peter Drucker has been arguing for half a century that the place where management theory is most needed is in the public sector. In most cases – the NYPD is a good example – even cynics have to admit that management theory has hardly made the public sector worse. Yet to many people – Drucker included – management theory in the public sector has proved a disappointment. Many of its easiest victories have come from privatising parts of the public sector that should never have been public in the first place. When management theory has been applied to areas which have to remain within the public sector – notably health and education – its results have often been patchy. The peculiar circumstances of the public sector have only exaggerated the contradictions within private-sector management theory; and there has been precious little good, new public-sector management theory. A victory has been won, but it has often been a Pyrrhic one.

How they met

In Britain, Australasia, Canada and now Scandinavia the public sector's love-affair with management theory started at the top. Shocked by the state of their public finances, governments called for help from the private sector. For example, in Britain Margaret Thatcher and her ministers set up a succession of powerful bodies, some of them staffed by businessmen and consultants, to improve the management of the public sector: the Efficiency Unit (under Lord Rayner, head of Marks & Spencer), the Financial Management Unit, the National Audit Office and the Audit Commission. Thatcher also introduced a wide range of 'market-oriented' reforms, including privatisation.

In the United States, on the other hand, the love-affair with management theory started with lower-level bureaucrats who were increasingly frustrated by the foot-dragging of the public sector. In the early 1980s, Bob Stone was deputy assistant secretary for installations at the Department of Defense, and he was furious with the way that bureaucratic regulations were producing lousy services for his troops. For Stone, *In Search of Excellence* (1982) by Tom Peters and Robert Waterman was a revelation. Using the book which he still describes as 'a bible', Stone tried to get rid of all the rules which kept him from staying close to his customer. He handed power to front-line managers, condensed thick Pentagon manuals into page-long mission statements and turned one outpost into a 'regulation-free' installation, modelled on a store he had read about in *In Search of Excellence*. He also invited Peters to give lectures to the top brass.

At roughly the same time that Stone was discovering excellence, 'total quality management' (which means anything from reorganising workers into teams to taking notice of customers) became a quasi-religion among local government officials. One of the first nationally known figures to join the movement in the 1980s was Bill Clinton, then governor of Arkansas, who took to making speeches praising W. Edwards Deming and other quality gurus. By 1992 consultants at Coopers & Lybrand could count more than 200 local government 'quality initiatives' in the United States.

By the late 1980s the federal government too had become a convert – albeit in its own ponderous way. In 1988 Executive Order 12,637 ordained a government-wide TQM programme and established a Federal Quality Initiative housed in the Office of Personnel Management. Four years later a twenty-eight-volume report on federal management problems appeared. But public-sector management theory really went into overdrive in March 1993 when Bill Clinton established the National Performance Review under Al Gore's leadership. One of the first people it hired was Bob Stone, the disciple of Excellence.

Regardless of who first sponsored them, management ideas are now an institutionalised part of government. The Clinton administration has established a public-sector equivalent of the Baldridge Award for quality. British civil servants can win awards called Charter Marks for things such as successful staff suggestions. Britain has also established a public-sector MBA to ensure that civil servants are *au fait* with the latest in management thinking. There are even special Internet sites to which bureaucrats of all nations can log on to discuss subjects such as 'TQM for public servants'.

All this has proved a bonanza for management consultancies. In mid-1995 John Major's government admitted in a series of parliamentary questions that it had spent at least £320m on management consultants – almost certainly a fraction of the real figure. British consultancies are doing so well out of the public sector that they have started hiring former councillors to give them advice: Margaret Hodge, once head of the notoriously badly managed Islington Council, became a consultant to Price Waterhouse before returning to politics as a Labour MP. In America the public sector has proved such a lucrative client that most big consultancies now have several departments devoted to its needs: one firm, CSC Index, even has a special centre that concentrates on federal customers, such as the Department of Defense and NASA.

Fatal attraction

To the cynical eye, this may look conclusive proof of a honey-trap. Talk to many consultants privately and they will admit that governments have offered them a wonderful chance to resell (expensively) products and theories that they have already dished out to the private sector. Yet they will also insist that they were relatively late to realise its potential: on the whole, most of the enthusiasm for the affair has come from the public sector, which has shown a blind affection for management theory that is rarely seen in the private sector.

That obsession has three roots. The first is a crisis in faith in the public sector and a resurgence of faith in the private. In Britain, Margaret Thatcher instinctively regarded civil servants as muddle-headed do-gooders, who went into public service because they were too stupid or left-wing to make money in the private sector, and habitually called in friends from the private sector, such as Lord Rayner or Lord King, who was put in charge of British Airways, to solve difficult problems. In his direst hour, John Major brought in a consultant from McKinsey to head his Policy Unit. In America, Newt Gingrich takes a similar, simplistic line:

'Things that are making American business more competitive can be applied to the federal government.'

Nor is the Clinton administration much of a slouch when it comes to entrepreneur worship. If nothing else, Hillary Clinton's appetite for commodity trading and the Whitewater investment scheme have shown that the Clintons have never frowned on the quick buck. The Clinton family has always had strong ties to Arkansas businesses, notably Wal-Mart, Tyson Foods and the Stephens financial empire. Al Gore has been spotted doing all the right things – touring Southwest Airlines and General Motors's Saturn factory, and holding seminars with business luminaries such as Vaughan Beals, chairman of Harley-Davidson, and Jack Welch of General Electric.

Indeed, it is often liberals who are most passionate about management theory because they think it will help salvage government from public disillusionment. By the mid-1990s only 20 per cent of the American public trusted the federal government to 'do the right thing', compared with 76 per cent thirty years ago. Elaine Kamark, Gore's chief policy adviser, blames this on the fact that the public sector is stuck with a '1950s' attitude to its customers: workers continue to treat customers with surly indifference, whereas the private sector is increasingly competing on the basis of 'customer satisfaction'.

The second reason why governments of all persuasions are obsessed with management theory is a common desire to do 'more with less': to continue to provide reasonable public services without spending a higher proportion of GDP on the state. Politicians have noted that companies have been cutting their workforces while producing more and better products. Watchdogs like Britain's Audit Commission and America's Office of Management and Budget have repeatedly detailed public-sector inefficiencies. It is only natural for politicians to conclude that they can put off making hard decisions about raising taxes or cutting services by managing things better.

In America, Al Gore has said that agencies will have to 'justify why they should continue to exist at all'. In 1993–95 a Democrat presidency cut the Federal workforce by 100,000. Britain has slimmed its civil service to a central core and contracted out everything else to some 100 agencies, which operate on short-term contracts, or the private sector. Throughout the world, local government is a particular target. 'Inside every fat and bloated local authority is a slim one struggling to get out,' Nicholas Ridley, one of Thatcher's favourite ministers, once proclaimed.

Many politicians, including the late Mr Ridley, have been fascinated by California's 'contract cities' which buy in most of their public services. The usual model is a city called Lakewood, which, when it was first incorporated in 1954, supposedly needed only three employees to monitor the contractors who provided its 70,000 inhabitants with their hospitals, police and so on. Nowadays Lakewood is a little less streamlined – it employs 160 people and the council has to meet every two weeks, rather than once a year – but independent studies suggest that *per capita* spending on public services in contract cities is roughly half that in towns where the local authority provides the service itself.[3]

The third reason why governments have turned to management theory is a vague feeling that, regardless of the need to cut budgets, the public sector must move with the times. Just as the private sector has to take account of the spread of information technology and the emergence of much fussier, value-conscious consumers, so must the state. Al Gore once complained that Americans suffered 'from a quill-pen government in the age of Word Perfect'. Many high-ranking officials in Washington have had extensive experience of the private sector as it turned itself around in the 1980s. Listen to Newt Gingrich talk about Drucker or Alvin Toffler, and even his worst enemy would have to admit that the speaker's enthusiasm for change in the public sector is motivated by more than just a desire to cut welfare.

Any new ideas?

All this implies that there is something in what the consultants say: that, by and large, the politicians' feet have been so firmly on the accelerator that the management industry has usually been happy just to be taken along for the ride. This applies particularly to the gurus themselves who, by and large, have failed to produce new ideas for the public sector. For instance, Tom Peters, usually no slouch when it comes to selling his ideas, initially ignored it. It was not until 1989 that he produced a film about 'excellence in the public sector'. True, all the gurus pay lip service to Drucker's idea that the public sector is crying out for good management. True, they have begun to include a few more public-sector case-studies in their books. But, from Drucker onwards, their interest has largely been in the big picture, rather than the niceties of how to run particular government organisations.

A case in point is the guru who has most obviously involved himself in the public sector: Michael Porter of the Harvard Business School. He first got interested in the public sector in the 1980s when Ronald Reagan asked him to sit on the President's Commission on Industrial Competitiveness.[4] At the time busi-ness-magazine wisdom held that the globalisation of trade was making nations less and less important. Indeed Robert Reich, then Porter's colleague at Harvard, later put the case in its most sophisticated form in *The Work of Nations* in 1991, arguing that education and training were the only real source of national competitive advantage, because labour is the least mobile of all the factors of production.[5]

However, as the commission deliberated Porter became impressed by the huge role that nation states and national differences play in determining the success of companies. The result of this conversion in 1989 was *The Competitive Advantage of Nations*. Over 800 pages long, lavishly illustrated with charts, cluster maps and the like, littered with details about British biscuit makers and Korean piano companies, the book is a general inquiry into what makes national economies successful, and how governments should act to improve their country's competitive-ness. The book, which was read (or at least bought) by aspiring intellectuals everywhere, led to Porter himself doing consulting work for a large number of governments, writing reports on the competitive positions of New Zealand, Canada and Portugal.

Following similar assignments in local government Porter produced *The Competitive Advantage of Massachusetts* and *The Competitive Advantage of the Inner-City*.

The Competitive Advantage of Nations is really a book about
globalisation (see pages 253–5). But it also shows why it is
legitimate for business people and business thinkers to worry
about the state's role. National environments have always played a
central role in making firms successful, Porter argued. Now, as
globalisation and free trade expose firms to ever more competitors, the effect of national peculiarities on companies counts for
more, not less.

A colleague of Porter's at Harvard, Rosabeth Moss Kanter, has
recently looked at the relationship between public policy and
what some would call 'the business community' from the other
way round. As globe-spanning firms move operations from, say,
Massachusetts to Manila in search of better workers, they force (or
should force) politicians to rethink public policy. *World Class:
Thriving Locally in the Global Economy* looks at the impact of
globalisation on local communities.[6] She insists that the best way
for any region to thrive is to become world class at one of three
activities: thinking, manufacturing or trading. Moss Kanter's basic
argument is that it is pointless to fight globalisation; far from
preserving local communities, nativism condemns them to
disintegration.

All this clearly shows that there is a good deal of common
ground between management theory and the public sector. But it
is hard to see how Porter and Moss Kanter are much help to, say,
a Postmaster General trying to redesign the mail service. Both
Porter and Moss Kanter seem fired up about issues that have more
to do with general economics and political philosophy than the
nitty-gritty of public-sector management. The same could be said
for Kenichi Ohmae and his crusade to reform Japanese politics or
Charles Handy and his concern for the quality of British public
life, or indeed for any other of the first-division gurus.

This lofty disdain for detail has left room for a new breed of
management gurus who specialise in the public sector. The most
influential of these are David Osborne, an American public-policy

consultant, and Ted Gaebler, a former city manager. Their *Reinventing Government: How the Entrepreneurial Spirit is Transforming the Public Sector* reached the top of the best-seller lists in 1992, spawned an influential pressure group, the Alliance for Redesigning Government, and provided the first Clinton administration with something of a model.[7] The book was originally going to be called *In Search of Excellence in Government*, in tribute to Peters and Waterman; but in the end they decided to name it after another management tome, *Reinventing the Corporation*, by John Naisbitt.

As their fascination with private-sector gurus hints, the problem with Osborne and Gaebler is that, for all the details, their book is really about recycling old ideas rather than creating new ones. *Reinventing Government* simply explains how private-sector management theory can be applied to the public sector.

In practice, the real 'gurus' to emerge out of the public sector are the practitioners – usually politicians implementing what they think management theory should be. Al Gore's report on reinventing government, which also reached the *New York Times* best-seller list, reads rather like a self-conscious attempt to do for the public sector what *In Search of Excellence* did for the private: inspire readers to follow the example of America's best organisations. Bill Creech, a four-star general who made his name for his innovative approach to running Tactical Air Command, including condensing a 440-page rule book into an eight-page guide book, has become a guru in his own right, with his *Five Pillars of TQM*.

As soon as retired generals start writing about the five pillars of quality sensible people brace themselves for a backlash. All the same, it is often such earthy types who do the original thinking in the public sector. When Wal-Mart, a retail giant, was thinking of introducing pharmacies, the firm looked around to see who was best at designing queuing systems for large numbers of customers and found, to its surprise, that the answer was Air Combat Command. The American army is one of the leaders in getting poorly educated people from different ethnic backgrounds to work together. In 1995 Charles Handy cited the British army as an example of a 'high commitment' organisation which has really re-engineered itself since the war by slimming down to a fighting force of 60,000 men – an organisation, he noted, that was now smaller than Royal Dutch/Shell.[8]

The view from the trenches

On the whole, though, cases of 'best practice' springing out of the public sector are rare. In general all the public sector does is borrow ideas from the private sector. It often seems like a bureaucratic version of Chinese Whispers, with one group of people applying what they think another group of people have said.

Many governments are introducing what Peter Drucker once called 'management by objectives': mission statements (laying out broad objectives), fixed contracts (specifying what employees are expected to do), and performance measures (measuring how well they were doing it). An even more common idea currently doing the rounds of the public sector is the notion that 'the customer is king' – something Theodore Levitt, a professor at the Harvard Business School, preached to the private sector in the 1960s and Tom Peters re-preached in the 1980s. Now the Danish and Canadian governments are trying to persuade civil servants to treat their clients like private-sector customers; so is the British government, with its Citizens' Charter initiative. Even the Chinese government has sent out orders instructing its bureaucrats not be rude to its citizens.

In one way this is a little fatuous. Phrases such as 'Remember that the customer always has a choice' do not make much sense in an unemployment office in Bradford, let alone Beijing. But governments are putting some substance to this rhetoric by offering people compensation if service falls below a certain performance measure. Even such notoriously customer-hostile organisations as America's Internal Revenue Service and London Underground have adopted 'customer service standards'. And, like many other things to do with management theory, merely going through the motions can reveal some things – even if they are largely for curiosity value. One of the few reasons why the

White House now knows that there is an 'eagle parts programme', which collects dead eagles partly to supply bits of them to Indians for ceremonial purposes, is because the practice was cited by managers in the Department of the Interior as an example of innovative, customer-driven government.

Moreover, just because an idea is old does not necessarily mean that it is a bad one. Most companies treat customer service as a starting point; there is no reason why the taxman should not do the same. The same goes for another 'old' management technique: employee motivation and performance pay. In Britain, Australia and New Zealand the heads of civil-service departments are appointed for limited terms and rewarded, in part, on the basis of their performance. In Sunnyvale, California, city managers can achieve bonuses of up to 10 per cent if their agencies exceed agreed targets.

London Underground now publishes information about the performance of various Tube lines both against targets, and against each other. The state of Oregon has introduced 270 benchmarks, measuring everything from cutting teenage pregnancies to cleaning up the environment, and moved to performance-based budgeting. Telling people how well or badly they are doing can have a dramatic effect. Southwark Council, traditionally one of the poorest and most left-wing boroughs in Britain, divided its housing department into nineteen neighbourhood offices and then pestered them with information about how well they were doing, both *vis à vis* each other and other councils. The council also made all the comparative data publicly available. By 1995 Southwark was processing housing benefit quicker than any other London council except Kensington and Chelsea, a far wealthier area.[9]

All this customer service is fine enough, but from most civil servants' point of view, management theory is synonymous with one thing: delayering. The NYPD apart, re-engineering has often been brutal in the public sector. One victim has been Britain's Treasury which is now urging the discipline on other departments. Al Gore would eventually like the federal government to hit Tom Peters' target of one manager for every 25–75 employees.

In 1992–95 the British civil service shrank by 11 per cent to 506,000; the target is to remove another 60,000 people by 1998 (a reduction equal to the total staff of the Royal Air Force).[10] Having turned various government departments into independent executive agencies, British ministers have been hacking away at the central administration in Whitehall. For instance, by merging the Departments of Education and Employment, they were able to make do with ninety-five top civil servants instead of 145.

And, as in the private sector, downsizing and cost-cutting programmes are increasingly accompanied by an appetite for more modern, 'soft' management techniques. Some American government officials carry around small gold business cards which 'empower' them to make decisions without first going to their superiors. Some departments are even giving out 'forgiveness coupons', which pre-forgive people their mistakes, in order to encourage them to adopt a less rule-bound approach to government. One division of the National Forest Service, at Ochoco Reserve, Oregon, has introduced 'Grue Awards', named after an employee, which workers can give to each other as a token of appreciation for outstanding work.

This affection for mixing hard and soft management theory reaches right into the White House. When he is not thinking up ideas for slimming government, Al Gore is coming up with visions, or handing out 'heroes of reinvention' awards. No sooner had Bill Clinton been first elected president in 1992 than he organised a bonding weekend, designed to encourage more effective team-building, at which two 'facilitators' tried to get everybody to confess to some hidden secret. (Warren Christopher, the Secretary of State, admitted that he enjoyed jazz and piano bars.) Clinton also bought in two 'peak-performance gurus', Anthony Robbins and Stephen Covey, to motivate him, and a businessman, Erskine Bowles, to do a time-and-motion study of his schedule. Bowles produced a business plan, 'Strategic Goals for 1995', which amongst other things resulted in the president spending 62.5 per cent more time shaping domestic and economic policy.

Although it is hard to imagine, say, Jack Welch or Rupert Murdoch tolerating this sort of thing, Clinton's infatuations are fairly normal inside the Beltway. Hazel O'Leary, President Clinton's first energy secretary, proclaimed herself a student of Stephen Covey, who, she claimed, allowed people to break the 'ring of fear' that prevented them from hitting their peak performance. Nor are the Republicans immune. Their leaders now hold a 'management retreat' at the beginning of every year to help them set the agenda. Newt Gingrich argued that his Contract with America was primarily designed as 'a management-training document that was politically useful, not simply as a political document'.

Future historians may find these enthusiasms endearing or ridiculous; but, from a management theorist's point of view, most of them are fairly old. Leaving aside the armed forces' prowess in some types of personnel management, there is only one area where civilian civil servants can claim to be in the front line: creating internal markets. Again, the idea itself is a fairly old one: divide up a big organisation into small entrepreneurial units and force them to buy and sell from each other. But in many places, particularly Britain and New Zealand, governments have taken the idea further than companies. Perhaps the best-known example is the British health service, which we deal with in considerable detail in the last part of this chapter. However, throughout Britain's public service, schoolmasters, mandarins and government agencies have been forced to think of themselves as independent entities, with their own budgets and their incomes linked to the number of customers they can attract. And in New Zealand, the government has even applied the idea to politicians. It charges ministers with 'purchasing' services from the heads of civil service departments (renamed Chief Executives).

The backlash begins

The 1995 meeting of the Academy of Management was treated to a coruscating attack on the influence of management theory on the public sector by Henry Mintzberg. The *Harvard Business Review*, he argued, should have a skull and crossbones stamped on the cover with the warning 'not to be taken by the public sector'.

In the same year, Peter Drucker wrote a long article for the

Atlantic Monthly. It began by ridiculing parts of Al Gore's reinventing government crusade, such as the consolidation of 'the application process' in welfare offices in Atlanta into a 'one-stop shop' (which was management-speak for getting phone calls answered) and the reinvention of the Export-Import Bank, which, Drucker dryly noted, 'is now expected to do what it was set up to do all of sixty years ago: help small businesses get export financing'.[11]

Like Mintzberg, Drucker puzzled why the government had to think of people as customers in order to do things that should come naturally. But his core complaint was that most public-sector management theory came down to two things: either endlessly patching up services or downsizing, both things that had not worked in private sector. Worse, these remedies were being applied to fossilised organisations that had changed little since Herbert Hoover. What was needed was to 'rethink' the public sector, to ask basic questions of each part of government such as 'What is your mission?', 'Is it still the right mission?' and so on. Why, wondered Drucker, did the Veterans Administration run 300 hospitals itself, instead of contracting out the job to the private sector? And why did agriculture deserve its own department when it provided work for only 3 per cent of the population? The point, argued Drucker, was not to shrink government but to make it more effective.

Mintzberg and Drucker's frustration with what passes for public-sector management theory is as nothing compared with the fury of those who have been affected by it. Mention management theory to Oxford professors who spend half their time reporting back to Whitehall or to doctors who are judged by how many 'illness episodes' they have treated and you are guaranteed a tirade. Everybody in the upper reaches of the public sector seems to agree on the awfulness of managers: on the hideousness of their language, the harmfulness of their methods and the sheer second-rateness of their intellects. The only question is why governments have allowed themselves to be hoodwinked by this bunch of failed businessmen into wasting so much money.

Indeed, in Britain, the country where management theory has probably been applied most enthusiastically, the idea has become something of a public joke. In the 1995 film *Goldeneye* Bond's beloved 'M' is replaced by an accountant whose obsession with cutting costs has earned her the nickname 'the evil queen of numbers'. A good portion of *Hemingway's Chair*, a novel by Michael Palin which also came out in 1995, is devoted to ridiculing the way that management theory is changing the post office. Watch any television drama set in a school or hospital and you will be treated to an attack on the 'internal market'. Indeed, it is hard to think of any organisation which hates management theory as passionately as the BBC. The use of management gobbledegook by John Birt, the BBC's director general, prompted a special 'Birtspeak' column in *Private Eye* which the satirical magazine later expanded to include 'management drivel of all kinds'.

Will the accused please stand?

The charge sheet against management theory in the public sector begins with its expense. Fancy new management systems usually involve sophisticated computers, to speed up the flow of information, and well-groomed managers, to handle the additional paperwork. Government departments frequently have to hire expensive consultants to advise on 'change management' and 'personnel management', as everything which used to be done by instinct is now done on the basis of 'flow charts' and 'action plans'. In the United States, cities often spend 20 per cent of the cost of a contracted-out service on managing the contract.

Public-sector employees and politicians have proved to be more enthusiastic than sophisticated in their use of management ideas. One of the reasons why the Clinton White House got into such a mess was that, on coming into office, Clinton 'downsized' his staff by a quarter without rethinking their jobs. Politicians are no less addicted to fads than their private-sector equivalents – the only difference being that public-sector fads seem to lag behind private-sector fads by about five years.

Similarly, because politicians and administrators have failed to distinguish between the different sorts of management theory they are often most exposed to its contradictions. The three most popular public-sector fads – downsizing, re-engineering and total quality management – are, on many points of substance, mutually incompatible. Downsizing argues that workers are expendable; TQM sees them as an invaluable resource. Re-engineering depends on ripping up the organisation and starting again; TQM is a doctrine of continuous, incremental improvement.

A typical public-sector management reform involves keeping the old departmental structure, but hoping to do it with fewer people; worse, it introduces a performance measure in the crudest possible way. These days academics may be promoted for writing a lot of articles despite the fact that they are all bunk, and surgeons can be demoted because so many of their patients die. Most 'normal' companies now do much of their creative work in self-governing teams; the public sector has largely ignored this – as it has ideas such as networking. It was not until November 1995 that Michael Heseltine, a successful publisher in the private sector, persuaded his colleagues in John Major's Cabinet to welcome in Cab-e-net, an on-line information system.

However, the idea that the public sector has ignored most conspicuously is trust. In November 1995 Britain's top mandarin, Sir Robin Butler, admitted that the pressures in Whitehall were creating 'a feeling of insecurity' as the civil service was being forced to reshape itself 'faster than perhaps we have ever had to before'.[12] This seemed an understatement in a service, previously known for its jobs-for-life mentality, that had recently seen the early departure of three permanent secretaries and two agency chief executives – not to mention some 70,000 other civil servants.

Mintzberg argues that the growing obsession with measurement and accountability is bringing governments into conflict with all that is best in the public-sector ethic. Civil-service professions have traditionally exercised control through shared values, inculcated through long training; now it is assumed that their only values are financial (Mintzberg once heard a business manager proclaim, in all seriousness, that 'through control, we can prevent people from falling in love with their business').

This sounds merely as if management theory has been misapplied by bureaucrats. However, there is plenty of evidence that private-sector managers are no better at running the public sector than civil servants. In Britain, for instance, there have been a few successes, such as Sir Peter Levene, who reorganised first the Ministry of Defence's procurement system and then the Docklands Light Railway. But Lord Rayner found improving efficiency in government much harder than at Marks & Spencer. And at British Rail, both Bob Horton (a former chairman of BP) and Bob Reid (of Shell) were given a far rougher ride from the railmen's unions than they ever faced within their oil fiefdoms.

When Derek Lewis, a former protégé of Lord Rayner's at Marks & Spencer and then a director at Granada, was called in to run Britain's prisons, one official said the reasoning was 'to import a hard-edged private-sector manager to deal with the prison shambles'.[13] In fact Lewis found himself anything but in charge, caught in a three-cornered battle between the powerful prison-guard unions, the Home Secretary, Michael Howard, and the media. Lewis was sacked after a report in 1995 into the escape of two top-security prisoners from Parkhurst prison, which included a damning verdict on the introduction of new management methods: 'Any organisation which boasts one Statement of Purpose, one Vision, five Values, six Goals, seven Strategic Priorities and eight Key Performance Indicators, without any clear correlation between them, is producing a recipe for confusion.'

These episodes are not confined to Britain. In 1994 Renato Riverso and Roberto Schisano, successful managers at, respectively, IBM and Texas Instruments, were given the job of turning around the Italian airline Alitalia. Like Lewis they increased operational efficiency. They also tried to push through a restructuring plan; but they failed to cover their backs politically and, by March 1996, the unions had managed to persuade the government to eject both of them. Speaking to Riverso, an IBM veteran, you get the impression that he simply could not believe some of the practices he encountered – such as Alitalia cabin crew refusing to let people with confirmed paid-for tickets on to the aircraft so that their friends and relations (needless to say travelling free) could have the seats. On the other hand, his critics say that he was naive to expect anything different.

However, the greatest example of political naivety was Hillary Clinton's attempt to reform America's health-care system. To help her Mrs Clinton hired Ira Magaziner, head of a management consultancy, Telesis, and erstwhile adviser to dozens of America's leading corporations. Mr Magaziner acted like a parody of a consultant, intent on producing a perfect plan and blind to the demands of democratic politics. He set up gigantic committees, composed of hundreds of experts from around the world, to consider the problem. He assembled documents and reports from around the country. He produced a gigantic blueprint for an entirely new health-care system. The legislature threw it out with contempt.

Such disasters hint at a more fundamental argument preached by Mintzberg (though not by Drucker): that there are such fundamental differences between the public sector and the private sector that management theory from one will never be applicable to the other. One of Mintzberg's starting points, for instance, is that we are not customers of governments but citizens. A citizen cannot opt out of the social contract in the same ways as he might a commercial one. In the name of the common good, reluctant citizens can be conscripted into the army.

In other words 'government' and 'management' are not interchangeable concepts. Private-sector managers live under the threat of bankruptcy if they shirk tough decisions; politicians usually have the option of printing money or raising taxes. Private-sector managers are answerable to just one dictator, the bottom line. Their public-sector equivalents are, as Derek Lewis, Roberto Schisano and Ira Magaziner all found out, answerable to everyone and no one. As John Kay pointed out during the Lewis saga, 'Where there is ambiguity about responsibility, there is no real accountability. And where there is neither accountability nor responsibility there is inefficiency and incompetence.'[14]

Nor are such dilemmas confined to expensively imported

bosses. Normal civil servants have to serve the party in power without degenerating into party functionaries. They have to bear in mind that large numbers of people did not vote for the government, and that an opposition party, with different policies and priorities, may soon take over. It is rather like running a firm which has several sets of contradictory accounts and lives on the edge of a hostile take-over.

Public-sector managers also live in a world of rules and regulations, which limit their freedom to control both their employees and their budgets. Employment laws mean that sacking public workers is expensive (because senior staff have to be given expensive retirement packages) or counter-productive (because the first to go are the youngest and brightest). When America's Department of Interior cut the staff of its computing facility by 20 per cent, for example, it was forced to dismiss all its youngest employees – i.e. the ones who actually knew something about modern computers. When private-sector managers are brought in to redesign this or reinvent that bit of the public sector, they are repeatedly shocked to find that they must meticulously obey laws and regulations, and that they are answerable to the legislature for their actions.

Nor are these necessarily bad things. The public sector has piled control system upon control system not just for the fun of it, but to protect the public from the abuse of its money. Too much 'flexibility' can easily be turned into a national scandal by the press, forcing civil servants to reintroduce rigorous top-down controls. There is a limit to how much we can 'empower' government employees. After all, the roll call of 'empowered' government employees so far includes not only Oliver North but Robert Citron, the former chief financial officer of Orange County.

A disappointment, not a mistake

Does all this mean that management theory and the public sector are incompatible? Or is it just a relationship that requires more thought than either side has yet given it? Many of the disasters are really just a horrible reminder of two problems which plague policy-making of all kinds. The first is that the state is an incredibly blunt instrument: it gets hold of one idea and imposes it without any sensitivity to context. The second is the desperate craving of politicians for a magical solution: management theory has been supposed to restore people's faith in government, allow governments to cut taxes without reducing services, and generally square all sorts of impossible circles.

The worst thing about the public sector's obsession with management theory is its penchant for managerialism: the idea that something will be fixed once it is managed well. This is the 'quackery' that Drucker condemned in the *Atlantic Monthly*. No amount of managing can make sense of America's Medicare programme or Europe's common agriculture policy. Drucker blames this on political theorists who since Machiavelli have neglected 'what the proper functions of governments might be' and 'what governments should be accountable for'. Even leaving aside Drucker's uncharacteristically bizarre reading of history (what on earth were Hegel and John Stuart Mill on about if not the proper limits and functions of government?), the idea that it is all political theory's fault looks like passing the buck. Management theory has remarkably strong views about what companies should do and what they shouldn't. It too should play a role in working out the core competencies of the state.

In other words, it is fair to castigate management theorists for what they have failed to do in the public sector. But what about what they have done? The answer is surely that management theory has proved a disappointment but not a failure. Most of its critics tend to ignore the state of the public sector before the theorists arrived. For example, the charge that management theory has 'destroyed' staff morale forgets that there has been a 'crisis in the civil service' in most countries in every decade since the Second World War (a book by that name was much discussed in Britain in the 1960s – a period now revered by the traditionalists as a golden age).

The most obvious example of management theory improving the public sector is privatisation. Look at the performance of any privatised telephone service from Buenos Aires to Birmingham and you discover that, although people moan about the profits being made by the new owners, few want to return to the days when (in Buenos Aires at least) you had to bribe an official just to get your phone connected. One reason for the problems of public-sector management in America is that local politicians (with a few notable exceptions such as Stephen Goldsmith, the mayor of Indianapolis) have been nervous about moving services into the private sector.

Fine, you might say, but what about those parts of the public sector that have remained public: schools, hospitals and so on. It is in this area – the heart of the public sector – that the list of disappointments lengthens and public dissatisfaction is most obvious. It is worth saying one thing at the start: that critics of management theory are often heroically blind to what would have happened without it. The outstanding example of this is the BBC. John Birt's reforms may have sometimes bordered on the absurd, but, without some sign of movement, the Corporation might well have been forced by the Conservatives to give up the licence fee.

In general, management theory has often been introduced ineptly and for the wrong reasons; it has also wreaked havoc with the morale of the organisations concerned. However, on balance, we would argue that it has brought progress – perhaps not as much as it could have done but certainly more than would have happened in the muddled world that preceded it; and that it has basically won the political argument, in that its opponents want to adapt its reforms rather than reverse them. As a case-study to support this thesis we offer one that opponents of public-sector management theory would probably also choose: the British National Health Service.

The reform of the NHS, in one way, shows the power of management theory. Here after all was the largest organisation in Europe beside the Red Army being transformed by the ideas of an obscure Californian management thinker. Yet it also shows how management theory in the public sector is as much about politics as about organisational logic; how presentation is frequently more important than fact.

Somebody call a doctor

To outsiders the NHS has been the jewel in the crown of Britain's welfare state. To insiders, however, it has been a managerial nightmare. This is partly because of its size, and partly because it has long seethed with discontent. 'One of the most striking features of the NHS,' noted Enoch Powell, Minister for Health in 1960–63, 'is the continual, deafening chorus of complaint which rises day and night from every part of it, a chorus only interrupted when someone suggests that a different system altogether might be preferable . . . It presents what must be a unique spectacle of an undertaking that is run down by everyone engaged in it.'

In theory an unhappy institution should welcome change; the NHS never has. The staff are convinced that, however bad things are, they will only be made worse by meddling politicians. And there is a dangerous mismatch between the power of the employees (who are concentrated and visible) and the interests of the customers (who are unorganised and dispersed). For all that, the Conservative party eventually decided to shake up the National Health Service in the late 1980s; and it decided to do so along lines suggested by a management theorist.

Its guru was Alain Enthoven, an American disciple of Robert McNamara. Having worked for his hero at the Defense Department, he discovered a second career as a health economist, holding a chair at Stanford University and becoming a key figure in the Jackson Hole Group, a collection of health-care specialists who met in the Wyoming resort every year. In June 1985, after a tour of the English National Health Service, Enthoven wrote an article for *The Economist* arguing for a comprehensive reform of the NHS which was widely circulated amongst the radical right of the Conservative party and was the basis for the eventual reforms.[15]

Enthoven argued that the NHS structure 'suffers from a lack of real incentives for good performance. It relies on dedication and idealism. It is propelled by the clash of the interests of different provider groups. But it offers few positive incentives to do a better job for patients . . .' Enthoven's solution was an internal market, based around three big structural changes.

The first was a division between the buyers of health care (usually health authorities) and a range of competing providers (hospitals and the like). In the old-fashioned NHS doctors made all the most important decisions about allocating resources: the result was pots of cash for high-tech surgery and peanuts for preventative medicine. In the market-based NHS the job of the buyers would be to assess the health needs of the population and to meet them as efficiently as possible; the providers would compete to produce the best combination of service and cost.

The second change was to introduce prices. In the old-fashioned NHS resources were allocated by historical accident and administrative fiat. This meant that too much money went to fast-emptying inner-cities (which boasted ancient hospitals) and too little to the flourishing suburbs. More worryingly still, it created an efficiency trap. Successful hospitals attracted more patients without attracting more resources; unsuccessful hospitals lost patients without losing resources. In the new NHS money would follow patients.

The third change was to devolve managerial decisions to the lowest possible level. The problem with the old-fashioned NHS was that it gave doctors few incentives to improve their efficiency but every incentive to lobby for more resources. The best way to solve a problem was to complain about underfunding in the hope that you might be given more money. Enthoven wanted hospitals to be self-managing.

This idea looked calculated to appeal to Margaret Thatcher. In fact, her instinct was to stay well clear of the 'political heffalump trap' as she called the NHS. Her policy was to spend more money – real expenditure on health increased by 33 per cent between 1979 and 1987 – rather than ask fundamental questions. The 1987 election manifesto, which included ideas like privatising water, had nothing but platitudes on the NHS.

All this changed in the winter of 1987. No sooner had Mrs Thatcher won the 1987 general election than the NHS seemed to fall apart. Hospitals up and down the country closed wards for lack of funds. Newspapers overdosed on stories of hole-in-the-heart babies killed by penny-pinching Thatcherism. Once again Thatcher tried to buy peace: she handed the NHS an extra £100m. Eventually on a television programme, *Panorama*, she was so needled by an interviewer that she announced plans for a prime ministerial review of the NHS, taking everybody by surprise, civil servants, ministers and even herself.

It is hard to claim that an idea seized in panic was the result of long-term planning. Yet, in other ways, the NHS Review represented a triumph of management theory. Traditionally, British government reviews had been more like job-creation schemes for the great and the good, addressing vague problems and taking years to appear; the NHS Review was much more like something a management consultancy might be happy with. The Review met in secret, and consisted only of the prime minister and four Cabinet members.

Enthoven's idea of an internal market was rapidly adopted. At first some right-wingers wanted to encourage people to 'opt out' of the NHS, taking their tax contributions with them. This idea was squashed by Kenneth Clarke, the new health secretary and a formidable politician whose belligerent manner obscured his centrist, pro-welfare state sympathies. Clarke also adapted Enthoven's internal market to British circumstances, handing more power to general practitioners, the most popular part of the NHS.

This was the blueprint for change that appeared as a White Paper in 1988. However, in politics, drawing up a plan is the easy part; selling it is the real challenge. In the private sector, all you need to do is persuade the chief executive. He or she can then impose the restructuring on the organisation and sack all those who disagree. Politicians not only face an organised opposition, but they need to carry the public with them.

One could argue that the Tories never stood a chance of launching any plan which had the words 'NHS' and 'reform' in it. Nevertheless, it soon became clear that the two things that had made the NHS Review relatively efficient – speed and secrecy – immediately counted against it in public-relations terms. One of the virtues of a long, boring Royal Commission is that it softens up vested interests by allowing them to present their point of view. The Review left the vested interests feeling snubbed as well as threatened. And the Tories failed to explain what was wrong with the Bevanite NHS: how hospitals kept patients waiting for scarce beds but sat on acres of land in the middle of booming cities; how health authorities complained that they could not afford expensive drugs but failed to use their buying power to drive down prices from all their suppliers; how the concentration of resources in London short-changed people in the growing provinces. Worst of all, the reformers used buzzwords like 'internal market' and 'opted-out' which seemed intended to flatter Mrs Thatcher rather than to inform Mr Average.

The Labour party was convinced that, this time, the Thatcherites really had gone too far. 'By God, the government is going to get it in the neck,' said Labour's health spokesman Robin Cook. The Tories had spent the last decade privatising everything from gas to water. Why not health? Why make hospitals self-governing if you do not plan to push them into the private sector? Repeated opinion polls revealed that the majority of voters believed that the Tories were bent on privatising the NHS.

Even more effective than the Labour party's campaign was that of the British Medical Association. The government had assumed that the association (once dubbed the British Money Association) was nothing more than the voice of thick-headed and wallet-conscious backwoodsmen. In fact the BMA's reputation had been bolstered by its campaign against smoking. Its footsoldiers, the doctors, who saw hundreds of thousands of patients a day, littered their waiting rooms with BMA leaflets and aired their grievances to anyone who would listen. One middle-ranking minister, on a routine visit to his GP, was subjected, before he could get his shirt off, to a twenty-five-minute harangue on the evils of the reforms.

Soon panic spread to the government's own ranks. People said that fixing a price tag on the 27m treatments the NHS provided each year would cost £200m in computers and £25m in accountants. 'What we have is a menu without prices,' argued Sir Barney Hayhoe, a former health minister. 'It is a menu with attractive dishes, some without recipes and others untried and untested.' With more than three-quarters of voters opposing the reforms, Margaret Thatcher panicked. In May 1990, just a few weeks before the NHS bill was due to become law, she decided that the restructuring of the health service should be put on hold until after the next election (due in 1992). The legislation would be passed but not put into practice. After Clarke protested, a compromise was reached. The reforms were to go ahead after all. But there was to be no 'big bang'. The internal market was to be carefully controlled from the centre. The new buzzwords were 'soft landing', 'no surprises' and 'smooth take-off'.

In fact this compromise proved the saving of the reforms. The government persuaded a surprisingly large section of the medical profession to opt into the new reforms, partly by offering generous incentives to participate. In December 1990 fifty-seven hospitals became self-governing trusts, and in April 1991, 306 general practices, containing 1,700 GPs, became 'fund-holders'. But the government also kept its foot firmly on the brake. The new health contracts did little more than redescribe traditional relations in new-fangled language. The move to funding health authorities on the basis of the number and health needs of the population was slowed down so that the London regions, with their well-connected teaching hospitals, enjoyed more generous resources than they deserved.

The government's presentational problems were eased when Kenneth Clarke, who was hated by the medical establishment, was replaced by William Waldegrave, a gentler patrician. But what really saved the reforms was the replacement of Margaret Thatcher with John Major. The voters never thought the NHS was safe in the hands of a woman who boasted that she used private health care to make more room in the public wards; under Major, Labour's talk about the government privatising the NHS sounded less convincing.

As a result the NHS reforms stumbled through their first test, the 1992 election, which Major won against all predictions. Major's government then gradually took its foot off the brake. In April 1992 the Department of Health created 100 more trusts and 300 more GP fund-holders. By April 1996, more than half of all doctors had been given control over their own budgets and most hospitals had become self-governing. The DoH had also moved nearer to basing funding on patient numbers rather than just on tradition (although London was always something of an exception) and instructed purchasers to shop around for the best care at the best prices in negotiating their contracts.

But was it worth the candle?

There must have been many times during the introduction of the NHS reforms when the Tories wished that they had never heard of Alain Enthoven and his 'internal market'. The policy-makers were constantly confronted by two serious criticisms of their efforts. The first was that, far from galvanising the NHS, the reforms have demoralised it. As we have already pointed out, the NHS has never been a particularly happy ship, but with the management theorists at the helm morale plummeted. Six years after the reforms were first introduced, the medical profession was still up in arms – about overworked young doctors, underpaid nurses, ancient hospitals that face closure despite overwhelming local support, and the proliferation of bureaucracy. The government might have expected a rough ride from nurses' unions. However, there are also plenty of doctors who would normally vote Conservative and who ought to feel 'empowered' by their new opportunities, who instead complain that the new system means that they now have to waste their weekends doing paperwork.

The second criticism was that the reforms have encouraged the worst sort of managerialism. In 1983 the official Griffiths Report into the NHS complained that 'If Florence Nightingale were carrying her lamp through the corridors of the NHS today, she would almost certainly be searching for the people in charge.' Nowadays you cannot shine your lamp in any part of the organisation without revealing a crowd of people who are supposed to be in charge. The number of NHS administrators leapt by 18,000 between 1989 and 1994 – a period when the number of nursing staff in hospitals fell by 27,000. The average annual pay of trust chief executives (as the heads of hospital trusts insisted on calling themselves) had risen to £65,000 in 1995 (and was growing at twice the rate of that of nurses). The total managerial pay bill for NHS managers rose from £158.8m in 1989–90 to £723.3m in 1994–5. Before the reforms, administration in all its guises took up around 6 per cent of all NHS spending. In 1996 the total stood at about 10.5 per cent, according to the Audit Commission, the public services watchdog.

Not only did the managers seem overpaid; they were also leaden-footed. Alternative comedians made jokes about the NHS 'Value For Money' unit that was responsible for producing a 200-word definition of a familiar piece of hospital equipment, which begins, 'Bed: a device or arrangement that may be used to permit a patient to lie down' – noting that the joke would be even funnier if it were not actually true. Nor were beds the only object of concern. In 1996 health chief executives received an 'urgent' three-page memo dealing with the wrongful use of chairs.

To some extent both the problems to do with morale and managerialism proved self-correcting. A growing number of health-service workers of all sorts eventually committed themselves, inadvertently or deliberately, to the reforms. By April 1996, when the final wave of changes took place, most doctors and hospitals had been given control of their own budgets. The government also did its best to combat the excesses of the new managerial class. Stephen Dorrell, the secretary of state for health until May 1997, won wild applause at the 1995 Conservative Party Conference when he announced that he intended to cut spending on management in the NHS by 5 per cent over the next year.

Besides, by the mid-1990s dispassionate observers (not a category including many Britons) were beginning to notice that the reforms had begun to produce some of the organisational results that were hoped for. A few of these successes had been fairly rapid. The proportion of children being immunised against various diseases rose from 75 per cent in the fiscal year 1989–90 to

90 per cent in 1990–91, thanks to the introduction of an element of performance-related pay for doctors who performed the injections. By the mid-1990s, most statistical measures of efficiency showed notable improvements. For instance, despite an increase in the number of people being treated (or a 'growing customer base' as the healthocrats would doubtless put it), waiting lists had declined. By the end of 1995 the number of people waiting for more than a year for an appointment at a hospital had fallen to 31,600, down from 200,000 five years earlier. In 1994 studies by both the King's Fund, a think-tank specialising in health care, and the London School of Economics found that resources were being more closely related to needs than ever before.

The two most important parts of the internal market – the new independent trust hospitals and general practitioner fund-holders – also proved to be more of a success than broad opinion polls might suggest. In 1994 a survey of hospital trusts discovered that 48 per cent of patients thought services had improved since their hospital had become a trust, and 60 per cent thought they got more punctual service. Only 7 per cent thought they had got worse. Opinion was even more favourable among staff. In 1994 Julian Le Grande at the London School of Economics discovered a surprising amount of support for the reforms among NHS employees: 'If forced to choose between the new quasi-legal market NHS and the old command economy NHS, they would unhesitatingly prefer the new.'[16]

Meanwhile, GP fund-holders were so aggressive in forcing hospitals to treat their patients that Labour criticised them for it. In 1995 one survey of fund-holders found that 96 per cent felt that the quality of the service they offered had improved, and 81 per cent claimed to have introduced new services for patients. Many doctors used their increased freedom to improvise, laying on physiotherapists and chiropodists in their own surgeries. This reflects a wider concern within the NHS with prevention rather than cure – thanks in part to the various health targets the reforms introduced.

Such progress has won the NHS reforms a fair number of

admirers abroad. What impresses foreign observers is that the health-care reforms have managed to combine two elements that elsewhere have proved incompatible. On the one hand, the NHS continues to be paid for by the taxpayer and to be (largely) free at the point of delivery. But within the NHS market mechanisms are used to ensure the swift and flexible distribution of resources. An OECD report in 1995 held up the British system as a model for how to use market mechanisms to improve the efficiency of a public service. Hillary Clinton tried to reach the same goal of 'managed competition' from the opposite starting point of America's largely private health-care system. Throughout Europe and Australasia governments are trying to introduce a division between purchasers and providers into their health-care systems. The New Zealand government, which has gone furthest in the British direction, encourages regional health authorities to purchase health care from both public hospitals (rechristened Crown Health Enterprises) and private ones.

But what about the political pay-off? It would be naive to imagine that Margaret Thatcher and her Cabinet embarked on these great changes for purely altruistic reasons. To be judged successful, all public-sector management theory has to pay off at the ballot box. From this point of view, the NHS reforms have not been a vote winner. On the other hand, the reforms have not quite proved 'the own-goal' that people predicted. Throughout the whole debate the Labour party has been put in the unenviable position of having to say what it would do instead. One example of this was the 1992 election. Yes, there were a few problems for the Tories: two NHS trusts – Guy's in London and Bradford General – created a media debauch when they used their new-found freedom to sack hundreds of surplus staff. But as it became clear that, whatever they were doing, the Tories were not privatising the NHS, the Labour party had to come up with a new policy of its own. After much dithering, the Labour spokesman Robin Cook came up with an enfeebled version of the Tory idea: an internal market without the engine. He accepted the purchaser-provider split. But he refused to accept the case for NHS trusts or GP budget holders (despite the growing success of both).

The only really firm ideas Mr Cook produced were about introducing minimum wages and getting rid of compulsory competitive tendering – in other words handing money over to the public-sector unions.

Tony Blair went even further then Neil Kinnock in accepting the Tories' reforms. Throughout the May 1997 election, he put paid to any idea that Labour would return to its previous role as a cat's-paw of the health unions. True, in public he accused the Tories of closing hospitals and underfunding the health service; but in private he made it clear that he intended to preserve most of the ideas behind the reforms, including hospital trusts, GP fund-holders and the split between purchasers and providers. The paradox is that, if the reforms ever do yield a political dividend, the beneficiaries will not be the Tories, who courted unpopularity by implementing them, but Mr Blair's Labour government.

Management theory in the public sector has clearly not lived up to the exaggerated claims of its acolytes. Politicians have demanded that the theorists achieve all sorts of impossible feats: cut expenditure while improving services, or boost morale while slashing workforces. The more unscrupulous theorists have played on these self-contradictory fantasies by overselling their products. Yet, for all the inevitable disappointments, management theory has clearly brought more good than harm to the public sector. Thanks in part to the gurus' ideas, organisations are leaner, lines of authority are clearer and objectives more sharply defined. The future lies in pushing ideas such as delayering and contracting out farther still, not in returning to the old world of theory-free administration.

14

A WALK ON THE WILD SIDE

Most chapters in this book have, we hope, been organised around a theme or a collection of arguments. In the heartlands of management theory there is usually either an established debate or one that gradually emerges to anybody prepared to trudge through the literature. Once, however, you wander off towards the frontiers of management theory, the wilder areas where it mixes with self-help, philosophy, futurology or downright quackery, this structure disappears. Like Oakland, there is often no 'there' there. Coincidentally, these clouds of unknowing are often where the greatest fortunes are to be made. Present your publisher with a long, well-argued treatise on supply-chain management and, with luck, you may be able to build a new kitchen. Shave off your hair, cobble together a few thoughts based on what your last girlfriend shouted at you or on some article you read about population trends, come up with a catchy title (*Unhinge Your Soul, Supertrends 2010*), and, with a bit of luck and a lot of nerve, you should be able to buy your own island. Or so it seems.

This chapter is a brief survey of these strange but annoyingly wealthy creatures. It is, to be honest, a bit of a rag bag, stretching as it does all the way from the former English rugby captain to Alvin Toffler and Bill Gates. Is it also a rogues' gallery? Not entirely. Yes, in many cases the marketing is more interesting than the product. Yes, whether through accident or design, the thinkers' appeal rests to an unusual extent on the fear or greed of their audience. But, no, there is occasionally something of value in what they are saying. Moreover, the gap between orthodox management theory and its flakier fringe seems to be narrowing.

Consider first the man who has made a fortune by mixing together America's three great obsessions: management theory, religion and self-help.

A very effective person

In the early 1970s, flush with cash from *Butch Cassidy and the Sundance Kid*, Robert Redford started to build his own small chunk of paradise fifty miles north of Salt Lake City amidst several hundred acres of soaring rockfaces, giant redwoods and ice-clear streams. Redford still uses one part of the Sundance estate as his own base; the rest of his mountain retreat has become a resort, offering trekking, riding, skiing, fishing – and, of course, self-improvement.

The ranch's best client is the Covey Leadership Centre, an organisation set up by Stephen Covey, an earnest bald-headed Mormon and sometime professor of management at Brigham Young University. Throughout the year high-flying executives, politicians and public servants flock to the ranch to attend a week-long seminar. They watch films of the Berlin Wall collapsing. They read 'wisdom literature' – books by the likes of Plato, Confucius and Ben Franklin. They discuss the problems that prevent their companies attaining peak performance and their personal relationships from going smoothly. They learn how to husband their time and order their priorities by using Covey's patented personal organiser. They climb the mountain and rescue each other from various contrived calamities. Above all – for this is America and these are 'high-potential individuals' – they break down and weep.

Most of the Leadership Centre's activities take place twenty minutes' drive down the mountain, in Provo. Despite its strait-laced Mormon roots, epitomised by Brigham Young University, Provo is now one of the world's liveliest technological centres. Almost every young person you meet seems to be working for Novell or for some small software house – or for Covey. Indeed, another way to look at the town is as an archipelago of small islands of Coveyism: in one building Covey's lieutenants plan his campaign in the American South; in another they wonder how he will conquer the Asian market; in yet another they produce books, magazines, videotapes and personal organisers. Soon all these operations will be bundled together in their own brand-new 'campus' on the outskirts of Provo.

By 1997 Covey's management training business, founded in 1985 with a staff of two, employed 700 people and had revenues of close to $100m. Its clients include more than half of the Fortune 500 companies – names such as AT&T, Ford, Xerox and Merck. The centre works with 2,900 school districts and was helping ten of them, including, extraordinarily, Detroit, Dallas and the Bronx, to become 'principle-centred places'. Covey's ideas have also been embraced by institutions as diverse as the Idaho Minimum Security Prison and the Oneida Indian Nation, which was keen to break the Indian cycle of dependence on legalised gambling.

The foundation stone of this gigantic business is a single management book, *The Seven Habits of Highly Effective People*, which has sold about five million copies since it was published in 1989. The message of the book is simple enough: in order for you to reach your full potential, you have to build 'character'. Unlike other self-help creeds that just provide a set of excuses for people's failings, Coveyism is actually quite a tough discipline: people have to take responsibility for their actions, not blame them on others.

Unfortunately, this rigour does not extend to the book's style. The first six words of *The Seven Habits* are: 'To my colleagues, empowered and empowering'. Worse is to come. The first of Covey's seven habits is 'be proactive'; the sixth is 'synergise'. (Indeed, in conversation, 'synergy' vies with 'paradigm shift' as his favourite phrase.) He is forever referring to things like 'emotional bank accounts' and 'deposits of unconditional love'.

This is disturbing territory. How can you respect a man who restates Aesop's fable about the goose that laid the golden egg as 'the P/Pc Balance' for production/production capability? Can you really take seriously a man who claims, straight-faced, to have identified 'the universal value system of all mankind'? The instinctive response of any cynical British journalist, or perhaps just anybody whose bank account (either financial or emotional) is a little less plentiful than Covey's, is to reach for the critical hatchet.

In fact this reaction, whilst wholly excusable, is not entirely fair. (To begin with, there are plenty of people who are considerably flakier than Covey – as we shall see later.) The best way to appreciate Covey is to consider exactly why he has been so successful. The first reason is simple enough: he means it. Whatever its weaknesses, Coveyism's emphasis on personal responsibility comes from the heart. Covey's own Mormonism has been lifelong and unflinching. He keeps a family mission statement on the wall of his sitting room, and he has never smoked or drunk alcohol. He cultivated his skills as a public orator, and his habit of getting people to learn by teaching, through five years of missionary work in England and Ireland. He is the sort of man who can say without a hint of embarrassment or self-consciousness: 'We are not human beings having a spiritual experience. We are spiritual beings having a human experience.'

Nor is Covey some cone-headed fanatic from the sticks. He studied business at both the University of Utah and Harvard Business School, before moving back to his local university, Brigham Young. It was whilst doing his PhD thesis on 'American success literature since 1776' that Covey discovered that, for the first 150 years of the republic, most success literature concentrated on questions of character. But shortly after the Second World War people became more interested in superficial things such as appearance and style. Covey started to preach that people needed to return to the ancient discipline of character building. Soon his classes at Brigham Young were attracting hundreds of students. In 1985 he gave up his professorship and gambled everything he owned on the Covey Leadership Centre.

The second explanation for Covey's success is less of an insult than it seems: he runs a damned efficient business. Covey is unapologetic about wanting to turn the centre into the world's biggest self-help multinational. In Provo, for instance, Covey has removed himself from the day-to-day operations of his company, handing power to a loyal cadre of lieutenants, many of them from his own huge family, so as to give himself more time to concentrate on 'high leverage opportunities' – dealing with company bosses, giving broadcasts by satellite and mixing with politicians. Meanwhile, on the ground *The Seven Habits* has ingeniously spawned its own sales force. Rather than just treating the book as a quick emotional work-out, readers are urged to put the structures and systems in place to make those changes into permanent habits. The best way to turn good intentions into habits is to start teaching what you have learned. The result is that all round the country Covey's acolytes are organising reading groups, becoming trainers, acting as coaches – and spreading the word.

Nor is there any shortage of products for this pipeline to suck up. The centre already has another best-seller on its hands, *Principle-Centred Leadership*, and, with the help of Covey's brother, is preparing *The Seven Habits of Highly Effective Families* (aimed at healing the American family). It is also expanding its personal-organiser business, teaming up with Microsoft to produce a software version. (The point of a Covey organiser as opposed to a normal one is that, each week, it forces you to set priorities as well as to organise your appointments.)

But Covey is determined to push the business in two directions. The first is overseas. Covey bridles at the idea that his ideas are peculiarly American, let alone Mormon. *The Seven Habits* is available in twenty-eight languages and thirty-five countries: almost as soon as it was translated into Korean it sold 650,000 copies and demand is swelling in both Japan and China. The second expansion will be deep into America's troubled public sector. Here Covey has powerful allies. Hazel O'Leary, the former energy secretary, caught the Covey bug when she was vice-president of Northern States Power: she went on to offer training in the seven habits to all the employees of the government's tenth-largest department. Bill Clinton (who spent Thanksgiving in 1994 holed up in Camp David with Covey) told a conference on the future of the American workplace that American productivity would soar if people would just read *The Seven*

Habits. Nor are the Republicans keen to be left behind: Covey penned a chapter in Newt Gingrich's book on American civilisation.

Perhaps mixing management, religion and self-help guaranteed a gigantic audience: after all, Covey is delivering the American dream – both economic success and spiritual salvation in one go. Certainly his ideas have attracted plenty of desperate people who think that reading a book and buying an organiser can transform them from time-wasting slobs into models of efficiency. But Covey has also persuaded plenty of respectable companies to part with their money too.

Put another way, merely meaning what you say and knowing how to sell it does not mean much if the message itself does not have some unique selling point. The third reason why Covey has been successful is that, underneath all that frightful talk about enabling, his ideas actually have some relevance to mainstream management theory.

Most management thinkers are obsessed with corporate organisation and its systems of control and reward. From Frederick Taylor to the re-engineers, there has been a long tradition of thinking about people as if they are soldiers on the parade ground: the theorists have concentrated on trying to put them into the most effective patterns. Even the 'human relations school' – thinkers such as Douglas McGregor who had a big influence on Covey when he was a student at Harvard – has mostly been concerned with things like improving career ladders and giving workers a stake in the company. Coveyism starts with the individual – and sets out to improve him or her before slotting them into their place. Coveyism is total quality management for the character, re-engineering for the soul.

Cynics argue that Covey serves the needs of corporations which want to shift the responsibility for coping with job turbulence to the citizenry at large. Jeremy Rifkin, the author of *The End of Work*, has criticised Covey for creating the psychological conditions for 'just-in-time employment'. Instead of spending the time between one short-term job and another drinking and going to seed, Covey's pupils spend it 'sharpening the saw' – his phrase for improving their mental and physical health. It would be interesting to know how many of the AT&T managers who scampered around the mountains with Covey were later downsized in the telephone giant's huge restructuring; and even more interesting to know how many returned from Provo to plot that restructuring.

All the same, 'character' does seem to be a valid topic for management theorists to discuss. One of the attractions of Covey is that he has tried to rescue 'character' from both the simple-minded purveyors of self-help (who imply that you can change your character as easily as your underpants) and the social-service establishment (which ignores questions of character by blaming everything on 'the system'). Meanwhile Covey's basic idea – that businesses should think about how individuals feel as well as about the organisational structures in which they work – is gaining ground. Witness the firms now sending re-engineered employees on motivational courses, or the business schools offering courses in such soft subjects as ethics and leadership.

Improve yourself

One reason why Covey has won the custom of organisations like IBM is that, by the standards of his area of management theory, he seems alarmingly well qualified. Consider one of his main rivals, Anthony Robbins, a school caretaker turned 'peak-performance coach' who makes $50m a year from his seminars alone (according to his own estimates) and whose clients include Bill Clinton, Andre Agassi and the Princess of Wales. 'Diana admires his drive, energy and optimism,' commented her biographer, Andrew Morton, 'while the American millionaire lecturer has sensed that beyond the suffering and sadness lurks a brave, strong woman.'[1]

Robbins is an even more arresting sight than the spectacularly bald Covey – almost seven feet tall and a dead ringer for Superman – and he shows none of his rival's self-restraint when it comes to enjoying the fruits of his labours. He divides his time between his castle in San Diego, California, which comes complete with a helicopter pad, and his island in Fiji. The essence of Robbins' message, laid down in books such as *Awaken the Giant*

Within and *Unlimited Power*, is that you can achieve anything you want just so long as you adopt the right attitude: just think and it will be yours. To drive home his case he uses a blend of homespun wisdom, positive-thinking techniques, uplifting case-studies and out-and-out showmanship.

Meditation and chanting, argues Robbins, can be used to unlock the creative capacities of the 'right brain'. However the main way to unleash your power seems to be attending an *Unleash the Power Within* seminar, given by Robbins. These attract thousands of people, and are a cross between an evangelical sermon and a magical extravaganza. The high point comes when the audience walks barefoot across thousands of burning coals, protected by nothing other than the power of positive thinking. (It is not known whether Clinton or Princess Diana completed this feat; their power was unleashed in private.)

If Robbins has any relevance to the wider world of management theory it has unfortunately passed us by. However, one attraction of the Robbins package (and, for that matter, of the Covey package too) is that you get the whole caboodle: they are both one-stop shops for self-improvement. One of the most irritating things about their peers in the self-help industry is that they usually offer to improve just one aspect of our performance. The market has become hopelessly segmented. For instance, Morris Shechtman, a 'corporate psychotherapist' (and yet another of the people to be admired by Newt Gingrich) specialises in reducing the 'trauma and distress' caused by corporate restructuring (he has been to the Capitol to help Republicans understand 'the impact of the grieving process on public policy'). There is even one part of the management industry which claims that you can radically improve your productivity by organising your desk properly – and the United States has a National Association of Professional Organisers to prove it.

One of the most fertile segments might be described as mental gymnastics. Here, the uncrowned king is Edward de Bono, the father of lateral thinking. De Bono is not short on self-confidence: the subtitle of one of his books is *From Socratic to de Bono Thinking*. De Bono's books are full of clever puzzles designed to make you realise that the best way to approach a problem is often from the side: 'the mind must wobble before it can leap,' he argues. Nevertheless, the most notable thing about the modern Plato is his ability to plough a single furrow long after lesser men would have wobbled into a different pasture out of sheer boredom. De Bono has been writing books and giving seminars on lateral thinking since 1967. Though lateral thinking has often been treated with disdain by academics, it has provided de Bono with both wealth and influence. From his private island in Venice he dispenses advice to giant corporations and the educational bureaucracies of Venezuela, Singapore and Bulgaria.

Today's most pervasive self-improvement philosophy comes under the general rubric of 'new age'. New agers disagree about technical questions, endlessly debating whether hand-holding, meditation or chanting are the best ways to get on in life; but they all seem to agree on the awfulness of something called 'the Newtonian paradigm'. Isaac Newton is condemned for legitimising an atomistic approach to the world where things can be looked at in isolation. New Agers – a category that includes Peter Senge (see Chapter Six) – are much more impressed by quantum physics, cybernets, chaos theory, cognitive science, eastern and western spiritual traditions – or indeed anything that reveals that everything is interconnected with everything else; that you can't change one bit of the world without affecting another.

This may all seem a long way away from management. But management consultancies peddling new-age cure-alls of one kind or another seem to be doing flourishing business. Some consultancies help managers to clarify their 'business visions' by persuading them to dance; others by dressing them up as druids and witches and setting them off on the mythical quest for 'Dungeons and Dragons'. The Esalen Institute, located at Big Sur in California, helps people do everything from reduce their stress to enhance their creativity. A British company, Decision Development, uses the American Indian Medicine Wheel to help managers discover their inner selves. In Japan an alternative think tank, the Mukta Institute in Tokyo, helps companies tap into Buddhist modes of thought. Predictably enough, the Maharishi

Foundation has set up a school of management, which specialises in 'training managers to bring unfailing success and continuing progress to their companies', through meditation and levitation.

For all their minor differences, these gurus all preach the same seductive message: that we achieve far less than we are capable of achieving; and that we can close the gap between promise and achievement if we understand ourselves, set appropriate goals, remove inner blockages, transform fear into strength and generally 'unleash the power within'. They also preach their message in more or less the same ways. They are forever drawing up lists. Covey has 'seven habits'; Robbins has 'five keys to wealth and happiness' and 365 lessons in self-mastery, of which the 364th is 'Remember to expect miracles . . . because you are one.' They are also addicted to metaphors, which they repeat throughout their writings and dwell on in loving detail. Covey likes metaphors from the natural world; indeed at times he seems worryingly like Chancy Gardiner, the character played by Peter Sellers in the film *Being There*: 'The sequential leadership development can be likened to a tree.'

Surfing the wave

Unleashing all this hidden power is not much good unless you know where to go to. As we have already noted, one of the most highly prized abilities among the gurus is the ability to see into the future. Most mainstream management theorists have concentrated just on trying to work out the best ways for companies to cope with a changing world (see Chapter Seven on 'Strategy') rather than trying to predict what will happen. However there is also a fringe school of futurologists.

Nearly all the futurologists are technological determinists, convinced that the motor of history lies in steam engines and computer chips. Futurology is full of excited talk about the transition from a mainframe society to a PC society, with the attendant collapse of giant bureaucracies and triumph of small, nimble organisations. On the whole, the genre is irredeemably pessimistic: there is a lot of guff about the inevitability of workers being pushed out of the way by machines (which we have dealt with in our chapter on work). The non-arrival of each disaster does no more to kill the genre than the non-arrival of the end of the world kills cults.

All the same, it is noticeable that it is often the more optimistic authors who do best. For instance, John Naisbitt, author of *Megatrends*, which has sold eight million copies, and sundry spin-offs, including *Megatrends Asia* [2], admits that the future may have its problems – governments in particular will be left in the dust by the quickening pace of technological change; but, in general, he says the future will make us all a good deal better off. This jaunty optimism has helped turn him into 'one of the world's top social forecasters'. However, reading his books, it is extremely difficult to think of anything in them that has not been said before – or anything that is not already established wisdom. Even a fleeting visit to, say, Bangkok should be enough to show you the Asian Megatrend 'that people are moving from the villages to megacities'; similarly a quick dinner with any Asian economist could have unearthed the Megatrend that many Asian industries are changing from 'labour intensive to high technology'.

While Naisbitt's chief skill is as a packager, Alvin Toffler is a little more daring. His first book, *Future Shock*, opened with a bold statement: 'In the three short decades between now and the twenty-first century, millions of ordinary, psychologically normal people will face an abrupt collision with the future.' In Toffler's case this collision took the form of gigantic amounts of money pouring into his bank account. The book sold in its millions and turned Toffler (and his wife Heidi) into a regular feature on the international lecture circuit. It also paved the way for two follow-ups, *The Third Wave* and *Powershift*.

Toffler's appeal lies in the impression that he understands the broad sweep of history. He started life as a Marxist (an appropriate beginning for any technological determinist); he organised civil rights protests in the South, and worked for years in a car factory. Nowadays he is worshipped by the libertarian right: he picked up dinner in the White House from both Ronald Reagan and George Bush, has given a keynote address to a meeting of

Republican governors and (inevitably) is worshipped by Newt Gingrich.

Toffler divides history into three stages (or waves): the agricultural, lasting to the 18th century; the industrial, lasting to the present; and, now, the information age. The information age is bringing the end of some of the most familiar features of the industrial age: massification (mass production, mass markets, mass political parties, mass media), conformity (company man and his Persil-using wife) and ushering in a very different world. The computer chip is simultaneously bringing globalisation (killing distance by putting us all at the end of the line) and demassification (dissolving crowds into tiny interest groups). Toffler is quite interesting about the future shape of commerce (he follows Drucker's line on the importance of knowledge workers and virtual companies). But his more original thoughts tend to be political. For instance, he suggests that majority rule should be replaced with a 'minority-based, 21st-century democracy', relying less on elected assemblies than on electronic referendums, and less on central than on local government.

Appropriately, by the mid-1990s the technological determinists were being pushed to one side by the technologists – a new group of 'digital gurus'. Most of these people seemed to have been born with a computer in their hands. The classical digital guru is Nicholas Negroponte, the high priest of multimedia who works at MIT's Media lab. But the group also includes Kevin Kelly, the executive editor of *Wired*, the Internet's trade paper, and George Guilder, an economist who seems to know more about computers than most people in Silicon Valley. The digital gurus are preoccupied by working out what the microchip, PC and Internet mean for everybody. Their attraction is that they are much closer to the cutting edge than people like Toffler and Naisbitt – and consequently far more original. Guilder, for instance, was one of the first people to realise the importance of computer networks. Yet this affection for technology can also be a weakness: they often seem to believe that nothing ill can come of it. They often remind you of the boy in glasses rushing out of the chemistry lab clutching a bomb and shouting, 'Look what I've made!'

This unabated optimism is certainly more convincing than the dreary 'end of work' crowd. But the technologists can seem irrepressibly upbeat – none more so than their most recent recruit, Bill Gates. *The Road Ahead* is Gates' guide to the information highway (a phrase he rightly dislikes).[3] Although he spells out a few problems for particular groups of people, his tone is optimistic. Yes, 'friction-free capitalism' on the Net will put many intermediaries, such as travel agents and retailers, out of business. But the consumer will gain – and different sorts of travel agents and retailers will arise. Yes, more rich people will work at home in the country, but that does not necessarily mean that they will leave ghettos behind. The book comes most alive when Gates talks about gizmos that will make our lives easier such as small computers that will act as phones, wallets and diaries.

But is there any link with management theory? Not really. Gates makes the interesting prediction that, although the computer revolution has generally so far helped small companies by putting information at their fingertips which was previously only available to larger companies, the next networking phase of the computer revolution may help big ones by providing a way to bring a large number of people together; but he does not really follow it up. Indeed, books such as *The Road Ahead* tend to fall into a category that runs parallel to management theory but never quite meets it. Guessing what the future will be is a very profitable (and entertaining) game. But management involves taking decisions in the present. Even if you know what the future will be, you have only won half the battle. You then have to put together an organisation to take advantage of it.

Come on down

In two respects Gates is not a typical new guru: he has no need of money and he knows how to run a company. Over the past few years, word seems to have got around that there is a huge pile of money to be made by simply picking up your word-processor and 'headin' into them thar hills'. Management theory feels much like a town in the middle of the goldrush: not only are you overwhelmed by the stench of greed, you also run into the most extraordinary people. Walk into a bookshop and alongside Drucker's *Concept of the Corporation* you can find titles such as *Jesus CEO: Using Ancient Wisdom for Visionary Leadership* and *Make It So: Leadership Lessons from Star Trek the Next Generation*, not to mention a menagerie of books with titles like *Swim with the Sharks* and *Roaring with the Lions*. This section is devoted to four groups of these interlopers.

The first are the philosophers. The recent boom in studying ethics, fuelled by worries about corruption, pollution and the escalating salaries of bosses, has encouraged business schools to invite philosophers across for the day to speculate about the link between their trade and management. Now they are leaving their ivory towers (with their low pay and bitchy politics), and selling their skills more directly. Europe boasts more than a hundred 'philosophic practices', staffed by refugees from academia willing to offer advice on a wide range of subjects, ranging from the changing nature of work to the right to be lazy.[4] The first practice was opened in Germany in 1989, but the country which has the greatest affinity for the approach is the Netherlands, with twenty practices. France, the home of the *philosophes*, has only three.

The second group (which really ought to know better) is the original 'unacknowledged legislators of mankind': poets. A few modern bards have felt the calling of the corporate cheque book. David Whyte, a Yorkshireman now based in Seattle, has written *The Heart Aroused: Poetry and the Preservation of the Soul in Corporate America*. His 'lectures' to corporations consist of recitals of poems and folk-tales, intended to stir managers' creative juices. He has consulted for AT&T, Boeing and Dana. Poets have been joined by novelists. One of the best-selling management books of the last few years is Eli Goldratt's *The Goal*, which tells of how a production manager grapples with the complexities of total quality management.

A third and much bigger group is composed of sports people.

Perhaps this meeting of minds was inevitable, given the enthusiasm of managers for sport and the fondness of management writers for sporting analogies. But the latest management fads, with their emphasis on coaching and team-building, have been an open invitation for ageing sporting figures to turn themselves into management gurus. Needless to say, coaches are in particular demand. In March 1996, the *New York Times* asked several conventional management writers to assess the content of two recent best-sellers, *The Winner Within: A Life Plan for Team Players* by Pat Riley (of New York Knicks and Miami Heat fame) and *Sacred Hoops* by Phil Jackson (Chicago Bulls).[5] The general conclusion of the audit was fairly unsurprising: that most of what the coaches were saying about the importance of goals and teamwork was familiar motivational stuff but that the coaches had an undoubted talent for getting their message across through memorable examples.

Will Carling, who gave up the captaincy of England's rugby team early in 1996, seems to take management more seriously. He co-wrote *The Way To Win: Strategies for Success in Business and Sport* with Robert Heller, a veteran management writer, and he also runs a management consultancy, Insights, which 'presents motivational seminars to Captains of Industry by Captains of Sport'. 'They start off regarding it as a boys' day out,' says Carling, 'but they get fascinated by subjects like how you pull teams together.' Carling's stock in trade is showing how to apply 'lessons from the playing field to the workplace'. His chief message is about the importance of 'vision': it is only when people can 'see' themselves winning that they have the strength to get there. All fairly routine stuff, but it is interesting that Carling tries to apply management theory to his sport. Having read management books by the likes of Tom Peter and Peter Drucker, the England captain used 360-degree assessment (getting his players to say what they thought of him) and Japanese discussion techniques for stopping the same people dominating all debates.

The fourth group of management interlopers might be described as intellectual traders – people who import ideas wholesale from other disciplines. For instance, chaos theory (which has already migrated from physics to financial economics, with mixed success) pops up from time to time in management theory too: some people argue that companies should no longer try to form strategies, because strategies are an artefact of linear thinking, and we now live in a non-linear world, because tiny events can cause gigantic triumphs or disasters. Recently, however, biology rather than physics seems to be in the ascendant.

The most prominent thinker in this field is Ichak Adizes. He argues that companies have life-cycles, just like individuals, enduring the normal difficulties of each stage of development and running the risk of such human ills as infant death and premature ageing. When young they are flexible but over-emotional; when old they have their emotions under control but tend to be set in their ways; the ideal is to be in their prime. Although this does not seem like a particularly startling insight, Adizes sells it with astonishing panache, through dozens of books, tapes, newsletters, an Adizes Institute in Bel Air and a network of 'certified Adizes Professionals' all round the world.

My generation

And so what? One could argue that there is nothing new about the likes of Covey, Robbins or Adizes. Half a century ago, Napoleon Hill made a fortune out of writing books such as *Think and Grow Rich*. Hill's capacity to make money was only equalled by his ability to lose it. Still, he also drew up plans to found 'the world's first university-sized success school' on his ranch in the Catskill mountains and acted as a consultant to major companies. And his influence reaches beyond the grave: Newt Gingrich lists *Think and Grow Rich* as one of the books that most influenced him.

The difference (and the answer to 'So what?') is that, these days, the gap between the latter-day Napoleon Hills and respectable business theorists seems to have narrowed. Take, for instance, Gemini, a well-known consultancy that lists some of the world's biggest companies amongst its clients. In 1995 two of its leading consultants, Francis Gouillart and James Kelly, produced a book intended to demonstrate the firm's intellectual credentials. However, anybody picking up *Transforming the Organisation* does not come away reinvigorated by the rigour of its arguments; rather, you feel as if you have wandered back through time to a tent at Woodstock: 'It is time to replace our mechanistic view of business with a more organic one, and to endow the recently discovered biological nature of our corporations with a new spirituality that recognises the sanctity of individual human life and has compassion for individuals.'[6]

The authors urge companies to forget about dominance and pre-eminence, and become 'loved and respected institutions'. But the path to this desirable end is not easy, they advise: 'Like people, corporations become more whole and more credible when they embrace both the hero and the villain within themselves, both their soul and its shadow.'[7] They talk about breaking through 'walls of reluctance and denial'[8] – a feat which they hope to accomplish with the help of something called bio-re-engineering.

Picking on the men from Gemini is a little unfair. Conventional management thinkers of all kinds are increasingly looking at touchy-feely themes where it is difficult to be intellectually rigorous, even if you want to be. Many of the ideas preached by the gurus of the 1990s might have been invented in a 1960s commune: shifting from command and control to flat organisations; handing power down to workers; dreaming up visions rather than planning strategies; thinking globally rather than just nationally. Besides, the thinkers are only responding to their market. Companies feel that they have re-engineered the soul out of their organisations – and that they need to restore that soul by sending their workers off on a spiritual quest.

The temptation to 'let it all go' is all the greater seeing that some of the most profitable companies of the last few years have had a decidedly 'new age' flavour. 'Lighten up . . . feel your bliss', implores a large sign in the reception area of the Body Shop in Littlehampton, on England's Sussex coast. Workers stroll around the place wearing T-shirts proclaiming 'Extinct is forever'. Body Shop trucks bear slogans like 'Practise random kindness and senseless acts of beauty.' Employees attend 'values meetings', where they discuss what makes the company special to them. The in-house phone list is alphabetised by first names: it's Anita, not Mrs Roddick.

Interest in this approach is spreading beyond the fringe. In the United States, a new-age think-tank, Global Business Network, is underwritten by companies such as AT&T, Volvo and Nissan. Procter & Gamble and Du Pont are offering their employees 'personal growth experiences', to encourage them to be more creative and give them a deeper sense of 'ownership' of company results. AT&T has sent hundreds of middle managers on courses at Transpective Business Consulting, a Woburn, Massachusetts company, which, for $1,650 a person, offers to help people become better leaders by getting them to tune in to themselves. IBM's 'fit for the future' seminars introduce employees to I Ching, a Chinese oracle. Lotus Development Corporation has a 'soul committee' that makes sure the company lives up to its values. Even old 'Neutron' Jack Welch babbles about how he wants people rewarded 'in both the pocket and the soul'.

In 1991, TV-am, a British breakfast television station, adopted a new-age strategy in its effort to regain its franchise when it was auctioned. Bruce Gyngell, the company's Australian chairman, arranged a 'personal-growth seminar and development workshop' for his staff, at which they were invited to focus their spiritual energy and inner peace, with a view to renewing not just themselves but their franchise. Unfortunately, the franchise went elsewhere. Nor are such high jinks confined to the private sector. The American army's current slogan, 'Be all that you can be', is borrowed from the human-potential movement. Every Wednesday, at the World Bank in Washington, a group of bank employees sits in a semi-circle and tries to 'connect'.

One reason for the narrowing gap between the fringe and the mainstream is that the generation that came of age in the 1960s, when Timothy Leary was regarded as a serious thinker, is moving into senior positions in business, consultancy and academia. Members of this generation are much more open to wacky ideas than their more cynical (or sensible) seniors. They have also reached a stage in their lives when they have built up successful careers, had several children, and started looking for the deeper meaning of life: even Hillary Clinton, as hard-faced a lawyer-cum-politician as you are likely to find anywhere, has taken to talking about the 'politics of meaning'.

This is all very well – except for two things. First (as the Gemini book shows) when management theory wanders off into these new territories it seems to lose whatever structure and coherence it had in the first place. And, second, these fringe areas rely even more extravagantly on marketing rather than content. The fringe figures are far more unrestrained in the fears they conjure up and the hopes they promise to satisfy. The hallmark of men such as Covey, Robbins, Toffler and Adizes is marketing panache. Nobody has ever accused Stephen Covey of buying up copies of his own books in order to propel them to the top of the best-seller list. He has no need to.

Conclusion

AN IMMATURE DISCIPLINE

Instead of going on ordinary holidays, the most fanatical managers relax by going on tours of the world's best-run companies. Experienced tourists have already visited Toyota City in Japan to see lean manufacturing or DisneyWorld in Florida to learn Uncle Walt's 'pixie dust' formula for managing people; now the hardened backpackers in their number are moving on to more exotic attractions such as Springfield ReManufacturing, a maker of diesel-engines that shows its employees all its financial figures, and Johnsonville, a sausage-maker renowned for its ability to put together teams.

Our tour of management theorists has been a bizarre experience. Drop in on Rosabeth Moss Kanter or Michael Porter at the Harvard Business School and you catch a sight of the theorist as a respectable academic, churning out articles for learned journals, arguing over the finer points of econometrics and even doing the regular grunt-work of marking their students' papers. Visit Stephen Covey's leadership centre, and you can see the theorist as therapist, encouraging his clients to talk about their innermost feelings. Stumble into a Tom Peters seminar, and you can see the theorist as preacher, telling his audience that the latest buzzword can mean the difference between bankruptcy and unimaginable riches.

In few other academic disciplines do personal peccadillos play such a large part. In writing about management, many of the gurus are simply writing about themselves – and their own decidedly abnormal lives. Believing in portfolio workers is so much easier if, like Charles Handy, you are one already. The conviction that the future belongs to those global firms that have an 'Anchorage mentality' comes easily to a bilingual Japanese, such as Kenichi Ohmae. If Tom Peters had ended up in Essen rather than Silicon Valley, the world might have ended up with *Thriving on Order*.

Even a brief encounter with the world of management theory leaves you with two immediate impressions. The first is of enormous commercial success. When not ministering to their students, the Harvard professors are jetting off to conferences or offering advice to giant companies. Covey's Leadership Centre vies with leading software companies as the most successful enterprise in Provo. Speakers of the calibre of Peters can earn as much giving a seminar for a day as many middle managers earn in a year. One casual conversation between the authors and one of the best known gurus on the subject of who was the greediest theorist produced too many suspects to name.

The second impression is that management theory is a mish-mash. The books of tenured professors rub shoulders with those of out-and-out charlatans. Management consultancies can spend a small fortune on some worthy piece of research, and then demean themselves with an exhibition of needless hucksterism. In conversation, every guru can move from a point of genuine insight or scholarship to one of extraordinary banality.

The gurus' enormous commercial success and the variability of their output are linked. So far, management theory has produced, at most, one 'great' thinker: Peter Drucker. However, even Drucker has found it impossible to produce breakthrough ideas year after year – as the industry now demands that he should. Lesser writers face an even harder task. Many jumped opportunistically to management theory from other academic disciplines. Their first or second book included perhaps one genuine insight. Now, surrounded by the paraphernalia of their trade – their own consultancy, the speaking tours, the book contract, the mortgage payments on their third home – they are obliged to churn out material, hoping to stumble across the next big idea. Even if they were capable of finding another insight (which in many cases looks unlikely), they are unlikely to stumble across it this way.

The case for the gurus

The existence of so much junk has understandably led many people to dismiss management theory lock, stock and barrel. Scott Adams, the cartoonist who invented Dilbert and Dogbert, has made millions out of poking fun at management theorists and their works. 'A consultant is a person who takes your money and annoys your employees while tirelessly searching for the best way to extend the consulting contract' is one of his gentler judgements. By mid-1997 his book, *The Dilbert Principle*, had been near the top of the *Business Week* bestseller list for more than a year; *Dogbert's Secret Management Handbook* had also become a bestseller; and Mr Adams' cartoons were syndicated in more than 1,500 newspapers around the world. In writing this book we have repeatedly come across the same reaction: how can you waste your time on such rubbish? We have listened to a long list of complaints, often delivered with striking vitriol, about management theory. That it is an apology for an academic subject, intellectually dead, methodologically sloppy and driven by little more than fashion. That it causes huge harm to companies, by persuading them to engage in perpetual revolution – and even worse harm to employees by subjecting them to constant uncertainty. And that its practitioners are charlatans of the worst sort, charging gargantuan fees for nothing more useful than translating common sense into grotesque jargon.

The first thing we hope to have established in this book is that there is such a thing as management theory: that general lessons can be extracted from what companies do and can be used to help other companies to operate better. Successful management ideas are not just bits of local knowledge, fixed by culture and circumstances. They can travel and, suitably modified, can be used to reproduce that success elsewhere, in other countries, industries or even vocations. The Japanese took American ideas about quality control and used them to create lean production; the Americans then reimported lean production and used it to galvanise their faltering car industry. The public sector has borrowed ideas from the private sector; good companies have borrowed ideas from management pace-makers, such as Motorola, Toyota and McDonald's. And in most cases the ideas have improved the institutions concerned.

The second thing we hope to have established is that management theory is not entirely devoid of intellectual content. The best theorists tackle big subjects that touch all our lives, from globalisation to how to husband intellectual capital. Indeed, political argument and popular debate might be improved if 'normal' people had a better grasp of management theory. For instance, in the European Union some Eurofederalists clearly regard nation states as little more than restraints on trade. Their aim is to eliminate national peculiarities in order to achieve the sort of economies of scale which (they think) have made the United States such a powerhouse. But management theorists such as Michael Porter have clearly shown that countries are actually sources of competitive advantage – generators of specific skills and creators of a unique way of working. Make Germany less German and you emasculate its machine-tool industry. By the same token, the fears of British xenophobes that a single European market will mean a mass of homogenised products might be quieted if they bothered to look at organisations such as Percy Barnevik's Asea Brown Boveri: the best way to run a multinational is to work with the grain of local differences rather than to try to conquer it.

The third thing we hope to have established is that, so far, the results coming back from management theory's continuously experimenting laboratory are broadly positive. Industry leaders such as Motorola, Merck and 3M (just to name American firms beginning with 'M') have all made a point of taking management theory seriously: not all the ideas work, but those that do, such as quality in Motorola's case, tend to give them an advantage. Microsoft is showing every sign of following suit. This picture is repeated in Europe and Asia. Frequently the most admired company in each country – be it Acer in Taiwan, Toyota in Japan or Marks & Spencer in Britain – is a pioneer in management theory. Contrast two companies in broadly the same business – such as America's General Electric and Westinghouse, or Citibank and Chase Manhattan – and you will often find that the company that has pulled ahead – General Electric and Citibank – is the management junkie.

This may even be true of countries too. There are plenty of reasons for Japan's emergence as an economic power, of course, but one of them was surely the way that its companies studied and adapted management ideas. Management theory also surely plays at least a small role in explaining the relative states of American and German industry. During the 1980s, American business restructured furiously, trying to keep up with the latest fashions like core competencies and outsourcing. German business people stood arrogantly aloof from such 'fads', believing that good technology and craftsmanship would see them through. By the mid-1990s, the Germans felt conspicuously outdated. They have now embraced the ideas they earlier rejected.

Teenage angst

So why does a discipline that contains so much sense contain so much nonsense as well? One answer is that management theory is still such a young discipline, in which the canonical texts and defining methodologies are still being developed. As we explained in the introduction, management theory feels as if it is around 100 years younger than disciplines such as economics. This teenage period is likely to go on for some time – if only because the enormous financial success and influence of the discipline have created a cocoon around the gurus.

Still, rather than fretting about management theory's excesses, perhaps we should be grateful that its adolescence has not been more harmful. Poor management theories have cost people their jobs, they have bankrupted companies: they may even (who really knows?) be doing irreparable damage to public organisations such as Britain's National Health Service and Argentina's telephone system. But set alongside the chaos and suffering caused by communist economies, management theory's encounter with puberty seems relatively benign.

A second explanation why management theory is so patchy is that its audience demands instant solutions. Anxious managers grasp at management literature as a panacea for all their worries.

Many firms turn to management theory only when they are desperate. Their minds clouded by panic, they start out with exaggerated expectations, put the theory into practice for a few months, start to despair when it fails to produce results, and then turn to a new theory. Two years and twenty theories later, the business may well be bankrupt. But who is to blame: the theorists who failed to save the firm or the managers who got it into trouble in the first place?

The third explanation is less charitable: the discipline, no less than astrology, is a magnet for charlatans. As we have already noted, the fortunes that can be made by the successful are gigantic and there are virtually no barriers to entry. And even people who are not out-and-out frauds seem to suffer from all sorts of problems, from an inability to write English to a compulsion to jump on the latest bandwagon.

How to choose a witch doctor

How can we distinguish between the charlatans and the rest? There are a few initial rules of thumb to follow. The first is that anything that you suspect is bunk almost certainly is. Similarly, beware of all authors who emblazon the covers of their books with their academic honours, or who argue entirely by analogy.

It would have been nice to come up with an approved list of good gurus, but, as we have shown, even the best theorists tend to be a little hit and miss, and even the worst ones sometimes have something to say. Most of the ideas covered in this book fall into the broader category of 'good' management theory – concepts that every manager should think about. That still leaves the question of which ones he or she should implement.

The trite but truthful answer is: be selective. Nothing is more witch-doctorish than the suggestion that one magic potion will cure all ills. By all means re-engineer your distribution system: but the same discipline will probably work less well if it is applied to your research-and-development arm. By all means empower your workers but think what you are giving them power over. One of AT&T's many attempts to turn round its NCR computer subsidiary involved 'empowering' salespeople to approve contracts; this only meant that the sales people, eager to add to their quota, started taking on plenty of low-margin business that NCR would normally have rejected. And always remember that the cure can be worse than the disease. The short-term gain from axing a small percentage of your workforce may well be eradicated by the long-term effect on morale; your wonderful new 'global' product may save money on packaging and advertising but it could put off more customers than it attracts.

Choosing between the different medicines is not easy, particularly when so few of the witch doctors' products come with any kind of health warning. As we have pointed out before, the management theory industry is peculiarly un-self-critical. Duly declaring our vested interest, we would like to point out that one glimmer of hope in this respect is the business press. Even though many media empires have a growing financial interest in promoting the gurus, a sufficient number of journalists seem to have kept their critical faculties. *Business Week* exposed CSC Index's manipulation of the sales of *The Discipline of Market Leaders*. It has also written some admirably tough reviews of the books in which consultancies have invested a good deal of their credibility, notably Kelly and Gouillart's *Transforming the Organisation*. In general, the reviews of management books are finally beginning to reflect the frustrations of readers.

Indeed, there are signs that this more critical attitude is spreading to other areas of the industry. Management consultancies used to be able to get away with a lack of transparency that would have been impossible in almost any other profession. Now clients are subjecting consultancies to much more probing interrogations before taking them on. They are also forcing them to share in the risks of major restructurings by paying them according to performance. Business schools have also become much more sensitive to criticism from students, alumni and employers, thanks to the rankings which now appear in magazines such as *Business Week*.

Contradictions and anxieties

This more critical attitude is commendable. But there are a number of problems that seem, if anything, to be getting worse. The first, which has cropped up time and again throughout this book, is the tendency of management theory to make today's contradictory corporation more contradictory still. As the pace of business increases around the world, the theorists are pulling companies in different directions, either by abandoning one nostrum for its opposite or by preaching completely contradictory things. Quite apart from the illogicality of trying, say, to force an organisation to be more flexible (by sacking people) whilst at the same time teaching the virtues of trust, there is the effect that such fad-surfing has on a company's culture.

One thing that has never been good for organisations of any sort at any time is to be buggered around. Before any boss starts reinventing his (or her) company one more time he should dismiss the consultants for the afternoon, unplug his telephone, lock the door and study Gaius Petronius's description of a period of rapid change in the Roman Empire. 'We trained hard to meet our challenges but it seemed as if every time we were beginning to form into teams we would be reorganised. I was to learn later in life that we tend to meet any new situation by reorganising; and a wonderful method it can be for creating the illusion of progress while producing confusion, ineffectiveness and demoralisation.'[1]

The second growing problem is management theory's insensitivity to language. It is hard to think of a subject in which sloppy writing is so prevalent. The average management book reads as if it had been translated from German, with nouns used as verbs and sentences that meander this way and that. Words like re-engineering have a pseudo-scientific air, meant to suggest that companies are machines, which can be re-tuned by clever technocrats. As we have already pointed out, the peculiar illiteracy of management theory matters. Increasingly, institutions around the world are being run by people who have been trained in business schools. And the language of the 'global cosmopolitans', as Rosabeth Moss Kanter dubs the new élite, is managementese. In *The End of History* Francis Fukuyama pointed out that all the big arguments about politics and economics have been won by democracy and free markets. That may be something of an exaggeration; but a growing number of arguments are all about management of one sort or another. It is no small thing if the language in which these debates are conducted is deformed.

The third problem is management theory's insensitivity to the wider effects of its ideas. Back in the 1940s, Peter Drucker's pioneering work on General Motors treated the company as a social organisation. Nowadays only a few thinkers see the big picture. Charles Handy is increasingly preoccupied with the idea that companies are political communities, and that the best way to look at them is through the prism of political theory. Rosabeth Moss Kanter, a sociologist by training, has an acute eye for the social dynamics of companies, as does Jay Forrester, an engineer by training. But most gurus are insensitive to the fact that businesses are social and political communities, with their distinctive mores, power struggles and social dynamics.

A quick look at this wider social context brings home a number of unpleasant lessons. Thirty years ago most Americans – particularly the managerial class – expected the future to bring increased leisure and certainty. On the whole, management theory has pushed companies and public-sector institutions to become ever leaner. Millions have been downsized out of jobs; millions more work harder. These may be unavoidable things, but they often have been presented in such an inarticulate way that few workers of any description understand what is going on. It is hardly surprising that, as the contradictory corporation pulls itself in opposing directions, fewer and fewer Americans trust either their employers or their politicians. Like all the best witch doctors, management gurus have predicted a future of chaos and uncertainty that their own work has only made more likely.

This is not to say that we are joining the popular clamour in favour of stakeholding. Shareholder capitalism makes it possible for companies to make difficult but necessary adjustments that its stakeholder brother fudges; downsizing, delayering and re-engineering a company is better than allowing it to die of obesity. But managers should remember that firms exist on the sufferance of their host communities. Downsizing may be necessary – but it is dangerous to raise the chairman's salary at the same time as you are laying off thousands of workers. Re-engineering may be essential – but it is essential, too, to realise that, however powerful, the company's engine will not work unless it is fuelled by the enthusiasm of the company's employees. The alternative is that you risk a popular backlash against big business (of the sort Pat Buchanan tried to unleash in the United States) which could lead to draconian restrictions on management's freedom to manage. A good management theorist is something of a political theorist too.

Up, up and away

Whatever the discipline's problems, there is no doubt that it will go from strength to strength. Look at the income of the consultancies, the sales of management books, or the intake of business schools and all the trends are up. Most managers in the West have realised that, in a world in which new products can be copied instantaneously and wages can easily be undercut, the only lasting source of advantage is superior management. This realisation is spreading to the East, too. The founders of business empires in places such as Hong Kong and Singapore might have been able to rely on personal connections and political influence to build their empires. Their successors, however, need more formal management skills to prevent those empires from falling apart or stagnating.

There is an even more important reason why the witch doctors will enjoy an ever expanding demand for their services. Even if managers do learn how to thrive on chaos or control their destiny they will still be confronted by that most intractable of all problems: the cussedness of human nature. Managers are constantly embracing techniques that promise to control the uncertainty at the heart of their jobs – and constantly having to embrace more new techniques when their charges refuse to do as they are bid. In looking at the fate of managers and their pitiful predilection for magic cures we are reminded of David Hume's insight: 'In proportion as any man's course of life is governed by accident, we always find that he increases in superstition.'

NOTES

Introduction

1 *Financial Times,*29 December 1994, p. 4
2 *Business Week*, 11 March 1996
3 *New York Times*, 3–10 March 1996
4 'Losers feel stress of playing executive games', *Daily Telegraph*, 4 January 1995, p. 1
5 Lucy Kellaway, 'Volumes of learning – take it as read', *Financial Times*, 12 September 1994
6 Mauro F. Guillen, *Models of Management: Work, Authority and Organisation in Comparative Perspective* (1994), p. 120
7 Bain & Co, 'The Planning Forum, "Management Tools and Techniques: Survey Results Summary" ' (1995)
8 J.A. Byrne, 'Business fads: what's in and what's out', *Business Week*, 20 January 1986

Chapter 1

1 'Re-engineering', *Wired*, August 1995, p. 125
2 'The struggle to create an organization for the 21st century', *Fortune*, 3 April 1995
3 'At Wharton they're practising what they preach', *New York Times*, 5 March 1995, p.F9
4 Michael Hammer, *The Re-engineering Revolution: The Handbook* (1995), p. xii
5 'What you really think about re-engineering', *CFO* magazine, May 1995
6 'When slimming is not enough', *The Economist*, 3 September 1994
7 'Thanks, Goodbye', *Wall Street Journal*, 8 May 1995

8 *Financial Times*, 14 January 1994, cited in *The Financial Times Handbook of Management* (FT Pitman Publishing, 1995)
9 'Business reengineering, the CSC Index approach to achieving operational excellence'
10 The Lloyds case-study is drawn from interviews by one of the authors; parts of the story also appeared in 'The black horse goes to the vet', *The Economist*, 22 July 1995
11 'The pain of downsizing', *Business Week*, 9 May 1994
12 'Charles Handy sees the future', *Fortune*, 31 October 1994
13 Gary Hamel and C.K. Prahalad, *Competing for the Future* (Harvard Business School Press, Boston, Mass., 1994), p. 5
14 *California Management Review*, vol. 37, no. 4
15 'When slimming is not enough', *The Economist*, 3 September 1994
16 'Thanks, Goodbye', *Wall Street Journal*, 8 May 1995, p.1
17 NOP Survey of 801 union workers for TUC Conference, released September 1995. (*Daily Telegraph*, 11 September 1995)
18 The Corning case-study is drawn from interviews by one of the authors; parts of the story appeared in 'Re-engineering, with love', in *The Economist,* 9 September 1995, p. 92.

Chapter 2

1 Figures are taken from Adrian Wooldridge's survey of management consulting in *The Economist*, 22 March 1997.
2 John Kotter, *The New Rules: How to Succeed in the Post-Corporate World* (Free Press, 1995)
3 Ronald Yeaple, *The MBA Advantage: Why it Pays to Get an MBA* (Bob Adams, Boston). However the discounted figures are from 'The MBA cost-benefit analysis', *The Economist*, 6 August 1994
4 'Leaping to the lectern', *New York Times*, 8 September 1995, p. D1
5 Survey of Asian business, *Far Eastern Economic Review*, 14 September 1995
6 Jean-Philippe Deschamps and P. Ranganath Nayak, *Product Juggernauts: How Companies Mobilize to Generate a Stream of Market Winners* (Harvard Business School Press, 1995)
7 Examples taken from *Business Week*, 18 September 1995
8 Andrzej Huczynski, *Management Gurus: What makes them and*

how to become one, (Routledge, London, 1992), pp.191–2

9   Thomas J. Peters and Robert H. Waterman, *In Search of Excellence: Lessons from America's Best-Run Companies* (Harper & Row, New York, 1982), p. 56

10 Huczynski, *Management Gurus,* p. 163

Chapter 3

1   Quoted in Carol Kennedy, *Guide to the Management Gurus,* (Century Business), p. 41

2   C.S. George, *The History of Management Thought,* cited in David Clutterbuck and Stuart Crainer, *Makers of Management,* (Macmillan 1990)

3   'Pioneers and prophets', *Financial Times,* 19 December 1994

4   Lyndall Urwick and E.F.L. Breech, *The Making of Scientific Management,* quoted in Clutterbuck and Cramer, op. cit.

5   Guillen, op. cit., pp. 45–6

6   Pauline Graham (ed.), *Mary Parker Follett: Prophet of Management* (Harvard Business School Press, Boston, Mass., 1995), p. 27

7   Gullen op. cit., p. 224

8   Peter Drucker, *The Concept of the Corporation* (Mentor, New York, 1983 ed.), p. 3

9   Ibid., p. 78

10 Quoted by Kennedy, *Guide to the Management Gurus,* p. 41

11 Drucker, *Concept of the Corporation,* p. 132

12 Interview with authors, 10 October 1995

13 Breakfast with authors, 17 October 1994

14 'Megachurches', *New York Times,* 18 April 1995

15 Drucker, *The Concept of the Corporation,* p. 241

16 Ibid., p. 185

17 Peter Drucker, *Managing in Turbulent Times* (Butterworth Heinemann, 1980 ed.), p. 104

18 Ibid., p. 226

Chapter 4

1   Example taken from Economist Conference Unit, 'Tom Peters: The Pursuit of Wow!', 27 October 1995, London

2 Interview with author, 27 October 1995
3 For examples of this sort of argument, see 'Europe outgrows management American-style,' *Fortune*, 20 October 1980, pp. 147–8; 'Don't blame the system, blame the managers', *Dun's Review*, September 1980, p. 88
4 Peters and Waterman, *In Search of Excellence*, op. cit., p. xxii
5 Ibid., p. xxv
  6 Peter Drucker, *Frontiers of Management*
7 David Clutterbuck and Stuart Crainer, *Makers of Management: Men and Women Who Changed the Business World* (Macmillan, 1990), p. 218
8 Tom Peters and Nancy Austin, *A Passion for Excellence* (Collins, London, 1985), Foreword
9 Ibid., Ch. 7
10 Tom Peters, *Liberation Management* (Macmillan, London, 1992), pp. 612–14
11 Homa Bahrami and Stuart Evans, 'Flexible re-cycling and high-technology entrepreneurship', *California Management Review*, vol. 37, no. 3, Spring 1995, pp. 62–89
12 Seminar, London, 27 October 1995
13 Tom Peters, TPG Communications, 1995, 'Maybe the theories need re-engineering'
14 Peters and Waterman, *In Search of Excellence*, op.cit., p. 215
15 Ibid., p. 270
16 Ibid., pp. 106–7
17 Ibid., p. 30
18 For a classic statement of this position, see Peter Drucker, *The Practice of Management* (Harper & Row, New York, 1954)
19 John A. Byrne, *The Whiz Kids: Ten Founding Fathers of American Business – and the Legacy They Left Us* (Currency Doubleday, New York, 1993)
20 Peters and Waterman, *In Search of Excellence*, op. cit., p. 48
21 Ibid., p. 55
22 Ibid., p. 75
23 'Corporate culture: the hard-to-change values that spell success or failure', *Business Week*, 27 October 1980, pp. 148–60
24 Sampson, *Company Man*, op. cit., p. 196
25 Letter to authors, 30 October 1995

Chapter 5

1 Sampson, *Company Man*, op.cit., p. 221
2 Tom Peters, 'New products, new markets, new competition, new thinking', *The Economist*, 4 March 1989, pp. 27–32
3 This argument has been made most persuasively in Bennett Harrison, *Lean and Mean: The Changing Landscape of Corporate America* (Basic Books, New York, 1994)
4 'The case against mergers', *Business Week*, 30 October 1995
5 Harrison, op. cit.
6 'The European Economist', *Wall Street Journal Europe*, 30 October 1995, p. 4
7 *N.C. Churchill and D.F. Muzyka, 'Entrepreneurial Management: A Converging Theory for Large and Small Enterprises', Insead Corporate Renewal Initiative Working Papers, p. 2*
8 William H. Whyte, *Organisation Man* (Doubleday, New York, 1957) and David Riesman, *The Lonely Crowd* (1950)
9 The best example of this is Anthony Sampson, *Company Man*, op. cit.
10 Sumantra Ghoshal and Christopher Bartlett, 'Building the entrepreneurial corporation', *The Financial Times Handbook of Management*, p. 41
11 Jordan Lewis, *The Connected Corporation* (Free Press, New York, 1995). See also 'Holding the hand that feeds', *The Economist*, 9 September 1995
12 William Bridges, *Jobshift* (Nicholas Brealey, 1995), p. 20
13 'Jack Welch lets fly on budgets, bonuses, and buddy boards', *Fortune*, 29 May 1995
14 Quoted in Carol Kennedy, *Managing with the Gurus: Top-Level Guidance on Twenty Management Techniques* (Century, 1994), p. 130

Chapter 6

1 'Your company's most valuable asset: Intellectual Capital', *Fortune*, 3 October 1994
2 See Philip Hodgson, 'The learning organisation', *The Financial Times Handbook of Management*, op. cit., p. 691
3 Dorothy Leonard-Barton, *Wellsprings of Knowledge: Building and Sustaining the Sources of Innovation* (Harvard Business

School Press, Boston, 1995), p. 21

4 Ibid., pp. 24–7
5 Ibid., pp. 159–60
6 Ibid., p. 156
7 Ibid., pp. 75–8
8 Ibid., p. 70
9 Ibid., p. 79
10 Fred Moody, *I Sing the Body Electronic: A Year with Microsoft on the Multimedia Frontier* (Viking, New York, 1995)
11 Quoted in Michael Treacy and Fred Wiersema, *The Discipline of Market Leaders* (HarperCollins, 1995)
12 Deschamps and Nayak, *Product Juggernauts*, op. cit.
13 Quoted in conference booklet, Tom Peters, 'The Pursuit of Wow!', 27 October 1995
14 'The mass production of ideas and other impossibilities', *The Economist*, 28 March 1995
15 John Seely Brown, 'Research that reinvents the corporation', in Robert Howard (ed.), *The Learning Imperative*, (Harvard Business School Press, Boston, Mass., 1993), p. 89
16 *Forbes*, 7 November 1994, quoted in conference booklet, Tom Peters, 'Theory of Wow!', 27 October 1995
17 Quoted in Tom Peters Seminar, 27 October 1995
18 Gary Hamel, 'The prize that lies in foreseeing the future', *Financial Times*, 5 June 1995
19 Anthony Sampson, *Company Man: The Rise and Fall of Corporate Life* (1995), p. 197

Chapter 7

1 Michael Porter, 'The state of strategic thinking', *The Economist*, 23 May 1987, p. 21.
2 Henry Mintzberg, *The Rise and Fall of Strategic Planning* (Prentice Hall, New York, 1994), pp. 21–3
3 For a brief history of strategy, see ch. 21 of John Kay, *The Foundations of Corporate Success: How Strategies Add Value* (Oxford University Press, Oxford, 1993)
4 Mintzberg, op. cit., pp. 46–7.
5 Ibid., pp. 62–3
6 Michael Porter, *Strategic Thinking*, p. 22
7 Michael Goold, Andrew Campbell and Marcus Alexander,

Corporate-Level Strategy: Creating Value in the Multibusiness Company (John Wiley, New York, 1994), p. 54

8 Ibid., p. 100

9 Amar Bhide, 'How entrepreneurs craft strategies that work', *Harvard Business Review*, March/April 1994, pp. 150–61

10 Ibid., pp. 258–9 and numerous other places

11 Quoted in 'The CEO agenda', *Strategy & Business*, Fall 1995

12 Deschamps and Nayak, *Product Juggernauts*, op. cit., p. 131.

13 Stephen Rudolph *et al*, 'Emerging technologies: a novel approach to envisioning their development', *Prism*, fourth quarter, 1994, pp. 105–12

14 Mintzberg, op. cit., p. 295

15 Noel M. Tichy and Stratford Sherman, *Control Your Destiny or Someone Else Will: How Jack Welch is Making General Electric the World's Most Competitive Corporation* (HarperCollins, London, 1993), p. 11

16 Gerard Tellis and Peter Golder, 'First to market, first to fail: real causes of enduring market leadership', *Sloan Management Review*, vol. 37, no. 2

17 Goold, *et al*, op. cit.

18 'Hammer defends re-engineering', *The Economist*, 5 November 1994, p. 96

19 'As Sculley leaves Apple, image lingers of a leader distracted by his vision', *Wall Street Journal*, 18 October 1993

20 Gates quoted in *Financial Times*, 17 November

Chapter 8

1 Tichy and Sherman, op. cit.

2 David Packard, *The HP Way* (HarperBusiness, New York, 1995)

3 Breakfast with author, 17 October 1994

4 Wilshire Book Company, United Kingdom. Often out of print.

5 Mark H. McCormack, *What They Don't Teach You at Harvard Business School* (Collins, London, 1984), p. 207

6 Lee Iacocca with William Novak, *Iacocca* (Bantam, 1985), Prologue p. xiv

7 Doron Levin, *Behind the Wheel at Chrysler: The Iacocca Legacy*

(Harcourt Brace, New York, 1995)

8 Kennedy, *Managing with the Gurus*, op. cit., p. 98
9 'The wealth builders', *Fortune*, 11 December 1995
10 'Secrets of the Survivors', *Business Week*, 9 October 1995
11 Warren Bennis, *On Becoming a Leader* (1989)
12 See 'How tomorrow's best leaders are learning their stuff', *Fortune*, 27 November 1995
13 'The CEO as coach', *Harvard Business Review*, March/April 1995, p. 70
14 Peter Drucker, *Post-Capitalist Society* (HarperBusiness, New York, 1993), p. 71
15 'Britain's boardroom anatomy', *Management Today*, October 1995
16 'How high can CEO pay go?', *Business Week*, 22 April 1996
17 'Are they worth it?', *CFO* magazine, November 1995
18 'Are these ten stretched too thin?', *Business Week*, 17 November 1995
19 'France puts her affaires in order', *Financial Times*, 12 December 1994
20 'France's heirarchy must change to stop scandals', *Evening Standard*, 5 December 1995
21 'Business ethics: the view from the trenches', *California Management Review*, vol. 37, no. 2
22 'A company possessed', in Charles Handy, *Beyond Certainty*, op. cit., p. 105
23 Drucker, *Post-Capitalist Society*, op.cit., p. 73
24 Quoted in 'America's most admired companies,' *Fortune*, 6 March 1995
25 'Watching the boss', *The Economist*, 29 January 1994

Chapter 9

1 'The Temping of America', *Time*, 29 March 1993
2 William Bridges, 'The End of the Job', *Fortune*, 19 September 1994
3 Jeremy Rifkin, *The End of Work: The Decline of the Global Labor Force and the Dawn of the Post-Market Era* (Putnam, New York, 1995), pp. xvi–xvii
4 See an excellent special on technology and unemployment

(not written by the authors) in *The Economist*, 11 February 1995

5 Figures from Bureau of Labor Statistics study of job growth in different sectors, 1992–2005

6 R.A. Wilson with T.J. Webb, 'Occupational Assessment 1995" Institute for Employment Research, University of Warwick

7 *Financial Times* report on the changing British countryside, 14 October 1995

8 Charles Handy, *Beyond Certainty: The Changing Worlds of Organisations* (Hutchinson, 1995), p. 6

9 'Handy guide to corporate life', *Financial Times*, 17 August 1995

10 'Temporarily ahead of his time', *Herald Tribune*, 13 October 1995

11 'The temp biz boom: why it's good', *Fortune*, 16 October 1995

12 William Bridges, *Jobshift: How to Prosper in a Workplace without Jobs*' (Nicholas Brealey, 1995), p. 9

13 Philip Burgess and Paul and Sarah Edwards, 'Workshifting', special report (Center for the New West, Colorado), June 1995

14 John Kotter, *The New Rules: How to Succeed in Today's Post-Corporate World* (Free Press, New York, 1995)

15 'Special envoys' *Financial Times*, 8 September 1995

16 'Tales of the office nomad', *Financial Times*, 29 May 1995

17 'The Salaryman rides again',*The Economist*, 4 February 1995

18 Ibid.

19 Tom Peters, *The Tom Peters Seminar* (Macmillan, 1994), p. 91

20 'What do you expect if the work of millions is wiped out', *Herald Tribune*, 16 October 1995

21 'Rethinking work', *Business Week*, 17 October 1994

22 'Adapt or die', *The Economist*, 1 July 1995

Chapter 10

1 Survey of 750 companies by Arthur Andersen and National Small Business United. Quoted in 'It's a small (business) world', *Business Week*, 17 April 1995

2 Interview with the authors
3 Cited in 'Fast Track', *Financial Times*, March 1995
4 'Munching on change', *The Economist*, 6 January 1996
5 Tadahiro Sekimoto, 'Corporate Challenges in the New Century', paper prepared for the UK-Japan 2000 Group Conference, 17–19 March 1995
6 Interview with the authors

Chapter 11

1 James Womack, Daniel Jones and Daniel Roos, *The Machine that Changed the World. The Story of Lean Production* (Ranson Associates, New York, 1990), p. 225
2 Ibid.
3 Kenichi Ohmae, *The Mind of the Strategist* (Penguin Books, London, 1982), p. 221
4 Kennedy, *Managing with the Gurus*, op.cit., p. 222
5 Womack *et al*, *The Machine that Changed the World*, op. cit., p. 237
6 Jordan Lewis, 'Western Companies can Improve Upon the Japanese Keiretsu', *Wall Street Journal*, 12 December 1995
7 'Japan's new identity', *Business Week*, 10 April 1995, p. 37
8 'On the chin', *Far Eastern Economic Review*, p. 40
9 Tadahiro Sekimoto, 'Corporate Challenges in the New Century', op. cit., p. 3.
10 Ikujiro Nonaka and Hirotaka Takeuchi, *The Knowledge-Creating Company: How Japanese Companies Create the Dynamics of Innovation* (Oxford, 1994), p. 115
11 Ibid., p. 17
12 Ibid., p. 151
13 Ibid., p. 144

Chapter 12

1 For a fuller look at business in Asia, see a survey by John Micklethwait in *The Economist*, 9 March 1996
2 *Overseas Chinese Business Networks in Asia* by the East Asia Analytical Unit of Australia's Department of Foreign Affairs and Trade (1995)

Chapter 13

1 Interview with the authors
2 'A safer New York City', *Business Week*, 11 December 1995
3 'California's contract example', *Financial Times*, 13 November 1995
4 Michael Porter, *The Competitive Advantage of Nations* (Macmillan, London, 1989), p xii
5 Robert Reich, *The Work of Nations: Preparing Ourselves for 21st-Century Capitalism* (Vintage Books, New York, 1991)
6 Rosabeth Moss Kanter, *World Class: Thriving Locally in the Global Economy* (Simon & Schuster, New York, 1995)
7 David Osborne and Ted Gaebler, *Reinventing Government: How the Entrepreneurial Spirit is Transforming the Public Sector* (Addison-Wesley Publishing, 1992)
8 'An interview with Charles Handy', *Strategy & Business*, Fall 1995
9 'Benchmark in Southwark', *Financial Times*, 13 November 1995
10 'The revenge of the beancounters', *Financial Times*, 2 December 1995
11 'Really Reinventing Government', *Atlantic Monthly*, February 1995. Reprinted in Peter Drucker, *Managing in a Time of Great Change* (Truman Talley Books/Dutton, New York, 1995), pp. 285–301
12 Ibid.
13 *Financial Times*, 23 October 1995, p. 14
14 John Kay, 'Sharing responsibility for passing the buck', *Financial Times*, 17 November 1995
15 'Some reforms that might be politically feasible', *The Economist*, pp. 19–21, 22 June 1985
16 Quoted in Simon Jenkins, *Accountable to None: The Tory Nationalization of Britain* (Hamish Hamilton, London, 1995), p. 81

Chapter 14

1 Andrew Morton, 'A working Princess', *Sunday Times*, 13 November 1994
2 John Naisbitt, *Megatrends Asia: The Eight Asian Megatrends that*

are Changing the World (Nicholas Brealey, London, 1995)
3 Bill Gates, *The Road Ahead* (Viking, New York, 1995)
4 Max Berley, 'A move toward management by philosophy', *International Herald Tribune*, 12 February 1996
5 'Business advice from the sidelines', *New York Times*, March 1996
6 Francis Gouillart and James Kelly, *Transforming the Organisation* (McGraw Hill, New York, 1995), p. 4
7 Ibid., pp. 278-9
8 Ibid., p. 19

Conclusion

1 'Overview of Re-engineering', *The Financial Times Handbook of Management*, op. cit.

BIBLIOGRAPHY

Adair, John: *Effective Leadership* (Gower, Aldershot, 1983)

Ansoff, Igor: *Corporate Strategy* (Penguin, Harmondsworth, 1968)

Bartlett, Christopher (and Sumantra Ghoshal): *Managing Across Borders* (Harvard Business School Press, Boston, 1989)

Bennis, Warren and Nanis, B: *Leaders* (Harper & Row, New York, 1986)

Bennis, Warren: *On Becoming a Leader* (Hutchinson, London, 1989)

Blanchard, Kenneth and Johnson, S: *The One Minute Manager* (Fontana/Collins, Glasgow, 1983)

Bridges, William: *Jobshift: How to Prosper in a Workplace Without Jobs* (Nicholas Brealey, London, 1995)

Byrne, John: *The Whiz Kids: Ten Founding Fathers of American Business – and the Legacy They Left Us* (Currency Doubleday, New York, 1993)

Carling, Will (with Robert Heller): *The Way To Win: Strategies for Success in Business and Sport* (Little Brown, London, 1995)

Champy, James: *Reengineering Management: The Mandate for new Leadership* (HarperCollins, London, 1995)

Champy, James (and Michael Hammer): *Reengineering the Corporation* (Nicholas Brealey, London, 1993)

Clutterbuck, David (and Stuart Crainer): *Masters of Management* (Macmillan, London, 1990)

Cooper, Robin: *When Lean Enterprises Collide: Competing Through Confrontation* (Harvard Business School Press, Boston, 1995)

Covey, Stephen: *The Seven Habits of Highly Effective People* (Simon & Schuster, New York, 1989)

Covey, Stephen: *Principle-Centred Leadership* (Simon & Schuster, New York, 1992)

Cragg, Claudia: *The New Teipans* (Century, London, 1995)

Creech, Bill: *Five Pillars of TQM* (Dutton, New York, 1994)

Crosby, Philip: *Quality is Free* (McGraw Hill, New York, 1979)

Deschamps, Jean-Philippe (and Ranganath Nayak): *Product Juggernauts: How Companies Mobilize to Generate a Stream of Market Winners* (Harvard Business School Press, Boston, 1995)

Drucker, Peter: *The Concept of the Corporation* (First published, 1946) (Mentor, New York, 1983)

Drucker, Peter: *The Practice of Management* (Harper & Row, New York, 1954)

Drucker, Peter: *The Age of Discontinuity* (1969)

Drucker, Peter: *Management: Tasks, Responsibilities, Practices* (Butterworth-Heinemann, London, 1974)

Drucker, Peter: *Managing in Turbulent Times* (Butterworth-Heinemann, London, 1980)

Drucker, Peter: *Innovation and Entrepreneurship* (William Heinemann, London, 1985)

Drucker, Peter: *The New Realities* (Heinemann, London, 1989)

Drucker, Peter: *Adventures of a Bystander* (Harper & Row, New York, 1994)

Drucker, Peter: *Post-Capitalist Society* (HarperBusiness, New York, 1993/Butterworth-Heinemann, London, 1993)

Drucker, Peter: *Managing in a Time of Great Change* (Truman Talley, New York, 1996)

East Asia Analytical Unit, Australia's Department of Foreign Affairs and Trade: *Overseas Chinese Business Networks in Asia* (1995)

Emmott, Bill: *The Sun Also Sets: Why Japan will not be Number One* (Simon & Schuster, London, 1989)

Farkas, Charles (and Philippe De Backer & Allen Sheppard): *Maximum Leadership: The World's Top Leaders Discuss How They Add Values to Companies* (Orion, London, 1995)

Feigenbaum, A.V.: *Total Quality Control* (McGraw Hill, New York, 1983)

Financial Times Handbook of Management (FT Pitman Publishing, London, 1995)

Flannery, Thomas (and David Hofrichter and Paul Platten): *People, Performance and Pay* (Free Press, New York, 1996)

Fukuyama, Francis: *The End of History* (Free Press, New York, 1992)

Fukuyama, Francis: *Trust: the Social Virtues and the Creation of*

Prosperity (Free Press, New York, 1995)

Gates, Bill: *The Road Ahead* (Viking, New York, 1995)

Gertz, Dwight (and João Baptista): *Grow to be Great: Breaking the Downsizing Cycle* (1995)

Goldratt, Eliyahu (and Jeff Cox): *The Goal* (Gower, Aldershot, 1989).

Goold, Michael (and Andrew Campbell and Marcus Alexander) *Corporate-Level Strategy: Creating Value in the Multibusiness Company* (John Wiley & Sons, New York, 1994)

Gouillart, Francis (and James Kelly): *Transforming the Organisation. Reframing Corporate Issues. Restructuring the Company. Revitalizing the Spirit of Enterprise. Renewing People* (McGraw Hill, New York, 1995)

Graham, Pauline (ed.): *Mary Parker Follett: Prophet of Management* (Harvard Business School Press, Boston, 1995)

Guillen, Mauro: *Models of Management: Work, Authority and Organisation in Comparative Perspective* (University of Chicago Press, 1995)

Hamel, Gary (and C.K. Prahalad): *Competing For The Future* (Harvard Business School Press, Boston, 1994)

Hammer, Michael (and Steven Stanton): *The Re-engineering Revolution: The Handbook* (HarperCollins, New York, 1995)

Handy, Charles: *Understanding Organisations* (Penguin, London, 1976)

Handy, Charles: *The Future of Work* (Basil Blackwell, Oxford, 1984)

Handy, Charles: *The Age of Unreason* (Arrow Books, London, 1989)

Handy, Charles: *Beyond Certainty: The Changing World of Organisations* (Hutchinson, London, 1995)

Harrison, Bennett: *Lean and Mean: The Changing Landscape of Corporate America* (Basic Books, New York, 1994)

Harvey-Jones, Sir John: *Making it Happen* (Collins, Glasgow, 1988)

Harvey-Jones, Sir John: *Troubleshooter* (BBC Books, London, 1990)

Harvey-Jones, Sir John: *Troubleshooter 2* (Penguin, London, 1993)

Harvey-Jones, Sir John: *Managing to Survive* (Heinemann, London, 1993)

Heller, Robert: *The Naked Manager for the Nineties* (Little Brown,

London, 1995)

Hill, Napoleon: *Think and Grow Rich* (1937)

Hofstede, Geert: *Cultures and Organisations* (McGraw Hill, Maidenhead, 1991)

Howard, Robert (ed.): *The Learning Imperative* (Harvard Business School Press, Boston, 1993)

Huczynski, Andrzej: *Management Gurus: What makes them and how to become one* (Routledge, London, 1992)

Hurst, David: *Crisis & Renewal: Meeting the Challenge of Organisational Change* (Harvard Business School Press, Boston, 1995)

Iacocca, Lee (with Bill Novak): *Iacocca: An Autobiography* (Sidgwick & Jackson, London, 1985)

Jenkins, Simon: *Accountable to None: The Tory Nationalisation of Britain* (Hamish Hamilton, London, 1995)

Jones, Daniel (with James Womack and Daniel Roos): *The Machine That Changed The World: The Story of Lean Production* (Ranson Associates, New York, 1990)

Kanter, Rosabeth Moss: *The Change Masters: Corporate Entrepreneurs at Work* (Allen and Unwin, London, 1985)

Kanter, Rosabeth Moss: *When Giants Learn to Dance: Mastering the Challenges of Strategy, Management and Careers in the 1990s* (Simon & Schuster, London, 1989)

Kanter, Rosabeth Moss: *World Class: Thriving Locally in the Global Economy* (Simon & Schuster, New York, 1995)

Kay, John: *The Foundations of Corporate Success* (Oxford University Press, Oxford, 1993)

Kennedy, Carol: *Guide to the Management Gurus* (Century Business, London, 1991)

Kennedy, Carol: *Managing With the Gurus: Top level guidance on 20 management techniques* (Century Business, London, 1994)

Kidder, Tracy: *The Soul of a New Machine*. (Atlantic/Little Brown, Boston, 1981)

Kotkin, Joel: *Tribes: How Race, Religion and Identity Determine Success in the New Global Economy* (Random House, New York, 1992)

Kotter, John: *The New Rules: How to Succeed in Today's Post-Corporate World* (Free Press, New York, 1995)

Laserre, Philippe (and Hellmut Schütte): *Strategies for Asia Pacific* (Macmillan Business, London, 1995)

Levin, Doron: *Behind the Wheel at Chrysler: The Iacocca Legacy* (Harcourt Brace, New York, 1995)

Leonard-Barton, Dorothy: *Wellsprings of Knowledge: Building and sustaining the sources of innovation* (Harvard Business School Press, Boston, Mass., 1995)

Lewis, Jordan: *The Connected Corporation* (Free Press, New York, 1995)

Lorenz, Christopher (and Nicholas Leslie), ed: *The Financial Times on Management* (FT Pitman Publishing, London, 1992)

Machiavelli, Niccolò: *The Prince*

Meyer, G.J.: *Executive Blues: Down and out in Corporate America* (Franklin Square Press, New York, 1995)

McCormack, Mark: *What They Don't Teach You At Harvard Business School* (William Collins, London, 1984)

McGregor D: *The Human Side of the Enterprise* (McGraw Hill, New York, 1960)

Mintzberg, Henry: *Mintzberg on Management* (The Free Press, New York, 1989)

Mintzberg, Henry: *The Rise and Fall of Strategic Planning* (Prentice-Hall, Hemel Hempstead, 1994)

Monks, Robert (and Nell Minow): *Watching the Watchers: Corporate Governance for the Twenty-First Century* (Blackwell Business, Cambridge, Mass., 1996)

Moody, Fred: *I Sing the Body Electronic: A Year With Microsoft on the Multimedia Frontier* (Viking, New York, 1995)

Moore, James: *The Death of Competition: Leadership and Strategy in the Age of Business Ecosystems* (HarperBusiness, New York, 1996)

Naisbitt, John: *Megatrends: Ten New Directions Transforming Our Lives* (Warner Books, New York, 1983)

Naisbitt, John: *Reinventing the Corporation* (Warner Books, New York, 1985)

Naisbitt, John: *Megatrends Asia* (Simon & Schuster, New York, 1995)

Negroponte, Nicholas: *Being Digital* (Hodder & Stoughton, London, 1995)

Nonaka, Ikujiro (and Hirotaka Takeuchi): *The Knowledge-Creating Company: How Japanese Companies Create the Dynamics of Innovation* (Oxford, 1994)

Ohmae, Kenichi: *The Mind of the Strategist* (Penguin,

Harmondsworth, 1982)

Ohmae, Kenichi: *Triad Power* (The Free Press, New York, 1985)

Ohmae, Kenichi: *The Borderless World: Power and Strategy in the Interlinked Economy* (HarperBusiness, New York, 1990)

Ohmae, Kenichi: *The End of the Nation State: The Rise of Regional Economies* (Free Press, New York, 1995)

Ohmae, Kenichi (ed.): *The Evolving Global Economy: Making Sense of the New Global Order* (Harvard Business School Press, Boston, Mass., 1995)

Osborne, David (with Ted Gaebler): *Reinventing Government: How the Entrepreneurial Spirit is Transforming the Public Sector* (1992)

Packard, David: *The HP Way: How Bill Hewlett and I Built Our Company* (HarperBusiness, New York, 1995)

Pascale, Richard, and Athos, Anthony: *The Art of Japanese Management* (Penguin, Harmondsworth, 1982)

Pascale, Richard: *Managing on the Edge* (Penguin, Harmondsworth, 1991)

Peters, Tom (and Robert Waterman): *In Search of Excellence: Lessons From America's Best Run Companies* (Harper & Row, New York, 1982)

Peters, Tom (and Nancy Austin): *A Passion for Excellence* (Collins, London, 1985).

Peters, Tom: *Thriving on Chaos* (Macmillan, London, 1989)

Peters, Tom, *Liberation Management* (Macmillan, London, 1992)

Peters, Tom: *The Tom Peters Seminar: Crazy Times Call for Crazy Organisations* (Macmillan, London, 1994/Vintage Books, New York, 1994)

Peters, Tom: *The Pursuit of Wow! Every Person's Guide to Topsy-Turvy Times* (Macmillan, London, 1994/Vintage, New York, 1994)

Poras, Jerry (and James Collins): *Built to last: successful habits of visionary companies* (HarperBusiness, New York, 1995)

Porter, Michael: *Competitive Strategy* (The Free Press, New York, 1980)

Porter, Michael: *Competitive Advantage* (The Free Press, New York, 1985)

Porter, Michael: *The Competitive Advantage of Nations* (Macmillan, London, 1989)

Reich, Robert: *The Work of Nations* (Alfred Knopf, New York, 1991)

Reichfield, Frederick: *The Loyalty Effect* (Harvard Business School Press, Boston, Mass., 1996)

Rifkin, Jeremy: *The End of Work: The Decline of the Global Labor Force and the Dawn of the Post-Market Era* (Putnam, New York, 1995)

Robbins, Anthony: *Awaken the Giant Within* (Simon & Schuster, New York, 1991)

Robbins, Anthony: *Unlimited Power* (Simon & Schuster, New York, 1987)

Rohwer, Jim: *Asia Rising: Why America Will Prosper as Asia's Economies Boom* (Simon & Schuster, New York, 1995)

Sampson, Anthony: *Company Man: The Rise and Fall of Corporate Life* (HarperCollins, London, 1995)

Seagrave, Sterling: *Lords of the Rim: The Invisible Empire of the Overseas Chinese* (Bantam, London, 1995)

Senge, Peter: *The Fifth Discipline* (Doubleday, New York, 1990)

Senge, Peter, *et al*: *The Fifth Discipline Handbook* (Nicholas Brealey, London, 1994)

Simon, Hermann: *Hidden Champions: Lessons from 500 of the World's Best Unknown Companies* (Harvard Business School Press, Boston, Mass., 1996)

Tichy, Noel (with Stratford Sherman): *Control Your Destiny or Someone Else Will: How Jack Welch is making the world's most competitive corporation* (HarperCollins, London, 1995/Currency Doubleday, New York, 1993)

Toffler, Alvin: *Future Shock* (Random House, New York, 1970)

Toffler, Alvin: *The Third Wave* (Morrow, New York, 1980)

Toffler, Alvin: *Powershift* (Bantam, New York, 1990)

Treacy, Michael (and Fred Wiersema): *The Discipline of Market Leaders: Choose your customers, Narrow your focus, Dominate your market* (Addison–Wesley, New York, 1995)

Warner, Malcolm: *The Management of Human Resources in Chinese Industry* (Macmillan, London, 1995)

Waterman, Robert: *Frontiers of Excellence: Learning From Companies That Put People First* (Nicholas Brealey, London, 1995)

Whyte, William: *Organisation Man* (New York, Doubleday, 1957)

Zuboff, Shoshana: *In the Age of the Smart Machine: The Future of Work and Power* (Basic Books, New York, 1988)

INDEX